Ned Snell

SAMS

Teach Yourself to Create Web Pages in 24 Hours

THIRD EDITION

SAMS

201 West 103rd St., Indianapolis, Indiana, 46290 USA

Sams Teach Yourself to Create Web Pages in 24 Hours, Third Edition

International Standard Book Number: 0-672-32075-4

Library of Congress Catalog Card Number: 2001093349

Printed in the United States of America

First Printing: August 2001

03 02 01 4 3 2 1

Trademarks

Warning and Disclaimer

Acquisitions Editor
Mark Taber

Managing Editor
Charlotte Clapp

Book Packager
Justak Literary Services

Copy Editor
Rebecca Whitney

Indexer
Sherry Massey

Software Development Specialist
Dan Scherf

Interior Design
Gary Adair

Cover Design
Aren Howell

Production
William J. Hartman

Contents at a Glance

Contents

About the Author

Ned Snell has been making technology make sense since 1986, when he began writing beginner's documentation for one of the world's largest software companies. After writing manuals and training materials for several major companies, he switched sides and became a computer journalist, serving as writer and eventually as an editor for two national magazines, *Edge* and *Art & Design News*.

A freelance writer since 1991, Snell has written 18 computer books (and co-authored four more) and hundreds of articles and served as Reviews Editor for *Inside Technology Training* magazine. Between books, Snell works as a professional actor in regional theater, commercials, and industrial films.

Dedication

For Jo, Joseph and John.

Acknowledgments

Thanks to the folks at Sams Publishing—especially Mark Taber and Dan Scherf—and to Marta Justak and her team.

Tell Us What You Think!

As the reader of this book, *you* are our most important critic and commentator. We value your opinion and want to know what we're doing right, what we could do better, what areas you would like to see us publish in, and any other words of wisdom you're willing to pass our way.

You can email or write me directly to let me know what you did or didn't like about this book—as well as what we can do to make our books stronger.

Please note that I cannot help you with technical problems related to the topic of this book and that, because of the high volume of mail I receive, I might not be able to reply to every message.

When you write, please be sure to include this book's title and author as well as your name and address. I will carefully review your comments and share them with the author and editors who worked on the book.

Email: `webdev@samspublishing.com`

Mail: Mark Taber
Associate Publisher
Sams Publishing
201 West 103rd Street
Indianapolis, IN 46290 USA

Introduction

Books that aim to teach beginners how to create a Web page almost always start out the same way: They tell you what a Web page is and why you might want one of your own.

I figure that if you've picked up this book, you've already been online (at least a little), you've seen a Web page, and you know why you want one. So I won't waste even one of our 24 hours together on that stuff. Instead, I'll get you creating your own Web pages as quickly and simply as possible.

In fact, before your first three hours are up, you'll already know your way around the easy-but-powerful Web page creation program (Netscape Composer) included on the CD-ROM that comes with this book, and you will already have created your first Web page. How's that for cutting to the chase?

> Before proceeding with the lessons in this book, you should go to Appendix A, "Setting Up the Programs on the CD-ROM," learn about the programs on the CD-ROM, and set them up on your PC. You'll begin using them in Hour 2, "Starting Out with a Web Authoring Program," so when you get to Hour 2 I'll remind you to set up the programs in case you have not already done so.

Who I Wrote This Thing For

To understand this book without even breaking a mental sweat, you do not need to be any kind of Internet expert or computer guru.

If you can operate basic programs (such as a word processor) in Microsoft Windows, and if you can surf from page to page on the Internet, you already know everything you need to know to get started with this book.

By the end of this book, you'll know not only how to create cool-looking Web pages for yourself or your business, but also how to publish them on the Web for all to see.

Why Do You Need the Programs on the CD-ROM?

Well, you don't need them, exactly. Technically, you can create a Web page using a simple text-editing program or word processing program—and here you'll learn a thing or two about how to do it that way.

But for nearly everybody, Web page creation is quickest and easiest when you use a top-notch Web page editor. That's why this book includes a complete copy of Netscape Composer, plus a set of other valuable tools for bringing your Web pages to life.

In fact, the CD-ROM at the back of this book contains the whole Netscape Communicator suite (see Figure I.1), which includes not only Composer, but also the Netscape Web browser, the email and newsgroup program Messenger, and more—everything you need to create Web pages *and* enjoy the Internet. (Although the Internet surfing stuff in Netscape is terrific, you don't have to use it. You can do your Web page authoring in Composer and still use another Web browser, such as Internet Explorer, for other Internet stuff, if you prefer.)

Because I know that you have Composer, I demonstrate many Web page creation techniques in that program to help you get started. By the end of this book, you'll know how to do just about anything in Composer.

But this book is not limited to Composer, and neither are you. Along the way, you'll explore important Web authoring concepts that will enable you to quickly learn and use just about any other Web authoring program. You'll also discover a number of powerful techniques that don't even involve Composer. And in the final hour of this tutorial, I'll introduce you to a variety of other popular Web page creation tools so that you can decide where to go if you outgrow Composer.

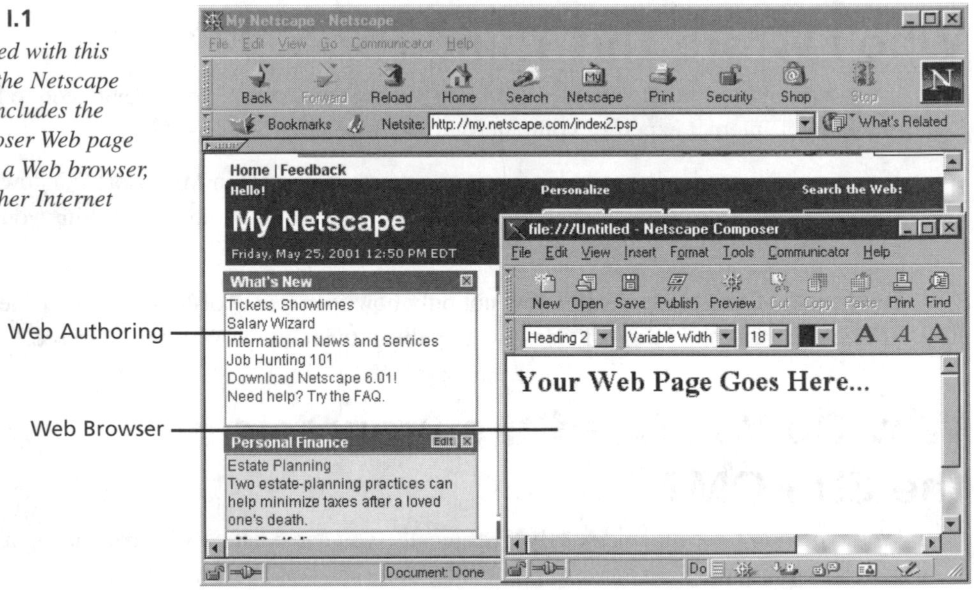

FIGURE I.1
Included with this book, the Netscape suite includes the Composer Web page editor, a Web browser, and other Internet tools.

How to Use This Book

This book is divided into six parts, each four hours long:

Part I, "First Steps, First Web Pages," kicks off with an easy primer on the technology behind a Web page and a Web page's basic anatomy. After that, you'll learn your way around in Composer and even create your very first Web pages.

Part II, "Titles, Text, and Tables," moves ahead to the nitty-gritty of Web authoring, getting your text into the page and making it look exactly the way you want it to look.

Part III, "Linking to Stuff," lays out for you the wonderful world of links. You'll find out not only how to add links to your Web pages, but also how to link to stuff other than Web pages, such as newsgroup messages or email addresses.

Part IV, "Adding Pizzazz with Multimedia," shows how to add audiovisual content to your page, including pictures, backgrounds, sound, video, and animation.

Part V, "Fine-Tuning Your Page," shows how to create those nifty fill-in-the-blanks forms *and* then takes you beyond Composer, showing how to use other tools on the CD-ROM to create frames, put multiple links in one picture, and add other advanced (but not too tough) Web page features.

Part VI, "Getting It Online," takes you step-by-step through publishing your pages on the Internet and shows you how to test, update, and publicize your pages. It also shows you how to expand your skills to new tools and techniques.

As you can see, the parts move logically from easy stuff to not-so-easy stuff—so it's generally best to read the hours in order. But here and there, I'll tip you to stuff you can skip if you're not immediately interested in a particular activity or technique.

After Hour 24, you'll discover two valuable appendixes:

Appendix A, "Setting Up the Programs on the CD-ROM," describes the programs on the free CD-ROM and shows how to set them up on your computer.

Appendix B, "Online Resources for Web Authors," contains a directory of Web pages you can visit to learn more about Web authoring, pick up great new Web authoring programs, or gather picture files, animations, and other fun stuff to spice up your own creations.

Finally, the book has a glossary, although I must point out that I use very, very little technical terminology, and I explain it to you whenever I do. So you'll probably never need the glossary. But just in case you want one, you've got one. I aim to please.

Things You Would Probably Figure Out By Yourself

As you go along, you'll run into a variety of different tip boxes and other special elements. When you do, you'll immediately recognize what each element offers—none of them really requires any explanation. But just for the record, you'll see the following:

"To Do's," New Terms, and Special Element Boxes

Here and there, I use step-by-step instructions, called "To Do's," to show you exactly how to do something. I generally explain how to do that thing in the text that precedes the steps, so feel free to skip 'em when you want to. However, whenever you feel like you don't completely understand something, do the steps and you'll probably get the picture before you're done. Sometimes, we learn only by doing.

NEW TERM I call attention to important new terms by tagging them with a New Term icon. It doesn't happen often, but when it does, it helps you remember the terms that will help you learn to create Web pages.

You'll also see three kinds of special element boxes:

A Tip box points out a faster, easier way to do something or another way to save time and effort. These boxes are completely optional.

A Note box pops out an important consideration or interesting tidbit related to the topic at hand. These boxes are optional, too, but always worth reading (otherwise, I wouldn't interrupt).

A Caution box alerts you to actions and situations where something bad could happen, like accidentally deleting an important file. Because you can do very little in Web authoring that's in any way dangerous, you'll see very few Cautions. But when you do see one, take it seriously.

Q&A Session

At the end of every hour, you'll find a few quick questions and answers explaining interesting stuff that wasn't included in the hour because it didn't directly contribute to teaching yourself how to create Web pages (even though it's interesting).

One More Thing

Actually, no more things. If you have not already done so, skip to Appendix A and follow the steps to set up the programs on the CD-ROM. Then start the clock and hit Hour 1. Twenty-four working hours from now, you'll know Web page authoring inside-out.

Thanks for spending a day with me.

Part I

First Steps, First Web Pages

Hour

Hour 1

Understanding Web Authoring

I can hear your motor running, so I know you're ready to dive in and start creating Web pages. But before building that first page, you need to acquire a rudimentary understanding of how Web pages are born and do some planning about what you want your page to be.

In this hour, you'll get a quick tour of what Web pages and Web sites are made of. At the end of the hour, you will be able to answer the following questions:

- What are Web pages made of, and how do they work?
- What's HTML, and why should I care?
- How does multimedia—pictures, sound, video, and animation—become part of a page?
- What are extensions, and why do they matter?
- How should I approach the organizing of multiple pages into a complete Web site?

Anatomy of a Web Page

Most Web pages contain, in addition to other optional parts, many of the elements described in this section. You should know what these parts are because the principal task in Web authoring is deciding what content to use for each standard part; a principal challenge is dealing with the different ways each browser treats the different parts. (More on that later in this hour.)

Parts You See

The following Web page elements are typically visible to visitors through a browser (see Figure 1.1):

- A *title*, which graphical browsers (most Windows, Macintosh, and X Windows browsers) typically display in the title bar of the window in which the page appears.

> The real title of a Web page does not appear within the page itself, but rather as the title of the browser window in which the page is displayed.
>
> However, most pages have another *title* of sorts—text or a graphic that is on the screen doing the job you typically associate with a title in books or magazines: sitting boldly and proudly near the top of the page to give it a name.

- *Headings*, which browsers typically display in large, bold, or otherwise emphasized type. A Web page can have many headings, and headings can be *nested* up to six levels deep; the page can have subheadings, sub-subheadings, and so on.
- *Normal text*, which makes up the basic, general-purpose text of the page. Traditionally, Web authors refer to lines or blocks of normal text as *paragraphs*. But in the parlance of the Netscape Editor, *any* discrete block of words on the page is a paragraph—whether the block is a heading, normal text, or something else determined by properties assigned to that paragraph.
- A *signature*, typically displayed at the bottom of the page. A signature usually identifies the page's author and often includes the author's (or Webmaster's) email address so that visitors can send comments or questions about the page. The email address is sometimes formatted as a mailto link so that visitors can click it to open their email program with a message preaddressed to the author.
- *Horizontal lines*, which dress up the page and separate it into logical sections.

1

FIGURE 1.1
Some common parts of a Web page.

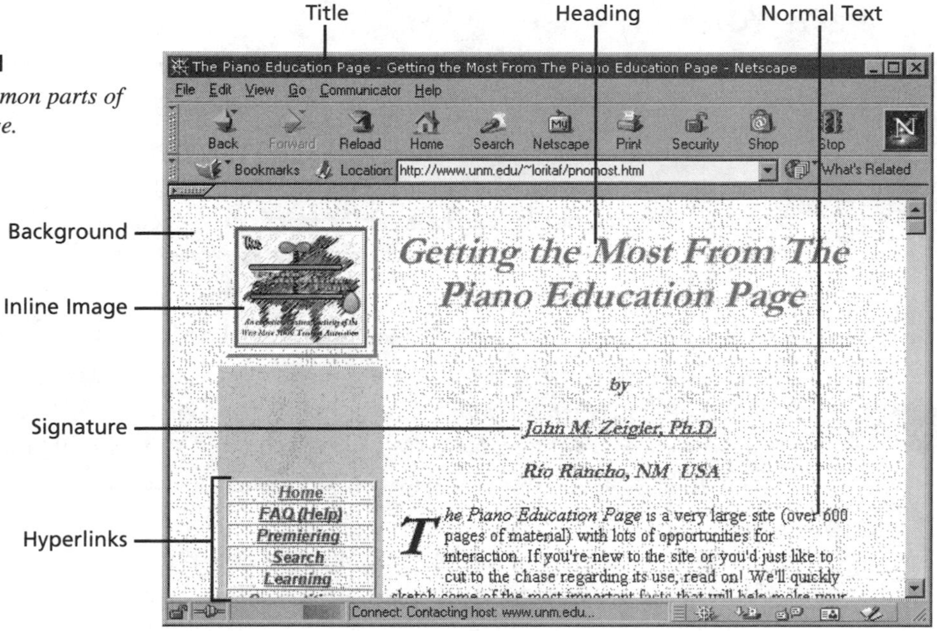

- *Inline images*, which are pictures incorporated into the layout of the page to jazz it up or make it more informative.
- *Background color or pattern*, which is a solid color or an inline image that, unlike regular images, covers the entire background of the page so that text and other images can be seen on top of it.
- *Animations*, which can be text or pictures that appear within the layout of the Web page but move in some way. Pictures can flash on and off or cycle through simple animations, and text can flash or scroll across the screen.
- *Hyperlinks* (or simply *links*) to many different things: other Web pages, multimedia files (external images, animation, sound, or video), document files, email addresses, and files or programs on other types of servers (such as Telnet, FTP, and Gopher). Links can also lead to specific spots within the current page.
- *Imagemaps*, which are inline images in which different areas of the image have different links beneath them.
- *Lists*, which can be bulleted (like this one), numbered, and otherwise.
- *Forms*, which are areas in which visitors can fill in the blanks to respond to an online questionnaire, order goods and services, and more.

Parts You *Don't* See

In addition to the stuff you see in a Web page, the page—or, rather, the set of files making up the page—has a number of other elements that can be included. These elements aren't usually visible to the visitor, but here are their effects:

- *Identification*—Web page files can include a variety of identification information, including the name (or email address) of the author and special coding that helps search engines determine the topic and content of the page.
- *Comments*—Comments are text the author wants to be seen when the HTML code of the page is read directly, not when the page is displayed in a browser. Comments generally include notes about the structure or organization of the HTML file.
- NEW TERM *HTML*, short for *Hyper Text Markup Language*, is the computer file format in which Web pages are stored. An HTML file is really just a text file with special codes in it that tells a browser how to display the file—the size to use for each block of text, where to put the pictures, and so on.
- *JavaScript code*—Within an HTML file, lines of JavaScript program code can add to the page special dynamic capabilities, like a time-sensitive message.
- *Java applets*—In separate files, Java program modules can enhance interaction between the visitor, the browser, and the server. Java is very popular for writing interactive games that can be played on the Web, for example.
- *Imagemap and forms processing code*—Program code used to process imagemaps and interactive forms.

To Do: Identify the parts of a Web page

1. Open your Web browser, connect to the Internet, and go to any Web page you like. (You can use the copy of Netscape included with this book or use most any other browser you have.)
2. Look at the title bar of the window in which the browser appears (the bar along the top, where you usually see the name of a program you're using). You probably see there the title of the Web page you're viewing and the name of the browser program you're using.
3. Explore the page (and others) and see whether you can identify any other parts described earlier in this hour. (Refer to Figure 1.1 if you need to.)

FIGURE 1.2
Step 1: Open your browser and view any page you like.

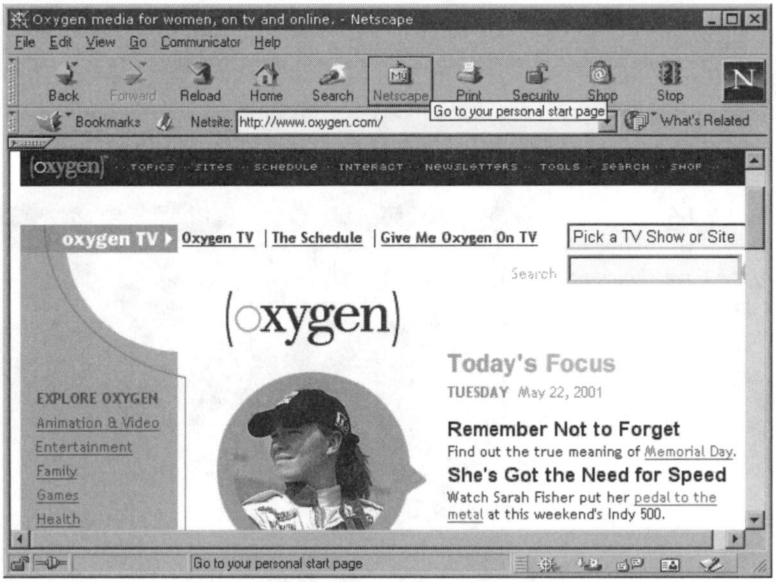

FIGURE 1.3
Step 2: Find the Web page's title in the browser's title bar.

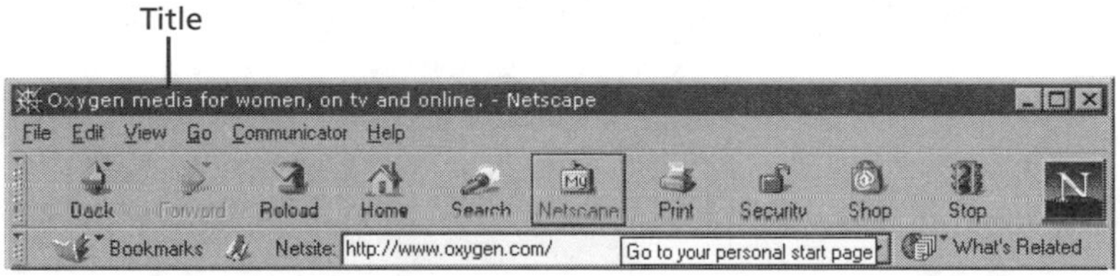

In most browsers, a status bar appears at the bottom of the window. Whenever you point to a link (without clicking), you may see in the status bar the address to which that link leads.

Besides exploring where links lead, you can learn about the picture files you see in a Web page. Point to a picture, right-click, and then choose Properties from the menu that appears. A dialog box appears and tells you the filename, file size, and file type of the picture to which you pointed.

Using these techniques, you can develop your Web authoring skills by learning more about the design of the Web pages you visit.

How a Web Page Works

When you write a Web page, no matter how you go about it, what you really end up with is an HTML file that can be published on a Web server.

An HTML file (see Figure 1.4) contains all the text that appears on the page, plus HTML tags.

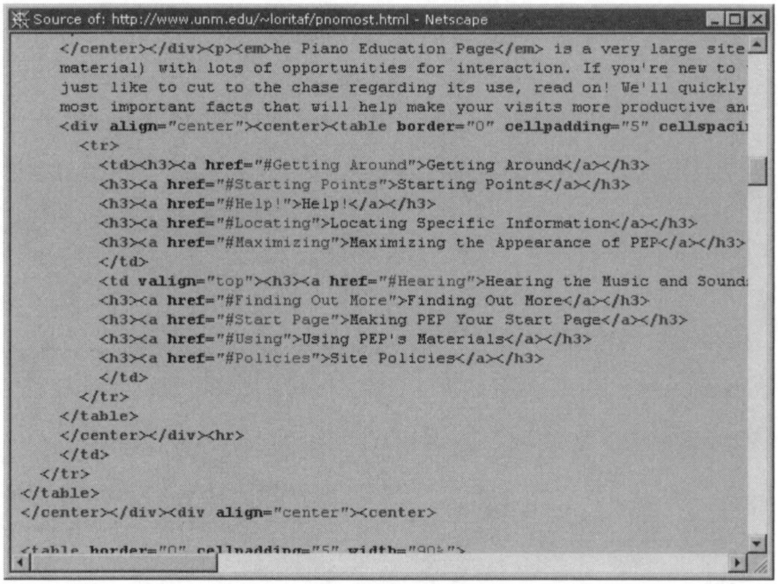

```
Source of: http://www.unm.edu/~loritaf/pnomost.html - Netscape
    </center></div><p><em>he Piano Education Page</em> is a very large site
    material) with lots of opportunities for interaction. If you're new to
    just like to cut to the chase regarding its use, read on! We'll quickly
    most important facts that will help make your visits more productive an
    <div align="center"><center><table border="0" cellpadding="5" cellspaci
      <tr>
        <td><h3><a href="#Getting Around">Getting Around</a></h3>
        <h3><a href="#Starting Points">Starting Points</a></h3>
        <h3><a href="#Help!">Help!</a></h3>
        <h3><a href="#Locating">Locating Specific Information</a></h3>
        <h3><a href="#Maximizing">Maximizing the Appearance of PEP</a></h3>
        </td>
        <td valign="top"><h3><a href="#Hearing">Hearing the Music and Sound
        <h3><a href="#Finding Out More">Finding Out More</a></h3>
        <h3><a href="#Start Page">Making PEP Your Start Page</a></h3>
        <h3><a href="#Using">Using PEP's Materials</a></h3>
        <h3><a href="#Policies">Site Policies</a></h3>
        </td>
      </tr>
    </table>
    </center></div><hr>
    </td>
  </tr>
</table>
</center></div><div align="center"><center>
```

FIGURE 1.4
The HTML source file of the page shown in Figure 1.1.

NEW TERM *Tags* are codes in an HTML file that tell a browser what to do. For example, if the tag `<b>` appears before a word and the tag `</b>` appears after the word, those tags tell browsers to show that word in bold type when displaying the page.

Besides controlling the formatting of the page, the tags in an HTML file label each chunk of text as a particular element of the page. For example, HTML tags identify one line of text as the page's title, blocks of text as paragraphs, certain lines or words as links, and so on. Other HTML tags designate the filenames of inline images to be incorporated into the page by the browser when the page is displayed.

A *Web browser* is a program that knows how to do at least two things:

- Retrieve HTML documents from remote Web servers (by using a communications protocol named HTTP, about which you need to know nothing right now)
- Interpret the HTML tags in the document to display a heading as a heading, treat a link like a link, and so on

What's important to remember is that the HTML tags do not offer you the kind of control over the precise formatting of a page that you would have in a word processor. HTML mostly just identifies what's what. Each browser decides differently how to format those elements onscreen, though the two major browsers—Netscape and Internet Explorer—tend to show most Web pages almost identically.

NEW TERM *Extensions* are special additions to the standard HTML language, usually created by a browser maker to enable that browser to do tasks not included in HTML. See "Extensions: Love 'Em!, Hate 'Em!," later in this hour.

At the time of this writing, the two most popular browsers—various versions of Netscape Navigator and Internet Explorer—comprise the overwhelming majority of the browser market. Although subtle differences exist in the HTML tags each one supports, the perpetual competition between these two has resulted in two browsers that display most Web pages identically. To most potential visitors on the Web, therefore, your Web page will look roughly the same as it does to you in Netscape as you work on it.

To folks using browsers other than the two big shots, your page will always show the same text content and general organization, but its graphical content and other aesthetics might vary dramatically from browser to browser. In fact, in some cases, pictures and any other graphical niceties might not even show up.

> You can download the browsers shown in Figures 1.5 and 1.6 and display your pages in them to see how your work appears in various browsers. Web addresses for getting these browsers appear in Hour 23, "Testing and Updating Your Page."

To illustrate this browser-to-browser variation, Figures 1.5 and 1.6 show exactly the same Web page as shown earlier, in Figure 1.1. That figure, however, displays the page through Netscape, and Figures 1.5 and 1.6 show it through two other browsers: Opera and DosLynx, respectively. Compare these two figures and observe how the presentation differs in each one.

DosLynx, the browser shown in Figure 1.6, is a *text-only* browser for DOS. (You remember DOS, don't you?) Disappearing rapidly from the Web (but still out there), these browsers cannot display inline graphics and display all text in the same-size typeface, although important elements, such as headings, can be made to stand out with bold type or underlining. Some people use text-only browsers out of choice, although most people do so because they lack the proper type of Internet account or the proper hardware for a graphical browser.

FIGURE 1.5
The same page as shown in Figure 1.1 is shown in Opera.

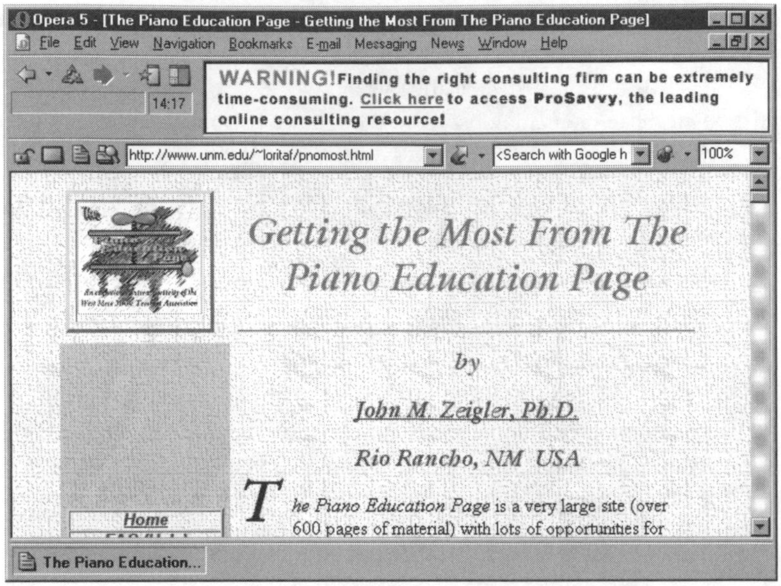

FIGURE 1.6
The same page, as shown in Figures 1.1 and 1.5, shown in DosLynx.

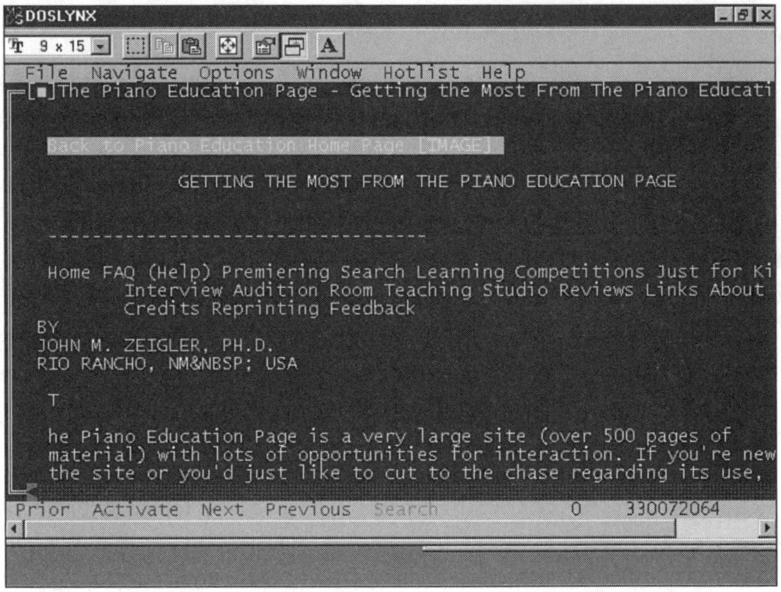

1

> In addition to those using text-only browsers, others online can't see graphics because they have used the customization features in their browsers to switch off the display of graphics (which speeds up the display of pages).

Although text-only browsers have all but disappeared, as a new Web author, you should keep in mind the possibility that some folks can't see the pictures in your pages. For them, you need to make sure that the text in the page gets the job done, whether the pictures appear or not.

▼ To Do

To Do: Examine the HTML source code of a Web page

1. View any Web page through your Web browser.
2. Change the view of your browser so that it shows the raw HTML source code of the page:

   In Netscape, choose View, Page Source.

   In Internet Explorer, choose View, Source.

   In another browser, look for a menu option that mentions Source or HTML.

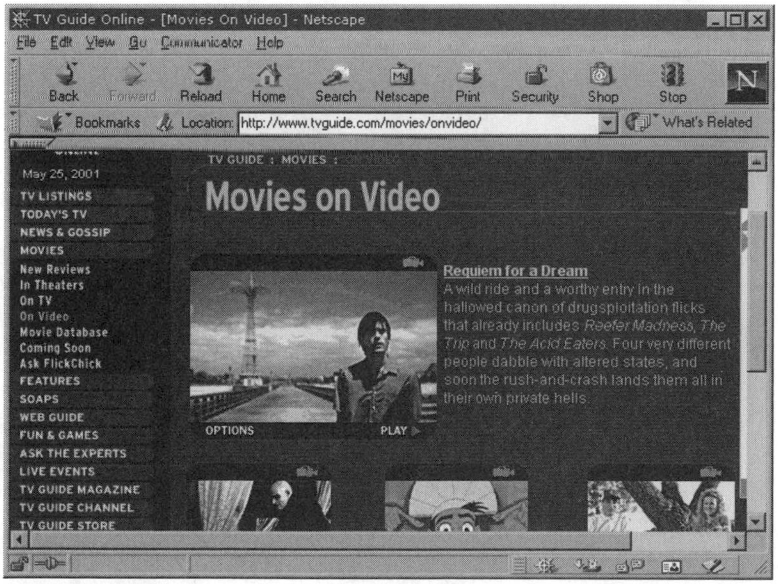

FIGURE 1.7
Step 1: View any page.

▼

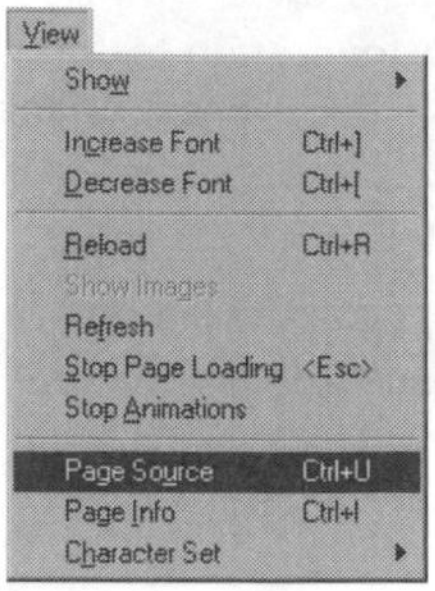

FIGURE 1.8
Step 2: Choose a menu item that displays the HTML source code of the page you're viewing.

3. Explore the HTML code. Don't worry if lots of it looks like gibberish—you don't really need to be able to "decode" an HTML file on sight. But if you look closely, you see the following within the various codes:
    - The actual text that appears on the page
    - Filenames of pictures in the page
    - Web addresses to which the links point
4. When finished examining the HTML source code, close the window in which the code appears so that the browser returns to its normal view.

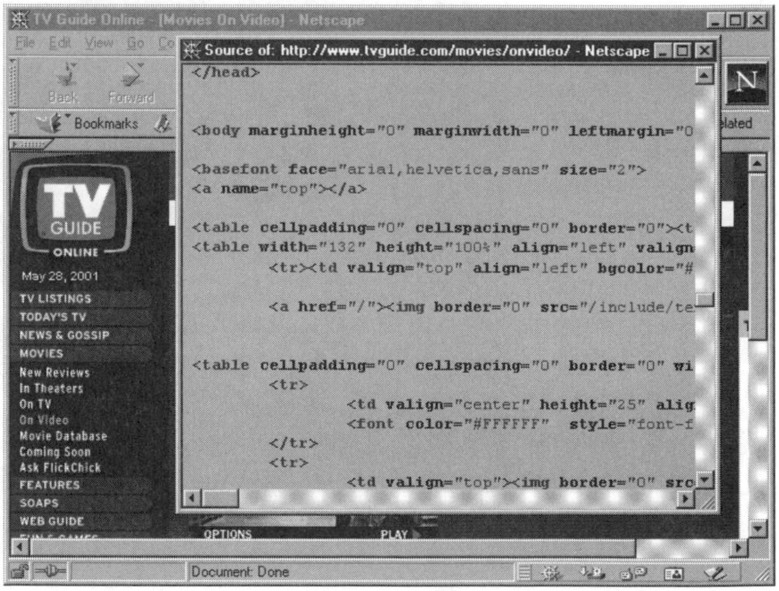

FIGURE 1.9
Step 3: Explore the code, just to get a feel for what a Web page is really made of.

Pictures, Sound, and Other Media

Because an HTML file contains only text, the graphics you see in Web pages—and the multimedia you can access from Web pages—are not exactly a part of the HTML source file itself. Rather, graphics are linked to the page in either of two ways:

- *Inline images* are graphics files whose filenames and locations are noted in the HTML file itself and identified as images by tags. Inline images are incorporated into the layout of the page—all the images you see through a browser when you access the page.
- *External media* are image, sound, or video files whose names and locations appear as links in the HTML file. These files do not appear or play automatically as part of the page. Instead, the page shows links that, when activated, download the file to play or display it.

Whether inline or external, the media files you use in your Web pages challenge the browsers that are used to view your page. The browser must be capable of displaying graphics to display inline graphics. External media files can be played by either the browser or, more commonly, helper applications (or plug-ins) opened by the browser.

When choosing to incorporate media into your page, you have to consider carefully the file types you use. The text-only rule of HTML files is what allows users of many different types of computers to access Web pages. Graphics files are less likely to be readable by a wide range of systems, and sound and video files, even less so. Even within the confines of PCs and Macintoshes, you need to consider whether your media will be supported by a broad spectrum of browsers or helper applications. You learn more about this topic in Hour 13, "Getting Pictures for Your Page."

Extensions: Love 'Em!, Hate 'Em!

HTML is standardized so that any Web browser can read any Web documents—sort of.

Here's the deal: All modern browsers support all of HTML 4, a well-established set of tags set by the committees that oversee Internet standards. Standardization is good because it provides Web authors with a way to ensure that most browsers can read what they publish. Because any browser can understand and interpret all the HTML 4 tags, authors need only stick within the confines of those tags to ensure that their pages are accessible to the biggest possible online audience.

> HTML 5 won't be created. Instead, the next major change in Web page standards is named XHTML. Similar to HTML in many respects, XHTML will give Web authors the level of control over page formatting that one sees in word processing and desktop publishing. XHTML is also being developed to accommodate the growing range of noncomputer devices that will be using the Web: portable phones and automobile Internet devices, for example.

The problem with standards, though, is that they evolve slowly. On the Web, only downloads are permitted to be slow; *evolution* is required to be *fast*. Think about it: The first graphical browser emerged seven years ago, and now we're talking real-time video. The entire birth and maturation of the Web as a graphical, interactive environment took place within the equivalent of a single Presidential administration. Yikes!

> When creating pages for a company intranet, where all users may have the same browser, you may not need to consider the extensions issue—you can apply all tags supported by the browser.

Leading browsers, including both Netscape and Internet Explorer, support all of HTML 4, the current standard. Still, the pace of Web page enhancement is so great that both Netscape and Microsoft continue to incorporate in their browsers extra tags and other capabilities that are not part of any approved HTML standard. These additional tags are extensions.

NEW TERM An *extension* is an HTML tag that makes possible some new capability in a Web page but is not yet part of the formal HTML standard.

The effects of these extensions, when used in a Web document, can usually be seen only through a browser that specifically supports them. Of course, Navigator supports many Netscape extensions, and Internet Explorer supports many Microsoft extensions. But subtle differences exist. For example, scrolling text banners that can appear in a box in the page layout in Internet Explorer appear instead in the status bar in some versions of Netscape. However, not all browsers support all extensions. That's why you need to be careful with 'em.

In general, whenever an incompatible browser accesses a page that uses these tags, nothing dire happens. The fancy extension-based formatting doesn't show up, but the meat of the page—its text and graphics—remain readable.

> Authors who want to take advantage of extensions are concerned that some visitors are not seeing the page in its full glory. That's why, more and more, you see messages like "Best when viewed through Netscape Navigator" or "Enhanced for Internet Explorer" on Web pages. That's the author's way of telling you that he or she has used extensions—and if you want to enjoy all the features of the page, you had better pick up a compatible browser.

Ways to Organize a Web Site

Finally, before you dive into creating Web pages, you must give some thought to the following issues:

- How can my message be broken down into an organized series of topics?
- How long of a Web page, or how many Web pages (linked together into a Web site), are required in order to say what I have to say?

> After you've developed and refined the topic breakdown and outline of your message, you might find that you've already composed the headings for your Web pages.

Jot down a list of the topics or subtopics your document will cover. How many do you have, and how much material is required for each topic? After this simple exercise, you begin to get a good sense of the size and scope of your document.

Now look at the topics. Do they proceed in a logical order from beginning to end, with each new part depending on knowledge of the earlier parts? Or, does the material seem to branch naturally to subtopics (and sub-subtopics)? How might you reorder the topics to make the flow more logical or group related topics together?

As you work on your breakdown (not *that* kind of breakdown—your topic breakdown), a simple outline begins to emerge. The more you refine the outline before you begin composing your document, the more focused and efficient your authoring becomes. More important, the resulting Web document presents your message in a way that's clear and easy to follow.

> To plan a document with three or more pages, *storyboard* it by roughing out each page on a piece of paper to decide which information belongs on each page. Tape the papers to a wall and draw lines or tape strings to plan links among the pages.

While you're building your outline, consider the logical organization of your presentation and how its material might fit into any of the common organizational structures seen on the Web:

Billboard—A single, simple page, usually describing a person, small business, or simple product. Most personal home pages are this type. They often contain links to related (or favorite) resources on the Web, but not to any further pages of the same document. (The Netscape Page Wizard builds this type of page.)

One-page linear—One Web page, short or long, designed to be read more or less from top to bottom. Rules are often used to divide up this type of page into virtual "pages." Readers can scroll through the entire page, but a table of contents and targets can be used to help readers jump down quickly to any section. This type is best used for fairly short documents (fewer than 10 screens full) wherein all the information flows naturally from a beginning to an end.

Multipage linear—The same general idea as the one-page linear type, but broken up into multiple pages that flow logically, one after the other, from beginning to end, like the pages of a story. You can lead the reader through the series by placing a link at the bottom of each page, leading to the next page.

Hierarchical—The classic Web structure. A top page (sometimes confusingly called a *home page*) contains links to other pages, each covering a major subject area. Each of those pages can have multiple links to still more pages, breaking the subject down further and getting into even more specific information. The result is a tree structure, like the one shown in Figure 1.10.

Web—As shown in Figure 1.11, a hierarchical structure without the hierarchy. In this multipage document, any page can have a link leading to any other page. It might be a "top" page, but from there, readers can wander around the Web in no particular path. Web structures are loose and free-flowing and are, therefore, best suited to fun, recreational subjects or to subjects that defy any kind of sequential or hierarchical breakdown. (*Hint:* Before you resort to using a Web structure, make sure that your message really calls for one—you might just be having trouble focusing.)

You can organize information in other ways; variations on each of the structures presented here. But one of these structures should resemble the general shape of your message, and

FIGURE 1.10
A hierarchical structure.

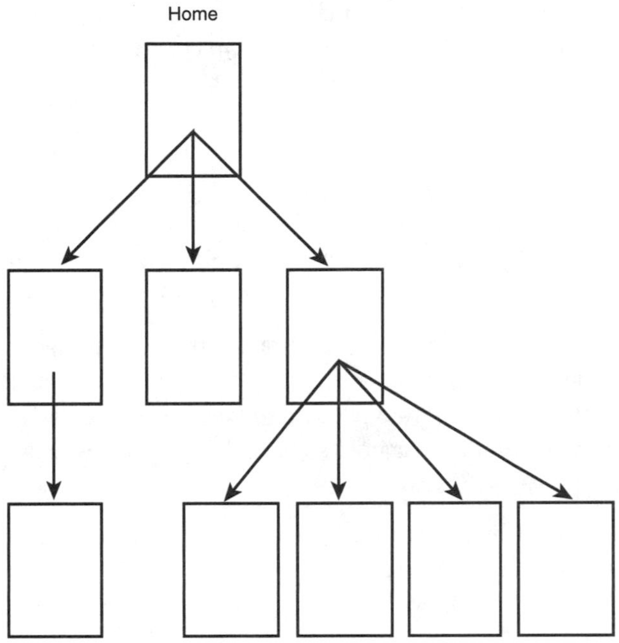

FIGURE 1.11
A Web structure.

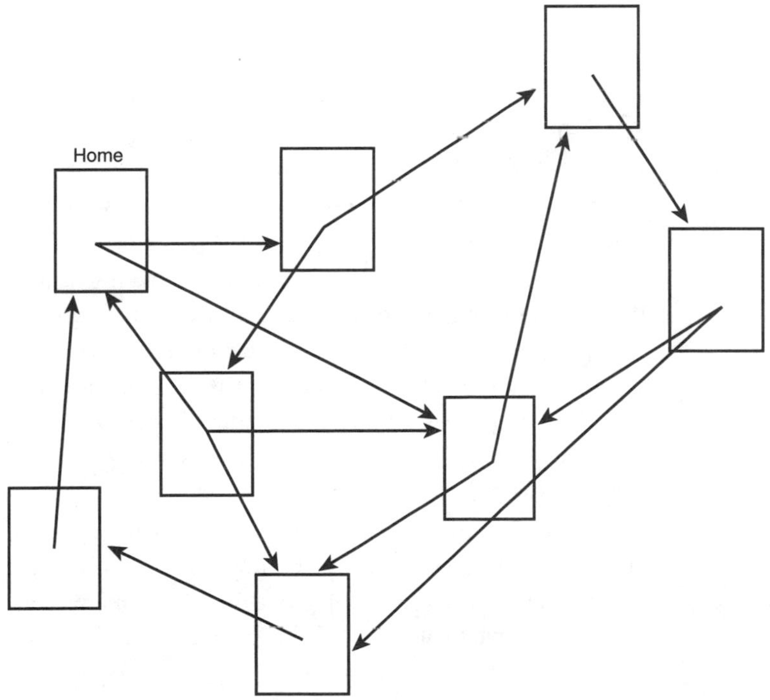

thus your document. To put it another way, if you haven't yet decided which of these structures is best for the Web page you want to create, you need to play with your message some more and break it down in different ways until a structure reveals itself to you.

Summary

You can, if you choose, create your Web page by getting some good coffee, sitting down, and fiddling for a while with a template (see Hour 3) or any Web page editor. In the end, you have an HTML file suitable for publishing (if not for reading).

But is it a file that achieves your goals for wanting a Web page in the first place? If you're looking for cyberfriends, will your page appeal to them? If you're looking for clients or customers, does your page make you look better than your competitors look? If you're offering useful information, are you doing so in a way that visitors to your page will find intuitive and easy to navigate?

To create a page that hits its mark, you must first ground yourself in the basics of how a Web document works and what it can and cannot do. That's what you've picked up in this hour. I didn't attempt to dictate how your document should look, feel, or operate—that has to be your inspiration. But I've tried to feed your thoughts so that you can make informed choices during whatever tasks you choose to take on next.

Q&A

Q So, basically, you're telling me that I can do all these cool things to my page, but I should stick with the boring stuff because the cool stuff is based on extensions and also some people can't see graphics. Isn't that, well, ever so slightly a bummer?

A Bummer—not. In practice, it's really not such a big deal. First of all, remember that the overwhelming majority of the folks browsing the Web can view graphics, and most use a browser that can cope with most extensions. So even if you go completely nuts with pictures and extension-based formatting, your page will look great to most people. By using techniques I show you in later hours, you can accommodate the graphics-impaired or extension-impaired so that your page is as useful to them as to everyone else.

Still, remember that just because you're writing a page *in* a Netscape Web page editor doesn't mean that you're writing it solely *for* users of the Netscape browser. A smart author makes his or her document informative and cool to look at *as well as* be accessible to all.

HOUR 2

Getting Started with a Web Authoring Program

When you work in a WYSIWYG Web page editor (like Netscape Composer, included with this book), your page looks (with minor exceptions) just the way it will look to most visitors on the Web.

That's a powerful convenience; without it, Web authors have had to guess about the appearance of their pages while fiddling with all the HTML code. To check their work, authors had to open the file in a browser and then go back to the HTML code to make adjustments. With a WYSIWYG editor, you can see and do it all in one window, live and in color.

This hour examines the general operation of Composer so that you know your way around when you approach the specific authoring tasks coming up in later hours. At the end of the hour, you will be able to answer the following questions:

- How do I open Composer?
- How do I fid my way around Composer's toolbars?

- How do I start, save, and reopen Web pages in Composer?
- How do I test the way my page will look online?
- Can I print my work?

> This hour assumes that you have already installed the programs from the CD-ROM included with this book, as described in Appendix A, "Setting Up the Programs on the CD-ROM."

Opening Composer

When you install Composer (as shown in Appendix A), a shortcut for opening the program is automatically added to your Windows Start menu.

- To open Composer, click the Start button and then choose Programs, Netscape Communicator, Netscape Composer (see Figure 2.1).
- To close Composer, choose File, Exit or click the X button in the upper-right corner of the Composer window (see Figure 2.2).

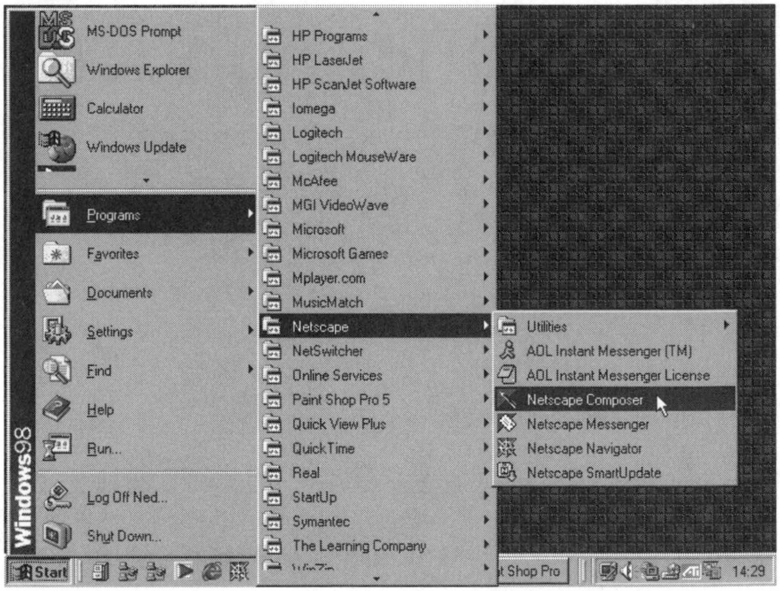

FIGURE 2.1
Opening Composer.

FIGURE 2.2
Closing Composer.

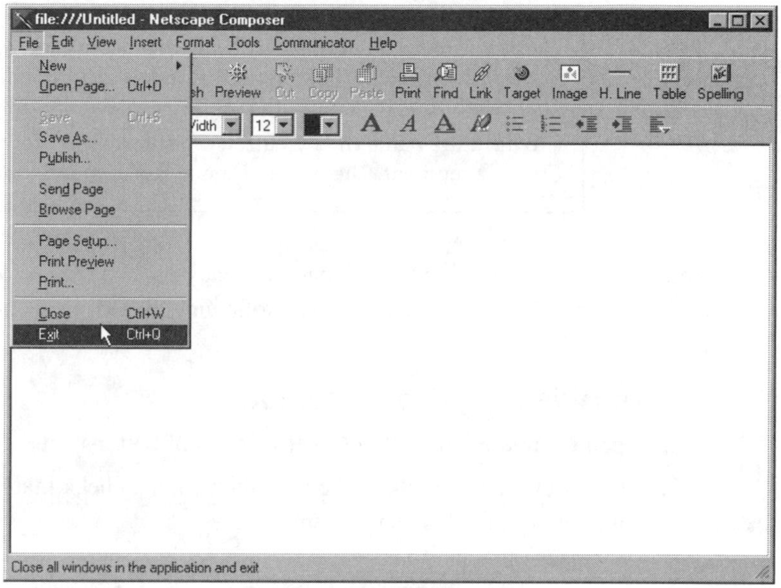

> When Composer opens, it automatically opens a new, blank Web page file. You can start typing right away to begin creating your first Web page.

Exploring the Composer Toolbars

You perform many activities in Composer by clicking buttons on its two main toolbars: Composition and Formatting (see Figure 2.3). Composer actually has four toolbars. It also has the taskbar, which appears at the bottom of the Composer window, but which has no role in Web authoring, and the Edit Mode toolbar, which you won't use until Hour 17, so ignore it for now. You learn much more about these toolbars over the next 22 hours; for now, it's enough just to know where they are.

FIGURE 2.3
You do most things in Composer by clicking buttons and picking from list boxes on the Composition and Formatting toolbars.

> Most buttons are easy to identify by their icons (and names, on the Composition toolbar). But note that every button (or list box) on the toolbars has a *tooltip*, a name that appears to identify the button.
>
> To learn the name of any button or list box, point to it (don't click) and pause a moment. The name of the button appears.

You can choose to display any toolbar (for ready use) or hide it (to free up more screen area for examining your creations). The following To Do shows how to hide and display toolbars.

To Do: Hide and display toolbars

1. Open Composer and look at the two rows of buttons beneath the menu bar.
2. Click View and then click Show. In the menu, a check mark appears next to the name of each toolbar that's displayed.

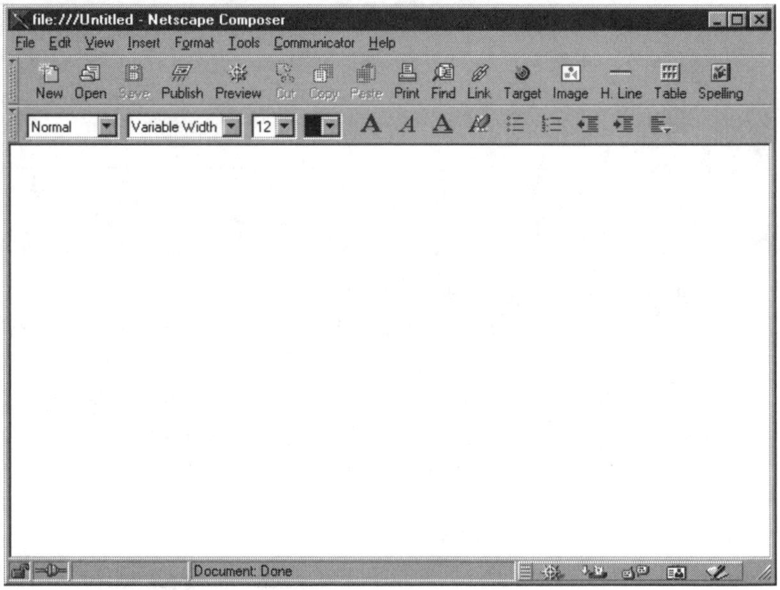

FIGURE 2.4
Step 1: Open Composer and check out the toolbars.

▼

FIGURE 2.5
Step 2: Open the View menu.

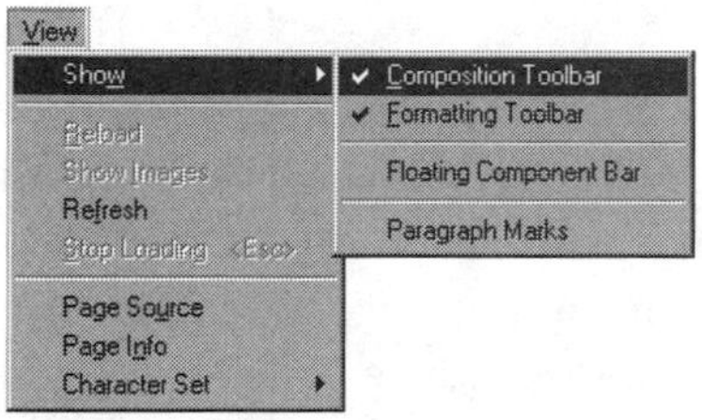

3. To hide a toolbar, click its name.

▲ 4. To redisplay a toolbar you've hidden, repeat Steps 2 and 3.

2

Starting a New Web Page

When you open Composer, it automatically opens to a new, blank page, so you can get right to work. As soon as Composer appears, you can begin applying the page-composition skills you learn in Part II.

But in Hour 3, you learn how to use templates to kick off a new page with a head start rather than begin with a blank slate.

> You can also start a new, blank web page at any time from within Composer, by choosing File, New, Blank Page.
>
> The new page opens in a new Composer window, so the page you were editing previously remains open behind it. You can go back and close the previous page, or switch back and forth between the pages as needed.

Saving and Naming Files

Whether you create it with a template (see Hour 3) or from scratch, you need to save your new Web page file early and often.

About Web Page Filenames

When you save a file in Composer, you give it a name—presumably the name by which it will be stored on a Web server when published. And when it comes time to publish a Web page, names can be tricky. For example, Windows 98, Windows 2000, Windows Me, and even the Macintosh all allow you to use spaces and punctuation in filenames, but you should not do so when naming Web page files. Composer permits you to do it, but when you attempt to publish the files, you will find that browsers cannot open them.

In general, as long as you use a filename extension of `.htm` or `.html` and eliminate spaces and punctuation, you can give your page files any name you like. However, you can avoid certain kinds of compatibility problems by making sure that your filenames conform to the "8.3" filename rule: The filename must be no more than eight characters long with an extension of no more than three (`.htm`, not `.html`); for example:

```
nedsnell.htm
```

Also, when a page will be the "top" page of a multipage Web presentation, standard practice is to name it `index.html` (or `index.htm`). Most Web servers are configured to open the file `index.html` automatically when a visitor specifies a Web site address or directory but not a specific file. However, this system works only if you have your own directory on the server. Usually, you will. But if you share a directory with others, odds are that you won't be the first to post a file named `index.html`, so the server won't accept your document. For this reason, sometimes you should choose your server (see Hour 21, "Publishing Your Site") and find out about its naming guidelines before settling on final names for your HTML files.

> When creating a multipage Web site, saving all the page files in the same folder on your PC is important. Doing so not only makes publishing easier, but it also simplifies other tasks, such as creating links between pages.
>
> The best approach is to create a new, empty folder on your PC and store in it all the files that make up the site—including not only the HTML files, but also other files that come into play, such as picture files.

To Do: Saving a file

1. Click the Save button on the Composition toolbar or choose File, Save.

FIGURE 2.6
Step 1: Click the Save button or choose File, Save.

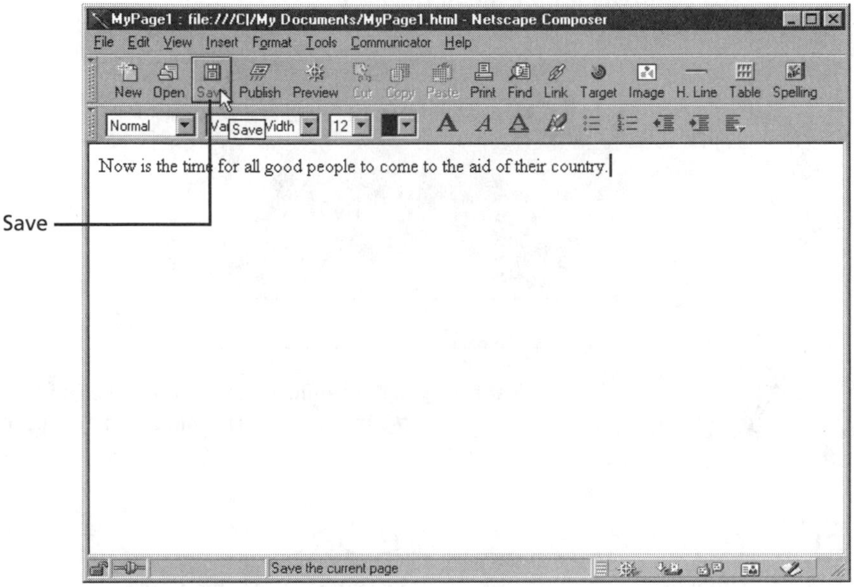

2. Choose a folder in which to save the page file. (To create a new folder to save in, click the Create New Folder button.) Then name the file as you would when saving a file in any Windows program and click the Save button.

FIGURE 2.7
Step 2: Pick a folder and type a filename.

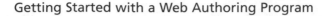

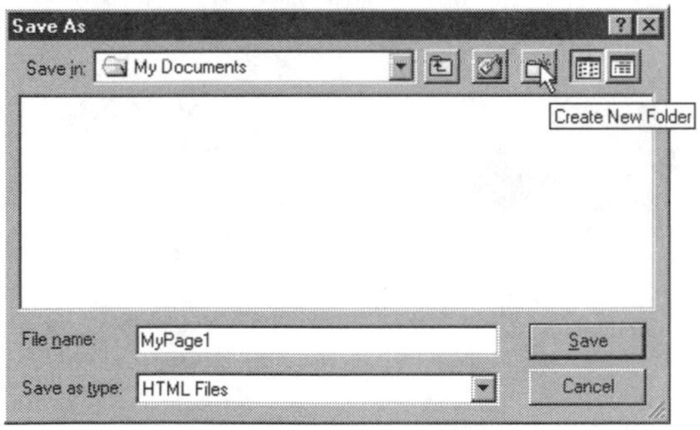

3. Enter a title for this page. (Don't feel pressured; you can always change the title later, as you learn to do in Hour 5.)

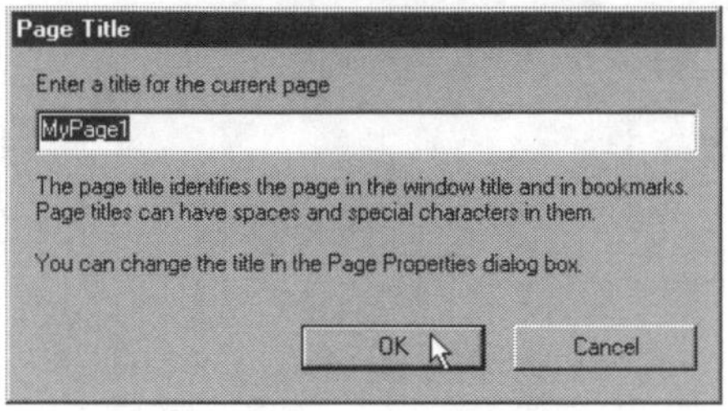

FIGURE 2.8
Step 3: Type a title.

> After the first time you save a file, you no longer need to perform Steps 2 and 3 when you save again. Simply performing Step 1 saves the file.

Editing Pages You've Saved

As you work on Web pages, you'll probably create them over a series of editing sessions. You need to open existing files and close them when you're done. The following To Do shows how to close files and to reopen them each time you want to work on them.

To Do: Closing and reopening pages

1. To close a page file (without closing Composer), choose File, Close.

FIGURE 2.9
Step 1: Choose File, Close to close a file.

2. To open a page file, choose File, Open Page.

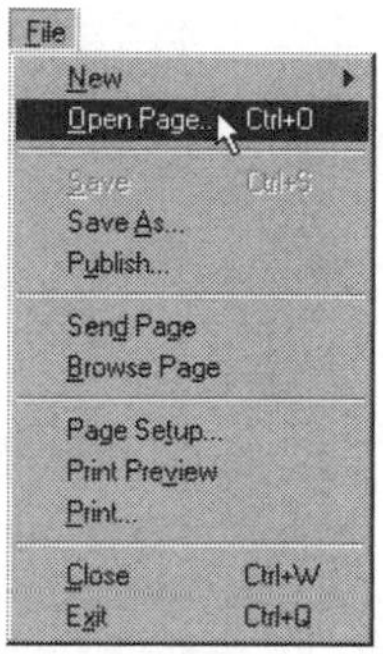

FIGURE 2.10
Step 2: Choose File, Open Page.

3. Click the Choose File button to navigate to the folder where you've stored the page file.

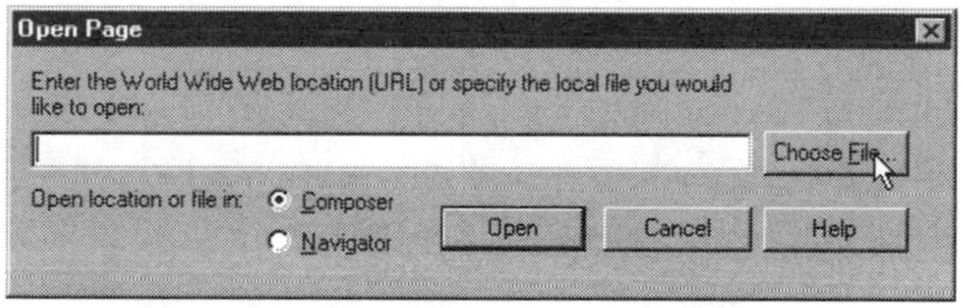

FIGURE 2.11
Step 3: Use Choose File to open the folder where the file is stored.

4. Choose the file's name from the Open HTML File dialog box and click Open.

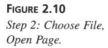

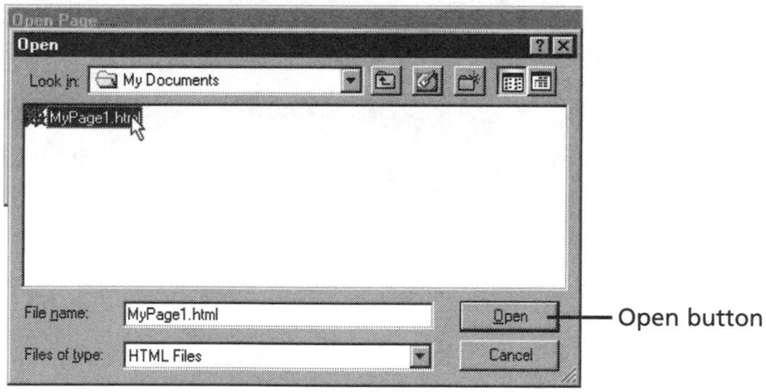

FIGURE 2.12
Step 4: Click the file's name and then click Open.

Checking Out Your New Page in a Web Browser

In Composer, your Web pages will appear pretty much the same as they will when viewed through a browser and the Internet. Still, you should preview your page through your Web browser from time to time to evaluate its true appearance.

> Check out the page in a few different browsers, to make sure that it looks okay to everyone online, no matter what browser they use. You learn more about testing your page's appearance in Part VI, "Getting It Online."

To Do: Opening your page in your Web browser

1. Save the file in Composer.
2. Click the Preview button on the Composition toolbar.

The page opens in Navigator, as shown in Figure 2.15. To return to editing your page, switch to Composer by clicking its button on the Windows taskbar.

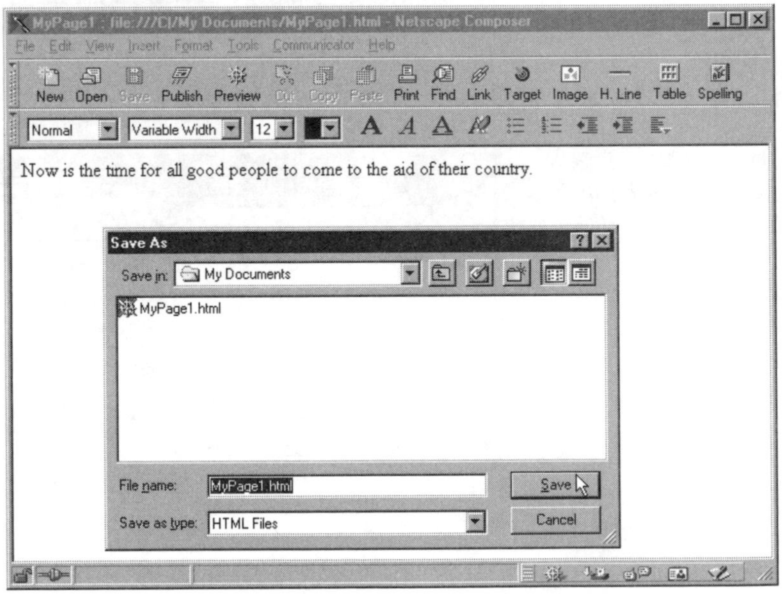

FIGURE 2.13
Step 1: Save the file.

FIGURE 2.14
Step 2: Click Preview.

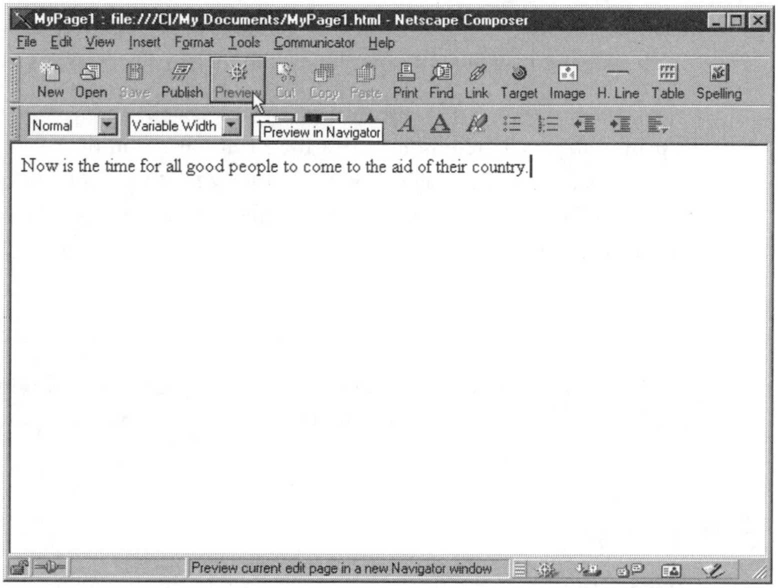

FIGURE 2.15
The page appears in Navigator.

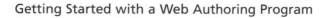

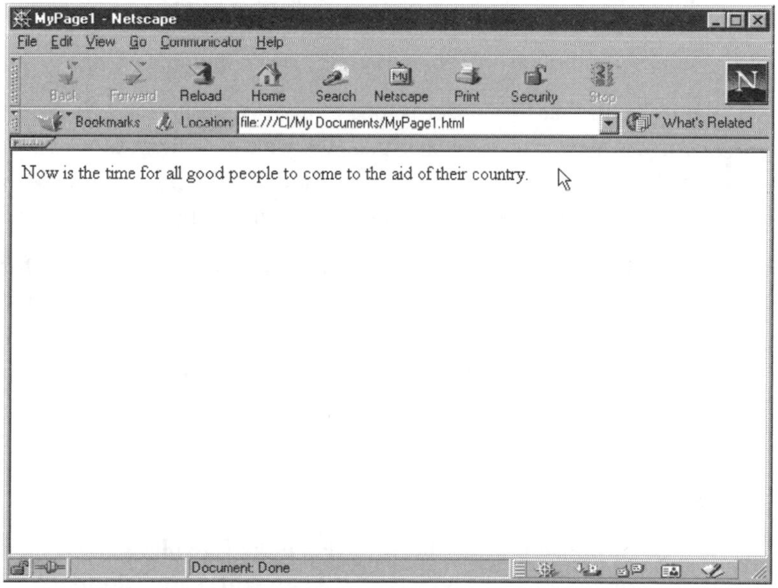

2

Printing Pages

When developing your pages, you may find that printing them from time to time is useful. Reviewing printouts of your pages may help you see typos or other errors you might miss when reading a page online (a trick of the eyes).

To print a page you're editing, click the Print button on the Composition toolbar or choose File, Print. The page is printed exactly as it would be from a Web browser—text formatting and pictures are included on the printout, but any background patterns you may have added are omitted to keep text legible. The page is broken up into appropriately sized chunks to fit on paper pages.

> Although you might want to print your pages for reference, do not rely on printouts as accurate representations of your page's appearance online.

Summary

Composer does a great deal—too much, in fact, for this hour to even scratch the surface. Still, in this hour, you've wrapped your arms around the job and learned how to get into, out of, and around Composer. As mundane as those tasks are, they're the essential foundation to productive Web authoring. You're on your way.

But for all that Composer is, one thing it is not is smart. It can't tell you whether the content you've created is well organized, well presented, or well written. And although it applies HTML tags to your document dutifully, it cannot tell you whether you've selected the most effective tags for presenting the content at hand.

Thus, Composer is a replacement for only time and labor, not for judgment. To author an effective Web document, you must acquire a sense of Web aesthetics. You pick up much of this sense as you work through this book. But you must also study other pages you see online and mentally catalog the design aspects and content approaches that sing to you—and those that annoy, bore, or baffle you.

Q&A

Q Suppose that I want to save a page I've already saved, but under a different name, to make a copy of it I can edit. Can I do that?

A Sure, that's a handy way to carry from one page to the next the common elements you've created for a site. When you want to do this, choose File, Save As (rather than File, Save or the Save button) and rename the file in the Save Page As box.

HOUR 3

Wizarding Up a Personal Home Page

The everyday, tried-and-true, best-case scenario for building a Web site is the one taught within this book: Use an authoring program offline to create HTML Web page files and then send them to a Web server.

But, for a variety of reasons, many folks are taking a different tack. Many Internet service providers, and also a gaggle of online communities, let visitors create and publish a Web page—and do the whole job, from start to finish, online, in their browsers, with no authoring program required. These online programs that help you build a Web site are called by many different names, but to make things easy, we can call them *wizards*.

These wizards have advantages and disadvantages, as you will soon see. Before diving in to the nitty-gritty of the best way to build a Web site, I thought it best to share with you the alternative so that you can make an informed choice.

At the end of this hour, you will be able to answer the following questions:

- What are the ups and downs of creating a page online with a wizard?
- Where can I find a wizard?
- What basic steps does it usually take to build a page this way?
- If I choose instead to go the offline Web authoring route described in the rest of this book, what do I need to know about the process of publishing my Web pages after I've created them?

Should I Create My Web Site Online?

That depends....

The benefit of a wizard is that it is a fast and easy way to get a decent-looking Web site up and running with a minimum of fuss. The problem is that you have far less control of the appearance of the results, and far less ability to make your page distinctive, than you would have if you created your page offline in a Web authoring program. Figure 3.1 shows a typical wizard-built page, although the actual appearance depends on which wizard you choose.

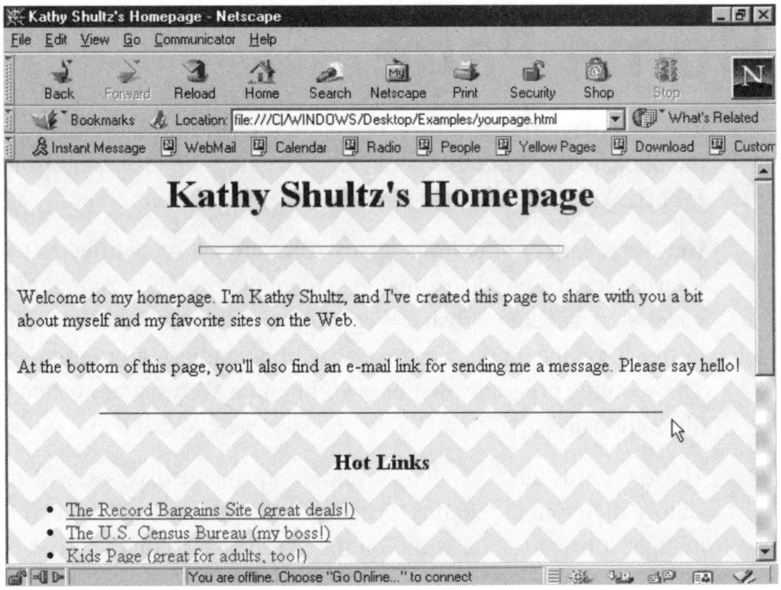
Kathy Shultz's Homepage - Netscape
File Edit View Go Communicator Help
Back Forward Reload Home Search Netscape Print Security Shop Stop
Bookmarks Location: file:///C|/WINDOWS/Desktop/Examples/yourpage.html What's Related
Instant Message WebMail Calendar Radio People Yellow Pages Download
Kathy Shultz's Homepage
Welcome to my homepage. I'm Kathy Shultz, and I've created this page to share with you a bit about myself and my favorite sites on the Web.
At the bottom of this page, you'll also find an e-mail link for sending me a message. Please say hello!
Hot Links
The Record Bargains Site (great deals!)
The U.S. Census Bureau (my boss!)
Kids Page (great for adults, too!)
You are offline. Choose "Go Online..." to connect

FIGURE 3.1
A wizard-built page tends to look generic.

You use a wizard by responding to questions and filling in choices in a series of online forms, using the same sorts of skills you would use to order a fruit basket from an online shop. Your entries in these forms are automatically plugged in to the appropriate spots in a Web page template. The template used is a simple, straightforward home page—no more, no less.

New Term A *template* is a finished Web page file that you can edit and customize to create a new page of your own much more quickly than starting from scratch. See Hour 4, "Starting Pages in Other Programs."

The templates used by most wizards are designed for personal home pages, or basic commercial pages, and are effective in that regard, even if they're a little short and overly simple.

Besides featuring limited layout options, most wizard-built pages have one more problem: *ads,* or banner advertisements that the server supplier inserts on your page (see Figure 3.2). With many wizards, your willingness to have ads on your page gets you the page for free.

3

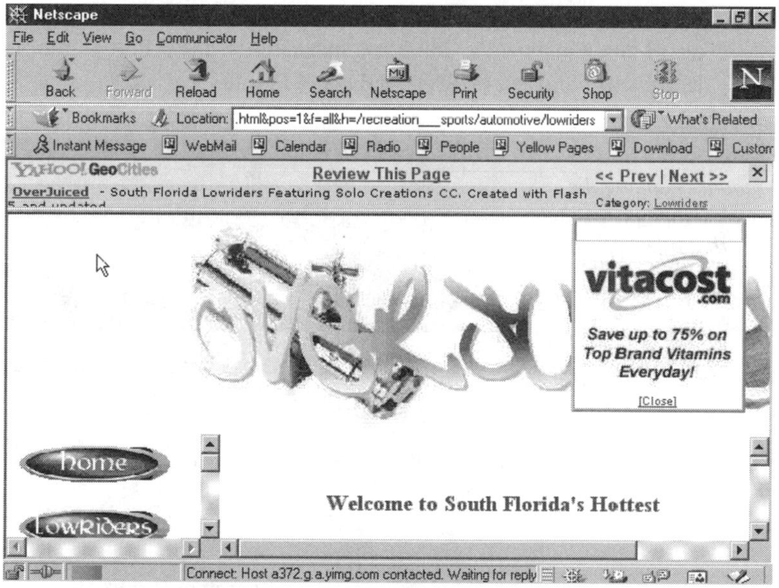

FIGURE 3.2
Most sites offering free Web space require you to carry their ads on your page.

Whether you should use a wizard depends on whether the overall organization of the resulting page is reasonably close to what you want to achieve—and on whether you can tolerate ads on your page. If you want a dramatically different look for your page, or if you plan to build an elaborate Web document made up of multiple linked pages and files, you might be better off with another startup strategy, such as the following:

- Transform into Web pages other documents you already have created in other programs (see Hour 4).
- Brave the void and start from scratch (see Hour 5, "Choosing a Title, Text Colors, and Other Page Basics").

Where Are the Wizards?

They're everywhere. The first, best place to look is the home page of your Internet provider. Many—particularly the big online services, such as AOL—provide page generators to make easy use of the "free" Web space included with your account. Look for links with names like Personal Web Site.

Another place to look for wizards is in any of the many online communities, sometimes also known as *portals,* that have sprouted up, including Yahoo! (see Figure 3.3), Microsoft Network (MSN), AOL, and Excite.

FIGURE 3.3
Yahoo! is among the many online communities that offer a free Web page.

Again, if you're looking for a fast page, start with your Internet provider. Failing that, try

Yahoo: `www.yahoo.com`

MSN: `www.msn.com`

Excite: `www.excite.com`

What Does It Take to Make a Basic Page with a Wizard?

That depends. Each of the many page generators online is a little different, but no matter. In every case, all you have to do is follow directions; every wizard tells you exactly what to do as you go along.

Just to give you a sense of what's involved in building a page online with a wizard, here are the basics of using the Web Site Builder, a wizard that AT&T WorldNet offers its subscribers.

As an AT&T subscriber, you start out at the AT&T WorldNet home page. On that page, you click the Free Web Page link and then read the guidelines page, as shown in Figure 3.4.

If you scroll to the bottom of that page and click the Signup button, a page appears on which you can click a Yes button to agree to the rules listed on the preceding page.

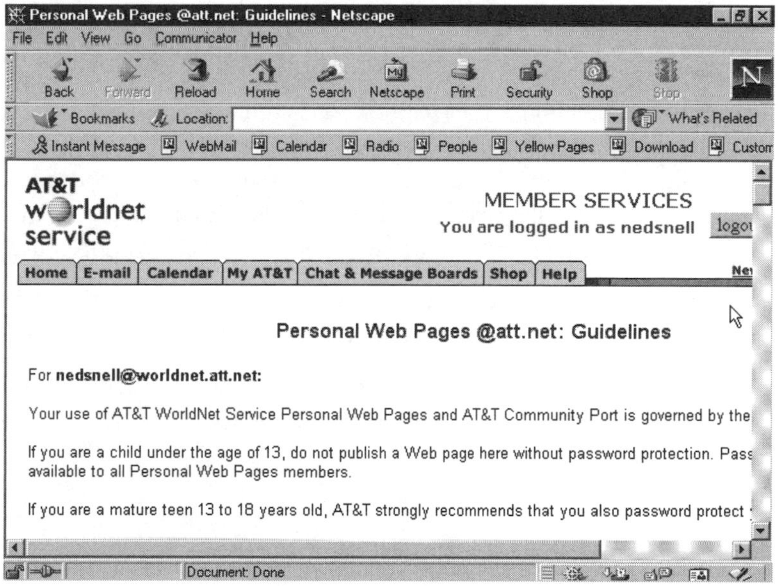
Personal Web Pages @att.net: Guidelines - Netscape
File Edit View Go Communicator Help
Back Forward Reload Home Search Netscape Print Security Shop Stop
Bookmarks Location: What's Related
Instant Message WebMail Calendar Radio People Yellow Pages Download
AT&T worldnet service
MEMBER SERVICES
You are logged in as nedsnell
Home E-mail Calendar My AT&T Chat & Message Boards Shop Help
Personal Web Pages @att.net: Guidelines
For nedsnell@worldnet.att.net:
Your use of AT&T WorldNet Service Personal Web Pages and AT&T Community Port is governed by the
If you are a child under the age of 13, do not publish a Web page here without password protection.
available to all Personal Web Pages members.
If you are a mature teen 13 to 18 years old, AT&T strongly recommends that you also password protect
Document: Done

FIGURE 3.4
Most wizards start off by telling you the rules.

Clicking on another Yes button gives you still another page (see Figure 3.5), explaining that you must agree to have cookies stored on your computer in order to create a Web page here. *Cookies* are small files that contain enough information that a Web site you interact with can identify you. Clicking the Continue button means that you will accept cookies, and you're then moved forward.

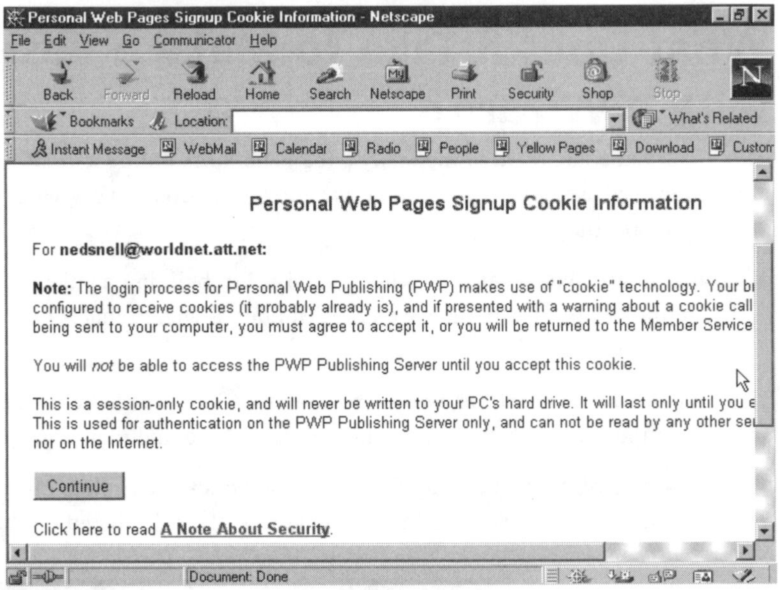
Personal Web Pages Signup Cookie Information - Netscape
File Edit View Go Communicator Help
Back Forward Reload Home Search Netscape Print Security Shop Stop
Bookmarks Location: What's Related
Instant Message WebMail Calendar Radio People Yellow Pages Download
Personal Web Pages Signup Cookie Information
For nedsnell@worldnet.att.net:
Note: The login process for Personal Web Publishing (PWP) makes use of "cookie" technology. Your
configured to receive cookies (it probably already is), and if presented with a warning about a cookie call
being sent to your computer, you must agree to accept it, or you will be returned to the Member Service
You will not be able to access the PWP Publishing Server until you accept this cookie.
This is a session-only cookie, and will never be written to your PC's hard drive. It will last only until you
This is used for authentication on the PWP Publishing Server only, and can not be read by any other
nor on the Internet.
Continue
Click here to read A Note About Security.
Document: Done

FIGURE 3.5
To build a Web site with some wizards, you must agree to the storing of cookie files on your computer.

At long last, you arrive at the Personal Web Pages @att.net page (see Figure 3.6), where you begin building your page. If you scroll halfway down the page, you have the chance to type keywords to describe your site. These keywords help search engines find your page whenever a visitor enters a search term related to your site. If you scroll down farther, you have the chance to enter all sorts of optional information about yourself and your site, used by the AT&T search engine to help WorldNet users find your page.

At the bottom of the page shown in Figure 3.6, clicking the Make Changes button opens the page on which you can choose layout options for your page (see Figure 3.7).

Begin by choosing the type of Web site you want to make: community, individual, family, or business. Your choice determines which of the AT&T templates the wizard uses for your page.

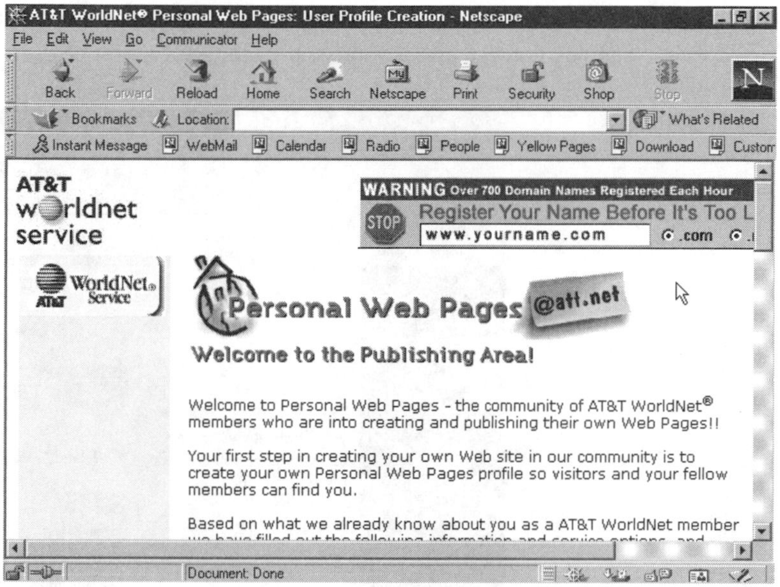

FIGURE 3.6
The Personal Web Pages page, where you begin building your page with the wizard.

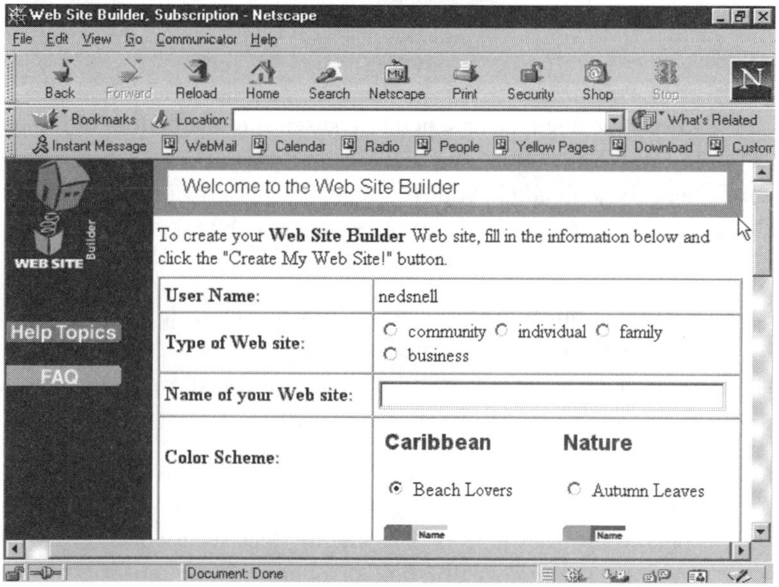

FIGURE 3.7
Choose your page's title, colors, and other options on this page.

You type a name for your page in the box provided and then scroll down to reveal the color schemes you can choose for your page (see Figure 3.8).

FIGURE 3.8
Choose colors for your page from the options provided.

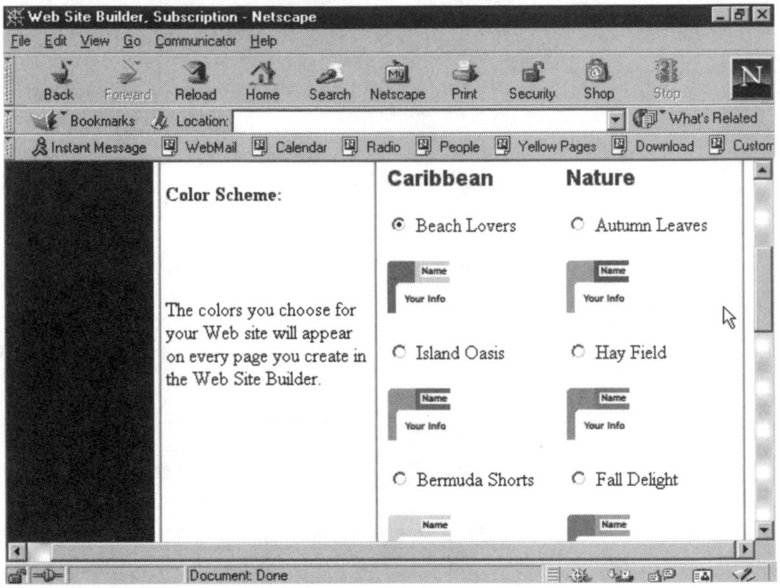

After choosing a color scheme, you scroll to the bottom of the page and click the Create My Web Site button. The Site Features page appears (see Figure 3.9). On this page, you can choose to add to your page any of a variety of useful objects. For example, you may choose to provide your visitors with a search tool or create a guest book so that users can tell you about themselves.

When you finish making changes to your site features, you click the Make Changes button at the bottom of the Site Features page. You can then click the Publish link near the top of the page to create and view your finished page, which at this point will look something like the one shown in Figure 3.10.

From here, you can click the Admin link at the top of the page to open dialog boxes in which you can add more to your page: Insert an image file for the photo (you will learn about image files in Hour 13, "Getting Pictures for Your Page") and add more text, for example. The main dialog box looks like the one shown in Figure 3.11.

FIGURE 3.9
Here, you can choose site features, such as a search tool on your Web page.

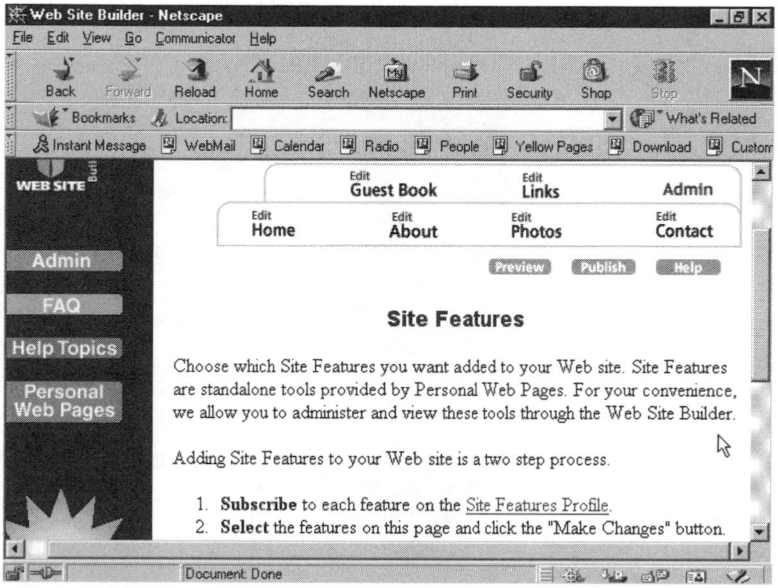
Web Site Builder - Netscape
Site Features
Choose which Site Features you want added to your Web site. Site Features are standalone tools provided by Personal Web Pages. For your convenience, we allow you to administer and view these tools through the Web Site Builder.
Adding Site Features to your Web site is a two step process.
1. Subscribe to each feature on the Site Features Profile.
2. Select the features on this page and click the "Make Changes" button.

FIGURE 3.10
Your new Web site, all done (sort of).

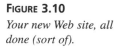

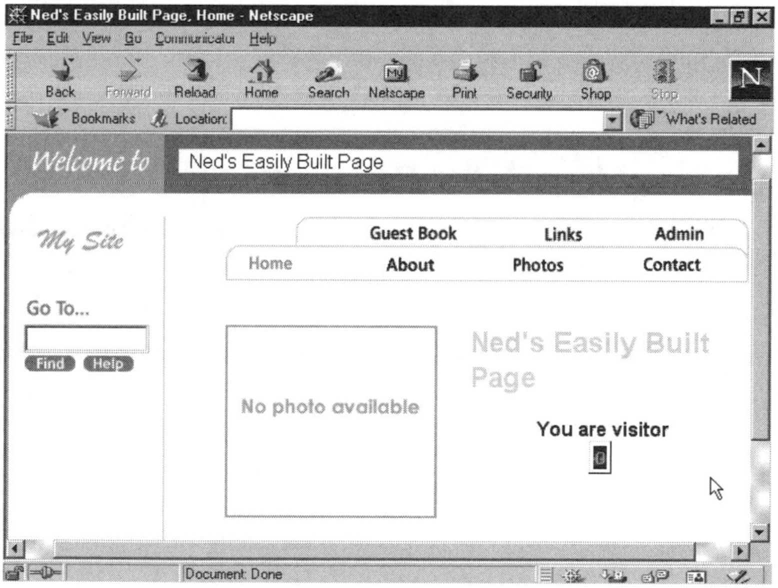
Ned's Easily Built Page, Home - Netscape
Welcome to
Ned's Easily Built Page
My Site
Go To...
Find
Help
Guest Book
Links
Admin
Home
About
Photos
Contact
No photo available
Ned's Easily Built Page
You are visitor

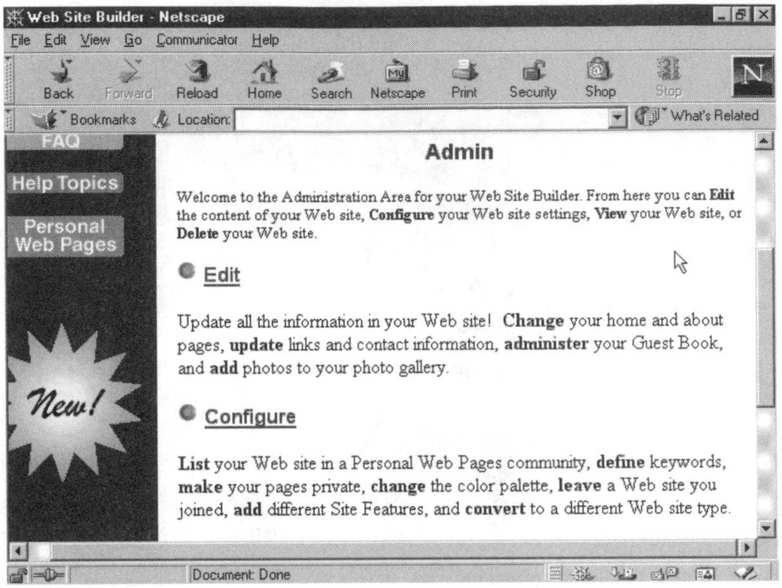
Web Site Builder - Netscape
File Edit View Go Communicator Help
Back Forward Reload Home Search Netscape Print Security Shop Stop
Bookmarks Location: What's Related
FAQ
Help Topics
Personal Web Pages
New!
Admin
Welcome to the Administration Area for your Web Site Builder. From here you can Edit the content of your Web site, Configure your Web site settings, View your Web site, or Delete your Web site.
Edit
Update all the information in your Web site! Change your home and about pages, update links and contact information, administer your Guest Book, and add photos to your photo gallery.
Configure
List your Web site in a Personal Web Pages community, define keywords, make your pages private, change the color palette, leave a Web site you joined, add different Site Features, and convert to a different Web site type.
Document: Done

FIGURE 3.11
The Admin page allows you to further customize your site.

Whattaya think? Yes, it's a Web page, online, and it took only a few minutes to make. It's not a bad way to start, but it comes nowhere near what you can create if you use a Web authoring program as described in the remainder of this book. Read on.

Understanding Publishing

You don't learn all the ins and outs of publishing your page online until Part VI of this book, "Getting It Online." But right now is a good time to begin learning what publishing is all about.

In a nutshell, publishing a Web page is a simple matter of uploading all the files that make up the page into a designated directory on a Web server (or intranet server, if you intend for your document to be used just by folks within a local intranet).

NEW TERM To *upload* is to send files from your computer to a server computer, such as a Web server. (It's the opposite of *downloading*—receiving files from a server). When you publish a Web page, you upload its files to a Web server.

Most servers—whether Web or intranet—are guarded by security systems that prevent unauthorized users from storing files there. To publish, you must contact the administrator of the server on which you want to publish and obtain the following:

- Permission to upload files to the server
- The name and path of the directory in which the administrator wants you to store your files
- The specific steps required for uploading files to the server (the exact procedure varies somewhat)
- A username and password that you will use while uploading to identify yourself properly to the server's security system (so that it will permit you to copy the files)

> If you obtain your Web server space from your Internet provider or online service, the username and password you use to upload Web pages to the server may be the same as the username and password you use to connect to the Internet.
>
> To learn more about getting server space for your Web page, see Hour 21, "Publishing Your Page."

When you are ready to upload files, you will do so through a *communications protocol* supported by the server. The required protocol is almost always either of the same two protocols most often used for downloading files on the Internet: FTP (used for downloading files from an FTP server) or HTTP (used for downloading Web pages and other files from Web and intranet servers to browsers).

Composer includes a built-in publishing tool that lets you publish your pages straight from Composer, using either the FTP or HTTP protocols. You learn how to publish from Composer—and to publish in other ways—in Hour 21.

Summary

Wizards offer a quick, easy way to build a complete, properly designed Web page, and are certainly worth a spin. To create a page that truly expresses you, you need more control than a wizard offers. Read on and learn how to create pages that are exactly what you want.

Q&A

Q Can I use the free Web space that communities offer but still publish a custom page built with an authoring program there?

A On many sites, including the AT&T WorldNet site described in this chapter, a link is provided for uploading HTML files into the Web space provided. You do have the option of foregoing the wizard, creating your page in a Web authoring program like the Composer program included with this book, and then uploading the page to the Web space.

Q Are other wizards available to create other kinds of basic pages?

A My, yes! In fact, dozens of these types of tools are available. Some are wizards and work very much like the Personal Home Page wizard. Others are not strictly wizards, but you use them the same way: You fill in the blanks and make a few choices, and out pops a finished HTML file, ready for editing.

All these tools—wizard and non—are sometimes collectively called *page generators*. Each builds a different kind of page, in a different style. (That's why you're smart to play around with several different ones, to discover the page generator whose output comes closest to the type and style of page you want).

Some page generators create pages that are far more sophisticated than those created by the Personal Home Page Wizard, featuring pictures, backgrounds, forms, and more. But all page generators have one thing in common: After you use any of them, you can open the files they create in Netscape Composer and edit them to your heart's content.

Some page generators are built into other programs; in Hour 4, you'll learn about page generators built into Microsoft Word, Publisher, and other programs. Other page generators are programs unto themselves, usually available as shareware you can download from the Web and run on your PC. Still other page generators run entirely online; only the resulting HTML file is saved on your PC, when you're done.

HOUR 4

Starting Pages in Other Programs

Time is tight for you—it's an issue. How do I know this about you? Well, of all the beginners' Web authoring books out there, you picked up the one that promises to deliver within a specific timeframe. Given what I know about you, I'm placing special emphasis on anything that can get you a great Web page quicker.

Aside from the page generators you discovered in the preceding hour, nothing saves time better than using a *template*, or using content you've already created in another program, such as a word processor. In this hour, you'll explore both these head-starts to Web pages. At the end of the hour, you will be able to answer the following questions:

- How can I turn stuff I already have on hand—such as a résumé or brochure I typed in my word processor—into a Web page without having to start over?

- Can I use a word processor or desktop publishing program to create a Web page?
- What are *templates*, where do I find 'em, and how can I use 'em to save time and effort in starting a page?

Starting in Your Word Processing, Desktop Publishing, or Other Program

A Web page, when you think about it, is just a document. It's a document that happens to be saved in the HTML file format, but, other than that, it's not different from documents created in other document-producing programs, such as word processors (Microsoft Word or WordPerfect, for example), desktop publishing programs (Microsoft Publisher or Adobe PageMaker), and presentation programs (Microsoft PowerPoint).

If these programs could save the documents you create as HTML files, the programs would be fully functional Web authoring tools, right? Well, in most cases (unless you're still using versions from a few years ago), these programs can optionally save the files you create as HTML files.

When you create a document in another program, save it as an HTML file, and then open it in Composer for further development, you might see a variety of little, yellow "tag" icons sprinkled about the page.

Though distracting, these icons usually do not indicate any real problem. They simply indicate in the file some formatting instructions that Composer does not know how to interpret. If you view the page in Netscape (or another browser), you see no yellow tags, and the formatting might look just great.

So, if you have these programs, you might be able to

- Open documents you've already created—your résumé, recipes, stories, ads, brochures, petitions, or whatever—and in a few clicks transform them into HTML files, ready to be edited and enhanced in Composer (with no retyping!).
- Start new Web pages in these programs, to take advantage of features in those programs before moving the job over to Composer. If you have Microsoft Word, for example, you should note that although Composer can spell-check, Word has spell-checking *and* grammar-checking. In a long page with lots of text, grammar mistakes are easy to miss. You might prefer to create such pages in Word and check 'em there before saving the file in HTML format and switching to Composer.

- Create and publish the file entirely in another program and never move over to Composer. If the Web authoring capabilities in the other program accomplish what you want, you always have that option. My feelings won't be hurt—honest.

The next few pages describe ways you can use a few popular programs to start Web pages. Recent versions of many other popular document-creation programs for Microsoft Windows offer similar capabilities.

> When you want to turn the entire contents of an existing document into a Web page, the techniques in this hour are a great way to begin.
>
> If all you want to do is to copy a portion of a document—a few paragraphs or a table—into a Web page, you need not bother with these techniques. Instead, you can easily copy text, tables, pictures, and links from any Windows program and paste that content into any Web page you're editing in Composer. See Hour 5, "Choosing a Title, Colors, and Other Page Basics," to learn how to use copy-and-paste.

Starting Web Pages in Word

With each new version, Microsoft turns Word into something more of a hybrid Web authoring and word processing program. Good Web authoring capabilities are built into Word 97, and even better ones are in Word 2000 and Word 2002.

In any version, you can save any file as an HTML file so that it can be published as a Web page or opened and edited in Microsoft FrontPage. In either program, you can create new Web pages from scratch, based on wizards and templates in Word. The following To Do's show how to use these features in Word 2000.

> Depending on the installation options you select when installing Word (or Microsoft Office, with Word included), the Web authoring capabilities in Word may or may not be included in the installation.
>
> If you find that you cannot perform the following To Do's, the Word Web authoring tools were probably left out of your installation. To add them, insert your Word or Office CD-ROM, start the installation program, choose Add/Remove Components, and be sure to select the Web authoring components when updating your installation.

To Do

To Do: Save a Word file as a Web page

1. Open the file in Word.
2. Choose File, Save As Web Page.
3. Make sure that the Save As Type list shows Web Page.

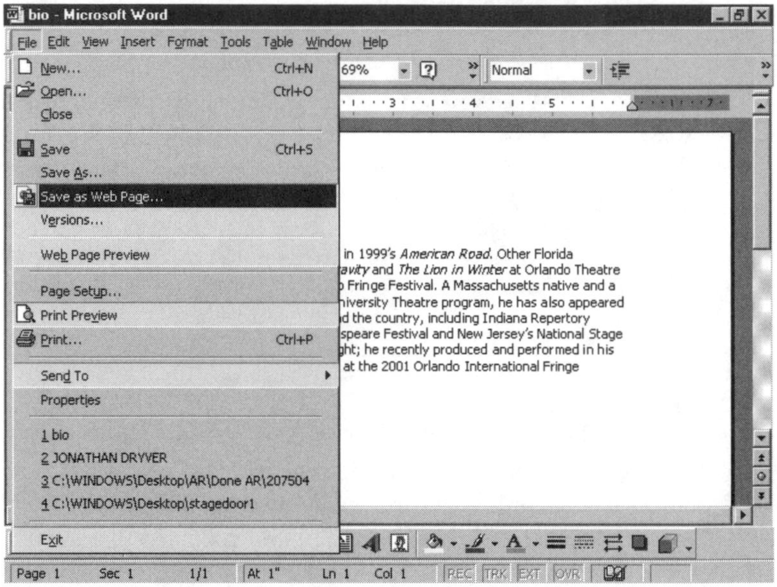

FIGURE 4.1
Step 2: In Word, choose File, Save As Web Page.

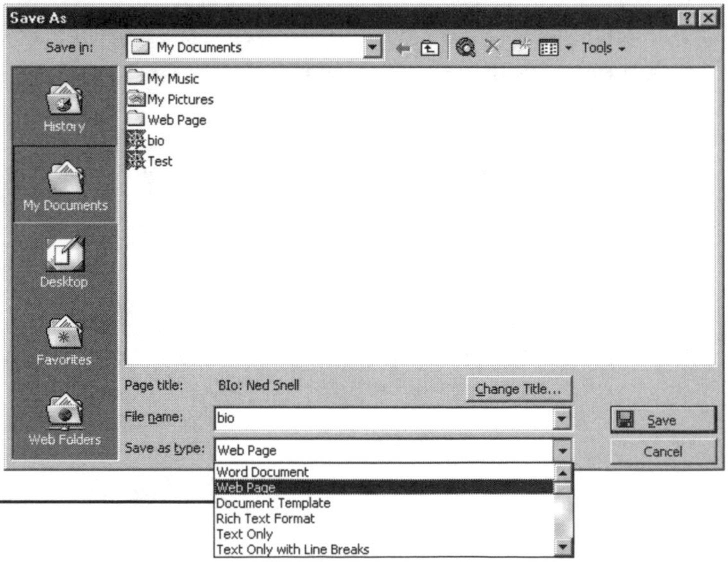

FIGURE 4.2
Step 3: Make sure that Web Page is chosen in the Save As Type list.

4. Choose a folder (and, optionally, rename your file) and click the Save button.

FIGURE 4.3
Step 4: Choose a folder and click Save.

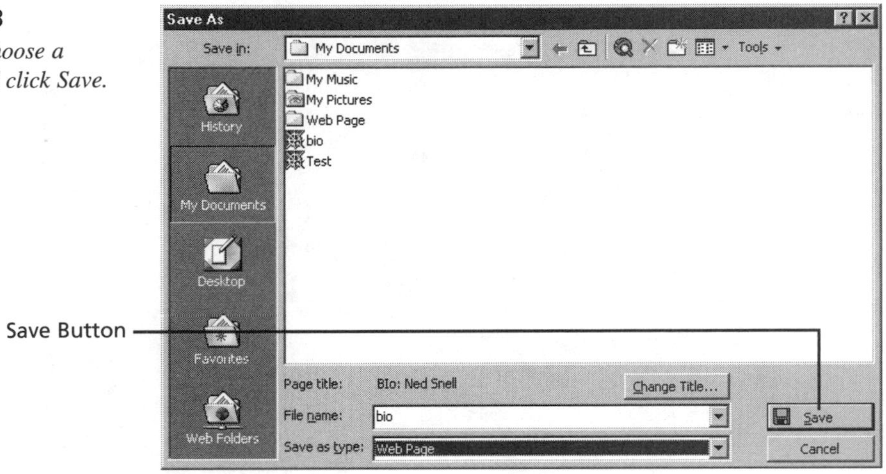

To Do: Start a new Web page in Word

1. Open Word.
2. Choose File, New.
3. In the New dialog box, click the Web Pages tab.

FIGURE 4.4
Step 3: Click the Web Pages tab.

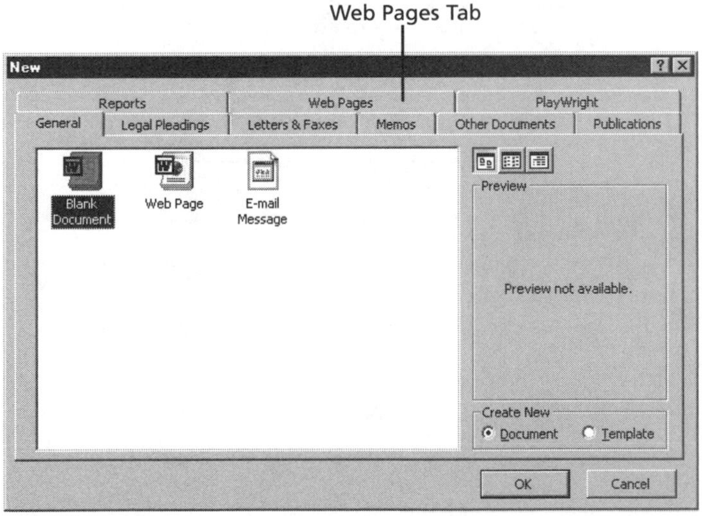

4. Choose the template icon whose name best matches the type of page you want to create and double-click it.

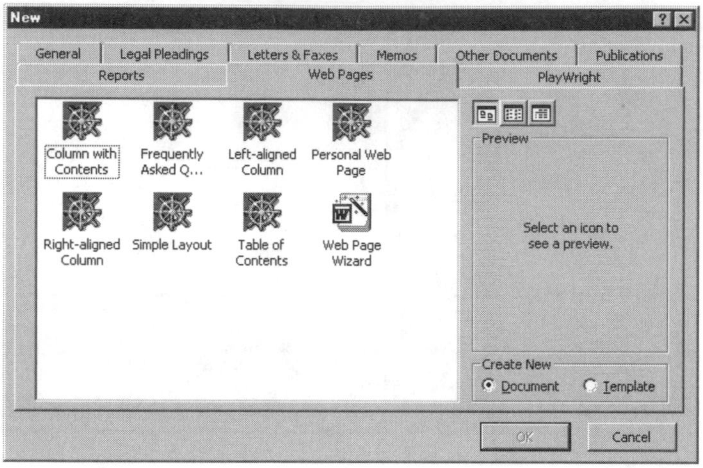

FIGURE 4.5
Step 4: Choose a template.

> In Step 4, observe, in addition to the various kinds of Web page templates, an icon for Web Page Wizard. Double-click that icon to open a wizard that leads you step-by-step through creating a new Web page.
>
> The results are slicker than what you get with most page generators (see Hour 3, "Getting a Head-Start with Templates"), but also much more complex and difficult to edit effectively.
>
> If you have Word, I recommend giving the Word Web Page Wizard a spin, just for practice. But I also advise not attempting to create anything critical with it until you gain some more experience.

5. Edit the file in Word as much as you like and save it. The file is already an HTML file, so at any time you can switch from Word and work on the page in Composer or publish it.

FIGURE 4.6
Step 5: Edit the file and save it.

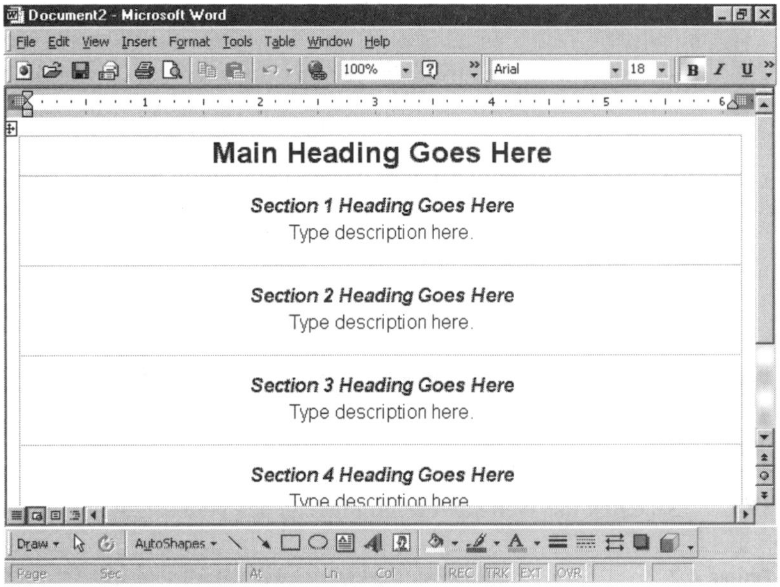

After your new Web page opens in Word, you might notice that Word looks a little different from what you're used to. It has toolbar buttons you don't recognize and new menu items.

These are the tools of Word's Web Layout view, a special view in which the Word tools are changed to those you need for working on a Web page. Word always switches to Web Layout view automatically when the file you're working on is an HTML file.

Making Web Pages in Publisher

Like Word, the desktop publishing program Microsoft Publisher (version 2000 or later) enables you to create new Web pages and convert existing publications to HTML files.

Given that Publisher is a program designed for creating print publications that have far more sophisticated layout and formatting than is possible in a Web page, don't be surprised if publications take on a much different appearance when you convert them.

What's a Template?

A *template* is simply an HTML file filled mostly with meaningless, boilerplate content rather than the real thing. The prefabricated file has already been organized and formatted with paragraph properties, horizontal lines, and other bells and whistles you learn to create later in this book. A template also can include many of the basic content elements of a Web page: title, headings, body, signature, and appropriate links, for example. (If you don't recognize these parts of a page, review Hour 1, "Understanding Web Authoring.")

> You might notice, in exploring Composer, that if you choose File, New from the menu bar, you see an option for creating a new "Page from Template."
>
> As with the Page from Wizard option described in the preceding hour, this option no longer functions as originally intended. Once upon a time, choosing the Page from Template option opened a free templates site at Netscape. Now, this option opens a site at Netscape designed to help you create and publish a free Web page within the Netscape online community.
>
> To learn more about creating a free Web page in the Netscape community (and in other, similar communities), see Hour 3.

By replacing the boilerplate content with your own content and leaving the decorative stuff alone, you can quickly create an attractive, effective Web page without having to fuss much over its organization or formatting. Of course, if you decide that you want to change the formatting or organization of a page created from a template, you can, just as you can edit any HTML file in Composer.

Figure 4.9 shows a template for a human resources department page. Figure 4.10 shows a page I created by replacing the template's text with my own. Compare the figures and observe that the only difference between the two is text content. Notice how I was able to take advantage of the template's organization, fancy horizontal lines, and character formatting while still making it my own.

FIGURE 4.9
An unedited template viewed in the browser window.

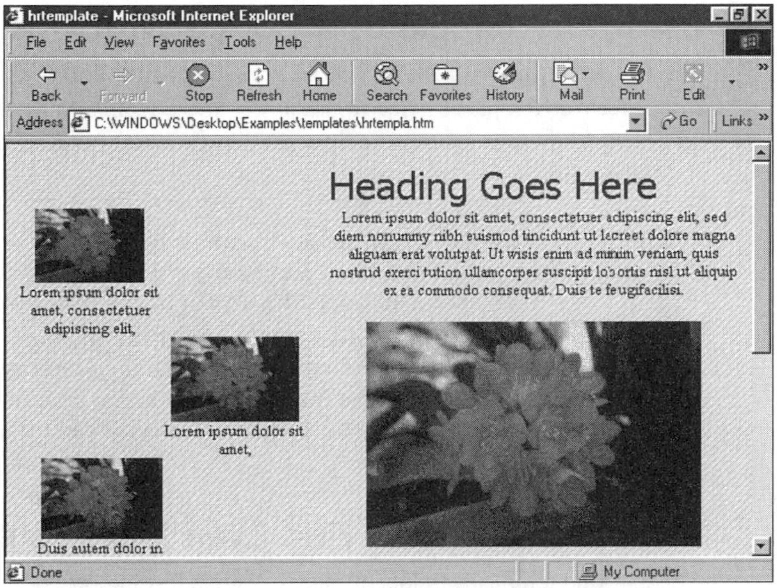
hrtemplate - Microsoft Internet Explorer
File Edit View Favorites Tools Help
Back Forward Stop Refresh Home Search Favorites History Mail Print Edit
Address C:\WINDOWS\Desktop\Examples\templates\hrtempla.htm
Go Links
Heading Goes Here
Lorem ipsum dolor sit amet, consectetuer adipiscing elit, sed diem nonummy nibh euismod tincidunt ut lacreet dolore magna aliguam erat volutpat. Ut wisis enim ad minim veniam, quis nostrud exerci tution ullamcorper suscipit lobortis nisl ut aliquip ex ea commodo consequat. Duis te feugifacilisi.
Lorem ipsum dolor sit amet, consectetuer adipiscing elit,
Lorem ipsum dolor sit amet,
Duis autem dolor in
Done
My Computer

FIGURE 4.10
The template edited into a real page with the addition of real content.

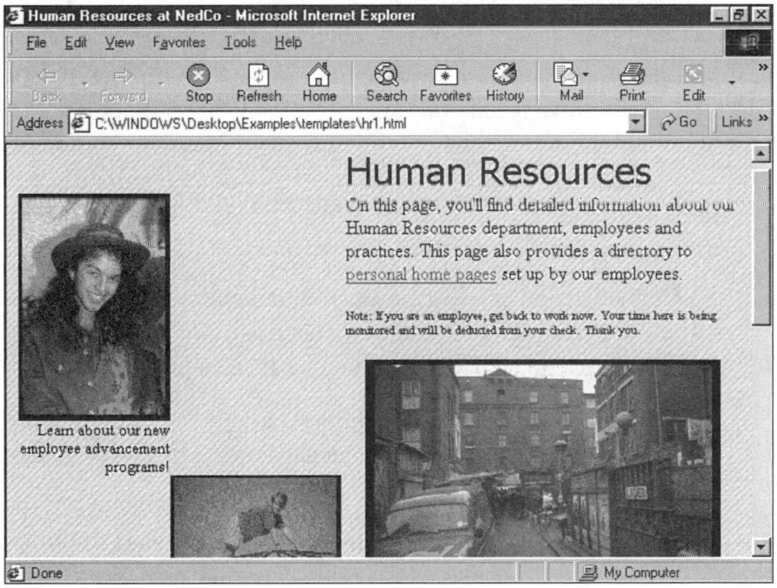
Human Resources at NedCo - Microsoft Internet Explorer
File Edit View Favorites Tools Help
Back Forward Stop Refresh Home Search Favorites History Mail Print Edit
Address C:\WINDOWS\Desktop\Examples\templates\hr1.html
Go Links
Human Resources
On this page, you'll find detailed information about our Human Resources department, employees and practices. This page also provides a directory to personal home pages set up by our employees.
Note: If you are an employee, get back to work now. Your time here is being monitored and will be deducted from your check. Thank you.
Learn about our new employee advancement programs!
Done
My Computer

Using the Templates Included with This Book

The CD-ROM included with this book contains a nifty library of Web page templates from FreeWebTemplates.com. To use any of these templates as a head-start to a Website, all you need to do is open the template file in Composer and save it on your hard disk.

> If you plan to make heavy use of the CD templates, you might find that copying all of them to your hard disk is more convenient so that you can easily open them as desired without having to futz with the CD.
>
> To copy all the templates to your hard disk, insert the CD-ROM and then open My Computer. Right-click the icon for your CD-ROM drive and then choose Explore from the menu that opens to display a folder of the CD's contents. Drag the Templates folder to your desktop or to another folder.

Knowing Where to Find Even More Templates

You can find templates in lots of places. Web authoring programs, like the full version of Microsoft FrontPage, usually contain a bunch, as do word processing programs designed to double as Web authoring programs (such as Microsoft Word).

At this point, your best bet is to look online. You can find plenty of good, copyright-free templates in Web authoring sites. The following URLs offer a few good starting points:

- `www.freewebtemplates.com`
- `freesources.net/templates` (see Figure 4.11)
- `www.icstars.com/hosting/templates.html`

Note that a copy of any template you find online must be saved to your hard drive before you can edit it. If the template is offered as a file (or, more likely, as a set of files in a ZIP archive), just download the file to your PC like any other file (and unzip it, if necessary).

If the template appears in your browser as a Web page, you need to save that page to your hard drive. While viewing the page online in your Netscape browser, you can do this in either of two easy ways:

- Choose File, Edit Page. This step opens the page in Composer. After the page is open in Composer, choose File, Save in Composer to save the page on your hard drive and edit away.
- Choose File, Save As to save the Web page on your hard disk without opening Composer. To edit the file later, open Composer, choose File, Open Page, and navigate to the saved file to open it.

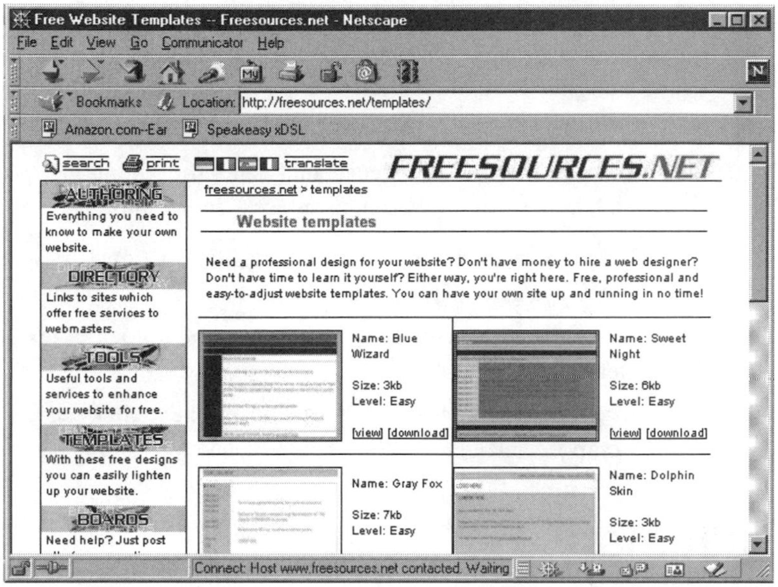
Free Website Templates -- Freesources.net - Netscape
File Edit View Go Communicator Help
Bookmarks Location: http://freesources.net/templates/
Amazon.com-Ear Speakeasy xDSL
search print translate
FREESOURCES.NET
AUTHORING
Everything you need to know to make your own website.
DIRECTORY
Links to sites which offer free services to webmasters.
TOOLS
Useful tools and services to enhance your website for free.
TEMPLATES
With these free designs you can easily lighten up your website.
BOARDS
Need help? Just post
freesources.net > templates
Website templates
Need a professional design for your website? Don't have money to hire a web designer? Don't have time to learn it yourself? Either way, you're right here. Free, professional and easy-to-adjust website templates. You can have your own site up and running in no time!
Name: Blue Wizard
Size: 3kb
Level: Easy
[view] [download]
Name: Sweet Night
Size: 6kb
Level: Easy
[view] [download]
Name: Gray Fox
Size: 7kb
Level: Easy
Name: Dolphin Skin
Size: 3kb
Level: Easy
Connect: Host www.freesources.net contacted. Waiting

FIGURE 4.11
FreeSources.net is one good resource for free Web page templates and other goodies.

Editing a Template into Your Own Page

After a template has been saved on your hard drive, you can edit, expand, reformat, or delete any part of it. In a few cases, you might find that you don't need to change much of anything—anywhere the template already says what you want to say, leave it alone.

Most of the text you see, however, must be replaced or deleted. You'll learn in detail how to edit Web pages in upcoming hours, but just to get you started (templates, after all, are for those who want to work quickly), the following are a few quick editing techniques:

- To replace an entire paragraph, highlight the paragraph from beginning to end by moving the mouse pointer to the left of the paragraph and clicking. Then type your new content. The paragraph is instantly deleted and replaced with whatever you type. Your new paragraph takes on the same paragraph properties as the one you've replaced.
- To replace only a portion of a paragraph, highlight the portion you want to replace (click and hold at the start of the selection, drag to the end, and release), and then type your content. The highlighted section is deleted and replaced with what you type.
- To replace a template image with one of your own, double-click the image and then use the dialog box that opens to insert a new image (see Hour 14, "Adding Pictures (and Picture Backgrounds)." To delete an image, click it once (to select it) and press the Delete key.

The only trick to editing a template is to change the content without screwing up the existing formatting. To that end, you might find it helpful to imagine that between each set of paragraphs are hidden formatting instructions that must not be lost or corrupted during editing.

To make sure that you don't accidentally alter the formatting, avoid doing anything that would delete the space between paragraphs; for example:

- When the edit cursor (the tall, vertical bar that appears whenever you type or edit text) appears at the beginning of a block of text, do not press the Backspace key.
- When the edit cursor appears at the end of a block of text, do not press the Delete key.
- If you do change the properties inadvertently, click the Undo button on the Composer Standard toolbar before you do anything else.

Summary

Talk about putting the cart before the horse! You've gone only four hours into the tutorial and you have yet to learn the basics of putting text, pictures, and links into a Web page. But you already know three ways—page generators, starting in other programs, and templates—to crank out a respectable page.

Because you've already experienced the rush of instant gratification, the next four hours provide an opportunity to settle down and work closely with the most important part of any Web page: the *words*.

Q&A

Q Can I make my own templates?

A Sure. In fact, doing so can save you lots of time if you create many similar pages.

To make your own templates, just build a page containing the elements that you tend to reuse from project to project. Create new pages by opening and editing that template file, making sure to save the creations with new filenames (using File, Save As) so that the template itself remains unaltered and ready to serve up the next new page.

Q Can I copy cool pages I visit online to use them as templates?

A Yes and no. (Don't you just *hate* answers like that?)

Technically, sure, you *can* grab any page you see online, save it on your PC, open it in Composer, and edit it. One way to do this task is to visit the page in Netscape and then choose File, Edit Page from the Netscape menu bar. Doing so opens the page in Composer so that you can edit it and save the edited version on your PC.

Another way to get the same result is to visit the page and then choose File, Save As from the Netscape menu bar. A dialog box for saving the Web page files (pictures and all) on your PC opens. After you save the files, you can disconnect from the Internet and open the files in Composer for editing.

Even though you *can* do this procedure, you usually shouldn't. For one thing, the page and its contents (including pictures) might be copyrighted, which means that using any part of it is a big, fat no-no. And even if the page is not copyrighted, it's someone else's work, so you bring bad karma on yourself if you steal it. You might be tempted to think that if you change all the words and pictures and just borrow the layout, it's okay. Well, in most cases the underlying HTML code might be copyrighted, too, so you're still busted.

For another thing, you don't *need* to copy anybody else's work. You have the tools to do anything you want, on your own, and within the next 20 hours, you'll have the skills. All you need after that is a little practice.

PART II

Titles, Text, and Tables

Hour

HOUR 5

Choosing a Title, Text Colors, and Other Page Basics

There's the forest, and then there's the trees.

In Web authoring, the trees are the content—the words, the pictures, the links. But before you start planting pines, you're smart to deal with a few quick, easy elements that affect your page at a higher level: the title, color scheme, and other stuff that defines the shape and function of the forest.

At the end of the hour, you will be able to answer the following questions:

- What are page properties, and how do I choose them?
- How can I change a page's title, and how do I know whether I've come up with a title that works?
- How do I apply custom colors to the text and background in my page?
- How can I add identification information to my page that will help it get listed properly in search pages online?

About Page Properties

Everything you learn in this hour has to do with stuff that's generally described as *page properties*, settings that affect the overall look and function of your page.

Unlike with all other parts of your page, such as the page's text and pictures, you do not create the page properties within the work area in Composer. Instead, you use two special dialog boxes: Page Properties and Page Colors and Background.

You use these dialog boxes to change your page's title, choose a scheme of complementary text and background colors, and embed special identification information that does not actually appear on the page but rather helps search tools (such as Yahoo! or Google) properly catalog your pages.

Choosing an Effective Page Title

You must enter a carefully worded title for each page you publish, because the title describes your page to the Web in myriad ways.

For example, when a visitor to your page creates a bookmark or favorite for your page in his or her browser, the title typically becomes the name of the bookmark or favorite.

Also, Web directories (such as Yahoo!) and *spiders* (programs that build Web directories by searching the Web and cataloging its contents) use the title as a primary reference for what the page is about. Give your page a poorly worded title, and it may not come up in the hit list when folks search on the very topic your page covers.

> When people use Yahoo!, Excite, and other Web-searching tools, you want them to find your page when your page really matches what they want, and *not* to find your page when it's not a good match. Entering a good, descriptive title is one step in ensuring that match.

Don't confuse the page title with any big, bold heading that may top a Web page and serve as its apparent title. Remember: By the time a visitor sees that top-level heading, he or she has already arrived at your page and is presumably already interested in its subject, so that top heading can be more creative than the real page title—even subtle. But the true title must be descriptive, not clever.

> Remember: The title entered in the Page Properties dialog box does not appear on the page itself, but rather in the title bar of the browser window in which the page is displayed.

An effective title should accurately describe the contents or purpose of your page. The title should also be fairly short—no more than six to eight words—and its most descriptive words should appear first.

A bookmark list or Web directory often has room for only the first few words of a title, so your title needs to be short, and those first few words must be meaningful.

The following are some good titles:

Sammy's Racquetball Directory

The Video Store Online

All About Trout Fishing

Marvin C. Able's Awesome Home Page

Weehauken, NJ, Events for July

In these good examples, notice that the most specific, important descriptor appears within the first three words: Racquetball, Video, Trout, Marvin C. Able, and Weehauken, NJ, Events.

Notice also that the fewest possible words are used to nail down the page. In the first example, you learn in three words that this page is a directory of racquetball-related information and that it's Sammy's directory (to distinguish it from any other racquetball directories). What more do you need to know?

The following, for comparison, are some lousy titles:

My Home Page

Things to Do

Schedule of Events

A Catalog of Links and Documents Provided As a Public Service for Persons Researching Population Trends

In the first three crummy examples, the titles are nondescript; they contain nothing about the specific contents of the page. The last example, although containing some useful information at the end, would be trimmed to its first four or five words in a bookmark list, and those first few words say nothing useful.

Now that you know a little more about effective titles, you may want to change the titles of pages you've already started developing. The following To Do shows how.

To Do: Change a page's title

1. In Composer, open (or create) the page file whose title you want to change.
2. Choose Format, Page Colors and Properties.
3. In the Title area, type (or edit to your liking) the title shown.

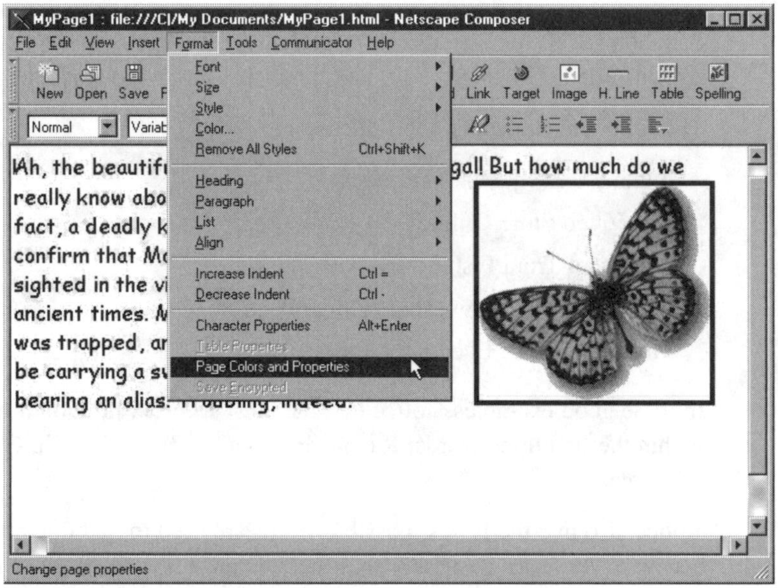

FIGURE 5.1
Step 1: Choose Format, Page Colors and Properties.

When typing your new title, be careful to capitalize and spell it exactly as you want it to appear in a title bar or bookmark list.

Don't bother trying to use character formatting, such as bold or italics, in the title. No character formatting is possible within the text-entry areas in the Page Properties dialog box, and even if it were, it wouldn't show up anywhere titles typically appear.

4. You may optionally type your name in the Author area, although this information will not appear anywhere on the page. Instead, it will appear within the HTML code to identify the author to anyone examining the code, usually a fellow Web author who admires your handiwork.

FIGURE 5.2
Step 2: Type your title.

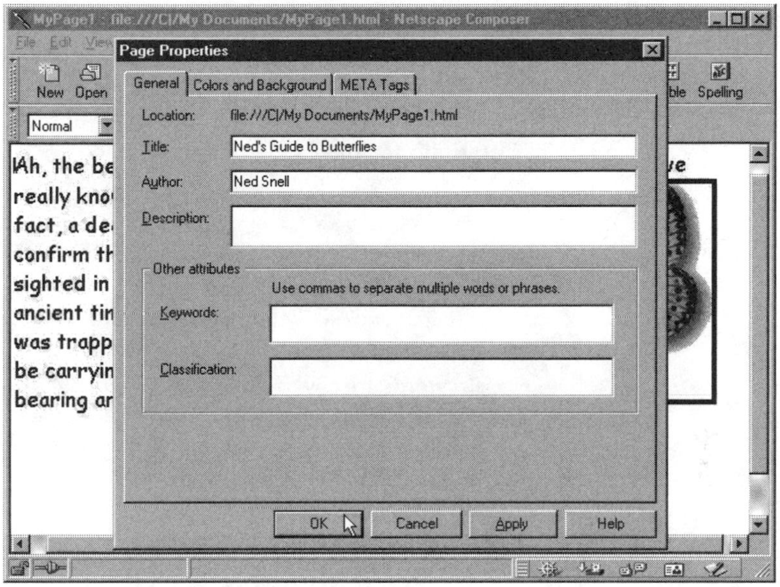

5. Finally, you may type a description for your page. To learn more about the description, see the next section, "Helping Search Pages Catalog Your Page."

Helping Search Pages Catalog Your Page

Most folks who publish a Web page want it found by everybody online who may have a remote interest in the page's topic. (If you intend to keep the Web page you're creating a big, fat secret, you can skip this part.)

Obviously, the key to exposing yourself is to ensure that the page shows up in the major (and minor) search pages, such as Yahoo! (`www.yahoo.com`), Excite (`www.excite.com`), and Alta Vista (`www.altavista.com`). If your page is about duck diseases, you want to be sure that whenever anyone enters the search term "sick duck," "duck illness," or "shaggy beak," a link to your page will appear high in the list of results.

In some cases, you must manually register your page with a search tool or use a Web promotion service to do it for you (you learn to do both in Hour 23, "Publicizing Your Site"). But many search pages catalog the contents of the Web automatically. These search pages use programs, sometimes called crawlers or spiders, that roam around the Web, give Web pages a quick glance, and then attempt (with varying success) to automatically assign each page to one or more related categories. The more accurately your pages are categorized by these programs, the more likely they are to be found by exactly the folks you want to attract.

The most important step in ensuring that the spiders categorize a page correctly is giving it a good, descriptive title, as described earlier in this hour (all spiders look at page titles). But in Composer, you can increase the accuracy with which you'll be categorized by typing a brief Description in the Page Properties dialog box (Format, Page Title and Properties).

> Besides title and description, there are two other ways you can describe your page to search engines, helping those engines do a better job of leading visitors to your pages: Keywords and Classification.
>
> - Keywords are any important terms with which your page might be associated. For example, the site for a reptile store might use the keywords pet, reptile, snake, herp, lizard, turtle, tortoise, etc. Think of words visitors might enter as search terms when seeking a site like yours; those are your keywords.
> - Classification is a category or class in which your site belongs: Shopping, business, recreation, and so on.
>
> To add keywords and/or a classification to your site, type them in the boxes provided on the General tab of the Page Properties dialog (refer back to Figure 5.2). As directed on the dialog, type a comma between each keyword in the Keywords box, or between multiple classifications in the Classification box. (In both boxes, insert dashes between multi-word terms; for example, `reptile-store` could be one keyword.)

Many spiders read the description and regard the words in it as clues to the page's proper category. If your page is about bicycles, including a description that contains words like *bicycle*, *bike*, *cycling*, *cycle*, *cyclist*, *Huffy*, and so on may increase the chances that those interested in cycling find your page through searches.

Also, when a search turns up your page, many search engines display the description along with the link to your site. A well-worded description helps ensure that folks who will be interested in your site get there.

Choosing Custom Colors for a Whole Page

In general, the visitor's browser—including Netscape and Internet Explorer—chooses the colors for the text and background of a page. Folks are then free to choose color schemes they find pleasing to their own eyes, and to have all Web pages show those colors, unless…

Unless the Web author (that's you) has applied custom colors. *Custom colors* are selected colors for the background and text that override the browser's color settings so that the Web author—not the browser—controls the color of text and the background.

> Note that custom colors affect only text and background colors. They have no effect on the colors in pictures or picture backgrounds [see Hour 14, "Adding Pictures (and Picture Backgrounds)"]. Pictures are always displayed with whatever colors they were created with, regardless of any settings in the page properties or the browser.

You can assign custom colors separately for each of the following page elements:

- *Normal text*—All text in the page that is not a link.
- *Link text*—All links in the page except those that are active or visited (described next).
- *Active Link text*—Immediately after a link has been clicked by the visitor, it may remain visible for a few moments while the browser retrieves the file to which the link points. While the link remains visible, it changes color to indicate that it has been activated.
- *Followed link text*—Links that the visitor has previously used through his or her browser. In your own travels online, you may have noticed that when you return to pages you've visited before, links you've used appear in a different color from those you've never clicked.
- *Background*—The entire background area of the page can be a solid custom color. The background color always sits behind text or images in the page, never covering them, obscuring them, or affecting their color.

> The text colors you select in the Page Properties box automatically affect the page elements they're supposed to, freeing you to forget about text color when composing your page.
>
> But note that, as you work on your page, you can selectively choose the color of any block of text, to give it special emphasis. The color you choose need not be one of the colors you selected in the Page Properties box; it can be any color you want. To learn how to choose the color of a selected block of text, see Hour 7, "Formatting Text."

To Do: Choose custom colors

1. Open the page whose colors you want to choose.
2. Choose Format, Page Colors and Properties.
3. In the Page Properties dialog, select the Colors and Background tab.

> Be careful that the text and link colors you choose stand out against the background color. For example, if you select a dark background color, all the text colors must be light so that the text will be legible atop the background.

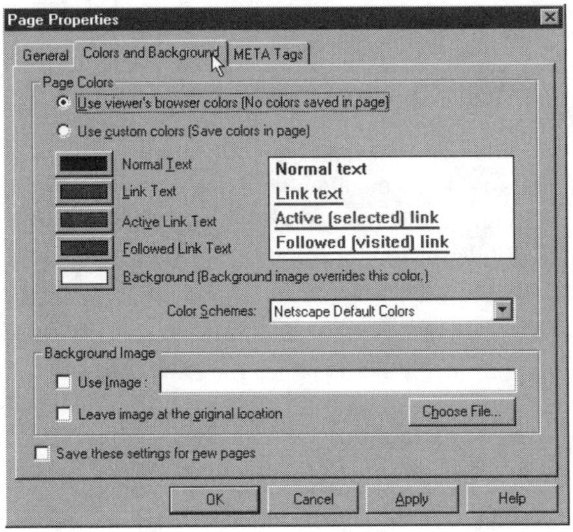

FIGURE 5.3
Step 3: Select the Colors and Background tab.

4. The default choice, Use viewer's browser colors, lets your visitor's browser determine the color scheme. Override this setting by clicking Use custom colors.
5. Click the button to the left of Normal Text. A chart of colors appears.
6. Click the box showing the color you want to use and then click OK.
7. Repeat Steps 4 and 5 for the other text types and background.

FIGURE 5.4
Step 4: Click a button next to any page element to display a list of colors to choose from.

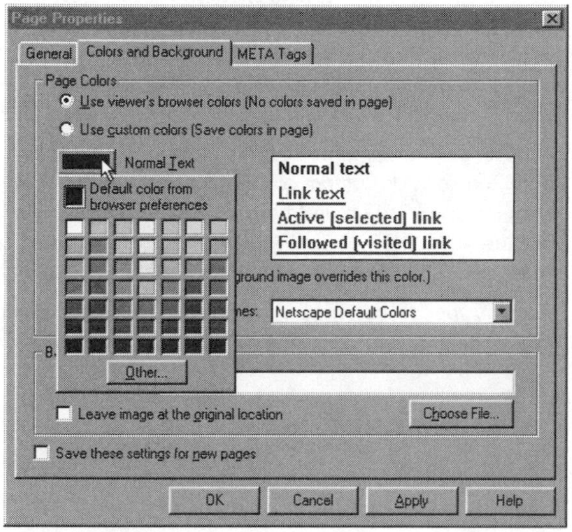

FIGURE 5.5
Step 5: Click a color.

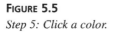

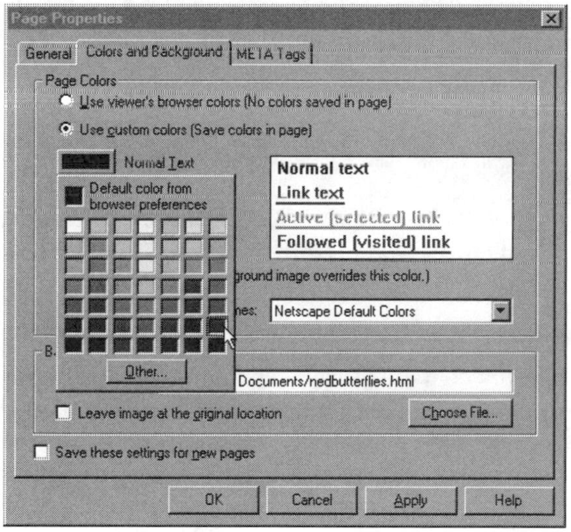

5

Do what you want, but bear in mind that it's sort of a waste of time to get too esoteric when choosing colors. Visitors will be running monitors with varying color capabilities and browsers with varying levels of support for colors, so it's unlikely that the colors will appear to others in the precise hue you choose.

In other words, it's meaningful to fuss over whether to make text red or blue. But to click Custom so that you can choose that *exact* shade of Mediterranean sea blue (the one the bridesmaids wore at your wedding) because it's a half-shade brighter than the blue that's in the color list...well, that's probably splitting hairs.

If a very specific color is essential to your design, it's better to use that color in a picture (or picture background) you create. See Hour 13, "Getting Pictures for Your Page."

Summary

Choosing your page properties is a snap, and it's also important. Doing it not only starts defining your page's appearance and purpose, but also forces you to begin thinking more clearly about those aspects. There's nothing like thinking up a title to help you focus your plans for your page.

Q&A

Q I've seen these cool backgrounds online, some that look like marble or other textures, and others that are pictures. How do I do those?

A Easy. Rather than use a background color, you can use a picture file to create a graphical background for a page, as you learn to do in Hour 14.

Note that if you do use an image for the background, the background color setting is irrelevant—an image background overrides a background color.

HOUR 6

Adding and Editing Text

Somebody once said to me, "Writing isn't so tough: All you have to do is find a quiet spot and open a vein."

That's true, actually, but to the extent that writing a Web page can be made less immediately life threatening, a WYSIWYG editor does just that. The principal job in creating the text of a Web page involves two main tasks: getting the text into the file (by typing it, copying it, or importing it) and assigning paragraph properties to each block of text. The properties tell browsers how to present that text.

In this hour, you learn how to get text into your Web page files, format it by assigning properties, and edit it. Dealing with the text first is usually the best way to build a Web page; it forces you to think about and resolve issues related to the organization and flow of content. At the end of the hour, you will be able to answer the following questions:

- What are the basics of creating the text elements of a Web page?
- How do I control the text's general appearance and position on the page?

- How do I type special characters that don't appear on my keyboard, such as copyright symbols?
- How do I edit the text?
- How do I check my spelling?
- How can I save time and typing with cut-and-paste, copy, and other text-entry tips?

Understanding Paragraphs and Their Properties

What makes a particular paragraph into a heading or something else is the properties you assign to the paragraph. Assigning properties to a paragraph is no different from assigning a style in a word processor, and usually it's just as easy. In a nutshell, you type a line or block of text and then assign properties to that paragraph to identify it as a heading, body text paragraph, or whatever. *Voilà*.

NEW TERM Composer calls each discrete chunk of text—all the text between paragraph marks (the character you type when you press Enter)—a *paragraph*, whether it's a heading, one line in a list, a multiline paragraph, or just a bunch of words.

Note that paragraph properties apply only to entire paragraphs. For example, you cannot format two words in the middle of a paragraph as an address and the rest of the paragraph as a heading. Either the whole paragraph is one thing, or the whole paragraph is something else.

Understanding What Each Paragraph Property Does

You assign paragraph properties through the Paragraph Format drop-down list on the Format toolbar (see Figure 6.1). The most important paragraph properties are described in the following sections and are shown in Netscape, Internet Explorer, and most other browsers as they appear in Figures 6.2 and 6.3.

Normal

Use the Normal property for general-purpose text—like what you're reading right now. Most browsers display Normal paragraphs in a plain font with no special emphasis (such as bold or special color). Normal is the meat and potatoes of your Web page.

FIGURE 6.1
You assign paragraph properties with the paragraph format list on the Format toolbar.

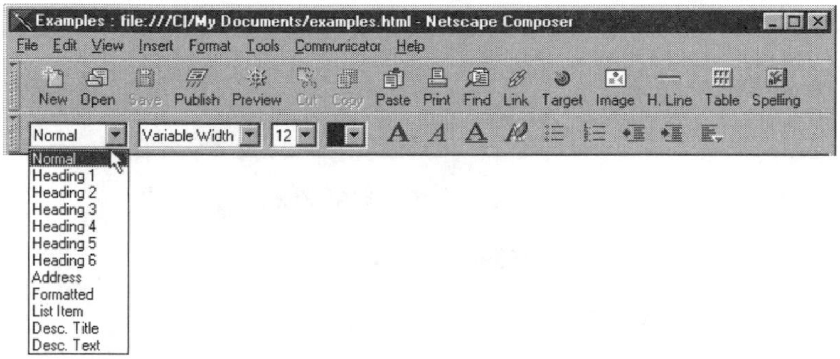

Headings (1-6)

Use headings the way you see them used in this book: to divide and label the logical sections of the page or Web page. You can use as many as six levels of headings, ranging in relative importance from 1 (most important or prominent) to 6 (least important or prominent).

> Because the level-1 heading is the most prominent, it is often reserved for the apparent title of your page—the one that appears within the page itself (not to be confused with the Web page title entered in the Page Properties dialog box).

In most browsers, a level-1 heading is displayed as the biggest, boldest text on the page. Level 2 headings are smaller and not bold, or they are de-emphasized in some other way. Level 3 gets less emphasis than 2 but more than 4, and so on. (Six levels require lots of variation, and the difference between headings only one level apart is barely distinguishable in some browsers, as you can see in Figure 6.2.)

Text-based browsers, which can't display varying font sizes, use bold, underline, or even numbers to show the varying heading levels.

You can use whatever heading levels you want, but, in general, obey the numbers. Subheadings within a section should have a higher-level number than the heading for the section. For example, a section that begins with a level-2 heading might have level-3 subheadings under it. The subsections under the level-3 heads might have sub-subsections with level-4 heads, and so on.

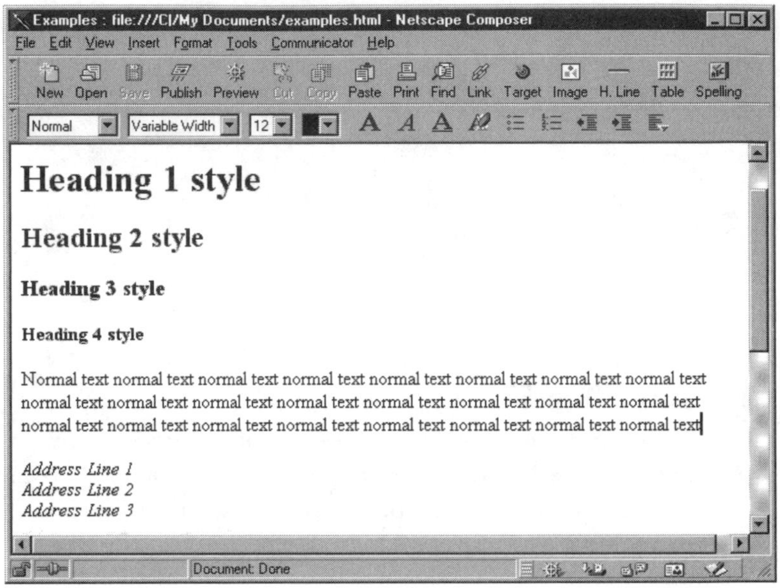

FIGURE 6.2
Paragraphs and their properties: headings, normal text, and address.

Address

Use the Address property for creating an *address block*, a line or many lines identifying someone, which usually lists an email address, a snail-mail address, or other contact information.

The Address property is used most often for the signature at the bottom of the page, but it can be used to give any address information on your page a unique style that sets it apart from other text. Most browsers display address blocks in italicized type.

> Assigning the Address property to an email address on your page does not, by itself, make the address a mail-to link that a visitor can click to send email. However, an email address with the Address property can be a mail-to link—you just have to make it one.
>
> To learn how to create a mail-to link, see Hour 10, "Making Links."

Formatted

"Formatted" might seem like a misnomer because text assigned the Preformatted property is in fact less formatted by the browser than any other kind. What *formatted* means in this context is *preformatted*—you have already lined up and spaced the text in a particular way, and you want browsers to leave that formatting alone.

Typically, browsers capable of displaying *proportionally spaced* fonts (such as the TrueType Arial or even the snappy font you're reading now) use those fonts for most text because they look better than typewriter-style *monospaced* fonts (such as Courier New). Also, browsers ignore tabs, extra spaces, and blank lines (extra paragraph marks) in HTML files.

Suppose that you want to show a text chart or table on your page, or words arranged in a certain way. Tabs are *verboten*, so you need to use spaces and a monospaced font to make the words line up right. But if browsers are permitted to do their regular thing with that text, they strip out the extra spaces, display the text in a proportional font, and generally screw up your lovely alignment job.

> You can use the Formatted property to create the effect of tables in your Web page, but you can also create real tables that look much better (see Hour 8, "Organizing Text with Tables and Rules").

For example, observe the careful alignment of columns and the use of a monospaced font in the simple table shown in Figure 6.3. This table uses the Formatted property. Notice how the browser's display font and regularity of spacing differ in the formatted table from the other text in the figure.

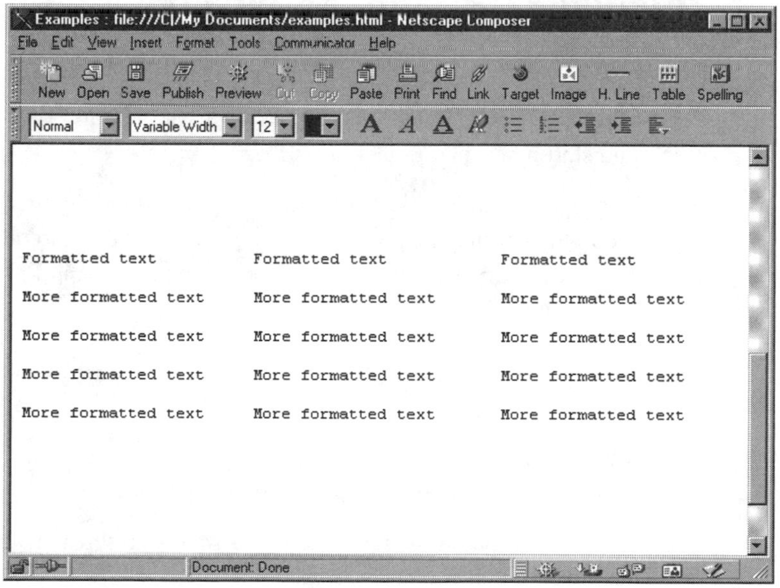

FIGURE 6.3
Paragraphs and their properties: "formatted" text.

You can apply paragraph properties in whatever way suits you. (No HTML police will stop you—at least not yet.) But it's good practice to think of these properties as a way to determine the role a paragraph plays in your page, not the appearance of the paragraph.

For example, there's no technical reason that you can't write a lengthy paragraph and make it a heading, rather than body text, to make it stand out on the page. But different browsers use different methods to make a heading look like a heading; some make headings big and bold, others underline, and some even number headings according to their levels. Some Web search engines catalog pages according to heading content because headings generally contain subject information. Putting ordinary paragraph information into a heading might generate some screwy hits on your page from Web searches.

Use properties conservatively, according to their designated roles. Save your artistry for character formatting, images, backgrounds, and other ways you can spice up a page.

Entering Text and Assigning Properties

You can add text to a page and assign properties to that text in several different ways, all of which are described in the following sections.

Entering Paragraphs By Typing

When you create a new Web page, the edit cursor appears automatically at the top of the Web page. Type away. To correct mistakes and make changes as you go, use the Backspace, Delete, and Insert keys just as you would in any Web page. To end a paragraph and start a new paragraph, press Enter.

By default, your paragraphs are all set as body text (unless you select a different property before you begin typing a paragraph). You can change them to other paragraph properties at any time, as described in the section "Assigning Paragraph Properties to Existing Text," later in this hour.

Typing Symbols and Special Characters

Sometimes, you need characters that don't appear on your keyboard, such as the copyright symbol or the accented characters used in languages other than English. For these types of occasions, Composer offers its Insert Special Characters menu.

1. Point to the spot in the text where you want to insert the character and click to position the edit cursor there.
2. Click Tools and then choose Character Tools, Insert Special Character.

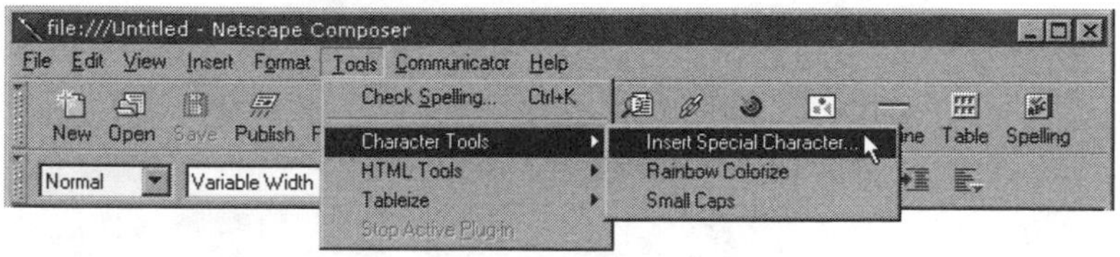

FIGURE 6.4
Step 2: Choose Tools, Character Tools, Insert Special Character.

3. Click the character or symbol you want to insert. After you click it, it appears on your page where you pointed the edit cursor.

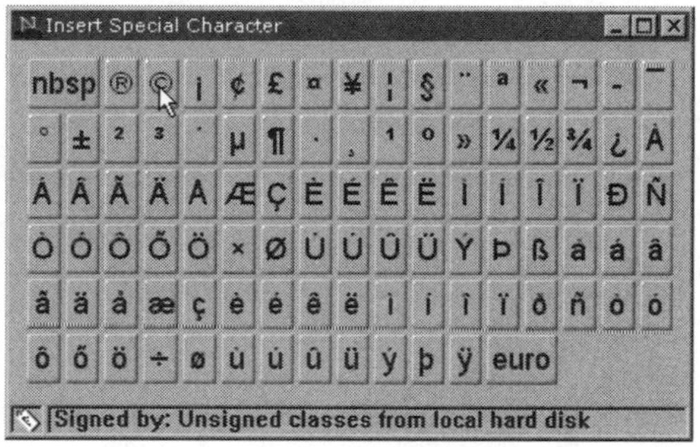

FIGURE 6.5
Step 3: Choose the character you want.

Copying Text from Another Document

The following To Do describes how to copy text from another document in Windows—such as a word-processing file or spreadsheet file—and place it in Composer so that it can be incorporated in your Web page. This method is a convenient way to use preexisting text, such as portions of your résumé or a description of your business, in your Web page without retyping it.

> If you want to use most or all of another document's contents in a new Web page, you may find that simply converting that document into a new Web page is more convenient than using copy-and-paste, as described here.
>
> To learn how to convert an existing word-processing file or other document into a new Web page, see Hour 4, "Starting Pages in Other Programs."

To Do: Enter text with copy-and-paste

1. Open the application normally used to edit or display the document from which you want to copy, and open the file.

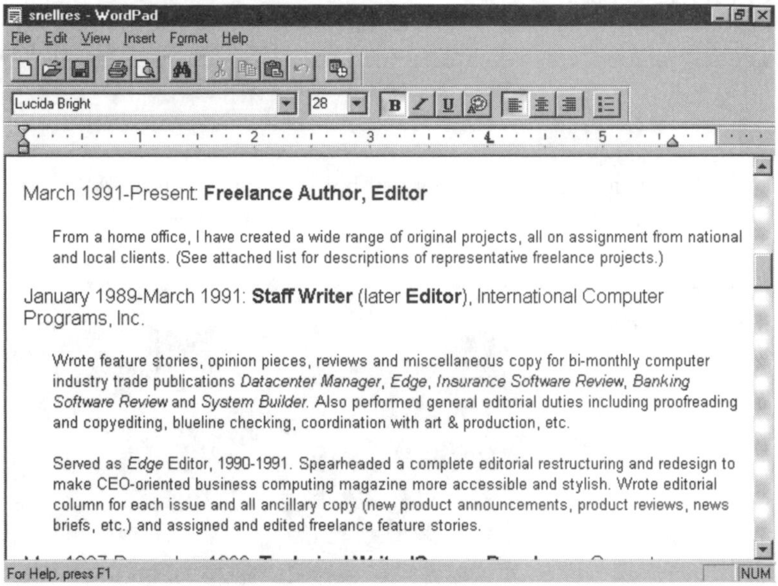
snellres - WordPad
File Edit View Insert Format Help
Lucida Bright
28
March 1991-Present: **Freelance Author, Editor**
From a home office, I have created a wide range of original projects, all on assignment from national and local clients. (See attached list for descriptions of representative freelance projects.)
January 1989-March 1991: **Staff Writer** (later **Editor**), International Computer Programs, Inc.
Wrote feature stories, opinion pieces, reviews and miscellaneous copy for bi-monthly computer industry trade publications *Datacenter Manager*, *Edge*, *Insurance Software Review*, *Banking Software Review* and *System Builder*. Also performed general editorial duties including proofreading and copyediting, blueline checking, coordination with art & production, etc.
Served as *Edge* Editor, 1990-1991. Spearheaded a complete editorial restructuring and redesign to make CEO-oriented business computing magazine more accessible and stylish. Wrote editorial column for each issue and all ancillary copy (new product announcements, product reviews, news briefs, etc.) and assigned and edited freelance feature stories.
For Help, press F1
NUM

FIGURE 6.6
Step 1: Open the application for the document from which you want to copy text.

2. Use your mouse to highlight the desired text. (To copy an entire document into your Web page, choose Edit, Select All in the application used to open the Web page.)

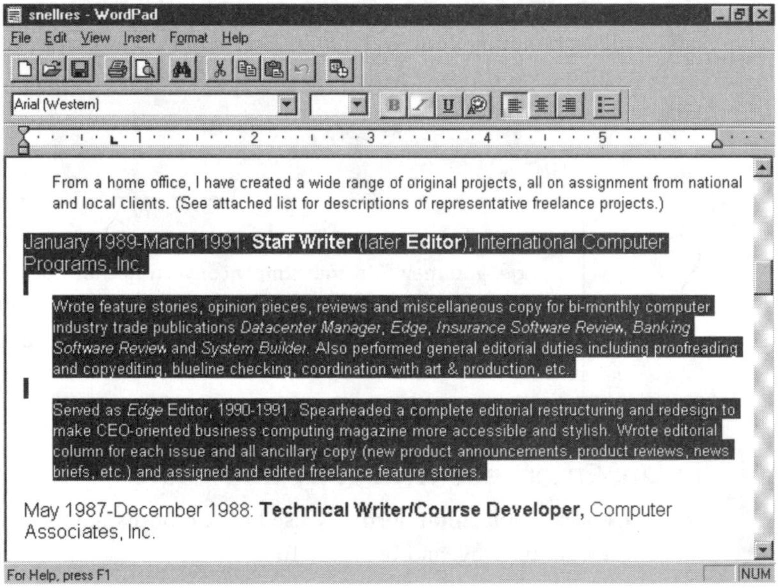
snellres - WordPad
File Edit View Insert Format Help
Arial (Western)
From a home office, I have created a wide range of original projects, all on assignment from national and local clients. (See attached list for descriptions of representative freelance projects.)
January 1989-March 1991: **Staff Writer** (later **Editor**), International Computer Programs, Inc.
Wrote feature stories, opinion pieces, reviews and miscellaneous copy for bi-monthly computer industry trade publications *Datacenter Manager*, *Edge*, *Insurance Software Review*, *Banking Software Review* and *System Builder*. Also performed general editorial duties including proofreading and copyediting, blueline checking, coordination with art & production, etc.
Served as *Edge* Editor, 1990-1991. Spearheaded a complete editorial restructuring and redesign to make CEO-oriented business computing magazine more accessible and stylish. Wrote editorial column for each issue and all ancillary copy (new product announcements, product reviews, news briefs, etc.) and assigned and edited freelance feature stories.
May 1987-December 1988: **Technical Writer/Course Developer,** Computer Associates, Inc.
For Help, press F1
NUM

FIGURE 6.7
Step 2: Highlight the text to copy.

3. Press Ctrl+C to copy the selection to the Windows Clipboard. (Alternatively, you can click the Copy button on the toolbar or choose Edit, Copy.)
4. Open Composer and open (or create) the Web page into which you want to copy the text.

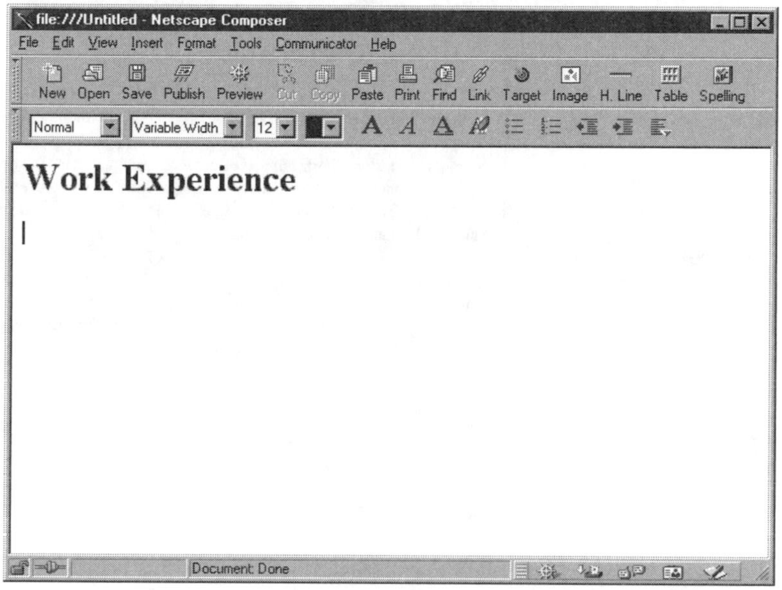

FIGURE 6.8
Step 4: Open the Web page in Composer.

5. In the page, click the general spot where you want to copy the text. (If you've just created the Web page, the text must be copied to the top of the Web page where the edit cursor is already located. In a page that already has text, you can click at the beginning or end of any paragraph to add the selection to that paragraph, or press Enter between paragraphs to start a new paragraph for the selection.)
6. Press Ctrl+V to copy the selection into the page. (Alternatively, you can click the Paste button on the Composer toolbar or choose Edit, Paste.)

When pasted into a blank Web page, the text is automatically assigned the Body Text paragraph property. You can then change it to any other paragraph property.

When pasted into a Web page with other paragraphs in it, the text is automatically assigned the same property as the paragraph it is inserted into or adjacent to.

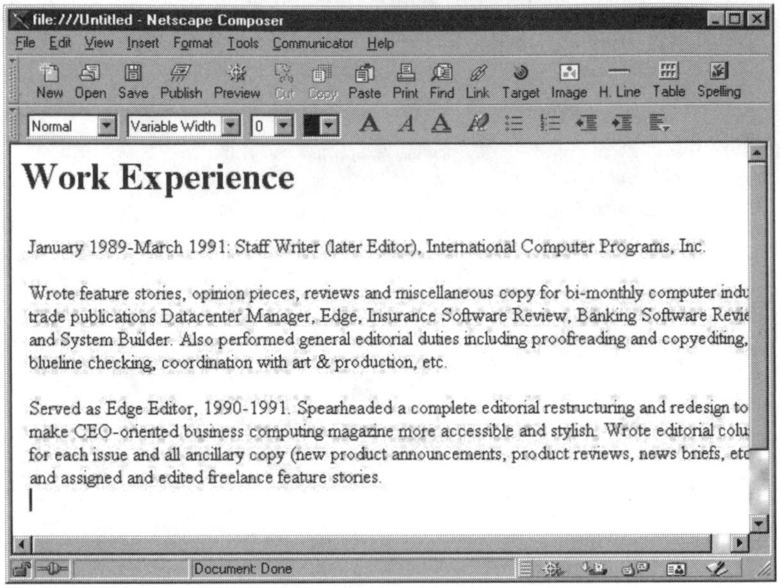
file:///Untitled - Netscape Composer
File Edit View Insert Format Tools Communicator Help
New Open Save Publish Preview Cut Copy Paste Print Find Link Target Image H. Line Table Spelling
Normal
Variable Width
0
Work Experience
January 1989-March 1991: Staff Writer (later Editor), International Computer Programs, Inc.
Wrote feature stories, opinion pieces, reviews and miscellaneous copy for bi-monthly computer indu
trade publications Datacenter Manager, Edge, Insurance Software Review, Banking Software Revie
and System Builder. Also performed general editorial duties including proofreading and copyediting,
blueline checking, coordination with art & production, etc.
Served as Edge Editor, 1990-1991. Spearheaded a complete editorial restructuring and redesign to
make CEO-oriented business computing magazine more accessible and stylish. Wrote editorial colu
for each issue and all ancillary copy (new product announcements, product reviews, news briefs, etc
and assigned and edited freelance feature stories.
Document: Done

FIGURE 6.9
Step 6: Insert the text.

Assigning Paragraph Properties to Existing Text

The process of assigning properties involves two steps. First, you select the paragraph or paragraphs, and then you choose the properties:

- To select one paragraph, position the edit cursor anywhere within it (by either clicking within the paragraph or pressing the arrow keys until the cursor arrives within the paragraph). Note that positioning the cursor within the paragraph is sufficient; you don't need to highlight the whole paragraph.

> If working *sans mouse*, you can select multiple paragraphs by positioning the edit cursor anywhere in the first paragraph and holding down the Shift key while using the arrow keys to move to anywhere in the last paragraph in the selection.

- To select two or more paragraphs, click anywhere in the first paragraph, drag to anywhere in the last paragraph, and release, as shown in Figure 6.10.

After the paragraphs are selected, you assign a paragraph property by clicking the Choose a Paragraph Format drop-down list (at the left end of the Format toolbar).

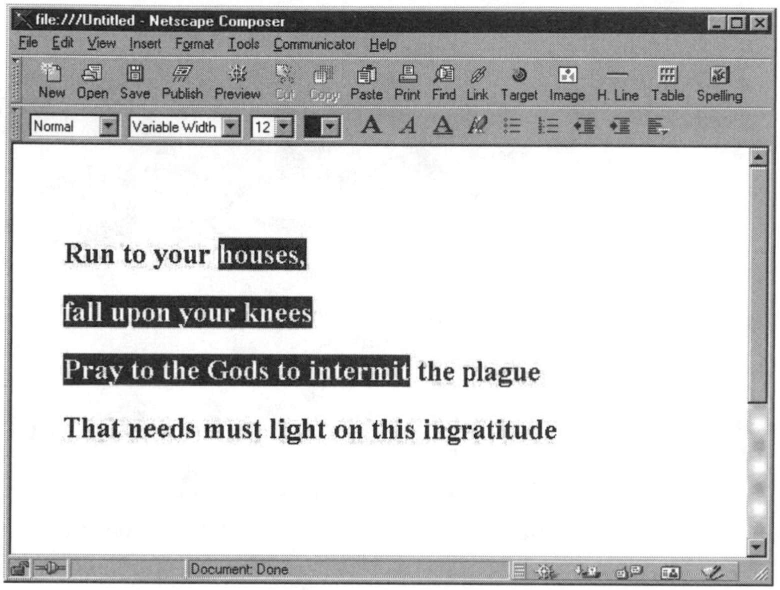
file:///Untitled - Netscape Composer
File Edit View Insert Format Tools Communicator Help
New Open Save Publish Preview Cut Copy Paste Print Find Link Target Image H. Line Table Spelling
Normal
Variable Width
12
Run to your houses,
fall upon your knees
Pray to the Gods to intermit the plague
That needs must light on this ingratitude
Document: Done

FIGURE 6.10
Selecting multiple paragraphs to assign them all the same paragraph property.

To Do: Assign properties and attributes as you type

Although a certain logic can help you enter your paragraphs and then assign properties, you can do the opposite. To assign properties as you type a paragraph:

1. Click the spot where you want the paragraph to go.

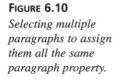

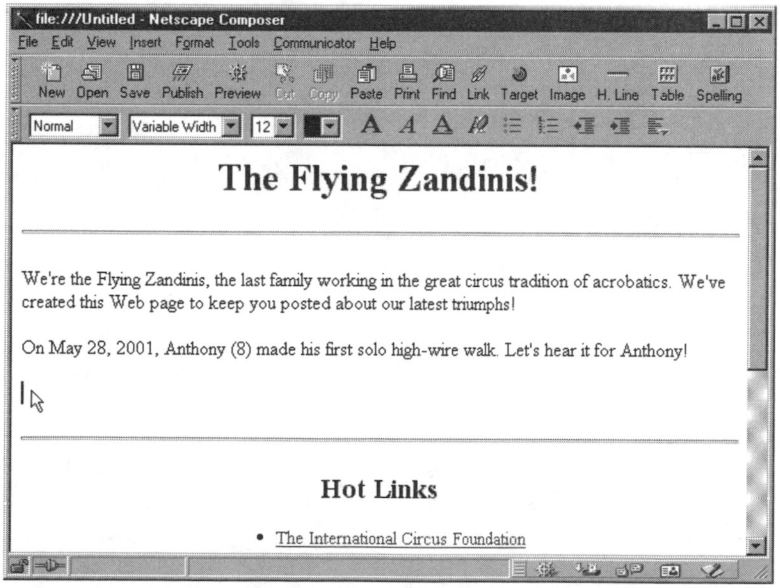
file:///Untitled - Netscape Composer
File Edit View Insert Format Tools Communicator Help
New Open Save Publish Preview Cut Copy Paste Print Find Link Target Image H. Line Table Spelling
Normal
Variable Width
12
The Flying Zandinis!
We're the Flying Zandinis, the last family working in the great circus tradition of acrobatics. We've created this Web page to keep you posted about our latest triumphs!
On May 28, 2001, Anthony (8) made his first solo high-wire walk. Let's hear it for Anthony!
Hot Links
The International Circus Foundation

FIGURE 6.11
Step 1: Click where you'll type the new text.

2. Click the Choose a Paragraph Format drop-down list on the Format toolbar and select a paragraph style.

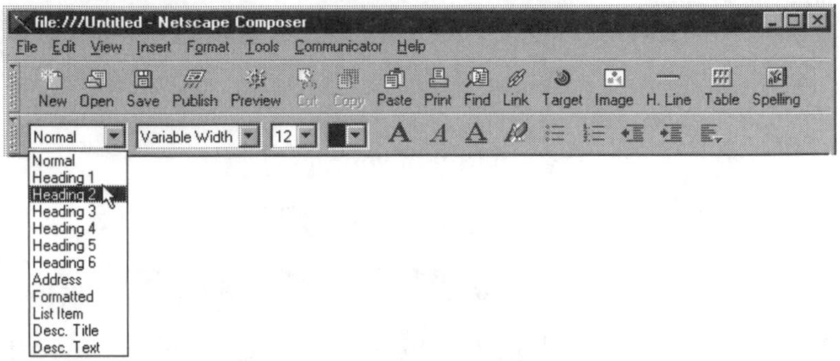

FIGURE 6.12
Step 2: Choose a style.

3. Type your paragraph. It appears on the page as you type it, formatted in the style you selected. If you press Enter (to end the paragraph and start a new one), the new paragraph reverts to the Body Text style.

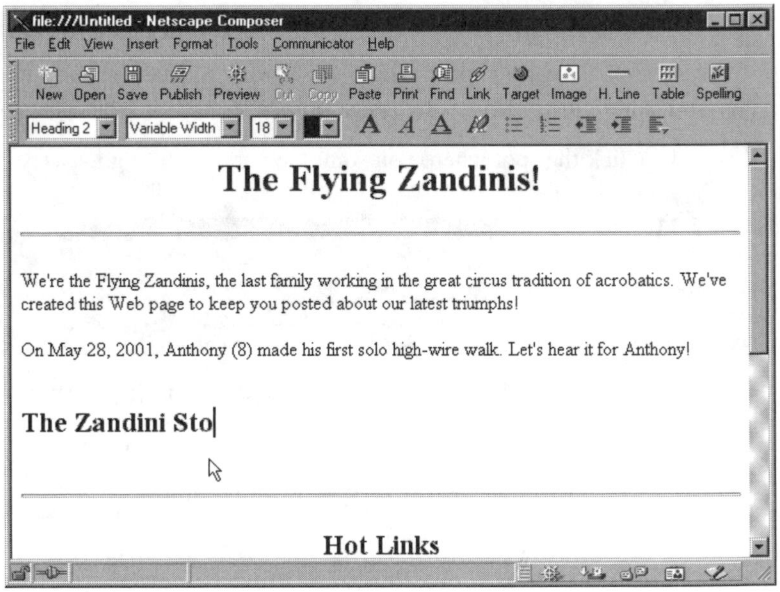

FIGURE 6.13
Step 3: Type away.

To learn the details of creating and formatting lists, see Hour 7, "Formatting Text."

Aligning and Indenting Text

On the Format toolbar, you find five buttons that control the position of a paragraph on the page (see Figure 6.14).

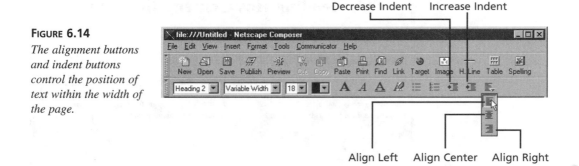

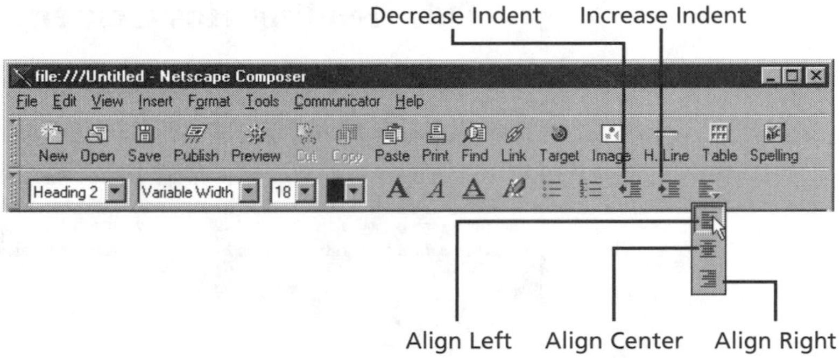

FIGURE 6.14
The alignment buttons and indent buttons control the position of text within the width of the page.

You can use these buttons (as described on the next few pages) on any paragraph, in any style. For example, you can use the Align Center button to center a paragraph whether the style of that paragraph is Body Text, List, Heading 2, or anything else.

Aligning Paragraphs

You can align any paragraph in any of three different ways (see Figure 6.15): tight against the left side of the page (the default choice), centered on the page (align center), and hard to the ride side (align right). The following To Do shows how.

Most of the time, left alignment is best, especially for Body Text paragraphs. Center can be nice for large headings (such as Heading 1 or Heading 2 style), especially if it is not used too much. Save right alignment for special needs.

Our eyes are accustomed to left-aligned text, especially for body text. A big, centered heading looks good on some pages, and right alignment can create a nice effect when text is put to the right of a graphic [see Hour 14, "Adding Pictures (and Picture Backgrounds)"]. However, centered Body Text paragraphs can appear a bit odd, and centered lists look downright strange.

6

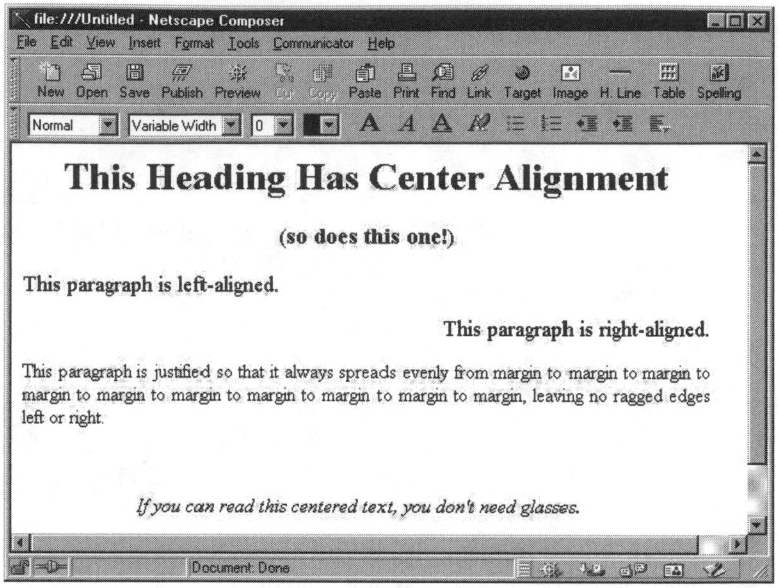
file:///Untitled - Netscape Composer
File Edit View Insert Format Tools Communicator Help
New Open Save Publish Preview Cut Copy Paste Print Find Link Target Image H. Line Table Spelling
Normal Variable Width 0
This Heading Has Center Alignment
(so does this one!)
This paragraph is left-aligned.
This paragraph is right-aligned.
This paragraph is justified so that it always spreads evenly from margin to margin to margin to margin to margin to margin to margin to margin to margin to margin, leaving no ragged edges left or right.
If you can read this centered text, you don't need glasses.
Document: Done

FIGURE 6.15
Left-aligned (the default), center-aligned, and right-aligned.

To Do: Align paragraphs

1. Select the paragraph or paragraphs you want to align.

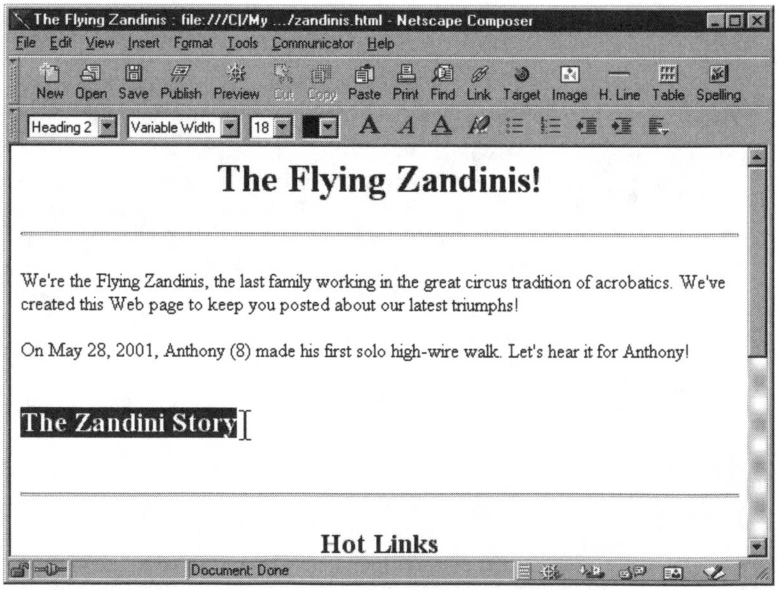
The Flying Zandinis : file:///C|/My .../zandinis.html - Netscape Composer
File Edit View Insert Format Tools Communicator Help
New Open Save Publish Preview Cut Copy Paste Print Find Link Target Image H. Line Table Spelling
Heading 2 Variable Width 18
The Flying Zandinis!
We're the Flying Zandinis, the last family working in the great circus tradition of acrobatics. We've created this Web page to keep you posted about our latest triumphs!
On May 28, 2001, Anthony (8) made his first solo high-wire walk. Let's hear it for Anthony!
The Zandini Story
Hot Links
Document: Done

FIGURE 6.16
Step 1: Select the paragraphs to align.

2. Click one of the alignment buttons on the Formatting toolbar: Align Left, Align Center, or Align Right. (If the paragraph is already aligned in any way other than left, you also see an Align Left button when you point to the toolbar.)

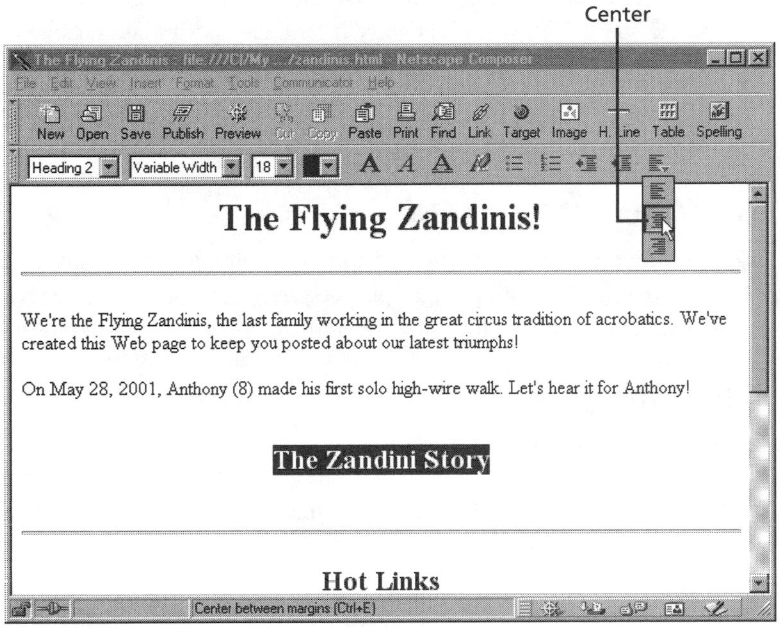
Center
The Flying Zandinis : file:///C|/My .../zandinis.html - Netscape Composer
File Edit View Insert Format Tools Communicator Help
New Open Save Publish Preview Cut Copy Paste Print Find Link Target Image H. Line Table Spelling
Heading 2
Variable Width
18
The Flying Zandinis!
We're the Flying Zandinis, the last family working in the great circus tradition of acrobatics. We've created this Web page to keep you posted about our latest triumphs!
On May 28, 2001, Anthony (8) made his first solo high-wire walk. Let's hear it for Anthony!
The Zandini Story
Hot Links
Center between margins (Ctrl+E)

FIGURE 6.17
Step 2: Click an alignment button.

Indenting Paragraphs

Besides choosing the alignment of paragraphs, you can *indent* them, pushing them away from the left margin just as you would in a word processor.

Composer supports multiple indent levels; you can increase the indent several times to push the paragraph farther away from the left margin. Decreasing the indent pulls the text back toward the left margin.

- To indent a paragraph, select it and then click the Increase Indent button on the Format toolbar. To indent even farther to the right, click the Increase Indent button again.
- To decrease the indent (move the left edge of the paragraph back toward the left margin), click the Decrease Indent button.

Adding Blank Line Spaces in a Page

Except within the Formatted paragraph style, HTML does not recognize paragraph marks in the HTML file as blank lines or extra blank spaces as extra blank spaces.

Thus, browsers generally ignore these characters when displaying a page. To create extra white space between paragraphs or extra spaces in a line, Web authors must use the HTML tags for line breaks and nonbreaking spaces, respectively.

Composer, however, figures that when you press Enter multiple times, you want to add white space—so it automatically inserts the appropriate tags.

So trust your word-processing instincts: To start a new paragraph, press Enter. To add a blank line, just press Enter again.

Editing Your Text

Editing a Web page is straightforward, much like editing any word-processing document. To do almost anything, highlight the text you want to change and then make the change. You can also search for a text string using the Composer Find in Page tool.

Highlighting Text

To highlight text with your mouse, position the cursor at the start of the area you want to highlight, and then click and hold the left mouse button. Drag to the end of the selection, and release the mouse button. Note that you can select as much text as you want in this way: a few characters, a word, a whole paragraph, or a group of paragraphs.

> When you drag through an area that includes both text and images, only the text is selected. Images must be selected separately (see Hour 14).

You can also highlight a selection for editing in other ways:

- Double-click a word to select it.
- Double-click at the beginning of a line to select the first word.
- Double-click at the end of a line to select the last word.
- Position the pointer to the left of a paragraph, double-click to select the entire paragraph, or single-click to select just the line the cursor is next to.

Replacing Selected Text

When text is selected, begin typing. The selection is deleted immediately and replaced with whatever you type. Any surrounding text that was not highlighted remains unaffected.

You can also replace a highlighted selection with the contents of the Clipboard by choosing Edit, Paste. (Of course, you must previously have cut or copied something to the Clipboard; see the section "Copying or Moving Selected Text," later in this hour.)

Deleting Selected Text

Press the Delete key to delete the selection.

> You can right-click selected text to display a context menu with choices for changing properties, for creating links, and for cutting, copying, and pasting (refer to Figure 6.5, shown earlier).

To delete the selection from its current location but copy it to the Windows Clipboard so that it can be pasted elsewhere in the page (or into another page or another Windows document), click the Cut button on the toolbar or choose Edit, Cut.

Copying or Moving Selected Text

To copy a highlighted selection, click the Copy button on the toolbar or choose Edit, Copy. Then click in the location where you want the copy to go, and click the Paste button or choose Edit, Paste.

To move a highlighted selection, click the Cut button on the toolbar or choose Edit, Cut. Then click in the location where you want the selection moved, and click the Paste button or choose Edit, Paste.

Undoing Edits ("Goofs")

If you goof on any edit and wish that you hadn't done it, you can undo it.

To undo the last edit you made, choose Edit, Undo.

Checking Your Spelling

Of course, some goofs go unnoticed too long for Undo to do much good—especially spelling errors. Fortunately, Composer has a spelling checker to rescue you.

To check spelling in a page, click the Spelling button on the Composition toolbar. Composer finds the first word it doesn't recognize (like all spelling checkers, it finds not so much misspelled words as words not in its dictionary), and displays the dialog box shown in Figure 6.18.

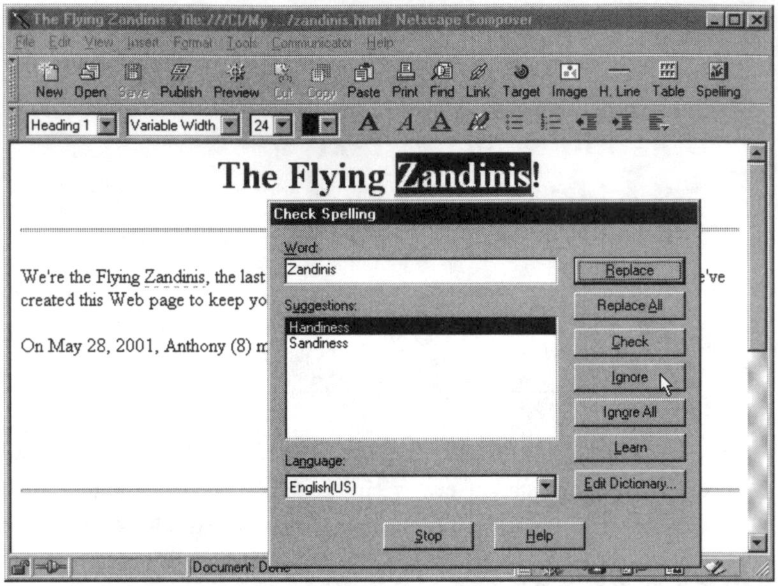

FIGURE 6.18
Click the Spelling button to open this box for fixxing yor speling.

In the Check Spelling box, you can

- Click any correct word listed in the Suggestions box and then click either the Replace button to change the misspelled word to the suggestion or Replace All to change all words spelled this way to the suggestion you chose.
- Edit or retype the word in the Word box to correct it and then click either the Replace button to change the misspelled word to the new version or Replace All to change all words spelled this way to the new version.
- Click Ignore to skip a word that's spelled correctly and just not recognized (like *Snell*).
- Click Ignore All to ignore this word everywhere in the page.
- Click Learn to add to the dictionary a correctly spelled but unrecognized word (like *Snell*) so that Composer no longer regards it as misspelled, in this or any other page you spell-check.

After you do any of these actions, the spelling checker moves on to the next word it doesn't recognize.

Tips for Good Text Design

It's your page, and far be it from me to tell you what it should look like. However, if you are interested in some of the accumulated wisdom of the Web masters, here are a few things to keep in mind when working with text on your page:

- Write clearly and be brief. Web surfers are an immediate-gratification, fast-food–type lot. To hold them, you must dole out your message in quick, efficient bites.
- Break up your message into pages of reasonable length, and break up pages into at least two or three sections (three is best) delineated by headings, pictures, or horizontal lines (see Hour 7, "Formatting Text"). This technique makes your page more attractive and inviting and also allows visitors to scan your page easily for items of interest.
- Don't overdo emphasis. Look through your page and watch for overuse of bold, italics, and custom font sizes and colors. Watch also for the use of headings or other properties used to pump up a paragraph that really belongs in body text. Let your page's organization (and pictures) create visual interest, and let your choice of words emphasize important ideas. Use bold to light up a word or two and use italics for things that belong in italics, such as book titles or foreign phrases.
- Proofread carefully on your own before publishing. In addition, have someone else check your spelling and critique your writing and layout. (See Hour 4, "Starting Pages in Other Programs," to learn how to use your word processor to spell-check a Web page.)
- Always use a signature (see Hour 10, "Making Links").

Summary

Composer provides simple toolbar buttons, dialog boxes, and menus for applying properties to paragraphs—the most important activity in building a Web page.

Q&A

Q In second grade, I was taught to type two blank spaces after a period, before starting the next sentence. When I try to do that in Composer (by pressing my keyboard's spacebar twice), it doesn't let me—I get just one space.

A Browsers generally ignore extra spaces, so it's a mistake to use extra spaces to change the appearance of type in a Web page—if you could type two spaces, most browsers omit the second space when displaying your page anyway. To help you avoid that error, Composer simply refuses to let you type more than one space character.

If you want that extra space because you're trying to line up rows or columns of text in a particular way, the spacebar isn't the way to do it. Instead, put the text in a table, as described in Hour 8, "Organizing Text with Tables and Rules."

If you absolutely must have multiple character spaces within a paragraph, you have two options: If you use the Change Style list to apply the Preformatted style to the paragraph, you can type all the spaces you want—Composer makes an exception for paragraphs in the Preformatted style, and browsers know to display all space characters in these types of paragraphs. The other method is to insert the HTML tag for a blank space; you learn to do that in Hour 17, "Editing HTML."

HOUR 7

Formatting Text

It's easy—too easy, in fact—to begin thinking that a Web page is made up of three basic parts: text, images, and links. Although that's generally true, it tends to imply that text is for content, images are for show, and links are for action.

The facts are a little muddier than that. Text is first and foremost a vehicle for information, but when text is dressed up in a fancy font or cool color, it contributes both content and design—feeding two brain hemispheres for the price of one. Similarly, organizing text into a bulleted or numbered list affects both content and style.

In this hour, you step beyond paragraph properties and into fancy text formatting. At the end of the hour, you will be able to answer the following questions:

- How do I make attractive lists?
- How do I choose the font and size for text, as I would in a word processor?
- Can I choose the color of text?

Working with Lists

You can use buttons on the Format toolbar to create two kinds of lists in Composer (see Figure 7.1):

Numbered list—A list whose items are numbered from top to bottom.

Bulleted list—An ordinary, indented bulleted list.

FIGURE 7.1
List styles you can create in Composer.

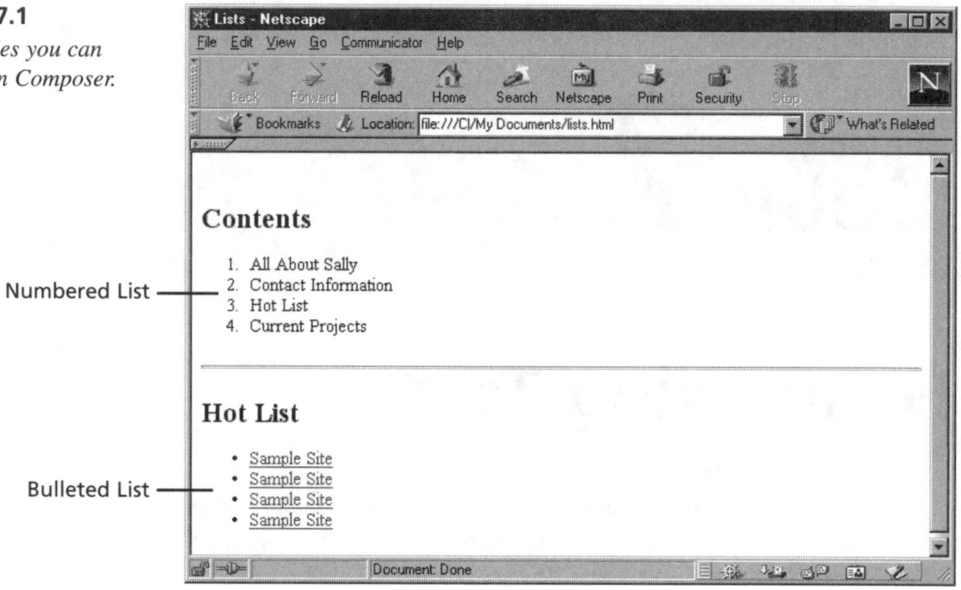

> Which kind of list should you create for a given purpose: bulleted or numbered? I dunno. It's your Web site. Do what you feel like.
>
> If you want a principle to guide you, try this technique: When the order of the items in the list is important, as in step-by-step instructions, use a numbered list. When the order doesn't matter, use a bulleted list.

But the choices don't stop there! You can change the bullet style or numbering type of your plain-vanilla bulleted or numbered list (see Figure 7.2).

FIGURE 7.2
Optional numbering and bullet styles.

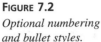

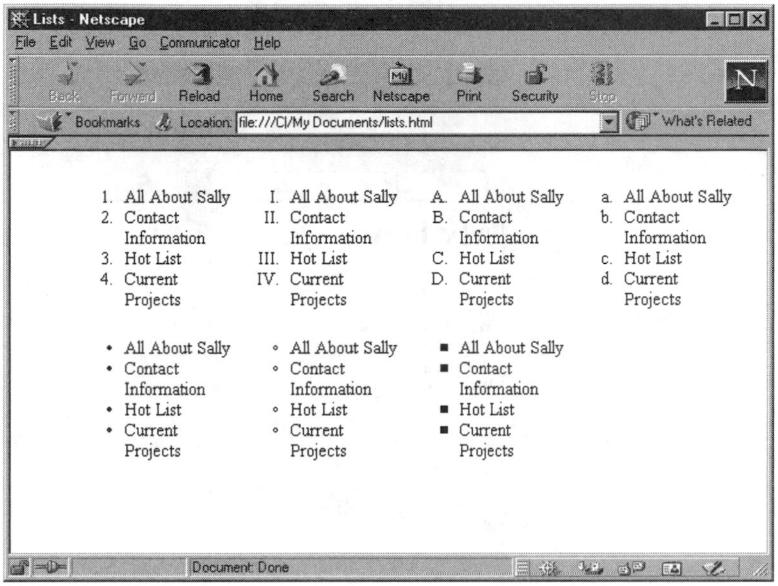

> In some pages you see online, you see cool list bullets that are geometrical, multicolored, and even animated.
>
> These are not real bullets assigned by a bullet style attribute, but rather images inserted right before each line of text [see Hour 14, "Adding Pictures (and Picture Backgrounds)"].

Creating Basic Lists

As with all other text formatting, you create a list by first typing the text of one or more list items; each item is a separate paragraph (press Enter after typing each item), and each item can be as long or as short as you choose. You then apply list formatting as described in the following To Do.

To Do: Create a list

1. Type the list items and press Enter after each one so that each list item is on a separate line.
2. Select the entire list.

7

FIGURE 7.3
Step 1: Type the list items.

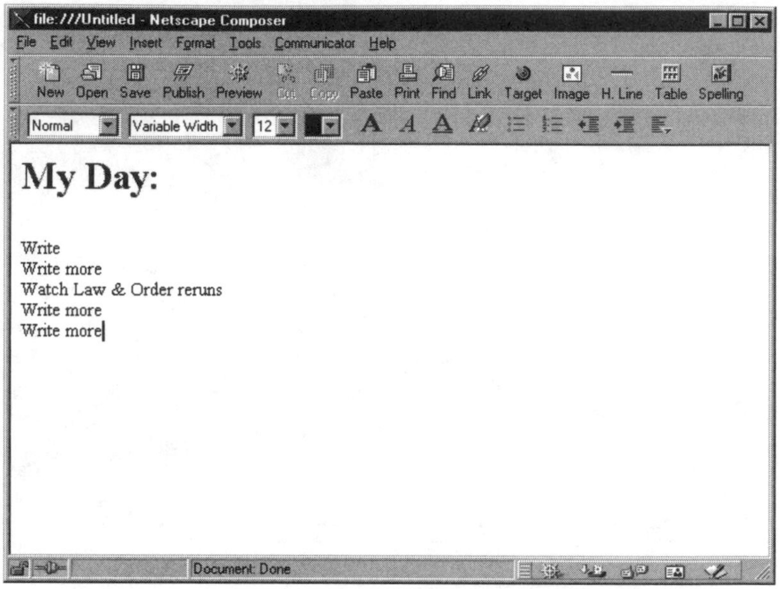
file:///Untitled - Netscape Composer
File Edit View Insert Format Tools Communicator Help
New Open Save Publish Preview Cut Copy Paste Print Find Link Target Image H. Line Table Spelling
Normal
Variable Width
12
My Day:
Write
Write more
Watch Law & Order reruns
Write more
Write more
Document: Done

FIGURE 7.4
Step 2: Select the list.

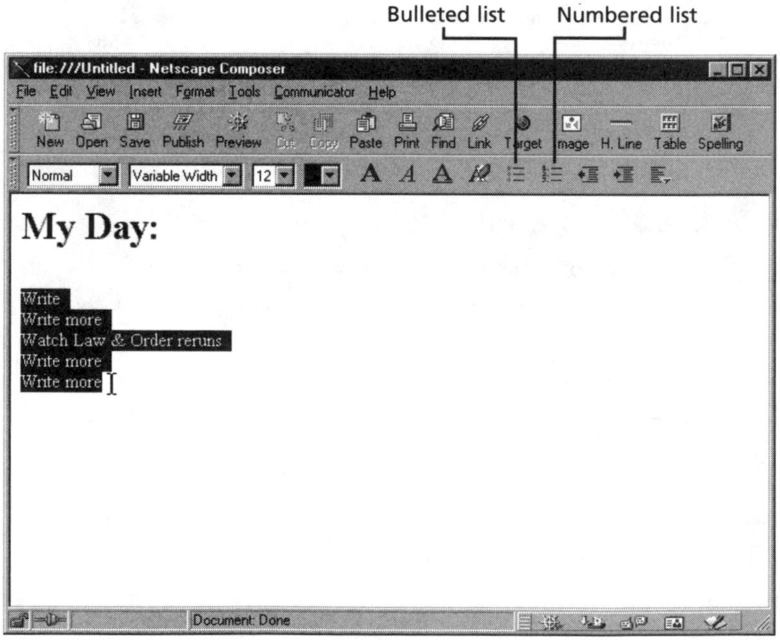
Bulleted list
Numbered list
file:///Untitled - Netscape Composer
File Edit View Insert Format Tools Communicator Help
New Open Save Publish Preview Cut Copy Paste Print Find Link Target Image H. Line Table Spelling
Normal
Variable Width
12
My Day:
Write
Write more
Watch Law & Order reruns
Write more
Write more
Document: Done

List formatting is paragraph formatting, so you can select a list by starting the selection anywhere in the first item and then dragging down to anywhere in the last item.

3. Click one of the two list buttons on the Format toolbar: Numbered List or Bulleted List.

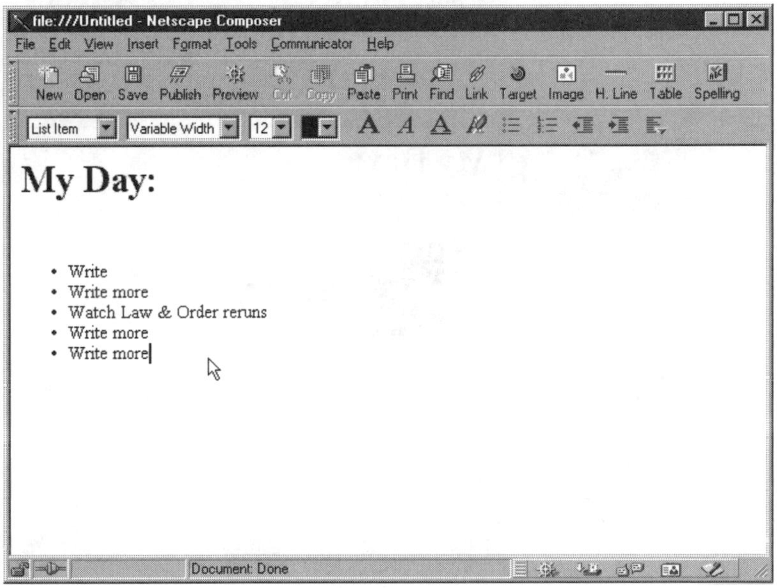

FIGURE 7.5
After Step 3, the list is formatted with the list style of your choice.

The items in a list can be formatted in any style. You can make a list of headings, for example.

However, note that the bullets and numbers at the beginning of the list usually do not change size, regardless of the size of the text. For that reason, you should keep list text in the Normal style or as a high-level heading (such as Heading 3 or 4).

If you want really big, bold text for list items, forget about regular list formatting and instead add graphical bullets (as described in Hour 14) that are big and bold enough to suit the power of the text.

Changing the Look of a List

You can make a pretty good-looking list just by clicking a button, as you did in the preceding To Do. But you don't have to settle for what you get. You can easily modify the appearance of a list, choosing the numbering style (A B C or I II III, for example) or bullet symbol.

1. Select the list.

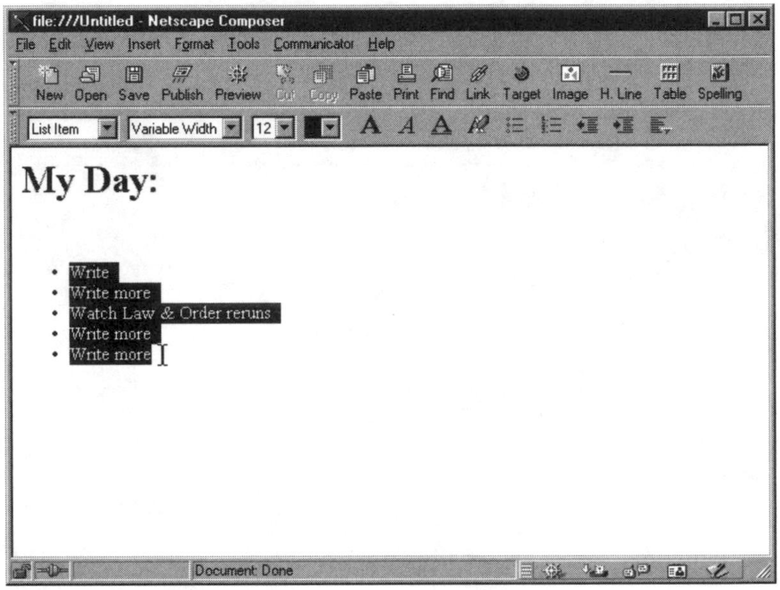

FIGURE 7.6
Step 1: Select the list.

2. Choose Format, Character Properties.
3. Select the Paragraph tab. The type of list you have assigned appears in the List Style box in the middle of the dialog box. You can leave it or change the list type using the drop-down list.
4. Depending on the selected list style, a list of options is available from a second drop-down list in the dialog box. If Bullet is the list style, you get a list of options for the Bullet style to use. If Numbered List is the list style, you get options for the Number style. Choose from the list the bullet or numbering style you want.

FIGURE 7.7
Step 2: Choose Format, Character Properties.

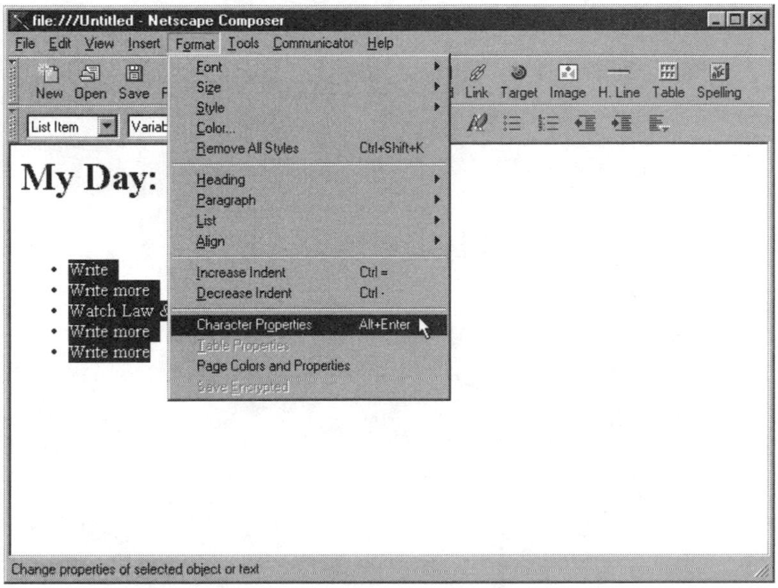

FIGURE 7.8
Step 4: Choose your style options from the list.

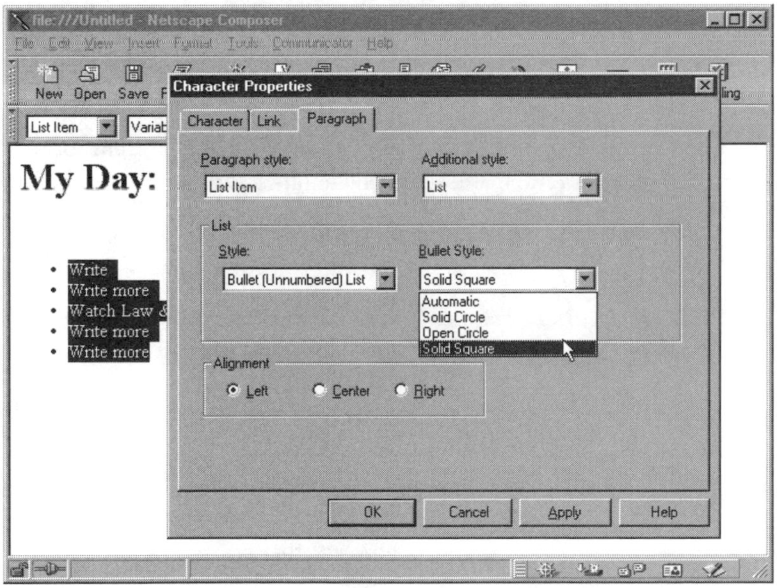

7

5. Click OK. The look of the list is changed.

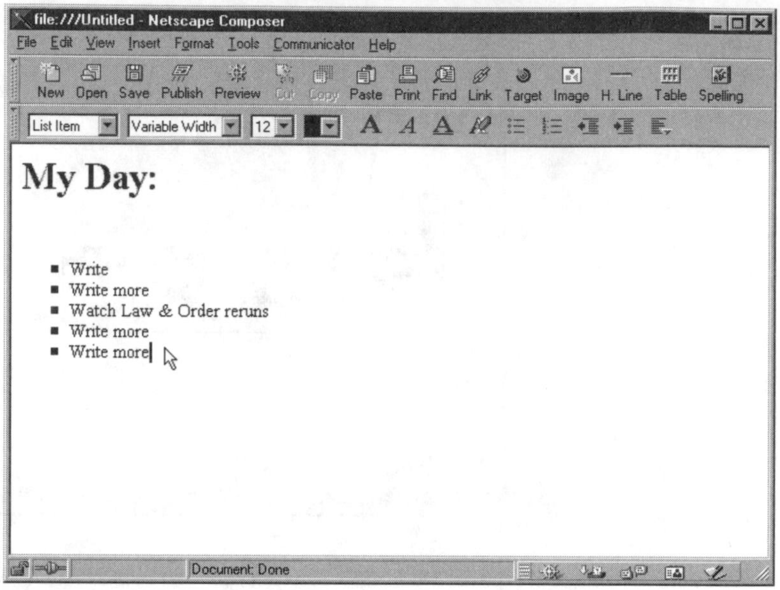

FIGURE 7.9
Old list, new look.

Dressing Up Text with Character Properties

Paragraph properties always apply to a whole paragraph; for example, you cannot make part of a paragraph a heading and another part normal text.

However, you can apply character properties to a single character in a paragraph, a few words, a whole paragraph, or a whole document.

NEW TERM *Character properties* are optional settings you apply to text to change its appearance, such as a particular font (typeface) or bold formatting.

> Paragraph properties (such as alignment and indenting) and character properties (such as font or boldfacing) generally work together to define the look of a paragraph and the text within it.
>
> Keep in mind, however, that browsers apply some character formatting to text based on paragraph style alone. For example, they automatically show headings in large, bold type. When you apply character formatting, you override any default formatting that the browser applies.

The most common use of character properties is to emphasize words by making them bold, italic, or underlined, just as you would when formatting a document in a word processor. But you can also change the color of characters, change the font (typeface) or size, and so on.

> Some character properties are based on extensions to HTML. As you might expect, anything you can do to text in Composer is fully supported by your popular friends Internet Explorer and Netscape Navigator. Among other browsers, however, you find a slippery slope of support levels.
>
> Nearly all graphical browsers support relative font sizes. Most support character styles such as bold, italic, and underline; however, some browsers interpret these styles as merely "emphasis" and decide on their own how to show that emphasis. For example, text you make italic might show up underlined (and not italic) in a browser that makes its own rules for emphasizing text. Unusual styles, such as superscript and blinking text, are not often supported outside the Netscape and Microsoft camps. Text color is an offshoot of custom colors and is supported in any browser that supports custom colors (as long as the visitor has not disabled that support).

Choosing Fonts

When you open Composer's font list, you'll see every Windows font installed on your PC, plus a few new choices. You can use any font in the list, but there are good reasons for self-limiting your font choices to a much narrower range than what Composer makes available.

Choosing a font instructs the browser to use the selected font (or, in a few cases, a font from the same family). The trick is that the font you choose, if it's not one of the very few built into Composer, must be installed on the visitor's computer (either PC or Macintosh), or the visitor's browser must have a special built-in font viewer.

For example, if you set text in Century Gothic, your visitors will see that font only if they happen to have Century Gothic installed on their computers. Otherwise, the text reverts to a font selected by the browser.

You'll have best luck with fonts if you keep the following guidelines in mind:

- The Variable Width and Fixed Width options each allow the visitor's browser to apply whatever variable or fixed-width font it happens to use by default.
- Helvetica/Arial are two proportionally spaced sans serif fonts. (*Sans serif* means that the font lacks the decorative lips or bars that appear at the points of characters

in serif fonts.) A browser on a computer lacking Helvetica or Arial can substitute another sans serif proportional font.

- Times is a serif proportional font for which a similar font, such as Century Schoolbook, can be substituted.
- Courier is a monospaced font (like that used to display text in the fixed-width character property or Preformatted paragraph property). Another monospaced font, such as Letter Gothic, can be substituted by the browser.

To Do: Choose a font for text

1. Select the exact characters to which you want to apply a new font.
2. Choose Format, Font.
3. Choose from the list of choices the font you want to apply.

Fonts are a form of character formatting, not paragraph formatting, so they affect only the exact characters you select. To apply a font to a whole paragraph, you must select the whole paragraph.

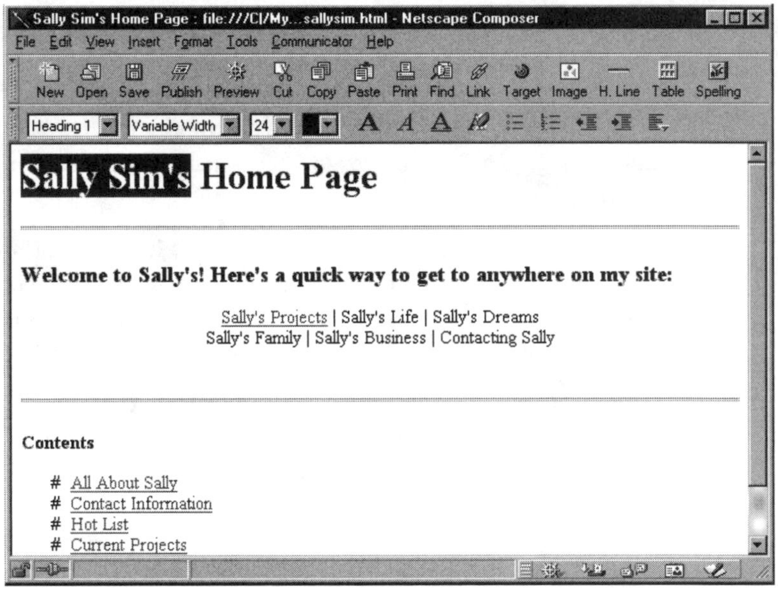

FIGURE 7.10
Step 1: Select the characters.

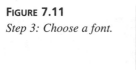

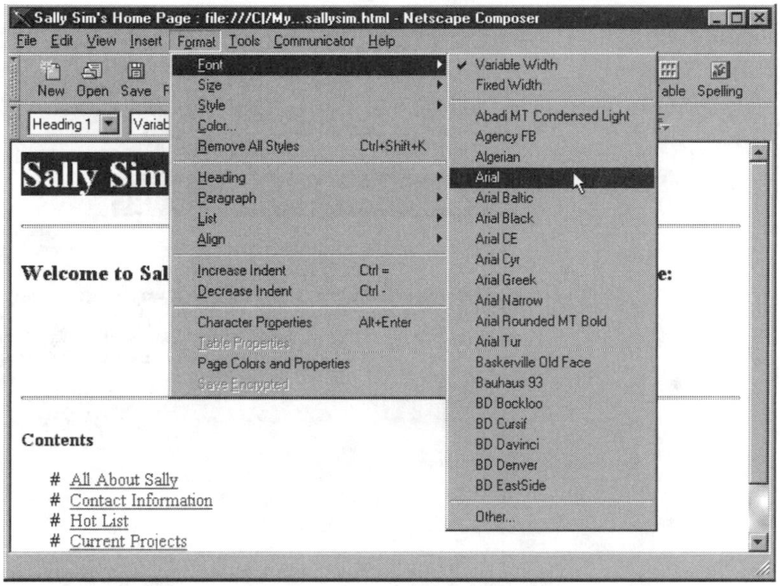

FIGURE 7.11
Step 3: Choose a font.

Choosing a Size for Text

The paragraph style determines size. For example, if text set in the Heading 3 style looks too small to you, the best solution is to change it to a bigger style, such as Heading 2 or Heading 1. Still, you can fine-tune the size of selected text easily, when the size chosen by the style isn't exactly what you want.

> If you click Larger Text Size and the selected text does not get any bigger, the text is already set at the largest size allowed. Similarly, if the Smaller Text Size option does nothing, the text is already set at the minimum size allowed.

▼ To Do

To Do: Choose the size of text

1. Select the exact characters you want to make bigger or smaller.
2. Locate the font size drop-down list on the Formatting toolbar.
3. To adjust the size of the selected text, select the font size.

FIGURE 7.12
Step 1: Select the characters.

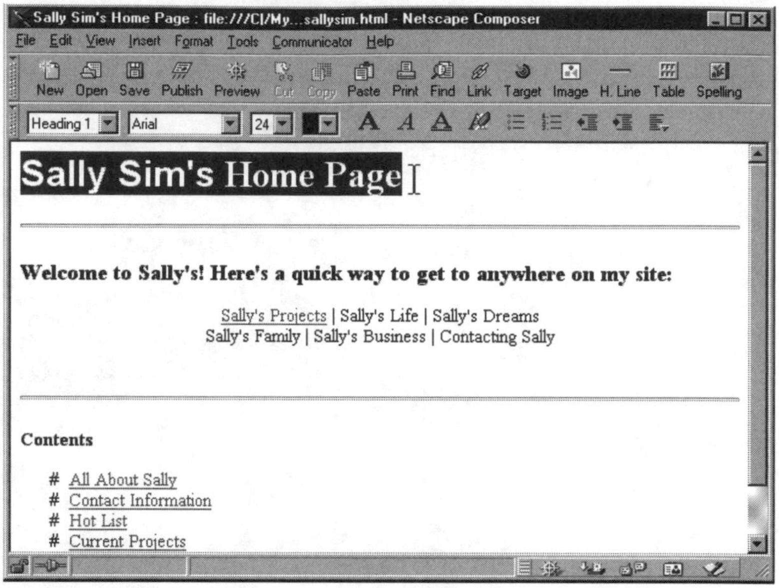

FIGURE 7.13
Step 3: Select a smaller or larger font size.

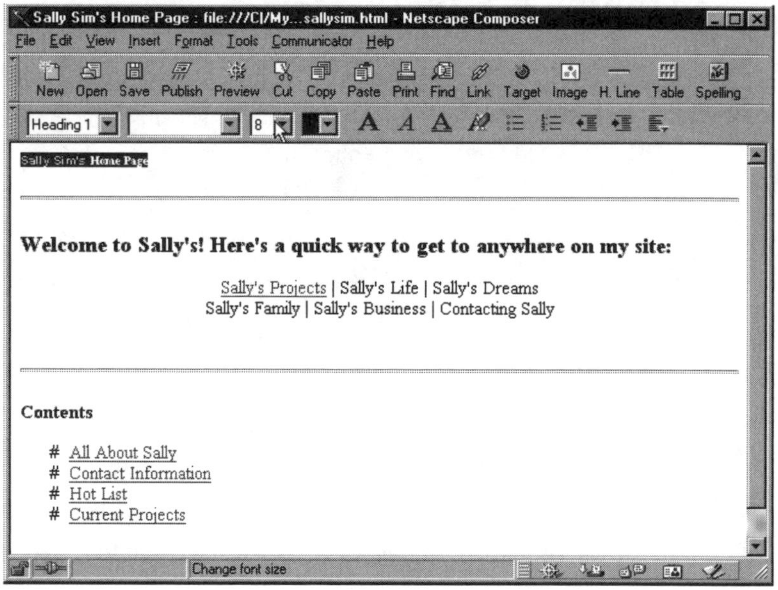

Making Text Bold, Italic, or Underlined

Just as in any letter or report you might create, bold, italic, and underlining are valuable tools in a Web page for making text stand out or for making it match editorial standards (such as setting book titles in italics). These styles are easy to use, but use them sparingly; too much of this stuff makes text busy and hard to read.

> You can combine these kinds of formatting; for example, you can make the selected text both bold and italic by clicking the Bold button and then the Italic button.

To Do: Apply bold, italic, or underline text formatting

1. Select the exact characters you want to format.
2. Click a button to format the selected characters: the Bold button, Italic button, or Underline button.

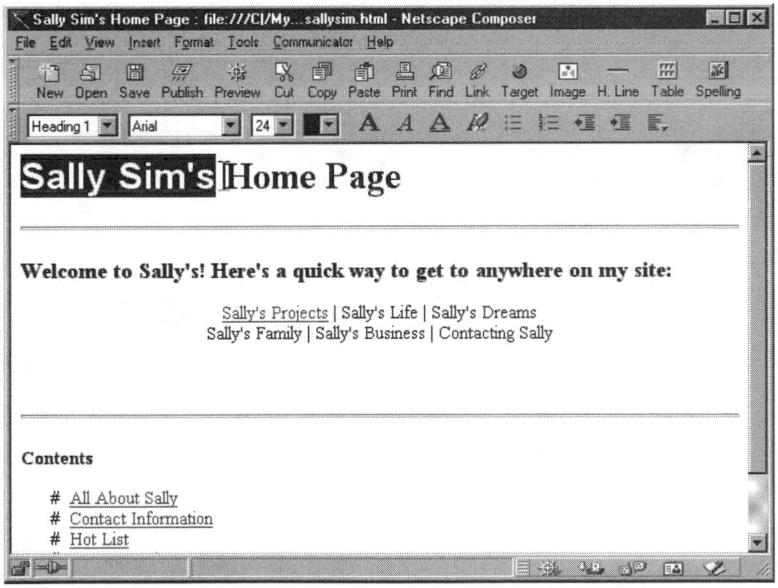

FIGURE 7.14
Step 1: Select the characters.

Rather than use the buttons, you can apply text styles by choosing Format, Style from the menu. The menu offers not only the familiar bold, italic, and underline choices, but also more esoteric character styles, such as strikethrough and subscript.

Use the esoteric stuff sparingly, though, because it is not supported in all browsers.

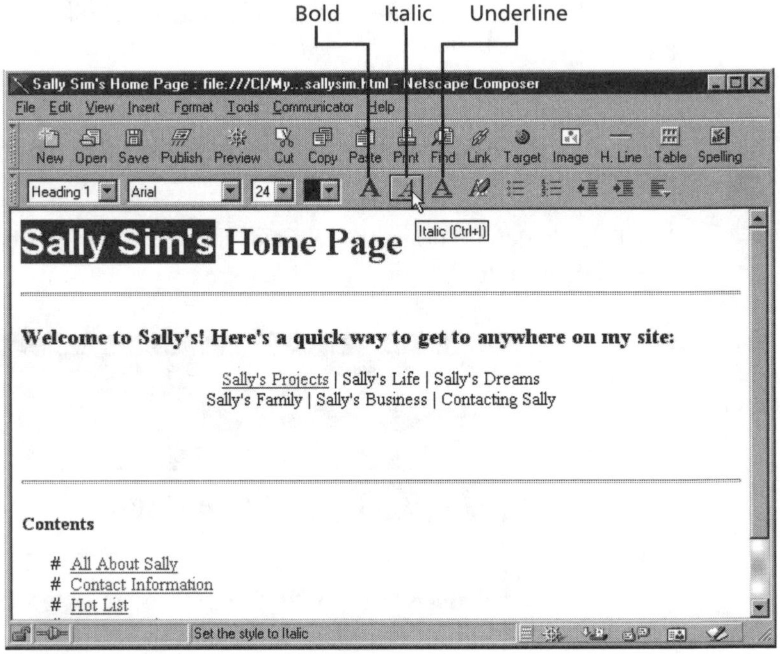

FIGURE 7.15
Step 2: Click Bold, Italic, or Underline.

To remove bold, italic, or underlining, select the text and click the button again. For example, to make some bold text not bold, select it and click the Bold button.

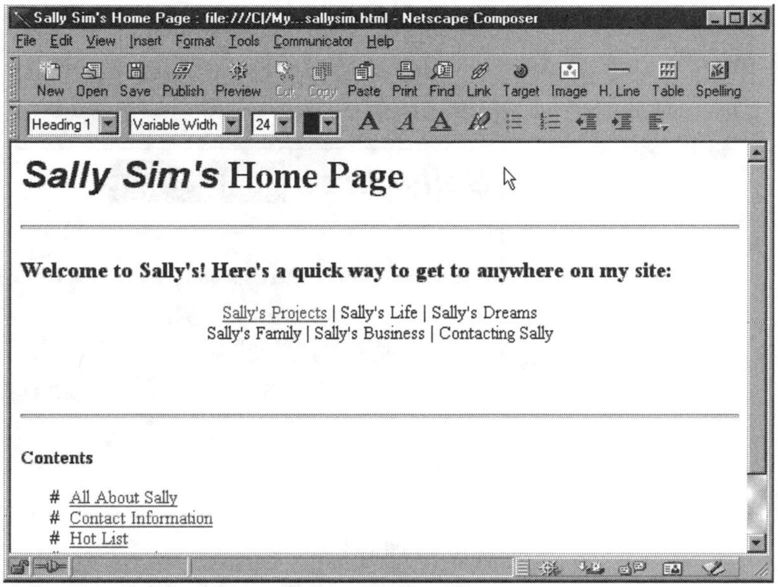

FIGURE 7.16
Italics applied.

Choosing the Color of Text

In Hour 5, "Choosing a Title, Colors, and Other Page Basics," you learned how to choose a coordinated color scheme for your Web page—a scheme for making sure that all the colors used for text, the background, and other objects all work together. If you do that, you probably won't be choosing colors selectively for blocks of text.

Still, you might want to give a heading or other selected text its own, unique color. The following To Do shows how.

To Do: Apply a color to text

1. Select the exact characters for which you want to choose a color.
2. Choose Format, Color.
3. Click the colored square containing the color you want to apply, and then click OK.

FIGURE 7.17
Step 1: Select the characters.

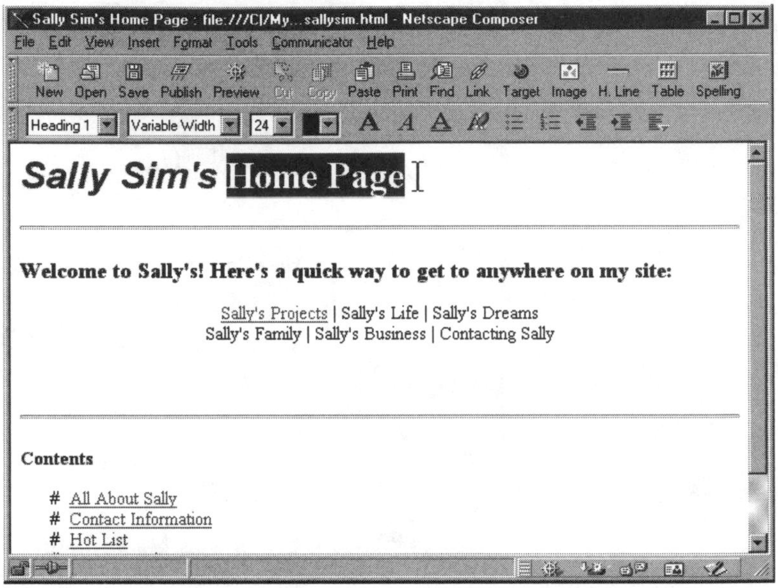

FIGURE 7.18
Step 3: Click the color you want.

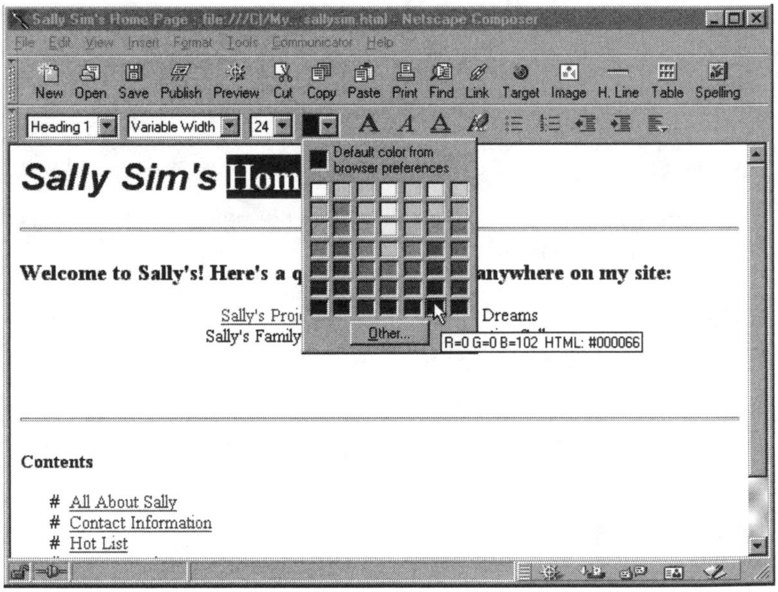

Summary

Still think that images are the meat of a page's looks? You haven't entered a single image, and yet you've discovered an easy arsenal of techniques for dressing up a page, including list formatting, custom colors, and fonts.

Sure, you still want to use images, but as your pages evolve, always remember that you have these simple but effective design tools available to you.

Q&A

Q Because I can't know what fonts my visitors might have on their computers, shouldn't I steer clear of fancy fonts—especially considering that some browsers don't even support them?

A Actually, fonts are a pretty safe bet. First, keep in mind that when you use fonts, nothing terrible will happen in browsers that can't support them—those browsers simply display the text in their default display fonts.

Second, all versions of Windows come with a default set of TrueType fonts, and Macintoshes are equipped with a similar list. If you use fonts from these default lists, you have a pretty good shot at getting your desired font displayed to most Netscape and Internet Explorer users on PCs and Macintoshes—and that's a majority of the Web surfers out there. You can better your odds by sticking with the three "super fonts"—Arial, Times New Roman, and Courier—so that computers lacking those fonts can substitute a similar font.

HOUR 8

Organizing Text with Tables and Rules

Between text and pictures is a gray area. The objects in this area affect the composition and organization of a Web page, but they aren't exactly text or pictures; they are tables and horizontal lines (sometimes also known as horizontal rules).

Tables are a great way to organize text in a meaningful, attractive way. And horizontal lines divide pages up visually into meaningful sections, making the page both more appealing and easier to read. In this hour—before moving ahead to pictures in Part IV—you'll learn how to apply these "gray area" techniques to make the most of text.

At the end of this hour, you will be able to answer the following questions:

- How do I insert horizontal lines in my page and control their appearance?
- How do I make a table?
- Can I customize table borders, headings, captions, and other things that affect the table's appearance?
- How can I create cool Web page layouts by making a table as big as a page?

About Horizontal Lines

The simple, straight lines running horizontally across many Web pages (see Figure 8.1) have always been known in Web parlance as *horizontal rules* because they're created by the HTML tag `<HR>`—`HR` for *h*orizontal *r*ule.

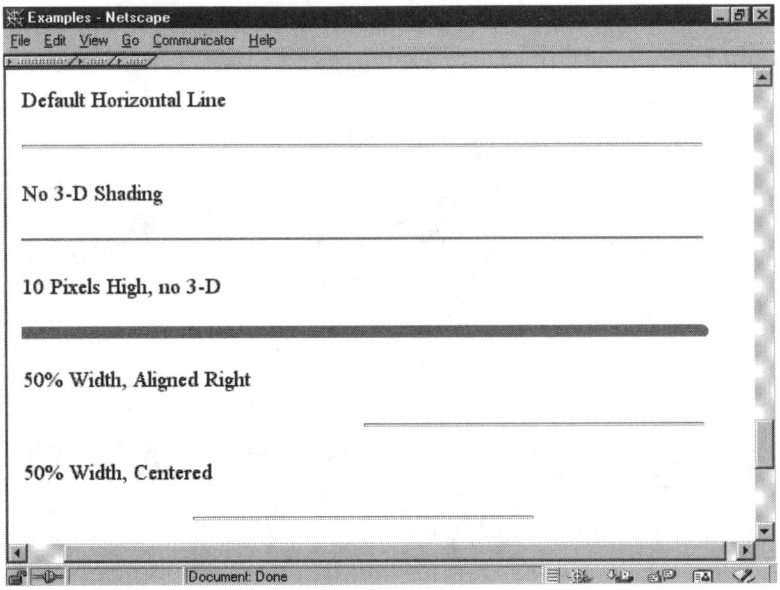

FIGURE 8.1
Horizontal lines are easy to create in various widths and thicknesses and offer an easy, attractive way to organize a page.

Netscape apparently thinks that the term *rule* is confusing, so in Composer it's a horizontal *line*. No matter. Rules are made to be broken, or lines, or something like that.

> In some pages, you see cool, graphical horizontal lines that zigzag, flash, or scroll. These are not real HTML "horizontal lines," but rather pictures inserted to achieve the same effect as a line (only cooler).
>
> You learn how to add these picture lines in Hour 14, "Adding Pictures (and Picture Backgrounds)." A nifty selection of pictures to use as cool lines is included on the CD-ROM with this book.

Virtually any browser (even a text-only browser) can show a horizontal line because any computer system can draw one across the screen (even if the line is made up of only underscores or dashes). Lines are a universal way to add some visual interest to your page and break up logical sections of a page or document to communicate more effectively.

To Do: Add horizontal lines

1. Click in your page at the spot where you want to insert the line.
2. Click the H. Line button on the Composer toolbar.

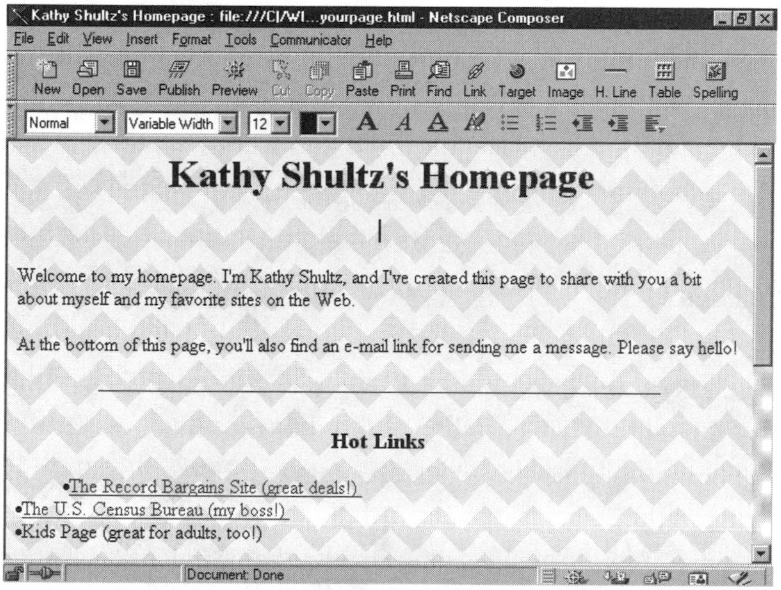
Kathy Shultz's Homepage : file:///C|/WI...yourpage.html - Netscape Composer
File Edit View Insert Format Tools Communicator Help
New Open Save Publish Preview Cut Copy Paste Print Find Link Target Image H. Line Table Spelling
Normal
Variable Width
12
Kathy Shultz's Homepage
Welcome to my homepage. I'm Kathy Shultz, and I've created this page to share with you a bit about myself and my favorite sites on the Web.
At the bottom of this page, you'll also find an e-mail link for sending me a message. Please say hello!
Hot Links
•The Record Bargains Site (great deals!)
•The U.S. Census Bureau (my boss!)
•Kids Page (great for adults, too!)
Document: Done

FIGURE 8.2
Step 1: Click where you want the line.

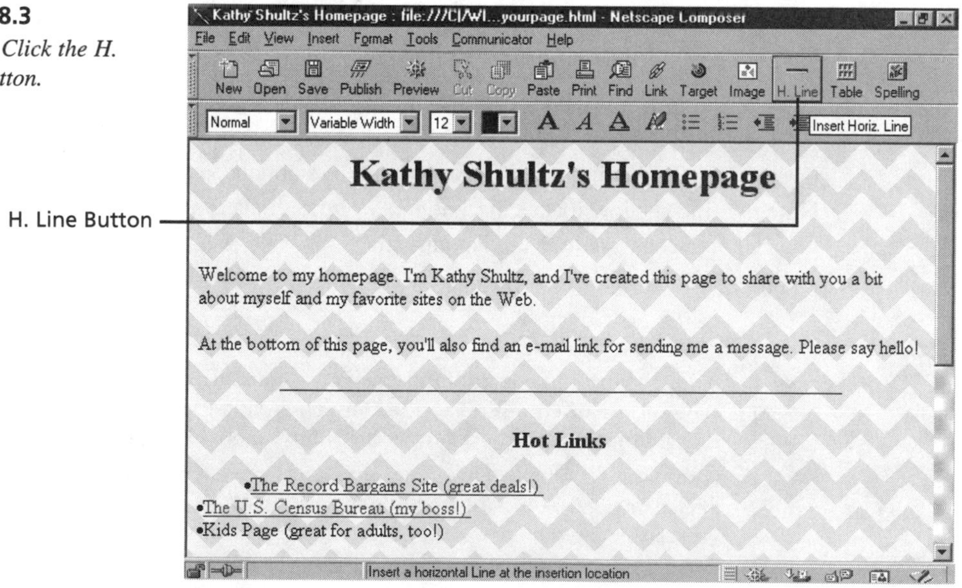
H. Line Button
Kathy Shultz's Homepage : file:///C|/WI...yourpage.html - Netscape Composer
File Edit View Insert Format Tools Communicator Help
New Open Save Publish Preview Cut Copy Paste Print Find Link Target Image H. Line Table Spelling
Normal
Variable Width
12
Insert Horiz. Line
Kathy Shultz's Homepage
Welcome to my homepage. I'm Kathy Shultz, and I've created this page to share with you a bit about myself and my favorite sites on the Web.
At the bottom of this page, you'll also find an e-mail link for sending me a message. Please say hello!
Hot Links
•The Record Bargains Site (great deals!)
•The U.S. Census Bureau (my boss!)
•Kids Page (great for adults, too!)
Insert a horizontal Line at the insertion location

FIGURE 8.3
Step 2: Click the H. Line button.

To Do: Change the look of a horizontal line

1. Double-click a line you've inserted to open the Horizontal Line Properties dialog box.
2. Type a number in the Height box to change the thickness of the line; a higher number makes a thicker line. A height of 2, 3 or 4 makes a good, everyday line. A height of 6 or 8 makes a fat, bold statement.

> In the Horizontal Line Properties dialog box, in the list box next to Width, always leave the choice % of Window selected. This option ensures that the number you type in the Width box expresses the width as a percentage of the page's width. Choosing the other option may produce unpredictable results on visitors' screens.

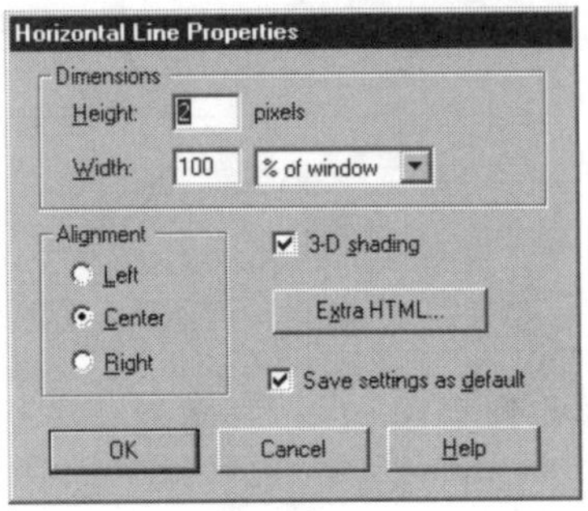

FIGURE 8.4
Step 1: Double-click any horizontal line to adjust its properties.

3. To make the line shorter than the full width of the page, type a Width value less than 100. For example, a width of 50 creates a line half the width of the page.
4. Choose an alignment (Left, Right, or Center) for your line. (Note that alignment is irrelevant if the width is 100.)
5. Check the 3-D shading box if you want the line enhanced with a nifty shadow. Note that the shadow makes the line look a little thicker; after adding 3-D shading, you may choose to reduce the Height value.
6. Click OK to see the results of your changes.

> If you *really* like the look of the line you've created and want to use the same style of line often, return to the Horizontal Line Properties box by double-clicking the line and checking the check box labeled Save Settings As Default.
>
> From then on, all new lines you create automatically take on that style you like so much. On those rare occasions when you want something different, you can simply change the properties for individual lines.

FIGURE 8.5
A line transformed.

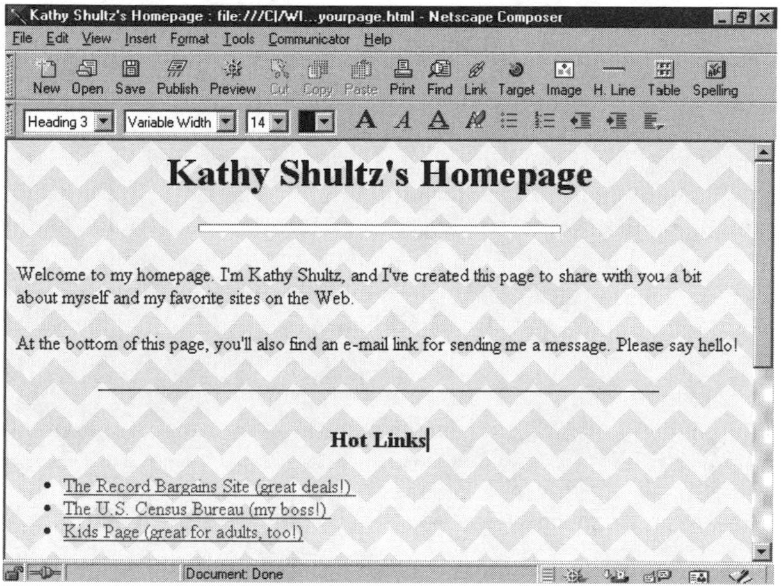
Kathy Shultz's Homepage : file:///C|/WI...yourpage.html - Netscape Composer
File Edit View Insert Format Tools Communicator Help
New Open Save Publish Preview Cut Copy Paste Print Find Link Target Image H. Line Table Spelling
Heading 3
Variable Width
14
Kathy Shultz's Homepage
Welcome to my homepage. I'm Kathy Shultz, and I've created this page to share with you a bit about myself and my favorite sites on the Web.
At the bottom of this page, you'll also find an e-mail link for sending me a message. Please say hello!
Hot Links
The Record Bargains Site (great deals!)
The U.S. Census Bureau (my boss!)
Kids Page (great for adults, too!)
Document: Done

About Tables

A table—regardless of the medium in which it appears—is composed of chunks of information arranged in rows and columns. The grid of rows and columns forms the cells in which you can organize text.

NEW TERM In a table, the box made by the intersection of a column and a row is a *cell*; cells contain the table content, or *data*.

> You can put text or pictures in a table cell. You learn how to put a picture in a table cell in Hour 14.

Although rows, columns, and data are the minimum requirements for any table, a more elaborate table contains additional elements (see Figure 8.6). It might have column or row headings and a caption above or below it. It might have solid lines, or *borders*, appearing on all sides and between cells to form a grid. Note, however, that the borders might be omitted so that cell data is neatly organized in rows and columns, but not boxed up (see Figure 8.7).

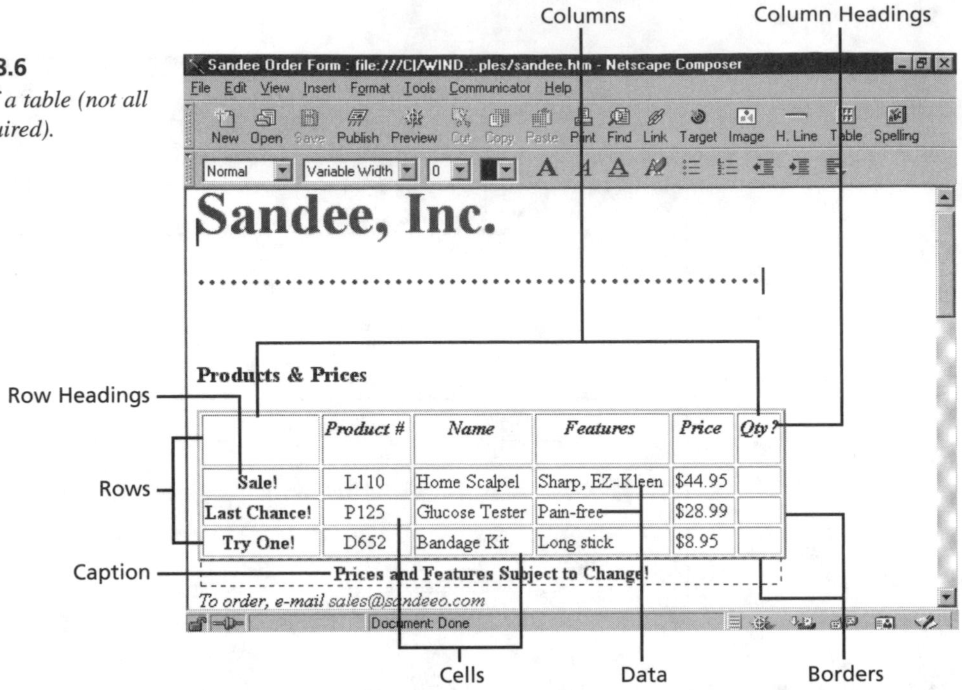

FIGURE 8.6
Parts of a table (not all are required).

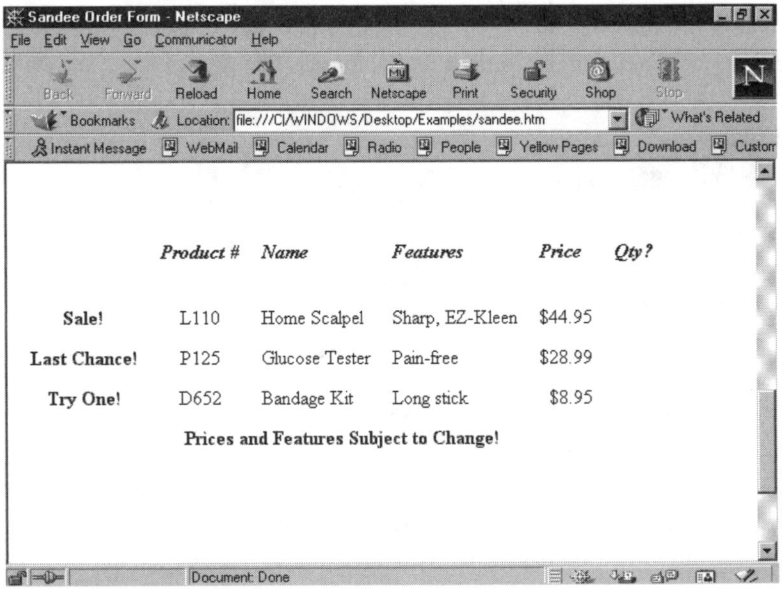

FIGURE 8.7
A table with no visible borders.

Tables are *transparent*—the page's background color or pattern shows through areas not covered by cell data or borders. However, a table can have its own background (see Figure 8.8), which does not cover the borders or cell data, but does cover the page's background.

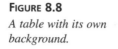

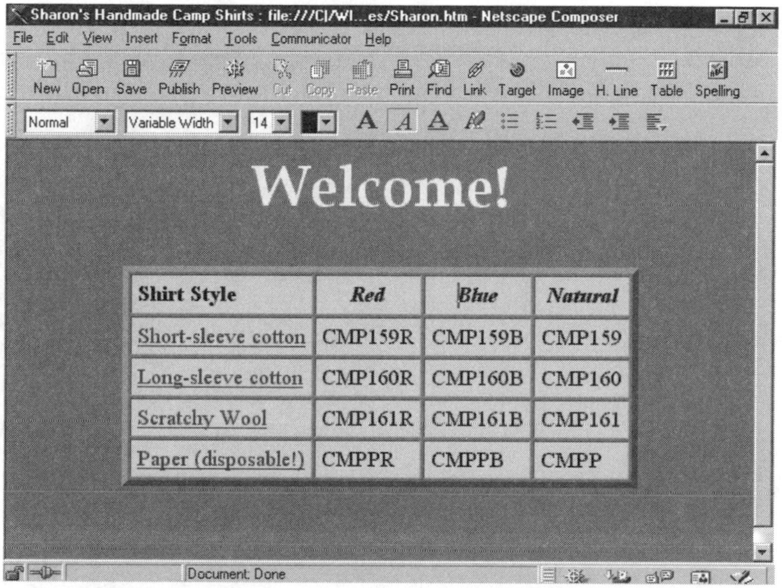

FIGURE 8.8
A table with its own background.

You can do a great deal to format tables to your liking. But keep in mind that the precise formatting of your tables is greatly controlled by the browser displaying it.

The height and width of cells are calculated automatically based on the number of columns and the length of the cell content. The width of a column is determined by the width necessary to contain the longest cell data in the column. When the data in a cell is long or when a table has many columns, the cell content may be wrapped automatically to allow the table to fit within the window.

Table Basics

The difficulty of creating tables is directly proportional to how fancy you wanna make 'em. A simple, basic table is a snap, as the following To Do's show. Fancier tables are a little more trouble (as you learn later in this hour), but then, shouldn't they be?

Keep your first tables simple and get more creative with tables only when you have the basics down pat. You'll do fine.

To Do: Insert a new table

1. Click at the spot in your page where you want to insert a table.
2. Click the Table button on the Composer toolbar or choose Table, Insert Table.

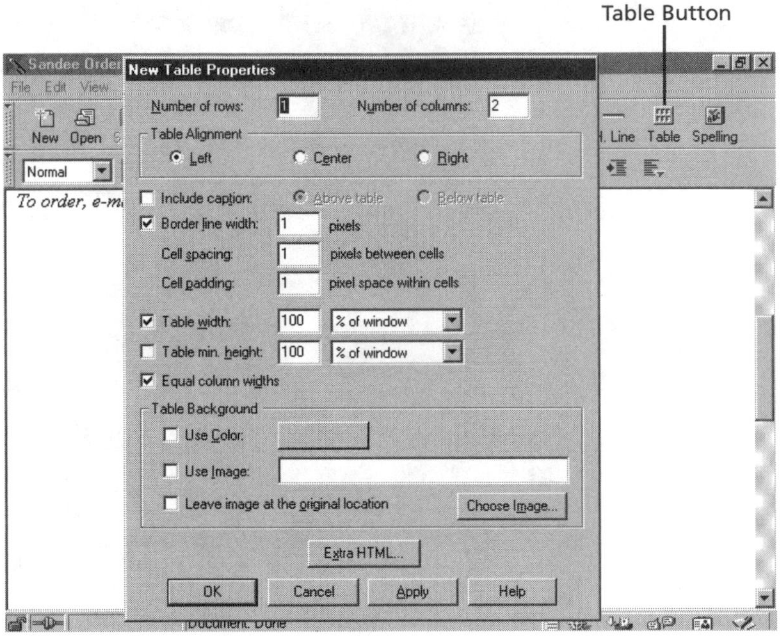

FIGURE 8.9
Step 2: Click the Table button.

3. In the Number of Rows and Number of Columns boxes, choose the number of rows and columns for the table.
4. Adjust in the dialog box any of the other options you want to change; you'll learn what all these options mean during the remainder of this hour. (Note that you can ignore these options for now and adjust them later in the Table Properties dialog box, as described later in this hour.)
5. Click OK.

> The dashed lines that show the table borders (see Figure 8.10) and gridlines appear just to show you where your table is—they don't show up when the page is viewed through a browser. That's okay—a table without borders still organizes its contents into rows and columns and can look pretty cool. But if you really *want* visible borders, you'll learn how to add them later in this hour.

8

FIGURE 8.10
A new table, ready for content or formatting.

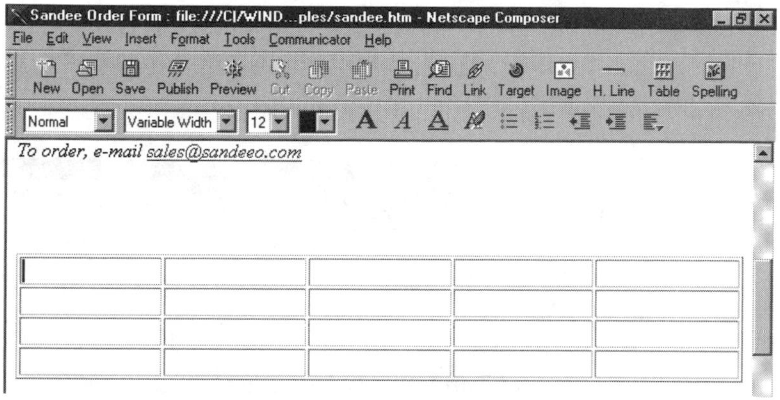

Filling in the Table

Filling in the cells of a table is simple—just click in the cell and type away, as the following To Do shows.

When typing in a cell, you can press Enter to start a new paragraph within the cell. You can also apply virtually any type of text formatting you would apply anywhere else in a Web page using the same selection techniques and formatting tools. Specifically, you can apply the following:

- Paragraph styles (normal or heading, for example)
- Fonts and attributes (bold, italic, and color, for example)
- List formatting (bulleted or numbered)
- Alignment (left, right, or center)
- Indenting

The thing to keep in mind about alignment and indenting in table cells is that the formatting is relative to the *cell*, not to the whole page or even the table. For example, if you apply Center alignment to text in a cell, the text is positioned in the center of the cell, not in the center of the table or page.

> In addition to being able to put ordinary text in table cells, you can also put pictures and links in them. To add a link, just type the text in the cell, highlight it, and then create the link as you would any other link (see Hour 10, "Making Links").
>
> To learn how to put pictures in table cells, see Hour 14.

To Do

To Do: Add text to table cells

1. Click in the cell in which you want to type.
2. Type whatever you want. Observe that the height of the cell expands as necessary to accommodate whatever you type.

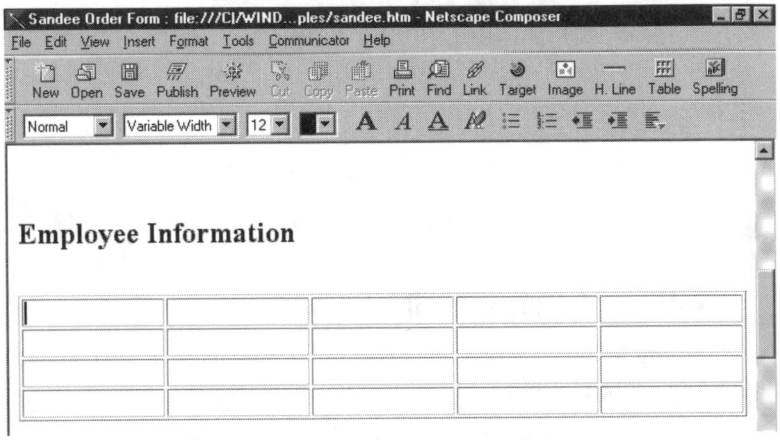

FIGURE 8.11
Step 1: Click in a cell.

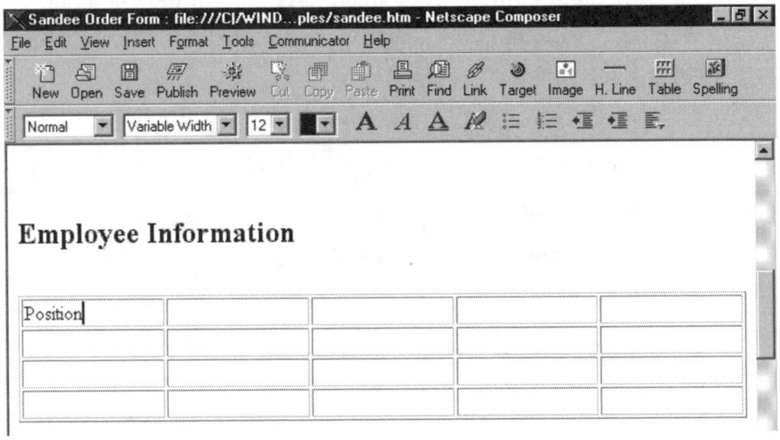

FIGURE 8.12
Step 2: Type away.

3. Press the Tab key to jump to the next cell (or click in the cell you want to fill next).

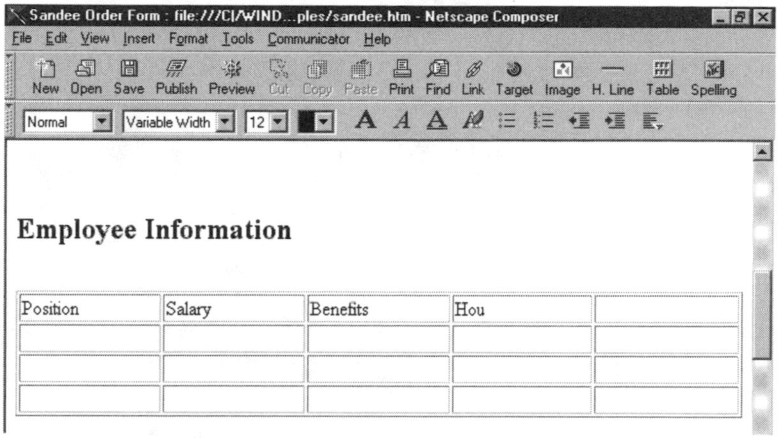

FIGURE 8.13
Step 3: Press the Tab key to jump to the next cell, and keep typing.

Editing and Formatting Tables

So now you've got a table, and you've got formatted text in it. Happy now? If so, congratulations—you're easy to please. If not, note that you can add cool borders to your table, add and delete columns and rows, add a background color, add a table caption above or below the table, and so on.

In short, creating the table is only the beginning. You can do so much more, mostly just by changing settings in the Table Properties dialog box (see Figure 8.14), as shown in the following To Do's.

> To experiment with borders, captions, and anything else in the Table Properties dialog box, make any changes in the dialog box and then click the Apply button rather than OK.
>
> The changes are made in the table, but the Table Properties dialog box remains open so that you can try different settings without having to reopen it.
>
> Keep experimenting, clicking Apply each time, and then click OK when you see what you want to keep, or click Cancel to close the dialog box without making any changes to the table.

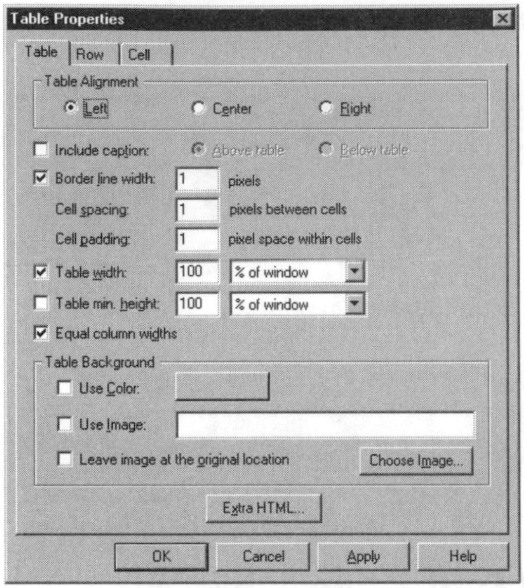

FIGURE 8.14
Use the three tabs of the Table Properties dialog box to change the look of your table.

Because that box is where it all happens, though, first you need to know how to open it. To open the Table Properties dialog box:

1. Click anywhere in the table.
2. Choose Format, Table Properties from the menu bar.

> You can also open the Table Properties box by right-clicking on the table and choosing Table Properties from the menu that appears.

To Do: Dress up tables with borders

1. In the Table tab of the Table Properties box, check the check box next to Border Line Width.
2. In the box to the right of Border Line Width, type a number for the width (line thickness). For example, type **4** to create a border that's four pixels wide. The higher the number, the thicker the border. A 1-pixel border is thin and delicate; a 6-pixel border is bold and sassy.
3. Click OK.

FIGURE 8.15
A nice, fat, 6-pixel border.

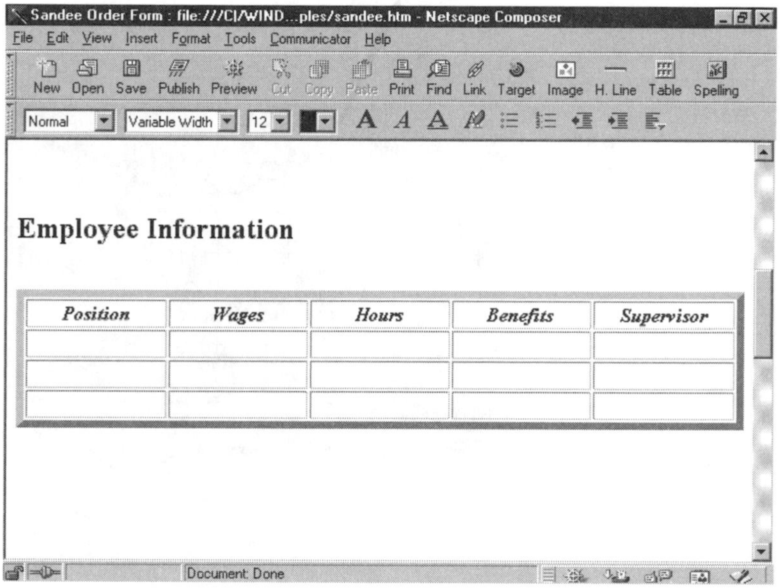

Unless you add a background to a table, the page's background color (or background picture) shows through the table (but does not obscure the table's content or borders). But a table can have its own background, different from that of the page, to make the table—and more important, its contents—really stand out.

The following To Do shows how to give a table its own background color. To learn how to give a table its own background picture, see Hour 14.

To Do: Give a table its own background color

1. In the Table tab of the Table Properties box, check the Use Color check box.
2. Click the button to the right of Use Color to display a list of basic colors to use for the table background.
3. Click the box containing your color choice and then click OK in the Tables Properties dialog box.

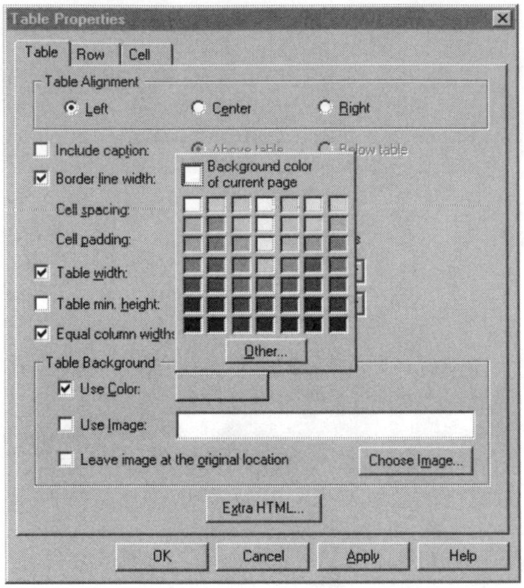

FIGURE 8.16
Step 2: Click the button to the right of Use Color to display a chart of colors to use for your table background.

You can use a different background for a selected cell or row than for the rest of the table; for example, you can give the top row its own, unique background color to make column headings stand out.

To begin, click in a cell whose background you want to choose (or any cell in the row or column whose background you want to choose) and open the Table Properties dialog box. Choose the Row tab (to choose a background color for the row) or the Cell tab (to choose a color for a cell). On the tab you selected, check the Use Color check box and choose a color.

Adding a Caption

NEW TERM A *caption* is a title or other label for a table that appears directly above or below the table (see Figure 8.17). Although the text of the caption does not appear within a table cell, the caption is a part of the table—if you move or delete the table, the caption goes with it.

To add a caption, check the Include Caption check box in the Table Properties dialog box, choose Above Table or Below Table, and then click OK. A dashed line (refer to Figure 8.17) appears where the caption will go. (The dashed line shows up only in Composer; it doesn't appear when the page is browsed.) Click in the box and type your caption.

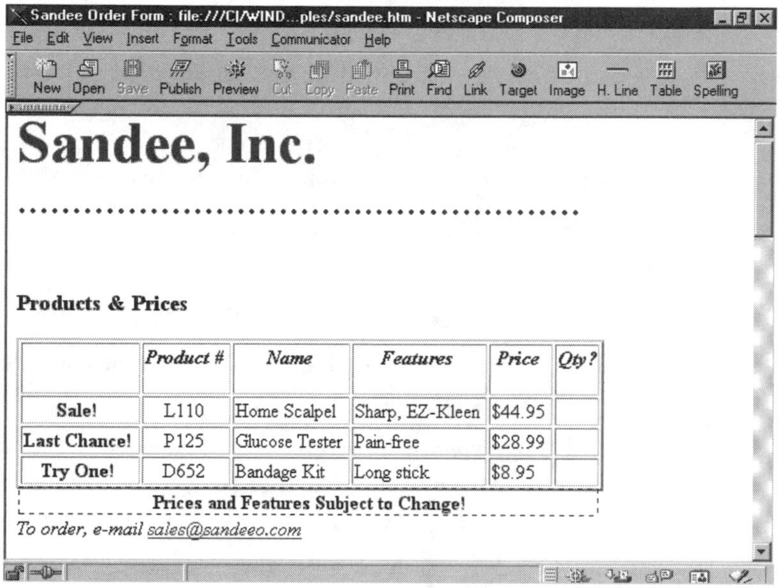

FIGURE 8.17
A caption titles a table.

Creating Column and Row Headings

What's a *heading*, anyway? It's text that's formatted differently from the rest of the table data (and maybe also enclosed in cells that are formatted differently) so that it is clearly not meant as table data, but rather as a descriptive label for a row or column (see Figure 8.18).

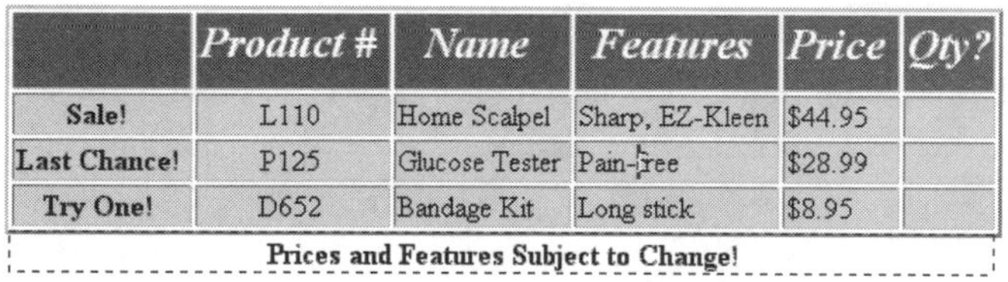

	Product #	Name	Features	Price	Qty?
Sale!	L110	Home Scalpel	Sharp, EZ-Kleen	$44.95	
Last Chance!	P125	Glucose Tester	Pain-free	$28.99	
Try One!	D652	Bandage Kit	Long stick	$8.95	

Prices and Features Subject to Change!

FIGURE 8.18
Apply unique text or cell formatting to a row or column to create headings.

You can create column or row headings by simply applying unique formatting to the text in the top or bottom rows (column headings) or leftmost or rightmost columns (row headings).

Applying bold or italic, making the font different, increasing the text size, giving the row containing the headings their own background (as you learn to do in the next section), choosing a unique text color, or doing all of the above is an easy way to create headings.

Working with Rows, Columns, and Cells

When you first create a table, as described earlier in this hour, you choose the number of rows and columns and you get a table that's a nice, regular grid. Often, that's just what you want. But, sometimes, after entering some of your data, you find that you need to add or delete rows or columns or change other aspects of the table's appearance.

In the next few sections, you learn how to manipulate rows, columns, and cells to create precisely the table you want.

Changing the Width or Alignment of a Table

By default, the tables you create fill the full width of the page. You can choose to make your tables narrower than that.

When a table is narrower than the full width of the page, you have another decision to make: alignment. Do you want the table to be positioned along the left side of the page (left alignment), on the right (right alignment), or in the center (center alignment)? The following To Do shows how to change table width and alignment.

To Do: Change a table's width and alignment

1. Click anywhere in the table and choose Format, Table Properties.
2. To change the width, make sure that the Table Width check box is checked on the Table tab and that the % of Window option is selected in the box to the right of Table Width. Then enter the percentage of the window you want the table to fill. (For example, enter **`50`** to make the table half as wide—50 percent—as the full width of the page.
3. If the width is less than 100 percent, you might select an alignment for the table. By default, tables are left-aligned. To change that, choose an option from the top of the Table tab: Center or Right.

> When choosing a width, avoid changing the % of Window option to its alternative, pixels. Choosing this option enables you to specify the table width as a number of pixels on a screen rather than as a percentage of the window.
>
> Different monitors and computers running at differing resolutions handle that instruction in unpredictable ways. For example, a table 240 pixels wide appears as about half the width of the screen on a computer configured to use the Windows minimum standard resolution (640×480). But the same table, on a computer configured for higher resolutions, might fill only 30 percent, 25 percent, or even less of the screen. Stick with percentages.

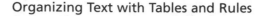

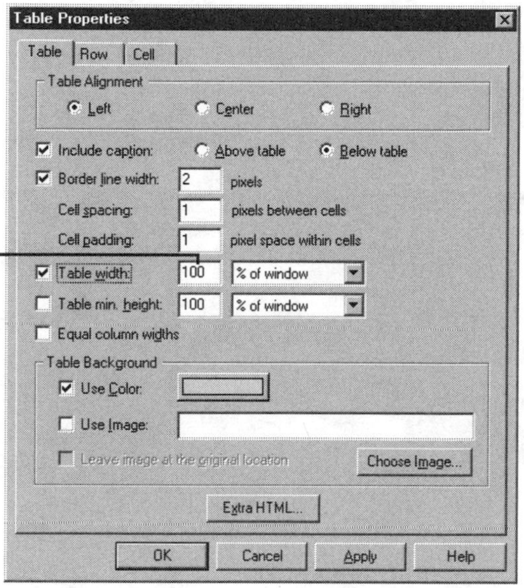

FIGURE **8.19**
Step 2: Change the percentage width.

Specify Width Here ——

Table Properties
Table | Row | Cell

Table Alignment
◉ Left ◯ Center ◯ Right

☑ Include caption: ◯ Above table ◉ Below table
☑ Border line width: `2` pixels
Cell spacing: `1` pixels between cells
Cell padding: `1` pixel space within cells
☑ Table width: `100` % of window
□ Table min. height: `100` % of window
□ Equal column widths

Table Background
☑ Use Color: []
□ Use Image: []
□ Leave image at the original location Choose Image...

Extra HTML...

OK Cancel Apply Help

FIGURE **8.20**
A changed table: 75 percent wide, center alignment.

	Product	Name	Features	Price	Qty?
Sale!	L110	Home Scalpel	Sharp, EZ-Kleen	$44.95	
Last Chance!	P125	Glucose Tester	Pain-free	$28.99	
Try One!	D652	Bandage Kit	Long stick	$8.95	

Prices and Features Subject to Change!

Adding and Deleting Rows and Columns

When entering data, you can jump from cell to cell by pressing the Tab key. The Tab key moves among the cells like a reader's eyes, moving from left to right across a row, and at the end of a row it jumps to the leftmost cell in the row below.

But guess what? When you reach the end of the final row and press Tab, a new row appears with the edit cursor positioned in its leftmost cell, ready for a cell entry. This feature enables you to define your table without knowing exactly how many rows it will have. You can simply keep entering data and using Tab to move forward until all the data has been entered. As you go, Composer keeps adding rows as they are needed.

Of course, you might sometimes want to add columns or add new rows between existing rows rather than at the bottom of the table. The following To Do shows how.

To Do: Add rows or columns

1. Click in a row directly above or below where you want the new row to appear, or in a column directly to the left or right of where you want the new column.
2. Choose Insert, Table.
3. Choose Row (to add a new row) or Column (to add a column).

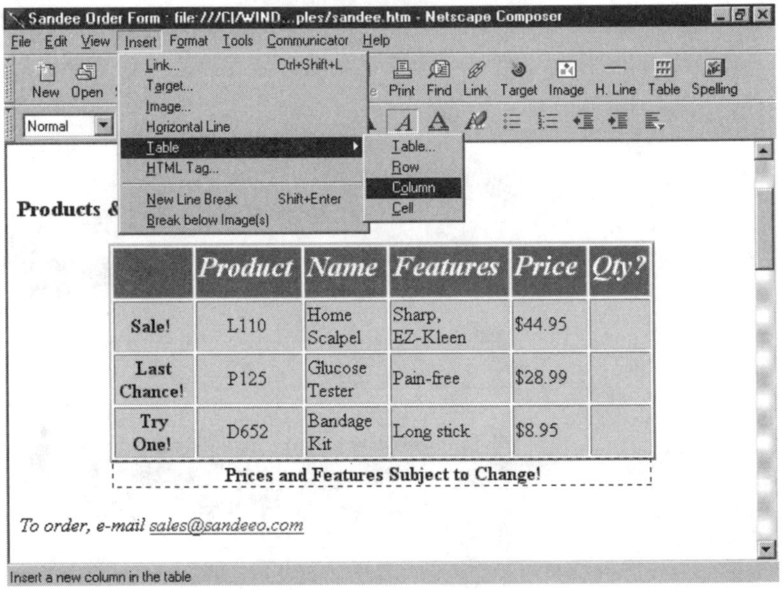

FIGURE 8.21
Step 2: Choose Insert, Table.

> To delete a whole table, click anywhere in the table and choose Edit, Delete Table, Table.

To delete rows or columns, always begin by positioning the edit cursor anywhere in the row or column you want to delete. Choose Edit, Delete Table and then choose Row or Column from the menu that appears.

When you delete rows or columns, keep in mind the following:

- Any data in the deleted row or column is deleted too.
- When you delete a row, rows below it shift upward to fill the gap.
- When you delete a column, rows to the right shift to the left to fill the gap.

Turning Table-Type Text to a Table

Say that you've already got some text—for example, rows and columns of text you've cut and pasted into Composer from another document, such as a word processing document. Using the Composer Tabelize feature, you can transform that text into a table in a snap.

To use Tabelize, the text must already be arranged in rows and columns. Each "row" of the text must end in a carriage return, just as if you had pressed Enter at the end of each line, to break the line. The columns might be formed by spaces or commas between what would be the contents of each cell.

For example, the following text uses spaces to form its columns (this formatting works best when each cell contains only a single word):

Blue Orange Gray

Purple Red Yellow

Aqua Maroon Fuchsia

When cells can contain two or more words, commas are used to mark the columns:

Mark Antony, Cleopatra, Julius Caesar

Romeo, King Lear, Hamlet

The following To Do shows how to tabelize this type of text.

▼ To Do

To Do: Changing organized text into a table

1. Create or copy-and-paste the text in Composer.
2. Select the text to be tabelized.
3. From the menu bar, choose Tools, Tabelize.
4. Choose By Commas (if commas separate the columns) or By Spaces (if spaces separate the columns).

▼

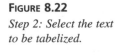

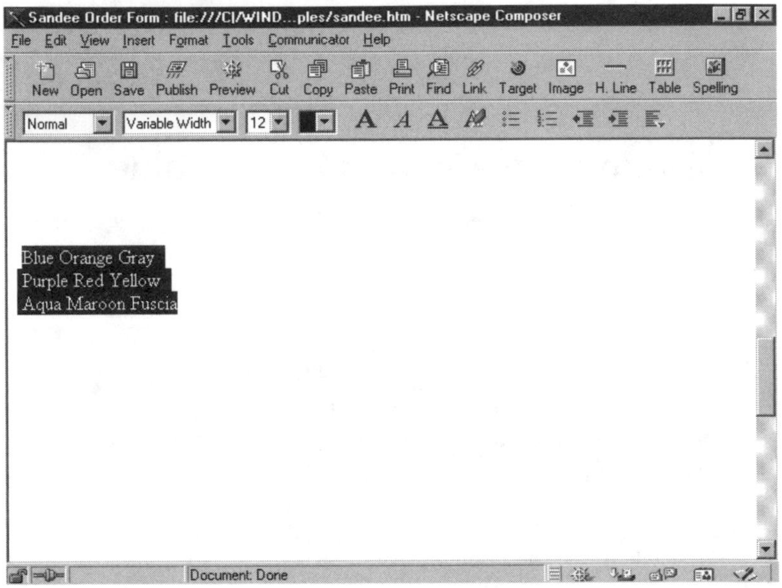

FIGURE 8.22
Step 2: Select the text to be tabelized.

FIGURE 8.23
A table from text.

Blue	Orange	Gray
Purple	Red	Yellow
Aqua	Maroon	Fuscia

Using a Big Table to Control Page Layout

As you move along through this book, you find that it's very difficult to control the exact location of objects in a Web page, the way you would in a desktop publishing program. Generally, you must settle for positioning pictures and paragraphs in rough association with another, leaving it up to the visitor's browser to arrange the page.

A popular way to get around this limitation is to create a table that fills the entire page and then put all the page's contents in table cells (see Figure 8.24). This approach gives you much better control of where objects appear in relation to one another.

If you use some kinds of templates (see Hour 4, "Starting Pages in Other Programs") or certain Web authoring programs (such as Microsoft Publisher), you find that these approaches might rely heavily on tables for page layout. For example, if you create a layout in Publisher and then use the Publisher tools to convert the layout into a Web page, you will discover that the resulting page is a big table. Publisher does this to preserve the organization of the page as faithfully as possible.

FIGURE 8.24
The dashed lines displayed by Composer reveal that this whole page is a table, which keeps the page elements neatly organized.

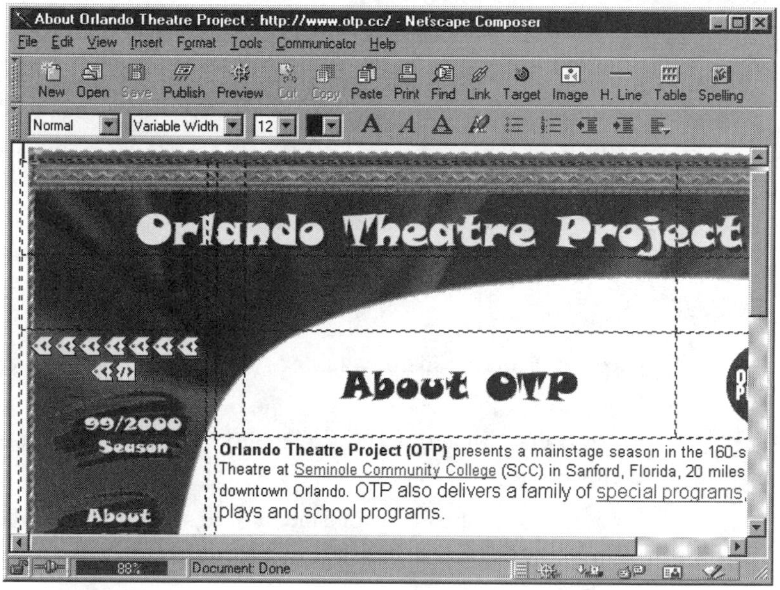

You needn't do anything special to use a big table for page layout. Just start with a blank, empty page and then insert a table. Use the Table Properties dialog box to make the table's width 100 percent of the window. The new table takes up the full width of the page, and its height expands as you add the page's contents to the cells.

When pages are formatted with tables this way, borders typically are not used. But you can add the borders if you want to. It's your page.

> Advanced Web authoring tools, such as Macromedia Dreamweaver and Microsoft FrontPage, do enable you to precisely position text and graphics in a Web page (without using a table), just as you would in a desktop publishing program. In FrontPage, this capability is called *absolute positioning*.
>
> The downside of absolute positioning is that it relies on a less-than-well-standardized set of technologies, collectively called Dynamic HTML (DHTML), that are supported in Internet Explorer 5 and in Netscape Navigator 4-6, but barely supported anywhere else.
>
> If you use absolute positioning or other DHTML tools, but still want your Web pages accessible to everybody, you must offer two versions of your pages online: One for those using browsers that support DHTML and another (without absolute positioning) for everybody else.
>
> See Hour 24, "Developing Your Authoring Skills," to learn more about advanced Web authoring tools and techniques.

Summary

A simple table is a simple deal. And that's the best way to start—simple. Don't get wrapped up in long, complex tables too soon. Try sticking with simple tables of just a dozen cells or so, not just because it's a good way to learn, but also because big, hairy tables defeat their own purpose: They confuse visitors rather than inform them. Eventually, you move up the table growth curve to tougher, smarter table techniques.

Q&A

Q Can I put a table inside a table?

A Certainly, and you can achieve some interesting effects by using a different border for the table inside (the "nested" table). You can even nest tables within tables within tables.

To nest a table, create the outside, or *parent*, table. Click the cell in which you want to nest a table and then choose Insert, Table, Table to create a new table inside the cell.

Observe that when creating and editing the nested table, some settings work a little differently. For example, you choose table width not as a percentage of the window, but rather as a percentage of the *parent cell*, the cell holding the nested table.

Q Sometimes, my table looks too crowded, and other times it looks too spaced out. Is there a way to adjust the spacing between cells or the amount of empty space between a cell's contents and the cell borders?

A In the Table Properties dialog box, two settings control the spacing in a table: Cell Padding and Cell Spacing.

Change the number in Cell Padding to adjust the spacing between the contents of a cell and the walls around that cell. Raising the number in Cell Padding—to 3 or 4, for example—creates more space around the cell contents, making the cell seem less crowded.

Change the number in Cell Spacing to adjust the amount of space between cells. A higher number moves cells farther apart.

PART III
Linking to Stuff

Hour

HOUR 9

Understanding Links

Links are one of the great mysteries of Web authoring. Everything else is up front and visible; everything else just has to look right. A link, on the other hand, has to do something—it has to act right. Links are mysterious because what they do when they are activated is not immediately visible to the naked eye.

Fortunately, creating links is surprisingly simple. The only tricky part is correctly phrasing the underlying URL. With an eye toward the real linking pitfalls, this hour shows what links are all about. At the end of the hour, you'll be able to answer the following questions:

- What are the two parts in every link?
- What kinds of stuff can a link lead to?
- How do I properly phrase the URLs for linking to all types of remote Internet resources, including Web pages, email addresses, and so on?
- What's the difference between a *relative* link and an *absolute* link, and why does it matter?

What's in a Link?

Every link has two parts. Creating links is a simple matter of choosing a spot on the page for the link and then supplying both parts:

- The *link text*—the actual text (or graphic) that appears on the page to represent the link. When a visitor activates a link, he or she clicks the link text to activate the unseen URL underneath.
- The *link location*—the URL describing the page, file, or Internet service to be accessed when the link is activated.

You can create menus or directories of links, like those shown in Figure 9.1, by making each link a separate line in a list. But links don't have to be on separate lines, as Figure 9.1 shows. You can use any words or phrases in your page as links, including headings (or words in headings), words in body text paragraphs, list items, or even single characters in any paragraph property.

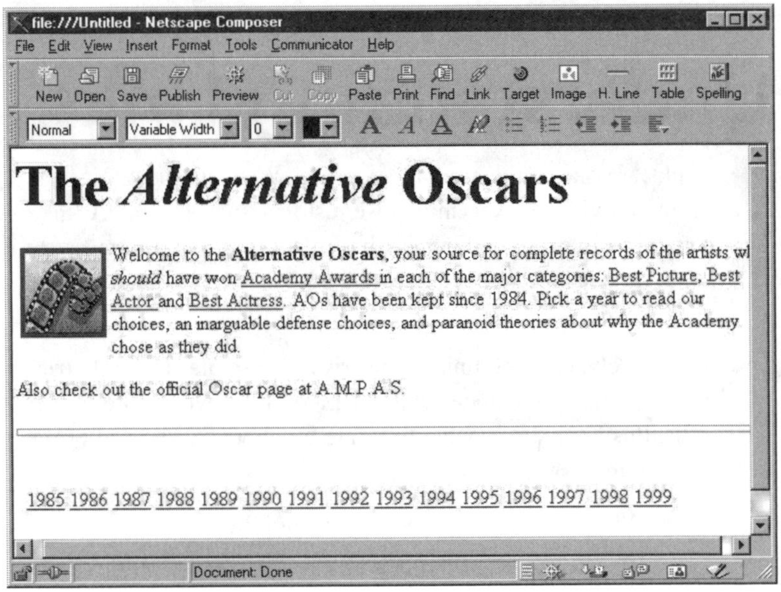
file:///Untitled - Netscape Composer
File Edit View Insert Format Tools Communicator Help
New Open Save Publish Preview Cut Copy Paste Print Find Link Target Image H. Line Table Spelling
Normal
Variable Width
0
The Alternative Oscars
Welcome to the Alternative Oscars, your source for complete records of the artists wl should have won Academy Awards in each of the major categories: Best Picture, Best Actor and Best Actress. AOs have been kept since 1984. Pick a year to read our choices, an inarguable defense choices, and paranoid theories about why the Academy chose as they did.
Also check out the official Oscar page at A.M.P.A.S.
1985 1986 1987 1988 1989 1990 1991 1992 1993 1994 1995 1996 1997 1998 1999
Document: Done

FIGURE 9.1
Links (underlined) in text and by themselves in a menu.

The link text takes on the paragraph properties of the text it is inserted into or closest to, but you can change the paragraph properties of the link text at any time, just as you would for any other text. The underlying link is undisturbed by such changes.

What's Linkable?

A link can point to any resource that can be expressed in a URL or to *local files* (files residing on the same server as the page containing the link). That includes not only remote Web pages and other pages and files residing on the same Web server as your document, but also newsgroups and articles within them, email messages, and FTP servers. In your travels on the Web, you've already encountered links pointing to all these types of resources.

9

NEW TERM A link can point to a specific location within a Web page—even to a specific location within the same page containing the link. For example, in a long Web page, each entry in a table of contents can be a link pointing to a specific section of the page (see Figure 9.2). This concept allows visitors to navigate quickly and easily within the page. The spots within pages to which a link can point are *anchors*.

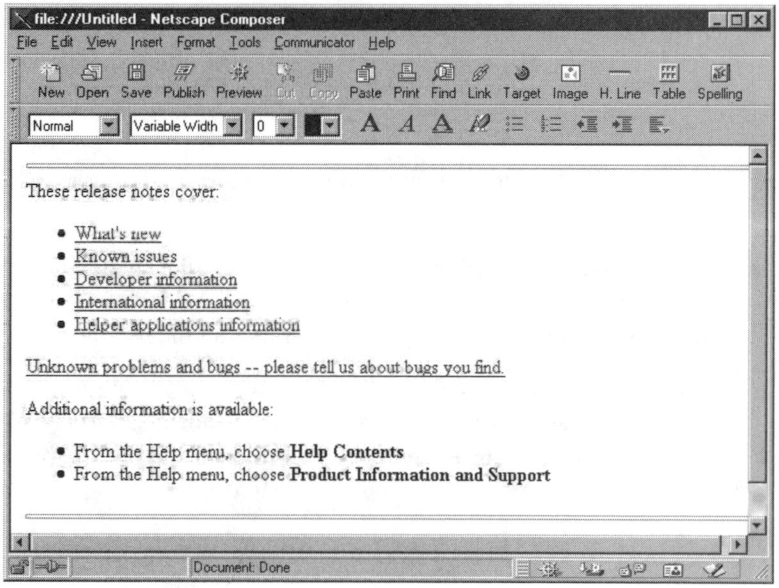
file:///Untitled - Netscape Composer
File Edit View Insert Format Tools Communicator Help
New Open Save Publish Preview Cut Copy Paste Print Find Link Target Image H. Line Table Spelling
Normal
Variable Width
0
These release notes cover:
What's new
Known issues
Developer information
International information
Helper applications information
Unknown problems and bugs -- please tell us about bugs you find.
Additional information is available:
From the Help menu, choose Help Contents
From the Help menu, choose Product Information and Support
Document: Done

FIGURE 9.2
A menu (table of contents) made up of links to pages within the same document or site.

To create a link, you use the same procedure regardless of the type of resource to which the link points. However, for each type of resource, you must consider certain issues when composing the URL for the link. The next several sections describe in detail the special considerations for each type of URL.

Web Pages

Web pages are the most commonly linked resource, and for good reason: You can bet that anybody viewing your Web page can view any other Web page, so links to Web pages are a reliable way to provide information. Linking to Web pages also allows your visitors to apply a consistent set of navigation techniques.

URLs pointing to Web pages always begin with the protocol designator `http://`. The protocol is followed by the Web server hostname, the directory path to the page file, and the actual HTML file of the page:

`http://`*`hostname/pathname/file.HTM`*

In some cases, you can omit the filename. Some Web servers have default files they display automatically whenever someone accesses the server or a directory without specifying a filename. For example,

`http://www.mcp.com/`

accesses the default page for the server `www.mcp.com`, and

`http://www.mcp.com/sams/`

accesses the default page for the directory `sams` on the server `www.mcp.com`.

Note that the preceding directory examples end in a slash. You should always use a slash to end an HTTP URL that does not end with a filename; the slash instructs the server to access the default file (usually `INDEX.HTML`). Some servers can still access the default file if you leave off the slash, but some don't. In a link, use the slash, for safety's sake.

Finally, always be careful to follow the exact capitalization of the URL as it would appear in the Navigator Location box when you view the page. Many Web servers are case sensitive and don't recognize the directory or filename if it is not properly capitalized.

Anchors in Pages

Web pages can contain predefined locations to which links can point. These spots are called *anchors* in HTML (and are created with the `<a>` tag—*A* for *a*nchor).

You can add anchors to your own Web pages and then link to those anchors from elsewhere in the same page or from other pages you create. In addition, you can create links to point to any existing anchors in other pages on the Web.

When you create an anchor (see Hour 11, "More Ways to Link"), give the anchor a name. You create links to anchors as you do to a Web page, with one difference: You add the name of the anchor to the URL you enter for the link.

> You can use a *relative pathname* to point to an anchor in another file stored on the same server (to link from one page of a multipage document to an anchor in another page in the document, for example). See the following section, "Local Files."

Local Files

Just as you can link to resources on any server, you can link to resources residing on the same server as your Web document. Obviously, you would do this when linking among the pages of a multipage presentation. But you might also choose to link to anything on your local Web server that relates to the topic of your page, such as another Web document or a text file containing related information.

> Technically, the pathnames you enter to create links to local files are not URLs. When you're creating a link, however, you enter these pathnames in the same place you would enter a URL for linking to a remote resource. That's why I refer to them generically as URLs.

When you phrase the URLs to create links to local resources, you have to consider the differences between *relative* pathnames and *absolute* pathnames.

Relative Pathnames

Relative pathnames include only the information necessary to find the linked resource from the document containing the link. In other words, the path given to the file is *relative* to the file containing the link; from outside that file, the information supplied as the URL for the link is insufficient to locate the file.

Suppose that all the pages of your multipage document share the same directory on the server and that one of those pages is named `FLORIDA.HTM`. To link from any page in your document to `FLORIDA.HTM`, you need to enter only the filename as the URL for the link; for example:

```
FLORIDA.HTM
```

Suppose that all pages except the top page reside in a folder or directory named `STATES` and that this folder is within the same folder containing the top page. To link from the top page to FLORIDA.HTM in the STATES directory, you would enter the directory and filename, separated by a slash; for example:

```
STATES/FLORIDA.HTM
```

This approach works as far into the folder hierarchy as you want. Just be sure to separate each step in the path with a slash. For a file several levels beneath the file containing the link, you might enter

```
ENVIRO/US/STATES/FLORIDA.HTM
```

Suppose that you're linking from a page lower in the directory hierarchy to a page that's higher. To do this, you must describe a path that moves up in the hierarchy. As in DOS (and in FTP servers), a double period (..) is used in a path to move up one level. For example, let's create a link from the FLORIDA page back to the top page (call it TOP.HTM), which you can assume is one level above FLORIDA. For the URL portions of the link, you would enter

```
../TOP.HTM
```

If TOP.HTM were three levels above FLORIDA, you would type

```
../../../TOP.HTM
```

> Use relative pathnames to link together the pages of a multipage document on your PC. Because the paths are relative, when you publish that document to a server, the interpage links still work properly. See Hour 12, "Using Links to Build a Web Site."

Finally, suppose that you want to link to a local file that resides in a folder that is not above or below the file containing the link but is elsewhere in the hierarchy. This link would require a path that moves up the hierarchy and then down a different branch to the file. In such a case, you use the double periods to move up and then specify the full directory path down to the file.

Suppose that you want to link from

```
ENVIRO/US/STATES/FLORIDA.HTM
```

to

```
ENVIRO/CANADA/PROVINCE/QUEBEC.HTM
```

The phrasing you need is

```
../../../CANADA/PROVINCE/QUEBEC.HTM
```

The three sets of double periods move up to the `ENVIRO` directory; then the path down from `ENVIRO` to `QUEBEC.HTM` follows.

> On DOS and Windows systems, a relative or absolute path might include the letter of the hard drive, but it must be followed by a vertical bar (|) rather than the standard colon; for example:
>
> `C|/STATS/ENVIRO/CANADA/PROVINCE/QUEBEC.HTM`

Absolute Pathnames

Absolute pathnames give the complete path to a file, beginning with the top level of the directory hierarchy of the system. Absolute pathnames are not portable from one system to another. In other words, while composing a multipage document on your PC, you can use absolute pathnames in links among the pages. However, after you publish that document, all the links become invalid because the server's directory hierarchy is not identical to your PC's.

In general, you use absolute pathnames only when linking to specific local resources (other than your own pages), such as FAQs, residing on the server where your page will be published.

Absolute pathnames are phrased just like relative pathnames, except that they always begin with a slash (/) and they always contain the full path from the top of the directory hierarchy to the file; for example:

```
/STATS/ENVIRO/CANADA/PROVINCE/QUEBEC.HTM
```

Other Internet Services

In addition to Web pages and their anchors, links can point to any other browser-accessible servers. But before linking to anything other than a Web page or an anchor, keep in mind that not all browsers—and, hence, not all visitors—can access all these other server types.

Nearly all browsers can handle FTP. Less common is mail access, and even less common is newsgroup access. Netscape Navigator has native support for both. Other browsers open helper applications for mail. For example, Internet Explorer opens Outlook Express when a mailto or news link is activated. Still, many browsers have no news or mail access.

FTP

Using a link to an FTP server, you can point to a directory or to a specific file. If the link points to a directory, clicking the link displays the list of files and subdirectories there (see Figure 9.3), and each listing is itself a link the visitor can click to navigate the directories or download a file. If the link points to a file, the file is downloaded to the visitor's PC when he or she activates the link.

> If you create a link to an HTML file residing on an FTP server, clicking the link downloads the file and displays it, just as though it were on a Web server.

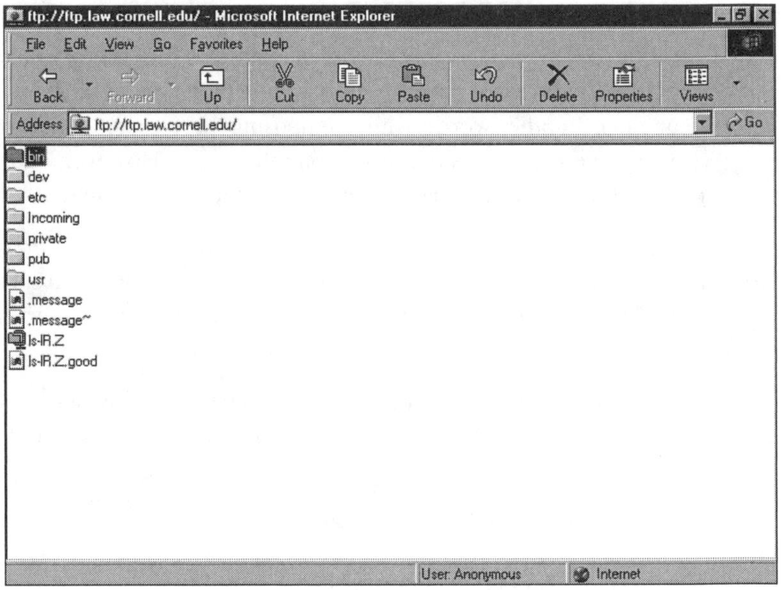

FIGURE 9.3
An FTP directory.

To link to an anonymous FTP server, use the protocol designator `ftp://`, followed by the name of the FTP server, the path, and the filename (if you are linking to a file), as the following examples show:

> Observe that you do not end an FTP URL with a slash when linking to a directory. This technique differs from an HTTP URL, where a slash is always advisable except when accessing a specific HTML file.

`ftp://ftp.zdnet.com` Links to the ZDNet anonymous FTP server and displays the top-level directory

`ftp://ftp.zdnet.com/pub` Links to the ZDNet anonymous FTP server and displays the contents of the `PUB` directory

`ftp://ftp.zdnet.com/pub/pcmag/support.txt` Links to the ZDNet anonymous FTP server and downloads the file SUPPORT.DOC from the PCMAG directory

> You can link to non-anonymous, password-protected FTP servers. However, in most cases, these types of servers have been set up precisely to prevent public access. A URL to a non-anonymous FTP server includes a username and password for accessing that server, so anyone who accesses your page can access the FTP server—or read the URL activated by the link to learn the password.
>
> Obviously, you should never create a link to a non-anonymous server unless you have express permission to do so from the server's administrators. Getting such permission is unlikely.
>
> To link to a non-anonymous FTP server for which you have permission to publish a link, you phrase the URL exactly as you would for anonymous FTP, except that you insert the username and password (separated by a colon) and an `@` sign between the protocol and the path, as shown in the following line:
>
> ```
> ftp://username:password@ftp.mcp.com/pub/secrets.doc
> ```
>
> This URL downloads the file `secrets.doc` from a password-protected server for which the username and password in the URL are valid.

News

A link can open a newsgroup article list or point to a specific article within that list. Although both newsgroups and the articles they carry come and go, a link to the article list might be valid for years. On the other hand, a link to a specific article might be valid for only a few days—until the article ages past the server's time limit for newsgroup messages, at which point the article is automatically deleted from the server.

Thus, the best use of news links is to point to the article list of a newsgroup whose topic relates to that of the Web document. If a newsgroup contains an article that you want to make a long-term part of the page, copy the article into a separate file and link to that file or simply copy it into a Web page.

Before copying a news article into a page, check for copyright notices in the article. Whether the article is copyrighted or not, email the author and request permission to use the article.

To link to a newsgroup to display the current article list, use the protocol designator `news:` followed by the name of the newsgroup. (Note that a `news:` URL omits the double slashes used in HTTP, and FTP.) For example, the following are valid news links:

```
news:alt.video.dvd
```

or

```
news:news.announce.newusers
```

To link to an article, find the message ID in the article's header; it's often enclosed between carats (< and >) or labeled *Message ID* by most newsreaders. (Exactly how it appears depends on which newsreader program you use.)

To phrase the URL, use the protocol designator `news:` followed by the message ID. Note that you do not include the carats, and you do not need to include the newsgroup name in the URL.

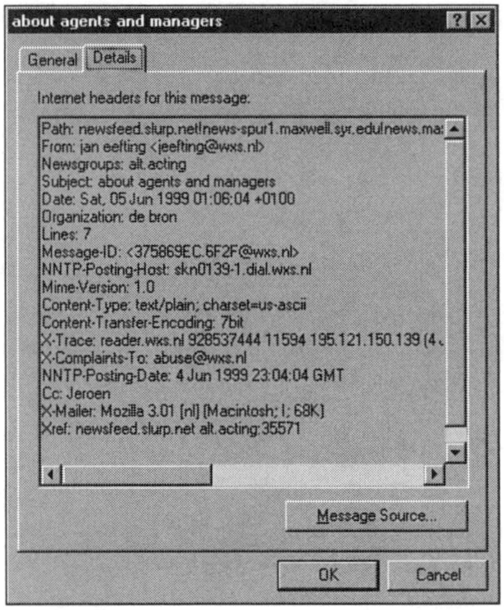

FIGURE 9.4
A news article header in Outlook Express, showing the message ID (it's labeled "Message-ID" and appears about halfway down the list).

Mail

Mail URLs can be the most difficult to goof up. You enter `mailto:` followed by an email address. That's it. (Note that a mailto: URL omits the double slashes used in HTTP, FTP, and Gopher URLs.) For example,

```
mailto:nsnell@mailserver.com
```


> Before putting an email address other than your own in a link, ask permission from the addressee.

The most common use of mailto: links is in a signature at the bottom of a page. (You learn how to create a signature in Hour 10.) But you can use a mailto: link anywhere it makes sense to offer your readers a way to contact you or someone else.

To Do: Study links

Follow these steps to explore the way the links you see online are phrased:

1. Connect to the Internet and open your Web browser. (Use either the Netscape Navigator browser included with this book or Internet Explorer. These steps may not work with other browsers.)
2. Go to any page you like and locate a link on it.
3. Point to the link (don't click) and then look in the status bar at the bottom of the browser window. The URL to which the link point appears there, shown exactly as it is phrased in the HTML file.
4. Explore other links this way. In Web pages you visit regularly, try to find links to
    - Other Web pages
    - Anchors
    - Files
    - FTP directories
    - Email addresses

Summary

As you discover in the next three hours, creating links is pretty easy. In fact, making the link is the easiest part, especially if you copy the link from elsewhere. Phrasing the URL just right is the hardest part. Now that you understand the ins and outs of URLs, in the next hours you'll pick up some tips for ensuring that you get 'em right when you make links.

Q&A

Q I'm still fuzzy on this whole relative path/absolute path business, and I have a headache. Can I just stay stupid on this one and hope that everything works out in the morning?

A To some extent, you can. Just trust Composer. When making links to local documents, use the Browse button in the Link Properties dialog box to choose files so that Composer can phrase the path for you. Then use the Composer publishing features (see Hour 22) to publish your document rather than handle the uploading on your own. Composer automatically adjusts the local file links and uploads all the linked files so that the links still work on the server.

Hour 10

Making Links

By design, this hour is an easy one. The only hard part about making links is understanding how they work and getting the URL right—and you learned all about that in Hour 9, "Understanding Links." In this hour, you'll put that knowledge to work.

But I haven't given up making things easy yet. You're also about to discover a variety of ways to make picking up the URLs for your links quicker, easier, and more accurate. At the end of the hour, you'll be able to answer the following questions:

- How do I create a new link?
- Can I create a signature for my page so that visitors can conveniently send me email?
- How can I make linking easier and more accurate by copying and pasting URLs?
- How do I get rid of a link?

As you know, links can be attached to text or pictures. However, you won't learn how to add pictures to your pages until Hour 14, "Adding Pictures (and Picture Backgrounds)."

Although most of what you learn in this hour applies to both text and pictures, you won't pick up the specifics of making picture links until Hour 14.

Creating New Links

Creating a new hyperlink is a two-part job:

1. First, you create the link text, the text that a visitor would click to activate the link.
2. Next, you attach the URL to the link text.

The following To Do shows how easy it is to create a new link to a Web page.

To Do: Create a new link to a Web page

1. Type and format the text that will serve as the link text.
2. Select the text.

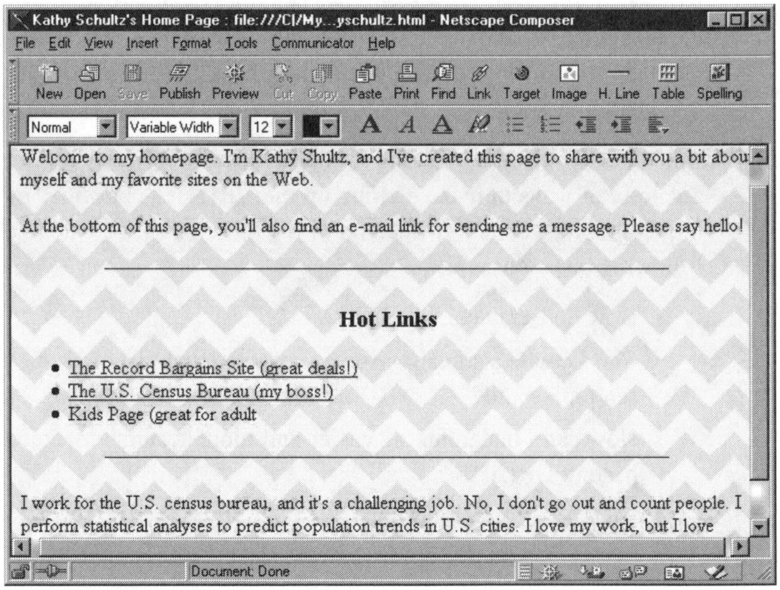
Kathy Schultz's Home Page : file:///C|/My...yschultz.html - Netscape Composer
File Edit View Insert Format Tools Communicator Help
New Open Save Publish Preview Cut Copy Paste Print Find Link Target Image H. Line Table Spelling
Normal
Variable Width
12
Welcome to my homepage. I'm Kathy Shultz, and I've created this page to share with you a bit abou
myself and my favorite sites on the Web.
At the bottom of this page, you'll also find an e-mail link for sending me a message. Please say hello!
Hot Links
The Record Bargains Site (great deals!)
The U.S. Census Bureau (my boss!)
Kids Page (great for adult
I work for the U.S. census bureau, and it's a challenging job. No, I don't go out and count people. I
perform statistical analyses to predict population trends in U.S. cities. I love my work, but I love
Document: Done

FIGURE 10.1
Step 1: Type the link text.

Although you can apply character formatting (such as fonts or italics) to the link text you create, don't do it. Just apply the paragraph style you want to use and leave it at that.

Browsers usually display link text with unique formatting (usually underlining and a blue color) to help visitors instantly identify links on a page. You don't want your character formatting to make finding links tricky for your visitors by changing the link text formatting they're accustomed to seeing.

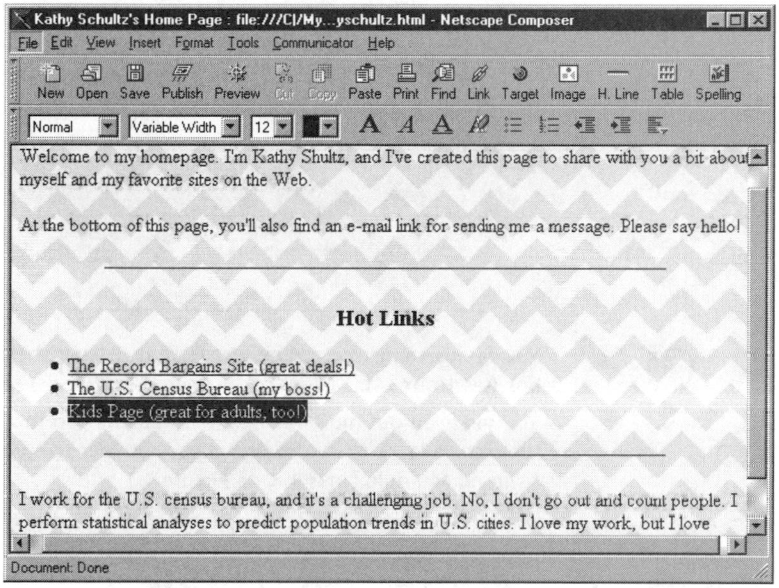
Kathy Schultz's Home Page : file:///C|/My...yschultz.html - Netscape Composer
File Edit View Insert Format Tools Communicator Help
New Open Save Publish Preview Cut Copy Paste Print Find Link Target Image H. Line Table Spelling
Normal Variable Width 12
Welcome to my homepage. I'm Kathy Shultz, and I've created this page to share with you a bit about myself and my favorite sites on the Web.
At the bottom of this page, you'll also find an e-mail link for sending me a message. Please say hello!
Hot Links
The Record Bargains Site (great deals!)
The U.S. Census Bureau (my boss!)
Kids Page (great for adults, too!)
I work for the U.S. census bureau, and it's a challenging job. No, I don't go out and count people. I perform statistical analyses to predict population trends in U.S. cities. I love my work, but I love
Document: Done

FIGURE 10.2
Step 2: Select the link text.

3. Click the Link button on the Standard toolbar.

Link Button
Kathy Schultz's Home Page : file:///C|/My...yschultz.html - Netscape Composer
File Edit View Insert Format Tools Communicator Help
New Open Save Publish Preview Cut Copy Paste Print Find Link Target Image H. Line Table Spelling
Normal Variable Width 12

FIGURE 10.3
Step 3: Click the Link button.

4. In the box labeled Link to, type the complete URL. Be sure to include the `http://` part at the beginning. Then click OK.

FIGURE 10.4
Step 4: Type the URL and click OK.

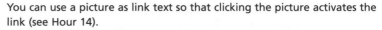

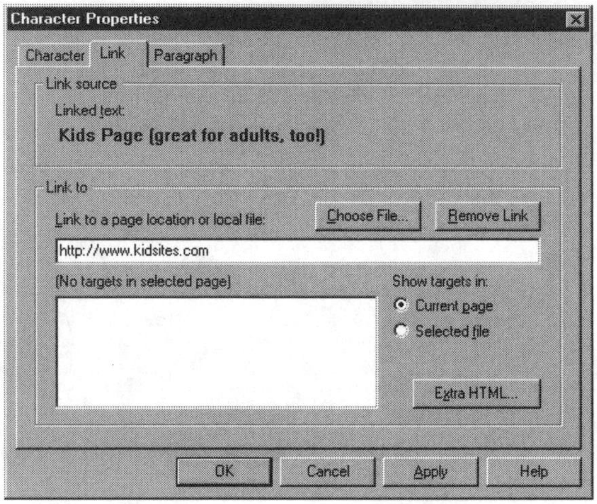

> You can use a picture as link text so that clicking the picture activates the link (see Hour 14).
>
> You can even put multiple links in one picture so that clicking each part of the picture leads to a different place. You learn how to do this in Hour 20, "Putting Multiple Links in One Picture."

Creating a Signature (Linking to Email)

A *signature* is nothing more than some sort of generic sign-off message that has an email address embedded within it. A few stock wording choices—in popular flavors—are:

Inviting—Comments? Questions? Email me at `nsnell@mailserver.com`.

Formal—If you have any comments or questions regarding this page, contact `nsnell@mailserver.com`.

Efficient—Feedback: `nsnell@mailserver.com`.

Traditionally, the paragraph containing the signature uses the Address property, although that is not required.

What is required is a *mailto link*—a link that, when clicked, opens the visitor's email program and starts a new message, preaddressed to an email address specified in the link. Mailto links let you provide your visitors with an easy way to contact you (or anyone else you choose).

> When you create the link text of a mailto link, the text does not have to show the exact email address because most visitors' email programs use the right address automatically when they click the link. So you may choose text such as "Contact Me," rather than your email address.
>
> However, some visitors use Internet software that doesn't support mailto links; these visitors see the link text okay, but nothing happens when they click it. So when you choose not to use the email address as the link text, be sure to show the email address elsewhere on the page, for the benefit of the "non-mailto-enabled."

To Do: Create a signature

1. Click where you want the signature to be located (usually at or near the end of the page) and type the signature message, including the email address.
2. Select some text in the message—your name or an email address—to serve as link text for the mailto link.

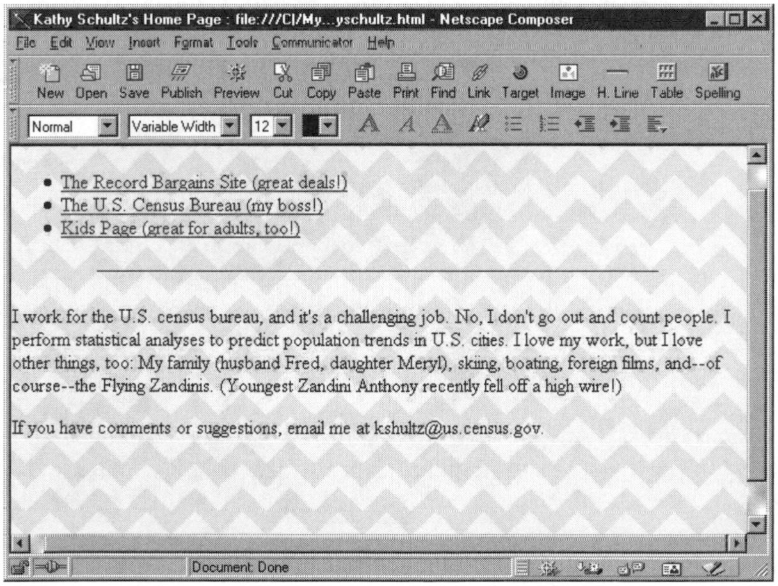
Kathy Schultz's Home Page : file:///C|/My...yschultz.html - Netscape Composer
File Edit View Insert Format Tools Communicator Help
New Open Save Publish Preview Cut Copy Paste Print Find Link Target Image H. Line Table Spelling
Normal
Variable Width
12
The Record Bargains Site (great deals!)
The U.S. Census Bureau (my boss!)
Kids Page (great for adults, too!)
I work for the U.S. census bureau, and it's a challenging job. No, I don't go out and count people. I perform statistical analyses to predict population trends in U.S. cities. I love my work, but I love other things, too: My family (husband Fred, daughter Meryl), skiing, boating, foreign films, and--of course--the Flying Zandinis. (Youngest Zandini Anthony recently fell off a high wire!)
If you have comments or suggestions, email me at kshultz@us.census.gov.
Document: Done

FIGURE 10.5
Step 1: Type the signature.

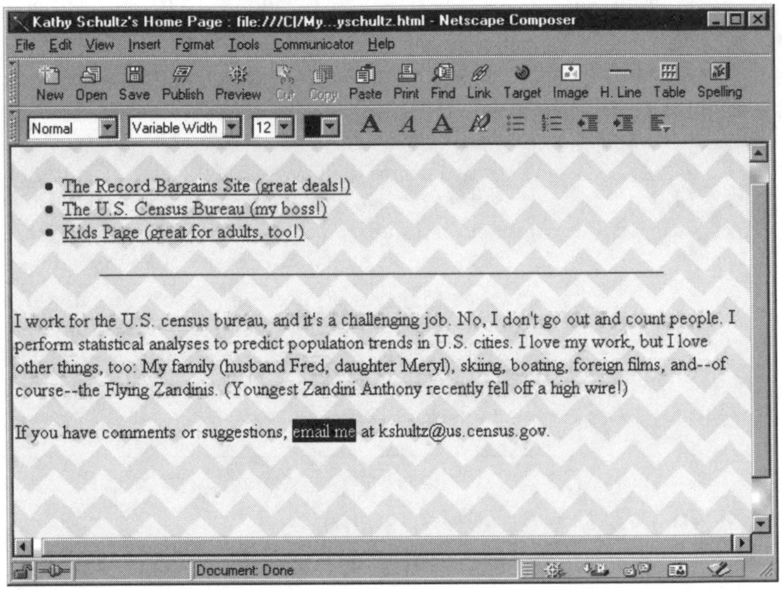

FIGURE 10.6
Step 2: Select the part of the signature that will be an email link.

3. Click the Link button.
4. In the Link Location box, type `mailto:`.
5. Right after the `mailto:` part, type the complete email address and click OK.

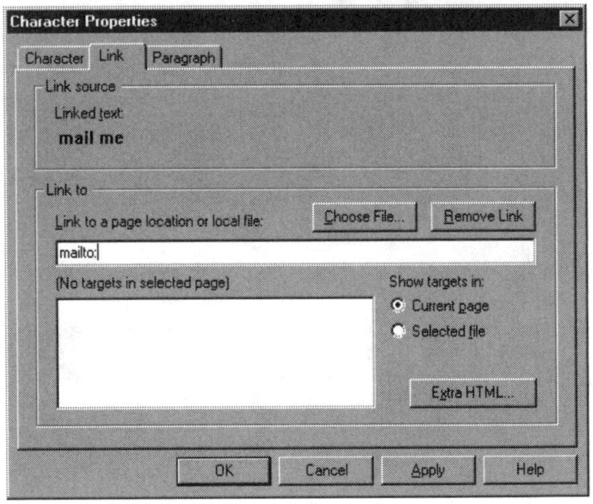

FIGURE 10.7
Step 4: Type mailto: to start the URL.

FIGURE 10.8
Step 5: Type the email address.

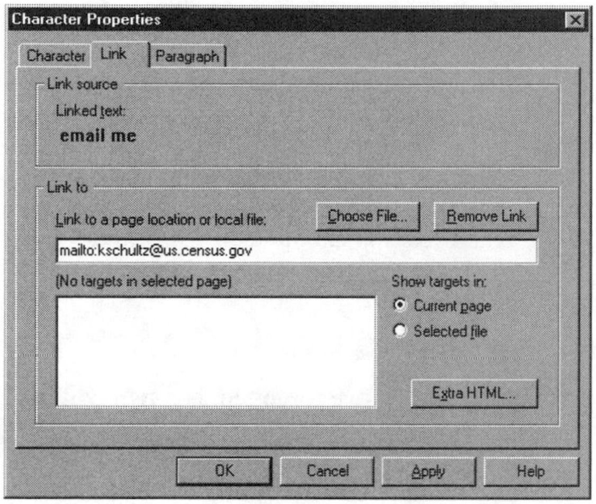

Copying Links from Other Pages

Anywhere you see a hyperlink, you can easily copy it from your Web browser right into a Composer page by using copy-and-paste techniques.

In fact, a page you've just accessed on the Web makes the most reliable source for a link. If you copy a file's URL while viewing it and paste it as a link into a page you're creating, you can trust that the link will probably work properly (until and unless the page or other resource is moved or removed).

Sources for copying links include

- The Address box in your browser (where the URL of the current page appears)
- The Bookmarks list (in Navigator) or the Favorites list (in Internet Explorer)
- The header of a news article in your Internet newsreader program
- The header of a mail message in your email program
- Any link appearing in a Web page

When copying a link into your page, keep in mind the following:

- The link text may or may not be copied, depending on what browser you use; instead, the link text that appears in Composer might sometimes be the URL itself. To give the link a name to appear instead of its URL, edit the link as described later in this hour (see the section "Editing Links".)

- The link takes on the paragraph properties of the paragraph in which it is inserted or the one closest to it. Remember, though, that a link can accept any paragraph properties or character properties—although in most browsers, the character properties cannot override the default way that links are displayed. That's a good thing because you don't want your formatting to disguise the fact that a link is a link.

To Do

To Do: Copy and paste a link

Copying and pasting, in case you've forgotten, is a two-part deal. First, you copy something to the Windows Clipboard, and then you paste it from the Clipboard into the place you want it to go. You can accomplish each half of the job in several ways. You have several ways to copy and several to paste, and you can combine any copy method with any paste method and get the same results.

To copy:

- *A link to the Web page appearing in your browser (Netscape or Internet Explorer)*—Right-click the URL in the Address box and then choose Copy from the menu that appears (see Figure 10.9).
- *A link shown in a Web page*—Right-click the link and choose Copy Link Location, if Navigator is your browser, or Copy Shortcut, if Internet Explorer is your browser (see Figure 10.10).
- *A link appearing in the Navigator Bookmarks list or the Internet Explorer Favorites list*—Right-click the desired bookmark and choose Copy Location from the menu.
- *A link appearing in the header of a news or mail message*—Open the message and locate the desired link in the message header. Right-click the link and choose Copy Link Location.

To paste a link from the Clipboard into your page, do the following:

1. Create and select the link text as usual, and then click the Link button.
2. Press Ctrl+V to copy the URL into the Link Location box.

FIGURE 10.9
Copying a link to the current Web page.

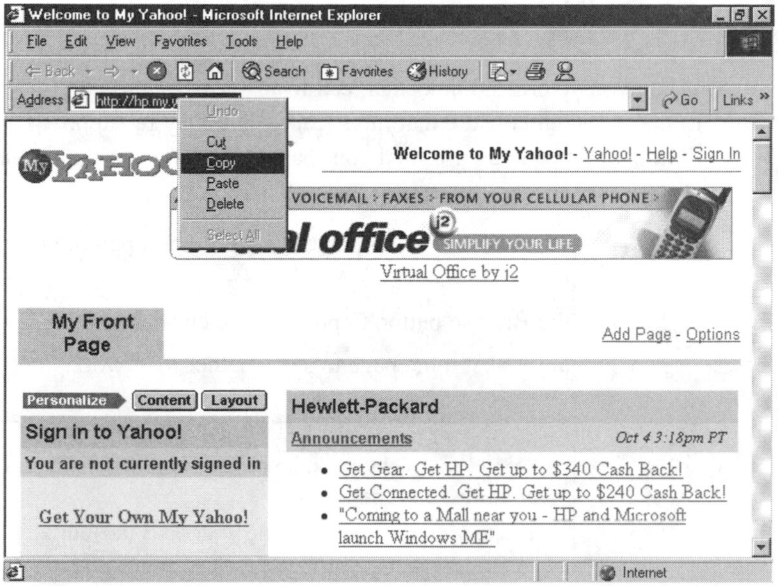

FIGURE 10.10
Copying a link from a link in a Web page.

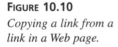

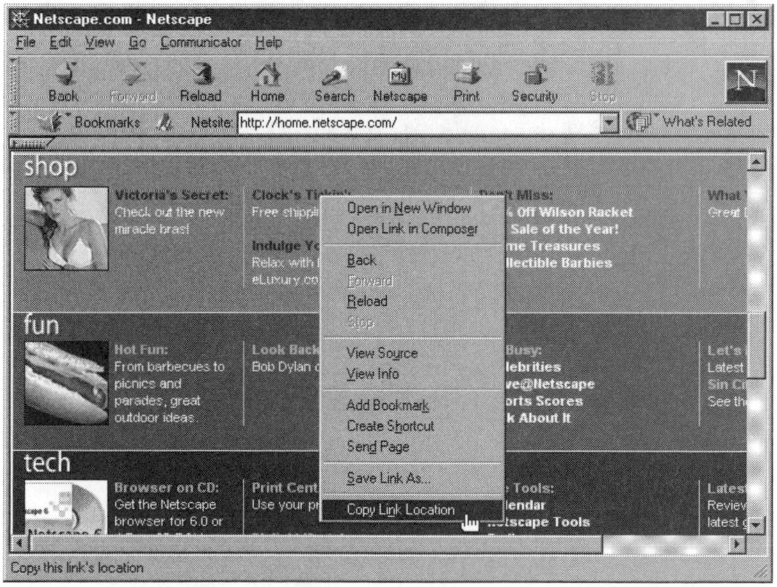

Checking That Links Lead Where They're Supposed To

When you've created links that lead from your page to other pages online, the only way to make absolutely sure that links lead where they're supposed to is to test the links online, *after* you've published your page. Still, you can do a reliable prepublishing link check at any time, right from within Composer:

1. Connect to the Internet, open Composer, and open the page file whose links you want to test.
2. Click the Browse button to preview the current page in Navigator.
3. Click any links in the page to see whether they work.

> Even if your links work, be careful to test them again, online, after you have published your page.
>
> You learn more about testing your links in Hour 22, "Publishing Your Site."

Editing Links

You can change anything about a link: the link text, the URL, the type of link, and more. That's handy if you decide to change the wording of the link text or if you need to update a link when the URL of the page it leads to changes:

- To change link text, just edit the text any way you want. Usually, the link behind the source is undisturbed by the editing. If, after editing the source, you see that the link is gone or that it is not connected any more to the exact words you want, just highlight the text and re-create the link.
- To change the URL or any other "behind the scenes" aspect of a link, right-click the link and choose Link Properties from the menu that appears (see Figure 10.11). On the dialog box that appears, change what needs changing, and click OK.

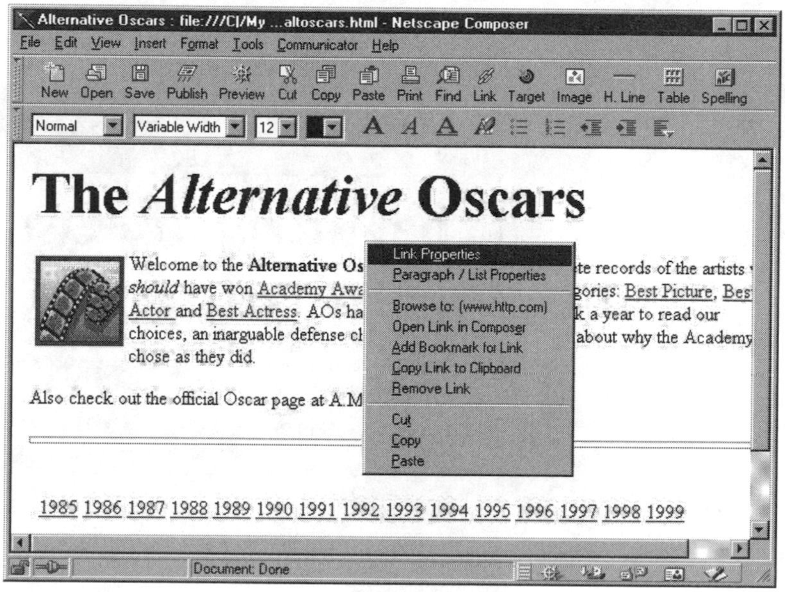

FIGURE 10.11
To edit a link, right-click it and choose Link Properties.

Delinking Text

Suppose that you want to remove a link from your page and keep its link text on the page. You could simply delete the link and retype the text. That's a solution for a link or two, but if you want to kill all the links in a large section or in an entire page, all the retyping would be tedious.

The following To Do shows how to revert a link into ordinary text on the page.

To Do: Remove a link (leave the link text)

1. Select the link, or select an entire section of a page containing multiple links you want to remove.
2. Right-click the selection and choose Remove Link or Remove All Links in Selection from the menu that appears.

▼

FIGURE 10.12
Step 1: Select the link or links.

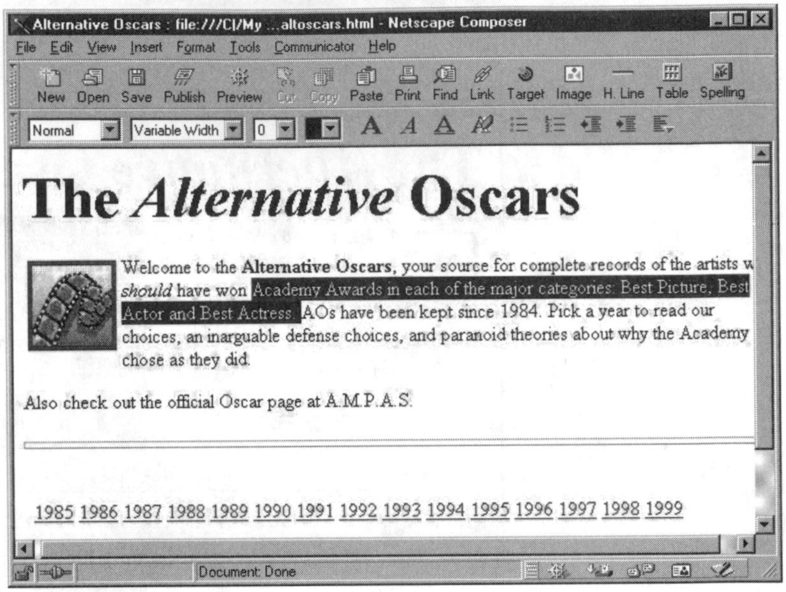

FIGURE 10.13
Step 2: Right-click and choose Remove Link.

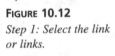

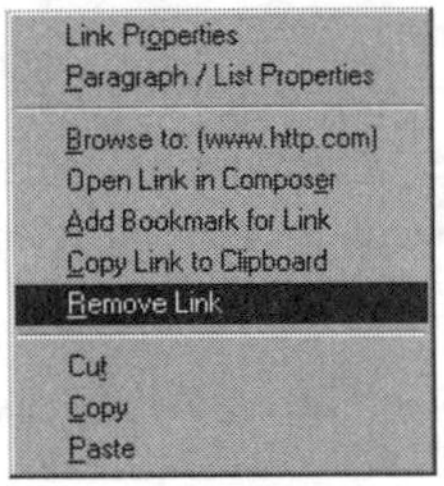

▲

Summary

Just because you can link everywhere doesn't mean that you should. Pages with extraneous links are no more useful than linkless ones. Carefully check out each place to which you will link. Is it really useful to your readers? Does it provide something new or simply duplicate material your other links already lead to? Does it appear to be on a reliable server or on one that's often inaccessible or slow?

Your goal should not be to provide your readers with as many links as possible, but rather with a choice selection. And you know that you must check, update, and add to your links often. Do that, and your visitors will return often.

Q&A

Q If I want to offer quick access to other resources related to my page, can I link directly to a category listing in a Web directory, such as Yahoo! or the WWW Virtual Library?

A Sure, and many people do that. As always, you should email the Webmaster of any directory you link to and request permission.

Also, try not to get too specific; link at the most general point in a directory's hierarchy that pertains to your topic, and let the visitor navigate down to the specifics. Broad categories in directories are fairly stable and remain in place for years. Very specific directory listings low in the hierarchy might disappear or change names, invalidating any links to them.

HOUR 11

More Ways to Link

If Web pages were books and links were a card catalog, targets would be thumbtabs.

Let me explain. Just like a card catalog entry, a link takes you only to a whole document—a Web page—not to any particular place *within* that document. That makes links great for general-purpose surfing, getting into the general ballpark of what you want.

But sometimes you want to take your visitors not just to a particular page, but also to an exact spot within that page. That's the job of *targets*. In this hour, you will expand on your linking skills from Hour 10, "Making Links," learning not only how to create and link to targets, but also how to link to any type of file so that your visitors can download the files you want to offer them.

At the end of the hour, you will be able to answer the following questions:

- Where and why would I use targets?
- How do I create a target in a page?
- How do I make existing text into a target?
- How do I create a link that takes the visitor to a particular spot within the page he's viewing?

- How do I create a link that takes the visitor from one page to a particular spot in another page?
- How do I create links that, when clicked, download a file?

Understanding Targets

A *target* is a hidden HTML tag—hidden in that it is not visible to the visitor, but is visible to you in Composer (see Figure 11.1) so that you can see where you put it. In Composer, a target in a file is indicated by a target icon, as shown in Figure 11.1).

> The target icons used to indicate a target location are visible in Composer only when you are working in Normal Edit mode. In Preview mode, the targets are invisible, just as they would be to a visitor browsing your page.

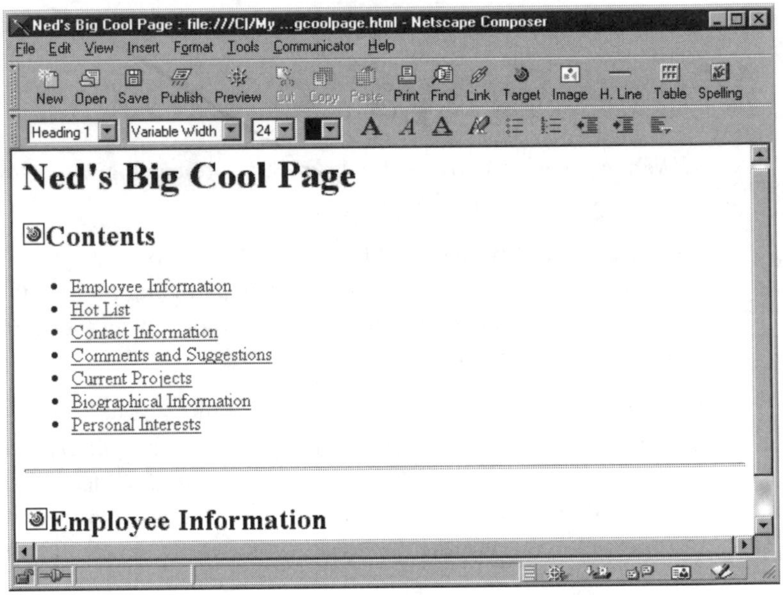

FIGURE 11.1
Target icons in a Composer page, as seen in Normal Edit mode.

A target provides a location in a page that a link can point to; clicking the link takes a visitor to that exact spot rather than just to the top of the page. A single page can have many targets, each one with a unique name so that a link can point to one and only one particular target. The link that points to a target can be in either the same page the target is in or another page.

Why use targets? Several common scenarios involve long Web pages where, without targets, the visitor would have to do lots of scrolling to locate particular information on a page:

- At the top of a very long Web page (such as a Frequently Asked Questions, or *FAQ*, file), you can include a list of links, each of which points to a different part of the file. The links enable the visitor to jump easily to any part of the file rather than have to scroll through it to find a particular section.
- You might want to use targets when links on one page refer to particular parts of another page that happens to be a long one. The links can point to targets in the long page, to take the visitor directly there in one click.
- In a frames-based page (see Hour 18, "Dividing a Page into Frames"), links in one frame can bring up particular parts of a file displayed in another frame. Like the other techniques, this one reduces the visitor's need to scroll, making a Web site easier to navigate.

Creating Targets in a Page

Before you can begin linking to targets, you must insert those targets in the page. The following To Do shows how to insert targets in a page in Composer. Note that you can choose from two basic methods: Create a target that marks a spot, and create a target that marks certain text.

> Which method should you use and when? It doesn't make much difference.
>
> Attaching targets to text makes the most sense when each section where you want to put a target begins with a unique heading, as in a FAQ. When that's the case, attaching targets to text saves you the extra step of having to name your targets.
>
> However, the text must be different for each target in the page; no two targets in a file can share the same name.

To Do

To Do: Create targets

1. Click at a spot where you want a link to lead, or select the text to which you want a target attached.

> If you select text when performing Step 1, make sure that your selection does not include a paragraph mark. If it does, you find that the Target Properties dialog box doesn't let you create the target.
>
> To avoid selecting a paragraph character, don't run the selection all the way to the end of a line. (Make sure that the selection ends with a character).

2. Click the Target button on the Composition toolbar.

FIGURE 11.2
Step 2: Click Target.

3. Type a name for this target and click OK.

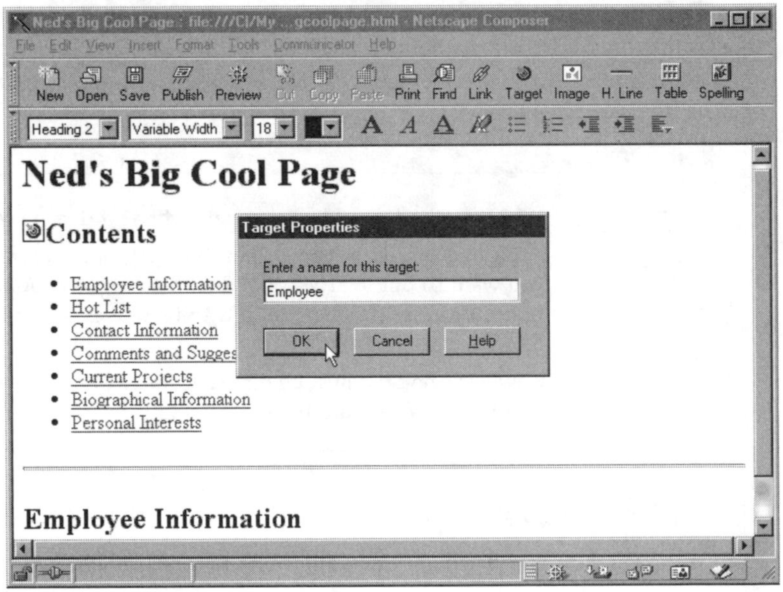

FIGURE 11.3
Step 3: Name the target and then click OK.

Deleting Targets

To delete a target, click the target icon to select it and press the Del key. If the target was attached to text, the text remains, but the target is gone.

Linking to Targets

You can create three kinds of links that point to targets:

- A link within the same page as the target to which it points.
- A link in one page that points to a target in another page in a multipage Web site you're creating in Composer.
- A link in one page that points to a target in another page online that's not one of yours.

In the following pages, you will learn how to link to targets in the same page and to targets in other pages online. See Hour 12, "Using Links to Build a Website," to learn how to link from one page of your own to a target in another page of your own.

> In Hour 14, "Adding Pictures (and Picture Backgrounds)," you learn not only how to add pictures to your pages, but also how to use a picture as a link.
>
> I'm jumping ahead a little, therefore, getting into pictures here, but I should tell you now that links using any type of link source—text, pictures, or even multilink imagemaps (see Hour 20, "Putting Multiple Links in One Picture")—can point to targets.

Linking to a Target in the Same Page

In Composer, creating links to targets in the same file is easier if you have only one file open, so that's where you begin, in the following To Do.

> As shown earlier in this hour, putting a table of contents at the top of a long page is customary, with each entry in the TOC linking to a target in a section of the page.
>
> If you create a long page of this type, you should also put a link on every section that jumps back to the TOC so that visitors can easily jump back and forth from the TOC to different sections.
>
> Put a target right over the TOC, and insert a link at every section that points back to that target, to get visitors back to the top.

To Do: Link to a target in the same page

1. Create and select the link text, as you would when creating any kind of link, and then click the Link button.
2. A list of targets in the current page appears in the box labeled Select a named target. Click the name of the target you want the link to point to, and then click OK.

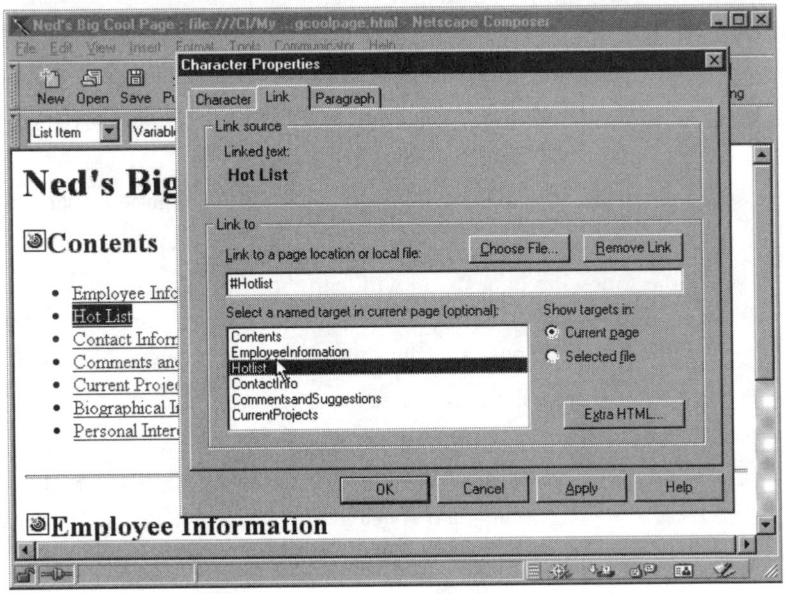

FIGURE 11.4
Step 2: Choose a target from the list.

> The list of targets is organized alphabetically, by target name, so find the target you want by name. Don't assume that the targets are listed in the same order in which they appear in the page—from top to bottom, unless you were careful when naming them to alphabetize them or number them consecutively, from top to bottom.

Linking to Targets in Other Pages Online

The easiest way to link to a target in someone else's page online is to find on that page a link that points to the target to which you want to link. For example, if you want to link to a particular part of a FAQ file online, find in the FAQ's table of contents a link that points to that part. Then copy that link from the Web page into your own page using copy and paste, as described in Hour 10.

> As always, when linking to pages that are not your own, you should email the Webmaster of the page to which you want to link and ask whether it's okay.
>
> Some Webmasters might say that it's okay to link to the page, but not to targets within the page. This situation might happen when the page contains advertising or other information that the Webmaster wants all visitors to see; linking to targets would allow them to bypass this type of material.

Another method is to learn the target's exact URL, which is made up of the page's URL, a pound sign (#), and the target name. For example, the following URL:

```
http://www.test.com/sample.htm#target1
```

points to a target named `target1` in a page file named `sample.htm` on a server named `www.test.com`.

The easiest way to learn the URLs of targets in an online document is to browse to the document in your Web browser and find in that document the links that point to the targets. When you point to a link (don't click), the status bar at the bottom of the browser window (in Navigator or Internet Explorer) shows the full URL to which that link points—including the target name.

After you know the complete URL, you can create a link to it like any other link to a Web page, by typing it in the URL box in the Link tab of the Character Properties dialog box (see Figure 11.5).

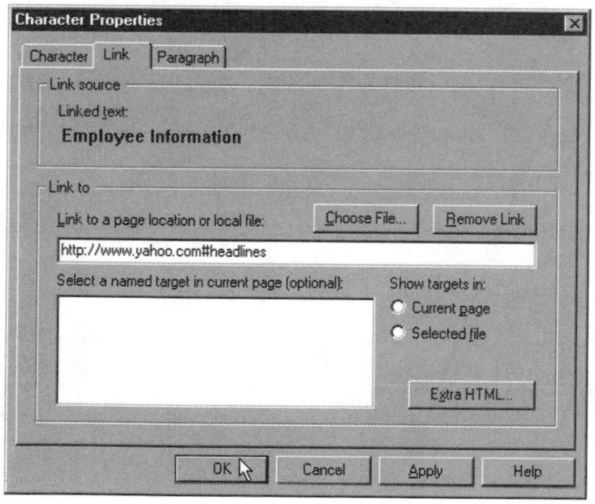

FIGURE 11.5
You can enter a URL that includes a target name directly in the Link tab on the Character Properties dialog box.

Creating Links that Download Files

You might have content that you want to offer your visitors, but don't want to turn into a Web page. For example, if you have a long story, report, or other document in a word processing file, you might want to offer that file for downloading rather than turn it into a Web page (or series of Web pages).

You can offer any kind of computer file for downloading—documents, sound clips, or pictures, for example. The steps for creating links to files are the same—no matter what type of file you want to offer—as the following To Do shows.

One caveat to keep in mind: To use a file you provide, the visitor must have the right program. For example, if you publish a Word file, the visitor must have a program that can display (or convert) Word files to view it. You cannot do much about this situation, except to try to offer only popular, widely used file types, such as Word (.doc) for documents, `.avi` for video clips, or `.wav` for sound clips (see Hour 15, "Snazzing Up Your Page with Sound, Video, and Special Effects").

To Do: Create links that download files

1. Get the file to which you want to link, and move or copy it to the folder where your Web page files are stored.
2. In the Web page in Composer, type and format the link text as usual.

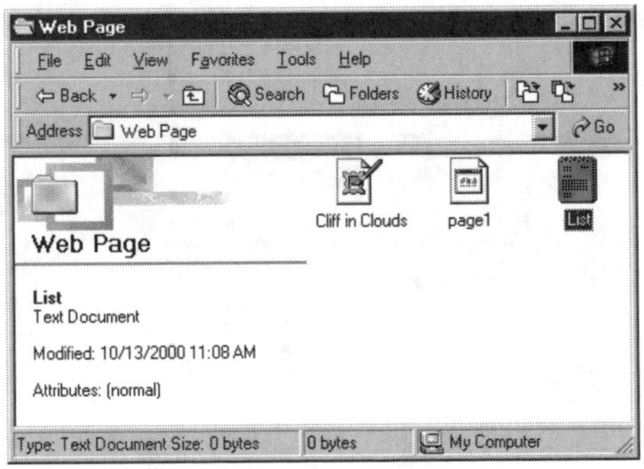

FIGURE 11.6
Step 1: Put the file in the same folder as the Web page file.

In the link text (or right next to it), be courteous and tell your visitors the file type (so that they can tell whether it's a file they're equipped to view) and size (so that they can "guesstimate" how long it will take to download at the speed of their Internet connection).

3. Select the link text and click the Link button on the Composition toolbar.
4. Click the Choose File button.

FIGURE 11.7
Step 4: Click Choose File.

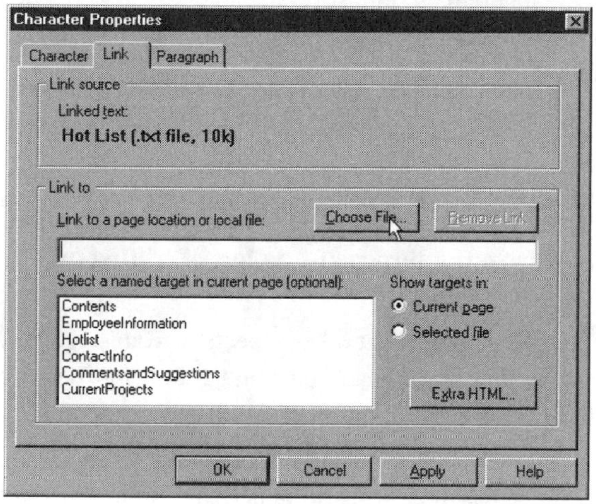

5. Use the dialog box to browse to the file you want this link to download, select that filename, and click Open.

FIGURE 11.8
Step 5: Browse to the file.

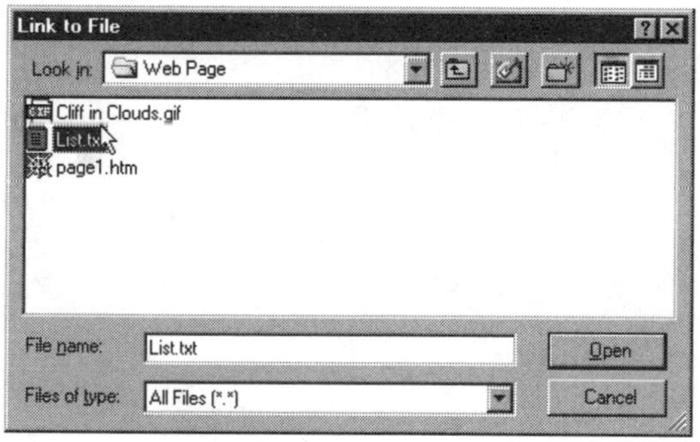

> When you publish this Web page online, you must remember to also publish the file to which the link points and make sure that it's stored in the same directory online as the page containing the link; otherwise, the link doesn't work. See Part VI, "Getting It Online."

Summary

You probably won't use targets often; if you feel that you need targets, you should first consider breaking up the page into several, smaller pages. But when it makes sense to publish lots of information in one file, targets help your visitors wade around in all that information conveniently.

Q&A

Q Should I finish the rest of my page before adding targets to it? I'm wondering what happens to the targets if I do lots of editing and formatting to the file after I've added them.

A In general, completing most other aspects of your page before adding targets makes sense. That way, the targets don't get all shuffled around to the wrong spots if you do heavy editing on the page later, such as adding, moving, or replacing large blocks of material.

However, note that most formatting activities don't hurt targets. If a block of text that includes a target has its font or alignment changed, for example, the target still works (although the icon appears to take on any alignment changes or indents you apply to the adjacent text).

HOUR 12

Using Links to Build a Web Site

There are pages, and then there are *sites*—groups of pages linked together. (The term *Web site* is also used to refer to the server on which those pages are published; see Hour 21, "Finding Webspace.")

Without carefully created links and targets, a set of Web pages is no site—it's just a bunch of individual, unrelated pages. Link those pages in just the right way, and they become a cohesive site your visitors can explore to enjoy all that's offered on every page.

In this hour, you'll revisit the various ways a Web site can be structured (first introduced in Hour 1, "Understanding Web Authoring") and learn how and when to deploy each method in your own projects. At the end of the hour, you will be able to answer the following questions:

- How do I link my own pages, to tie them together into an integrated Web site?
- Can I link from one page to a particular spot in another?

- What tips should I apply to make sure that my site is attractive, logical, and easy to use?
- For each type of structure, what links (and sometimes targets) do I need to insert to link my pages properly?
- How do I choose when and whether to build my site as a linear, hierarchical Web, or other site structure?

> What separates basic Web authoring tools like Composer from big leaguers like Microsoft FrontPage or Macromedia Dreamweaver? Well, other than a few bells and whistles, the most important difference is that pro tools include *site-management* features.
>
> With site management, you can display a diagram of all the interlinked pages in a Web site. You can add or delete pages or move pages around, and all the links among pages are automatically adjusted so that they still lead where they're supposed to. You can apply a *theme* to a Web site so that all its pages share a common style.
>
> Starting out, creating single pages and basic Web sites of maybe five pages or so, you don't need site-management capabilities. But as you move up to bigger, more complex sites, you should start hinting that, for your next birthday, you want a Web authoring program with site management.

The Basic Act: Linking One Page to Another

Composer makes it easy to link pages you've created while they're still on your PC. The trick is to create the pages first and then build the links as described in the following To Do.

To Do: Link one of your own pages to others

1. Create the Web pages that will make up your Web site, and save them all in the same folder.
2. Type and format the text that will serve as the various links.
3. Select the text of one link source.

FIGURE 12.1
Step 1: Create your pages and store them together in a folder.

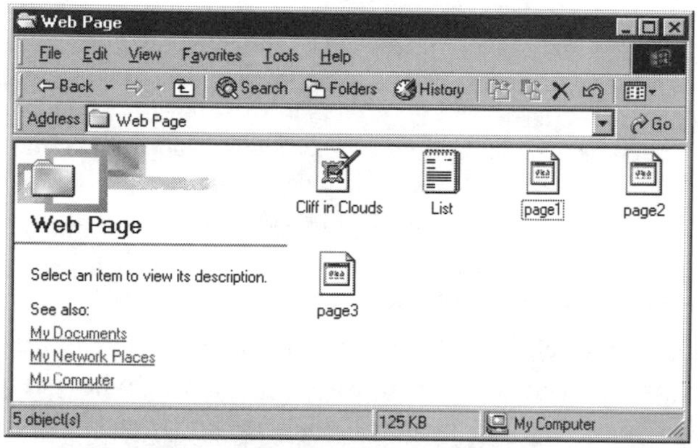

FIGURE 12.2
Step 3: Select a link source.

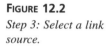

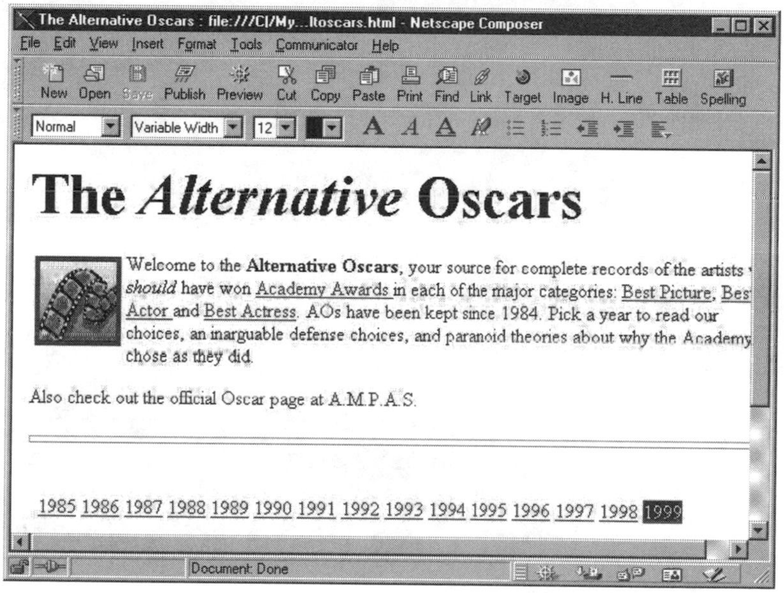

One good way to link pages is to create a block of links—containing a separate link for each page—and put it at the bottom of every page. That way, your visitors can jump from any page in your Web site to any other with just one click.

After you've created the block of links, you can use copy-and-paste to copy the block from one page to others (see Hour 6, "Adding and Editing Text").

> Or, you can build the block in one page and then use that page as a template (see Hour 4, "Starting Pages in Other Programs") for all the rest.
>
> Besides (or in addition to) using a block of text links, you can use picture links (see Hour 14, "Adding Pictures (and Picture Backgrounds)") or an imagemap (see Hour 18, "Dividing a Page into Frames") to create a navigation bar, a graphical link block for each page in the site.

4. Click the Link button on the Composition toolbar.
5. In the box labeled URL, type the complete filename of the page file to which this link points (including the `.htm` or `.html` part). Do not put `http://` or anything else at the beginning. The filename alone does it. Then click OK.

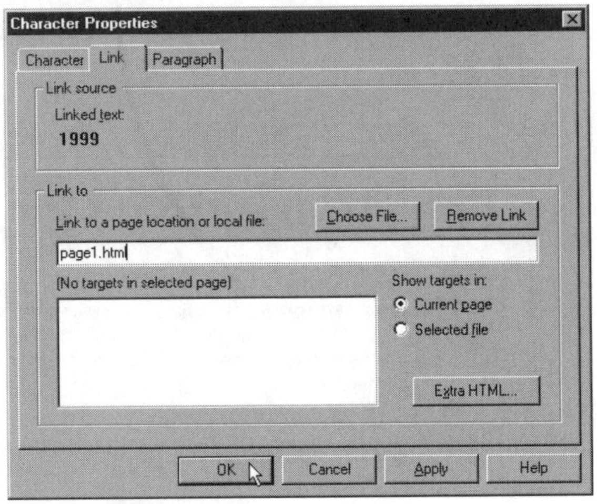

FIGURE 12.3
Step 5: For the link URL, type the filename of the page to which to link.

Linking from One Page to a Target in Another

In Hour 11, "More Ways to Link," you learned the fine art of linking to targets, a technique used most often to link from one part of a long page to another. But you can also jump from one of your pages to a particular target point in another of your pages. The procedure is essentially similar to linking from one page to another.

To Do: Link to a target in one of your own pages

1. Open the page containing the target and double-click the target icon of the target you want to link to, to display the Target Properties box. Jot down the target's name.
2. Open the page where the link will live, create and select the link text as you would when creating any kind of link, and then click the Link button.
3. In the Link to box, type the filename of the page containing the target. (Don't put `http://` or anything else in front of the filename.
4. Immediately following the filename, type # followed by the name of the target and then click OK.

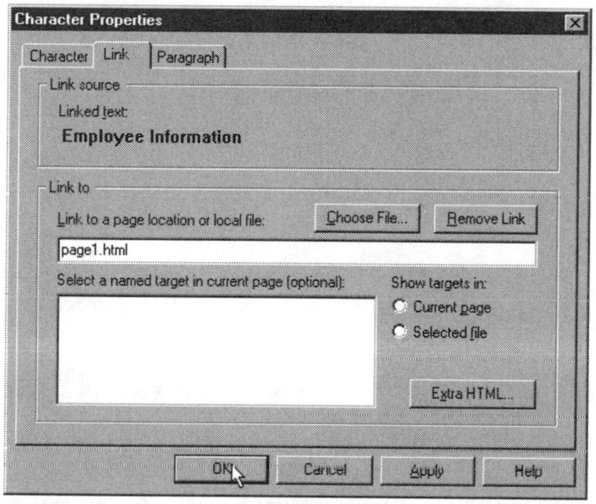

FIGURE 12.4
Step 3: Type the filename of the page containing the target.

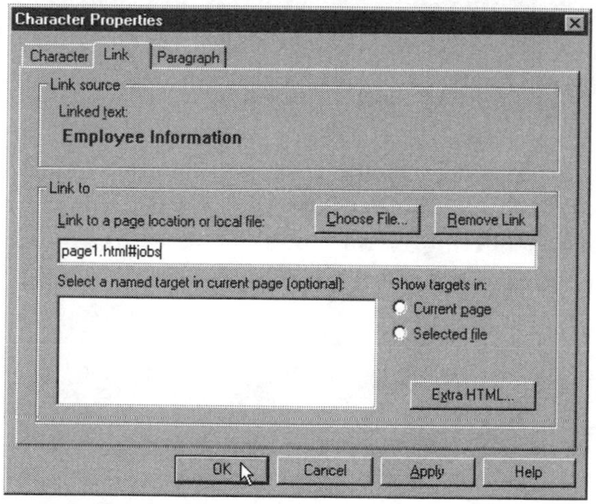

FIGURE 12.5
Step 4: Add a pound sign (#) and the target name to the filename.

Site-Design Tips

The skills outlined in the preceding To Dos are all you need to stitch multiple pages into a coordinated site. All you need now is a little guidance about ways you can organize information into a Web site. The remainder of this hour offers tips for choosing a site design.

Building a Multipage Linear Site

In a multipage linear site, the pages and links are set up in a way that encourages the reader to read a group of pages in a particular order, from start to finish (see Figure 12.6).

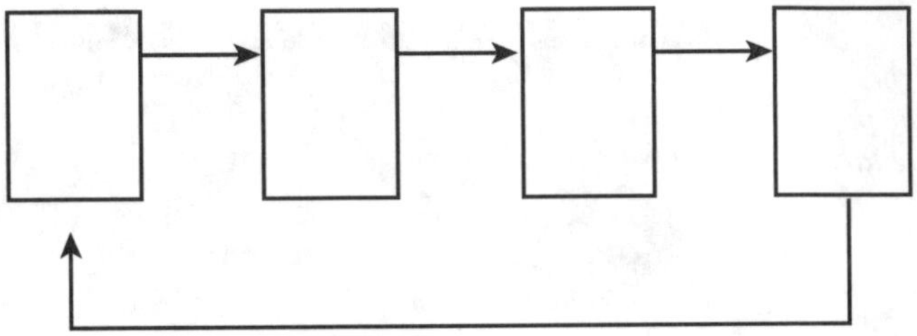

FIGURE 12.6
The structure of a multipage linear site.

This design makes sense when the content your site delivers is made up mostly of medium-size blocks of text (around one screen) that should be read in a particular sequential order, from beginning to end. (Some people call it a *slide show* structure because the visitor steps through the pages in order, as in a slide show.)

Suppose that this book were converted into a Web site. Its "hours" serve the reader best when they're read in order, because each chapter builds on material from the ones before it. To encourage readers to proceed in order, the site would be designed so that the natural flow from page to page (or from hour to hour) follows the proper order. Other content that fits this design includes a story that's too long to fit on one page or lengthy step-by-step instructions.

Each page in a multipage linear site features a prominent link, often labeled Next or Continue, that leads only to the next page in order. Other links can be offered as well, but be careful about offering too many links in these types of pages—the links enable the reader to stray from the order, defeating the purpose of the design.

> The Microsoft PowerPoint program (included in most versions of Microsoft Office) is designed to help you quickly build an attractive slide-show presentation.
>
> Recent versions of PowerPoint can convert their slide presentations into multipage linear Web sites. They convert each slide into a separate Web page and then automatically insert the navigation buttons (Back and Next, for example). It's a fast and easy way to make a Web site from content you might already have on hand.

Tips for Multipage Linear Site Design

When developing a multipage linear Web site, keep in mind the following tips for good design:

- Try to divide the material into pages that have just enough content (text and images) to fill the screen. Because the visitor is moving sequentially through the pages, he or she should not have to scroll, too. Putting just the right amount of text on each page enables visitors to conveniently explore the whole site just by clicking the Next link that you provide.
- A Next link on each page is the only link that's required and, often, the only one you want. However, if you can offer a Back link (pointing to the preceding page) without cluttering up the design, try to offer that link on each page after the first one so that the reader can review content, if necessary. Also handy is a Back to Start link that points to the first page, so that the reader can conveniently jump from any page to the beginning.
- The last page in the order should always contain a link back to the first page, even if you choose not to provide this type of link elsewhere.

Working with One-Page Linear Pages

When the following conditions are true, a one-page linear design is a terrific (and often overlooked) approach (see Figure 12.7):

- You have lots of text to deliver.
- That text is naturally divided into many small sections.
- You want to deliver the text in an efficient way.

FIGURE 12.7
A sample one-page linear design.

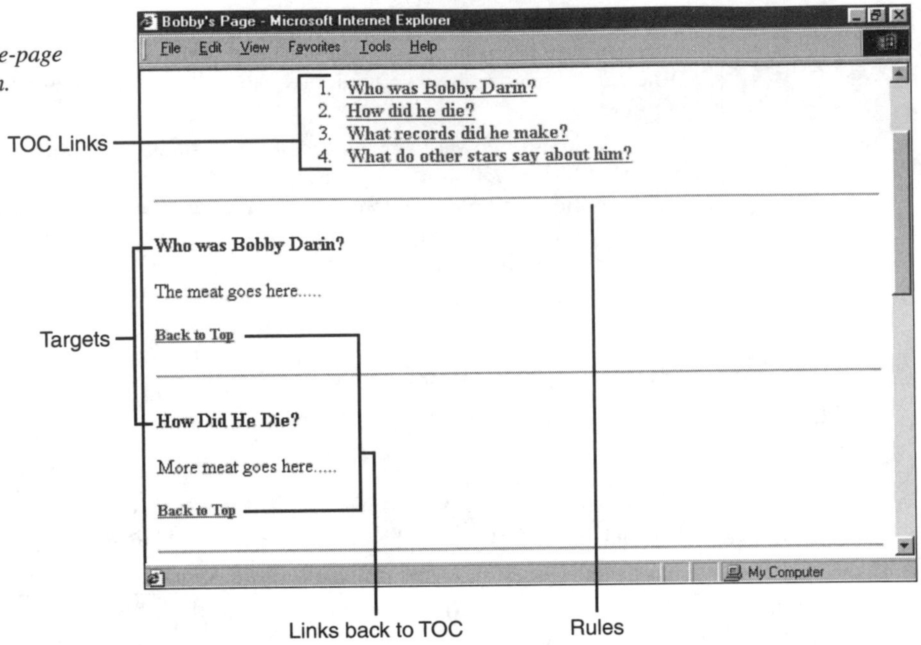

This structure is often applied to lengthy reference material provided as one part of a larger, multipage site, but a well-designed one-pager can actually serve as your whole site.

Although readers can always scroll through the entire page, the top of the page typically shows a list of links—a table of contents or index of sorts. Each link points to a target (see Hour 11) somewhere down in the page. The links help readers quickly find particular information without having to scroll for it.

> The longer the page and the more separate sections it has, the more important the table of links at the top is.
>
> If a page is only three or four screens long, the visitor can pretty easily explore it by scrolling. Five screens or longer, and you owe your visitors the assistance of some links.

Tips for One-Page Linear Design

When developing a one-page linear design, keep in mind the following tips for good design:

- At the top of the page, or adjacent to the table of contents, insert a target. Between each logical section of the page, insert a Back to Top link that points to the target at the top. This link enables the reader to conveniently return to the TOC after reading any section.
- Limit pictures (see Hour 14). The danger of this design is that the long page will contain so much data that it will take a long time to download to the visitor's browser. But text—even lots of text—moves through the Internet pretty quickly. If you limit yourself to an image or two, usually at the top of the page, you can lend some visual interest while still enabling the page to download quickly.
- Scroll through the page. If the total page exceeds 15 screens, consider breaking it up into a hierarchical or multipage sequential design.
- Use horizontal rules (see Hour 8, "Organizing Text with Tables and Rules") to divide sections of the text visually.

Making a Web-Style Site

In a Web structure, anything goes (see Figure 12.8). Any page can link to any other page, or to all other pages. This structure makes sense when the various pages contain information that is related to information on other pages, but there's no logical order or sequence to that information.

In a Web-style site, a "top" page might be provided as a starting point (as in a hierarchical site, as described later in this hour), but from there, readers can wander around the site in no particular path. Web structures are best suited to fun, recreational subjects or to subjects that defy any kind of sequential or hierarchical breakdown.

Typically, each page of a Web-style site contains a block of links—often in a column along one side of the page or in a block at the bottom—that lead to every other page in the site (see Figure 12.9).

Tips for Web-Style Design

When developing a Web-style site, keep in mind the following tips for good design:

- Before you resort to a Web structure, make sure that your message really calls for one—you might just be having trouble recognizing the logical organization of your content.
- Visitors can easily get lost in a Web-style site. I recommend always including a "top" page that serves as an all-purpose starting point and then making sure that every page in the site contains an easily identifiable link back to the top page. That way, lost visitors can easily get back to a landmark from which to set off down a new path.

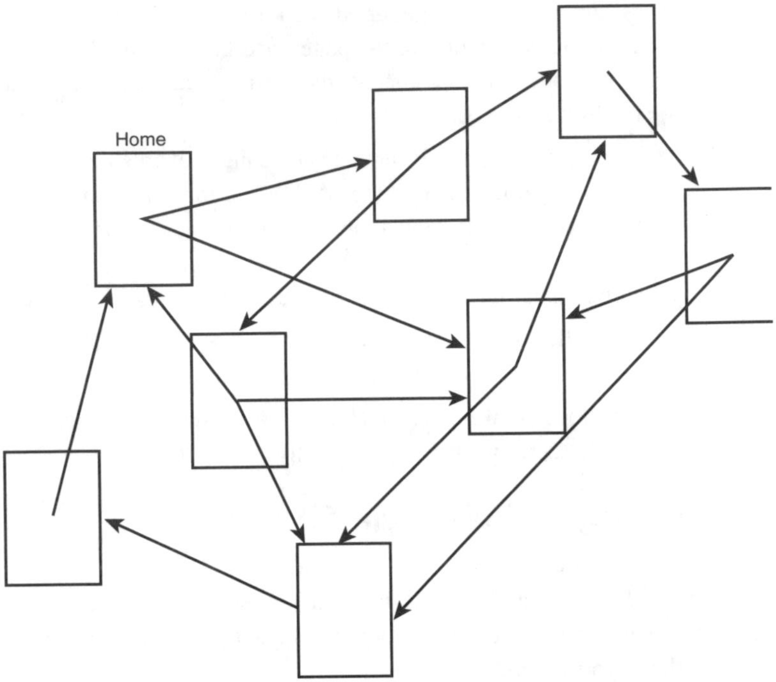

FIGURE 12.8
A Web-style structure.

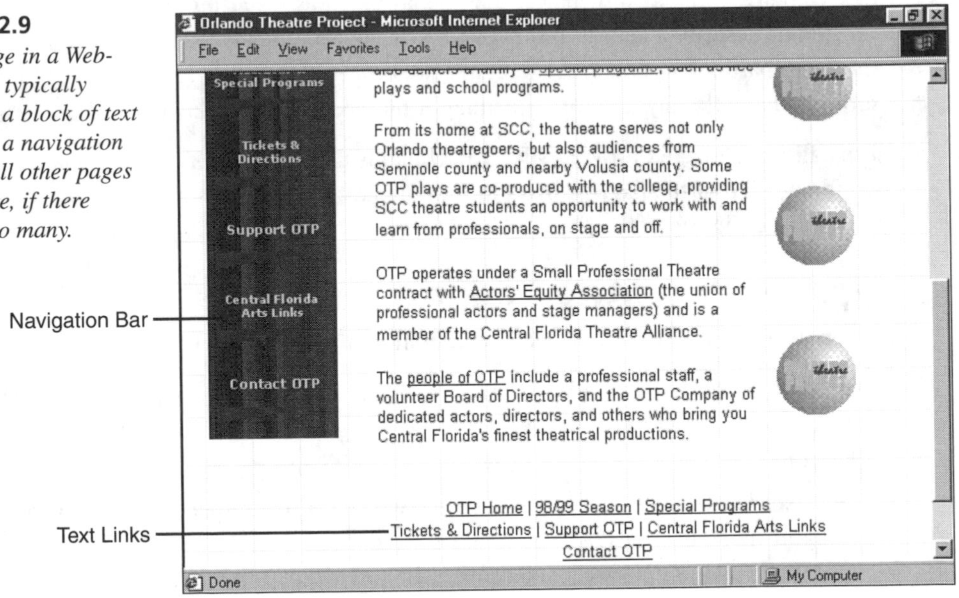

Orlando Theatre Project - Microsoft Internet Explorer
File Edit View Favorites Tools Help
Special Programs
Tickets & Directions
Support OTP
Central Florida Arts Links
Contact OTP
plays and school programs.
From its home at SCC, the theatre serves not only Orlando theatregoers, but also audiences from Seminole county and nearby Volusia county. Some OTP plays are co-produced with the college, providing SCC theatre students an opportunity to work with and learn from professionals, on stage and off.
OTP operates under a Small Professional Theatre contract with Actors' Equity Association (the union of professional actors and stage managers) and is a member of the Central Florida Theatre Alliance.
The people of OTP include a professional staff, a volunteer Board of Directors, and the OTP Company of dedicated actors, directors, and others who bring you Central Florida's finest theatrical productions.
OTP Home | 98/99 Season | Special Programs
Tickets & Directions | Support OTP | Central Florida Arts Links
Contact OTP
Done
My Computer
Navigation Bar
Text Links

FIGURE 12.9
Each page in a Web-style site typically contains a block of text links (or a navigation bar) to all other pages in the site, if there aren't too many.

Making a Hierarchical Site

The most well-organized design (see Figure 12.10), a hierarchical Web site starts out with a general, "top" page that leads to several second-level pages containing more specific information. Each of these second-level pages leads to third-level pages containing more specific info about the second-level page to which they are linked, and so on.

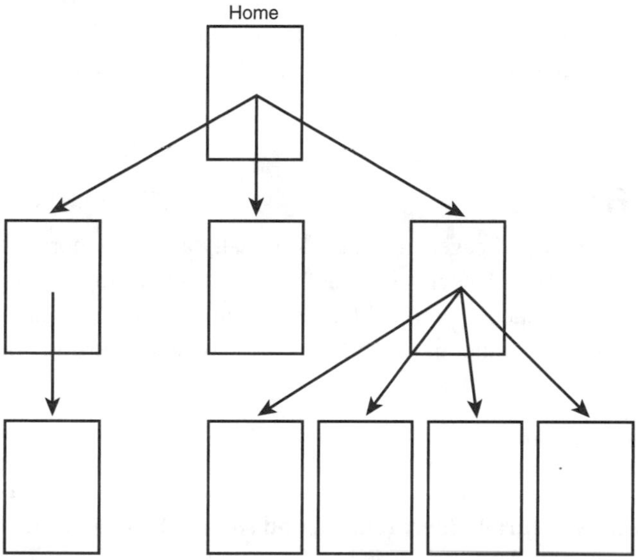

FIGURE 12.10
A hierarchical structure.

The careful organization of a hierarchical site is not for the mere sake of neatness. The structure of the page actually helps the visitor find what he or she wants, especially when the site carries lots of detailed information.

Suppose that the site sells clothes, and I want a dress shirt. The top page might show links to women's clothes and men's clothes. I choose the Men's link and arrive at a second-level page offering links to shirts, pants, and shoes. I choose Shirts, and I see a third-level page offering Dress and Casual. I choose Dress, and I'm there. The structure of the page makes my search easy, even though the site offers hundreds of items.

Tips for Hierarchical Design

When developing a hierarchical site, keep in mind the following tips for good design:

- As in a Web-style design, be sure that every page in the site contains an easily identifiable link back to the top page so that visitors can easily get back to the top without having to struggle up the hierarchy a level at a time.

- More than with any other design, a hierarchical structure demands that you think and plan carefully the content of each page and the organization of the pages so that the site flows logically. As with my shirt example, visitors should be able to drill intuitively down through the hierarchy to find specific information.
- Keep in mind that many levels are available to you. Don't try to link the top page to a dozen second-level pages—doing so suggests that you have not really figured out the organization. Ideally, each page should lead to no fewer than two pages and no more than seven or eight, in the level below it. Then again, don't follow arbitrary rules. Just be sure that the page organization and the natural organization of the content match.

Summary

The organization of pages in a site is not really a Web authoring challenge: It's a content-management issue. Understand exactly what you're trying to say and how to say it best, and the correct site structure will become immediately apparent to you. All that's left is adding some links (and maybe targets), and you know how to do that already, don't you?

Q&A

Q What if I'm planning to use some content that's naturally sequential, some that's naturally hierarchical, and some that's random? How do I make it all fit one model?

A You don't have to. For more elaborate Web sites, a *hybrid* approach is called for.

A hybrid approach generally starts out hierarchical, with an overview top page to serve as a starting point. But at the second level, that top page might link down to a one-page linear, or to the top page of what will then spread out into a Web structure, or to the first page of a multipage linear slide show, or to the top of a whole new hierarchy.

With a hybrid approach, you can make content at the second and lower levels conform to whatever structure suits it while still using the top page to hold the whole affair neatly together.

PART IV

Adding Pizzazz with Multimedia

Hour

HOUR 13

Getting Pictures for Your Page

In Hour 14, "Adding Pictures (and Picture Backgrounds)," you'll begin adding pictures to your page. But the trickiest part of adding pictures isn't the adding—it's getting the pictures in the first place and getting them in the proper format. In this hour, you'll learn how, where, and why to get pictures for your page.

At the end of the hour, you will be able to answer the following questions:

- Where can I get pictures for my Web page?
- How can I create pictures of my own?
- How do I preview the images in my page, to make sure they look the way I want them to look online?
- What rules—file type, resolution, and other factors—must my picture files follow to appear in a Web page?

About Inline Images

NEW TERM *Inline* images automatically appear within the layout of the page when a graphical browser accesses the page.

Computer image files come in many types. Common types include `.pcx` and `.bmp` files, which are used most often in Windows, and TIFF (`.tif`) files, which are often used on Macintoshes and in desktop publishing. However, the most common type of image file used for inline images is GIF (pronounced "jif" and using the file extension `.gif`). The next most popular type is JPEG (with a `.jpg` file extension in most systems).

> Although images in file types other than GIF or JPEG are inappropriate for use as inline images, most other file types can be used as *external* images, which are image files displayed outside the browser when the visitor clicks a link.

GIF files (see Figure 13.1) offer certain advantages (see the sections "Understanding Interlacing" and "Understanding Transparency," later in this hour), but they are limited to 256 colors (or 256 shades of gray in black-and-white images). For most graphics, especially those originally drawn on a computer, this "8-bit" color is plenty. But for photographs, paintings, and other images taken from life, 256 colors do not permit enough variation in color or shade to present a realistically shaded image; the results can look "computerish."

FIGURE 13.1
GIF images are usually best suited to highly graphical pictures, such as logos.

However, the GIF 256-color limitation is not necessarily a big disadvantage. This is true for two reasons:

- Images in 16-bit color (65,000 colors) or 24-bit *true color* (16 million colors) tend to occupy much larger files than 256-color graphics—so much so that they might be inappropriate as inline images because they take too long to download to the visitor's browser. (See the "File Size" section, later in this hour.)
- A proportion of your audience might be running their browsers in 256-color mode anyway, which cannot display the extra color depth and detail possible in 16-bit

and 24-bit color graphics. The picture still shows up, but it looks no better than a 256-color image, and possibly a little worse.

However, if you want to display more than 256 colors or grays, a JPEG file can handle it (see Figure 13.2). More importantly, a JPEG file of a photograph is often a smaller file, which means that it appears more quickly on the visitor's display.

FIGURE 13.2
JPEG is a better choice than GIF for photos.

All graphical Web browsers can display inline GIF images, and a few can display *only* GIF images. The most popular browsers—Netscape and Internet Explorer—can also display JPEG images.

> Another image file format, `.png`, is supported by some browsers. But GIF and JPEG are much more universally supported and are thus your best choice for Web graphics.

Creating and Acquiring Image Files

13

Where can you get images? You can create (or acquire) them in the following ways; the important issue is not where they come from, but rather their file type, size, and other factors:

Paint/Draw—You can use a paint or draw program to create your inline graphics. Ideally, the program should be able to save your picture as a GIF (or, optionally, JPEG) graphic. If not, you can *convert*…

Convert—If you want to use existing graphics in your page that are not in GIF or JPEG format, you can convert them to GIF or JPEG by using a paint program or conversion utility or a conversion utility built into your Web authoring program. (Composer, however, does not convert images from other formats to GIF or JPEG.)

> **Tip:** The software that comes with many scanners, digital cameras, and video capture devices can save images in GIF or JPEG format; when the software cannot save in these formats, you can almost always save the file in TIFF format and then use another program, such as Paint Shop Pro (a demo version is included on the CD-ROM), to convert a TIFF file to GIF or JPEG.

Scan—Using a hand scanner, sheetfed scanner, or flatbed scanner, you can scan photographs or other images and save them (using the scanning software) as GIF or JPEG images. This technique also enables you to draw, sketch, or paint pictures on paper (if you have such skills) and then convert them into computer graphics for use in Web pages.

Shoot—Using a digital camera or computer videocamera, you can capture an image from life.

Note, however, that you don't have to create your own images—you can pick up existing images for a wide range of purposes. Collections of clip art are available on the Web and in commercial and shareware software packages.

NEW TERM *Clip art* consists of image files (and sometimes other kinds of media files, such as animations or sound clips) that you did not create but that are made available to you for use in your Web pages or other documents. Clip art libraries can be found on the Web, bundled with some software packages, and on CD-ROM or disk at your local software store.

As a rule, clip art is offered copyright-free, and you can use it any way you want. Some clip art collections are copyright-protected for some uses; be sure to read any copyright notices accompanying any clip art before you publish it in a Web page.

> **Tip:** The CD-ROM with this book includes a collection of clip art images for use as list bullets, bars, and backgrounds, which you learn to add in Hour 14.
>
> Also, Appendix B, "Online Resources for Web Authors," shows the addresses of a variety of great clip art libraries online.

Clip art collections on the Web generally offer their wares by displaying the images in a Web page. You can copy these images directly from the Web page into your page by using the steps shown in the following To Do.

▼ To Do

To Do: Copy clip art from the Web

1. Using Netscape as your browser, visit one of the clip art sites listed in Appendix B. (If you don't feel like flipping to the appendix now, just go to `clipart.com`.)
2. Following links and instructions you see on the page, browse around the site until a picture you want to use appears on your screen.

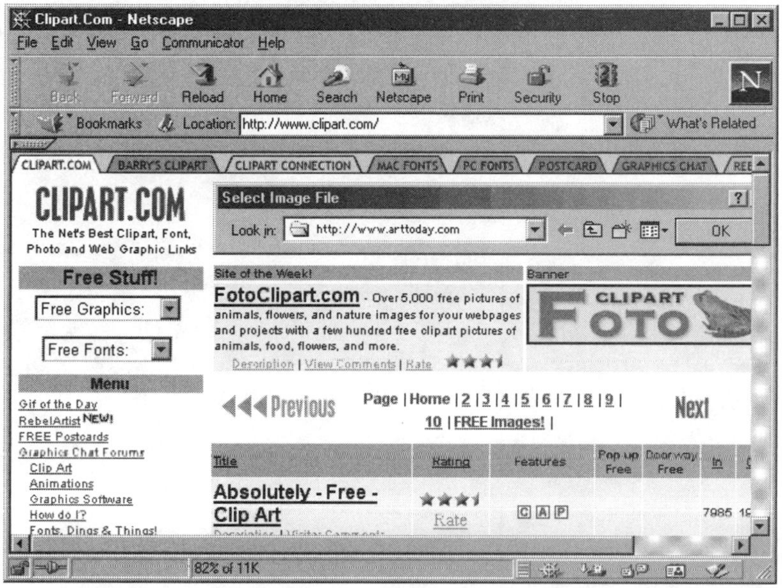

FIGURE 13.3
Step 1: Visit a clip art site.

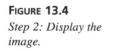

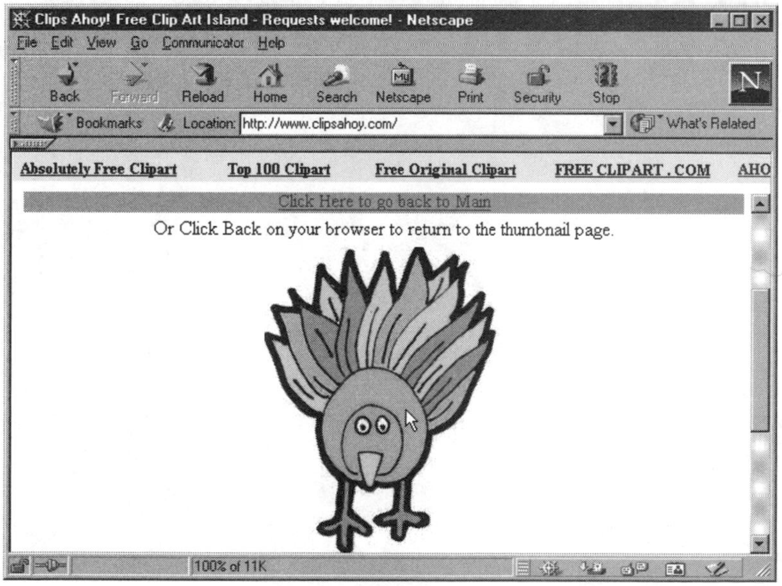

FIGURE 13.4
Step 2: Display the image.

▼

13

3. Right-click the desired image and choose Save Image As from the pop-up menu.
4. Save the file in the same folder in which you stored (or will store) the Web page in which you'll use the image (or be sure to move or copy it there later).
5. Switch to Composer and insert the image into your page as described in Hour 14.

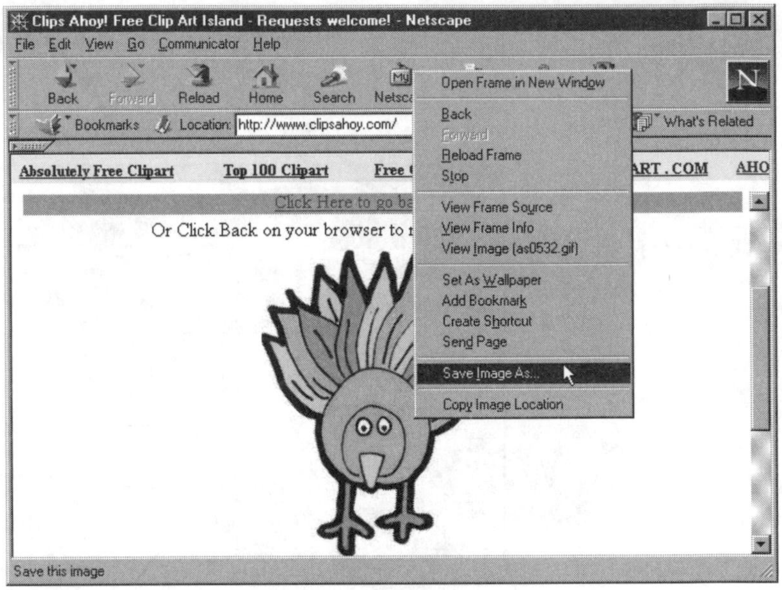

FIGURE 13.5
Step 3: Right-click and choose Save Image As.

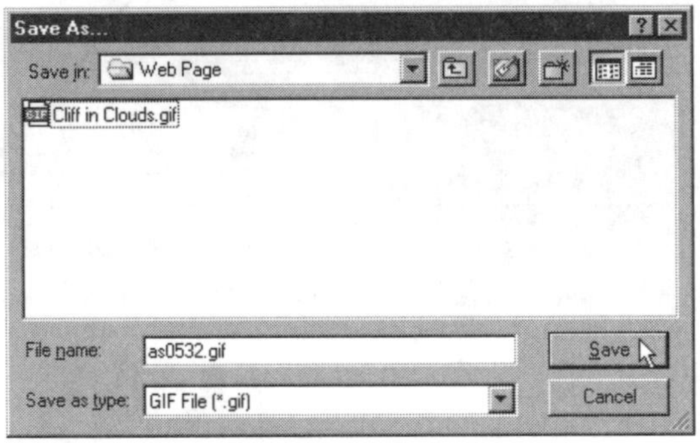

FIGURE 13.6
Step 4: Save the file on your hard drive.

Using Images from the CD-ROM

The CD-ROM included with this book features a handy collection of JPEG images for a range of uses, including some terrific background textures and cool bullets and rules.

In case you want to use the images in your practice pages (or real ones!) as you work through this hour, here's where you'll find them on the CD-ROM. (You can, of course, copy these folders from the CD-ROM to your own hard disk, if you want.)

> In the following disk paths, D: stands for the drive letter of the CD-ROM drive in your PC. For many people, that letter really is D:. But your CD-ROM drive letter might be E: or another letter, depending on how your PC is configured.

- D:\WebGfx contains three folders: Banners (Web banners), Buttons (various styles of navigation buttons you can attach links to), and Textures (background pictures).
- D:\Fun contains a collection of fun images.
- D:\Photos contains three folders of photographic images: Animals, Everyday, and People.
- D:\Backgrounds contains more great images for picture backgrounds.
- D:\Business contains business-related photographs.

> You can insert a picture directly from the CD-ROM into a page. When you publish, Composer publishes the image from the CD-ROM right along with the HTML file.
>
> However, I always recommend copying picture files to the same folder where the HTML file is stored (*before* inserting the picture in the page!), to avoid some kinds of complications that can crop up.
>
> Navigate to the CD folder where the image file is stored and locate the exact picture you want by using the techniques described in the next section, "Previewing Images in Windows." While previewing the image, choose Edit, Copy from the folder's menu bar. Then open the folder containing the Web page file in which you plan to insert the image and choose Edit, Paste.

Previewing Images in Windows

Sometimes, it can be tricky to find the image file you want just from its filename. Any number of terrific programs are available for browsing the images on your hard drive or on a CD-ROM—showing each picture to help you find the one you want.

If you have Windows 98, Windows 2000, Windows Me, or Windows XP (sorry—this feature doesn't work in Windows 95), you can preview any picture just by single-clicking its file icon in a folder; a preview of the picture appears in the folder window, to the left of the file icons, as shown in Figure 13.7. (If you see no preview, choose View, As Web Page from the folder's menu bar.) Previewing pictures this way makes finding and selecting the right picture easier when you plan to insert images in Composer.

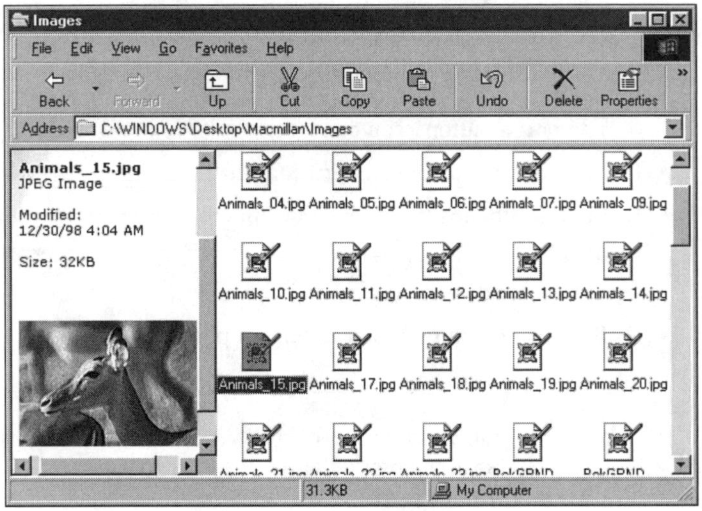

FIGURE 13.7
You can easily preview most image files in recent versions of Windows.

Important Stuff to Know About Inline Images

Before inserting an image into your page, consider the issues described in the next several sections.

File Type

As a rule, try to use GIF files whenever possible. Doing so ensures that almost any visitor using a graphical browser can see the image.

When you want to publish a more photorealistic image or you have a JPEG file you can't get converted to GIF, you can use a JPEG file as an inline image. If you do, be aware that you're hiding that picture from the folks using browsers that don't support JPEG (who are few).

With either GIF or JPEG, your image editor may give you a choice of color model and resolution. Choose RGB as the color model and 72 dpi as the resolution. These settings offer the best balance between appearance and file size.

File Size

In theory, a 20KB image file takes fewer than 5 seconds to travel from a server to a browser over a typical 53Kbps Internet connection. But a host of other factors affect the speed with which an image makes it to a visitor's optic nerve, including the disc access speed of the server, processor speed and available memory in the client PC, performance of the browser software, and multitasking speed.

Still, the one-second-per-4KB rule of thumb is a good way to estimate the speed with which your page will materialize on most visitors' screens. Given that, consider how long you want to make visitors wait to see your whole creation. Popular wisdom says that a typical Web surfer doesn't wait even 20 seconds before moving on—and, of course, popular wisdom is usually wrong. Unless visitors are highly motivated, they might depart early if your page takes as few as 10 seconds to shape up.

Add up the size of your HTML file and all the inline images you plan to add to it. (If you don't know how to do this, you'll learn how in Hour 21, "Publishing Your Page.") The recommended maximum is 30KB—such a page appears, images and all, in about 15 seconds or fewer. Realistically, though, you're wise to try to keep the whole package to around 20KB.

If you find that your page files are too big and slow, the obvious solution is to use fewer images. Other than that, here are some ways to keep your page compact:

- *Use images that take up less area on the page*—Smaller pictures generally mean smaller files.
- *Use fewer colors*—When drawing or painting an image, use as few colors as you can to achieve the desired effect. When working with clip art or scanned images that contain many colors, use an image editor to reduce the number of colors or the size of the *color palette*. Most editors offer options for making color images black and white or for "posterizing" a photograph to give it a graphical look. Either of these options tends to reduce file size dramatically and can result in some nifty effects.

- *Create text-only alternative Web pages*—When your page is heavily graphical, create a second set of all the pages beyond the top page, using the same general content but no graphics. On the top page, provide a link to this text-only version of your page. Visitors with text-only browsers and others who simply don't care to wait for images can use the text version instead.
- *Use thumbnails and external media*—Rather than display large GIF or JPEG images inline, use inline thumbnails (see Figure 13.8) or text as link sources to external versions of the images. That way, visitors have the option of viewing or ignoring the images. Visitors wait more patiently for images they choose to view.

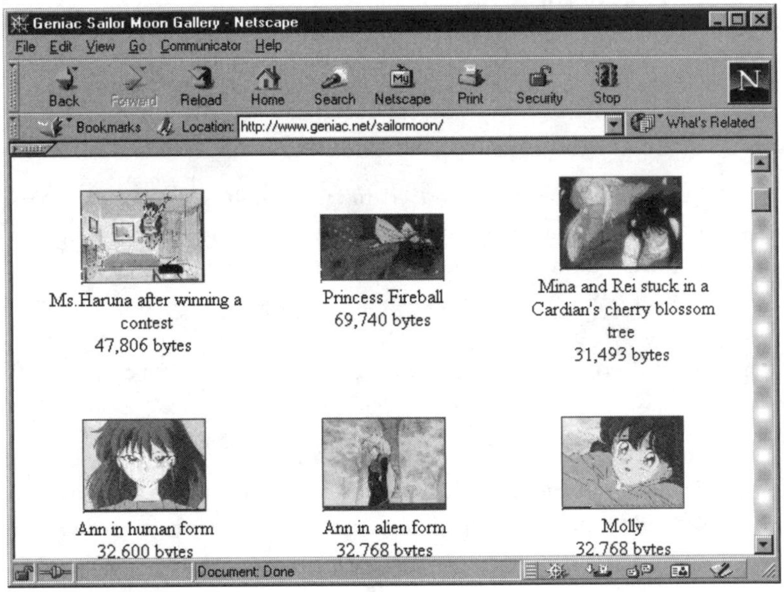

FIGURE 13.8
Thumbnails, small versions of images.

> When creating or editing a JPEG picture, you have the opportunity to choose a quality setting for the image file.
>
> What's "quality"? Well, JPEG files provide you with the option to sacrifice how good the picture looks in exchange for making the file smaller so that it appears on a visitor's screen more quickly. If you decrease the quality setting (as you learn to do in Hour 14), you might be able to dramatically speed up the performance of the Web page without noticeably degrading the appearance of the picture.

Copyrights

The ease with which images can be scanned, converted, copied, or even captured from the Web itself is a natural invitation to copyright infringement—and, in fact, the Web today is rampant with copyright violations. Smart authors are getting better about inserting copyright notices (see Figure 13.9) prominently on their pages to remind visitors that the work they see is not free for copying.

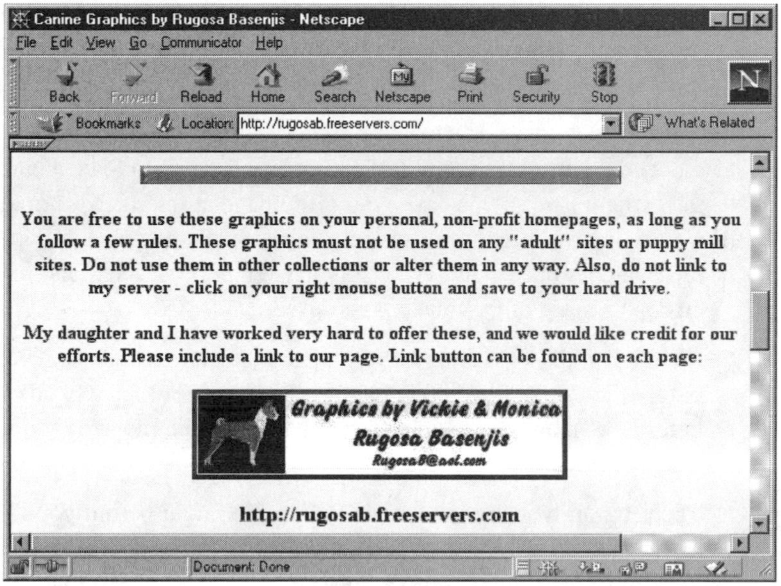
Canine Graphics by Rugosa Basenjis - Netscape
File Edit View Go Communicator Help
Back Forward Reload Home Search Netscape Print Security Stop
Bookmarks Location: http://rugosab.freeservers.com/
What's Related
You are free to use these graphics on your personal, non-profit homepages, as long as you follow a few rules. These graphics must not be used on any "adult" sites or puppy mill sites. Do not use them in other collections or alter them in any way. Also, do not link to my server - click on your right mouse button and save to your hard drive.
My daughter and I have worked very hard to offer these, and we would like credit for our efforts. Please include a link to our page. Link button can be found on each page:
Graphics by Vickie & Monica
Rugosa Basenjis
http://rugosab.freeservers.com
Document: Done

FIGURE 13.9
A copyright notice on a clip art page.

Regardless of whether it was accompanied by a copyright notice, do not publish any image unless

- You created it yourself by drawing or painting it or by photographing it with a digital camera. (Note, however, that publishing a photograph of copyrighted artwork—such as a snapshot of a copyrighted painting in a museum—might violate the copyright.)
- You scanned it from artwork you created or artwork you know to be copyright free.
- You acquired it from a clip art collection whose copyright notice specifically calls the images contained therein copyright-free or states clearly that you are authorized to publish the images. (If the copyright notice requires that you label the image with information about its creator, do it.)

13

If you publish your own artwork on the Web, include on your page a link to a copyright notice in which you reserve the rights to your artwork.

Understanding Interlacing

Interlacing your GIF images is one way to speed up the apparent display of images on your page. Interlacing doesn't affect the final look of the image in your page at all and requires no changes to the steps used to insert or format the image in your page. But interlacing does change the way the image materializes on the screen in some browsers.

A browser that is retrieving a non-interlaced GIF image typically displays an image placeholder until the entire GIF image has been downloaded, and then the browser displays the image. If you save your GIF image in interlaced format, browsers that support interlacing can begin to display the image while downloading it. As the image is retrieved, it appears quickly as a blurry rendition of itself and then incrementally sharpens up as more of the image is retrieved.

Interlacing allows visitors to your page to get an idea of what your images look like before they've finished downloading. If the visitor sees what he or she needs to see before the image comes into focus, the visitor can move on without waiting for the finished graphic.

The program you use to create a GIF image might permit you to save the image either as an interlaced GIF or as a non-interlaced GIF. If the program saves only non-interlaced GIF files, you can use a program such as Paint Shop Pro to convert the file to an interlaced GIF.

In the section "Creating Images in Paint Shop Pro," later in this hour, you'll learn how to save a file in interlaced GIF format.

Understanding Low-Res Versions

Another way to give visitors something to look at before the graphics show up is to use your image editor to save an alternative version of the image in a very low resolution (and with a different name from the high-resolution version). You can then define the *low-resolution version* as the image alternative representation when choosing Image Properties for the high-resolution version (as described in Hour 14).

In browsers that support alternative representations, the low-resolution, alternative image is displayed first, and it appears quickly because decreasing resolution makes the image file smaller. Although the visitor examines the low-res version, the browser loads the full-resolution image in the background and prepares it for display. When the full-resolution image is ready, it replaces the low-resolution version on the page. Like interlacing GIF images, this technique allows visitors to get an idea of what the image represents well before the final image shows up. You can use low-res alternatives for both GIF and JPEG images.

Understanding Transparency

In a GIF image, you have the option to make one color within the image *transparent*. In a Web page, the transparent parts of the image don't show, so whatever is behind the picture—usually a background color or pattern—shows through.

You have to deal with transparency more often than you might think. For example, when you paint a picture in most paint programs (including Paint Shop Pro), the file you create contains not only the parts you paint or draw, but also a white or colored background of a particular size. If you insert the picture in a Web page, the background shows up as a colored square or rectangle behind the parts you painted (see Figure 13.10). However, if you select the image's background color as the transparent color, the background square or rectangle is invisible in a Web page, allowing the page's background to show through.

FIGURE 13.10
In the bottom sample, the image background color is the GIF transparent color, so the page background shows through.

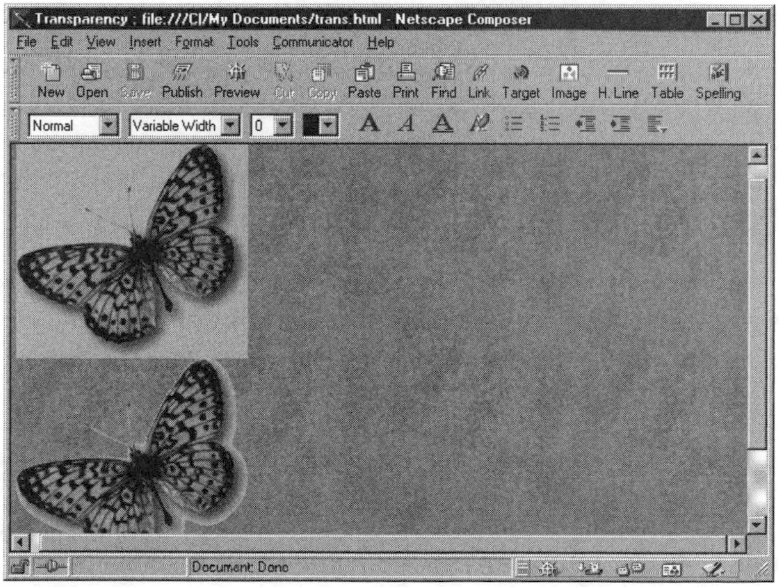

Composer offers no built-in control of transparency; you must select the transparent color when you're creating or editing the image. In the next section, you'll learn how to create images in Paint Shop Pro, including how to choose the transparency color. Many other programs also let you select the GIF transparency color. If your favorite paint program does not, you can simply create an image in that program and then open it in Paint Shop Pro to choose the transparency color.

Creating Images in Paint Shop Pro

The CD-ROM bundled with this book includes a trial version of Jasc Paint Shop Pro, a full-featured paint program you can use to create, edit, and convert images for your Web pages.

In fact, Paint Shop Pro is so sophisticated that I could devote a whole book to it. But you and I have Web pages to write, and, truthfully, if I give you just the basics to get you started, you'll discover the rest of Paint Shop Pro pretty easily on your own.

The next several pages explain the basics of using Paint Shop Pro to create, edit, and format images for use in Composer.

> The section that follows assumes that you have already installed the demo version of Paint Shop Pro from the CD-ROM bundled with this book. If you have not, see Appendix A.

Opening Paint Shop Pro

To open Paint Shop Pro in Windows, choose Start, Programs, Jasc Software, Paint Shop Pro 7 (see Figure 13.11).

Creating and Editing an Image File

To create a new image, open Paint Shop Pro and start a new image file by clicking the New button on the toolbar or choosing File, New.

The New Image dialog box opens, as shown in Figure 13.12.

> In Paint Shop Pro, you don't choose the file type (GIF, JPEG, and so on) when creating the image—you choose the file type when saving it.

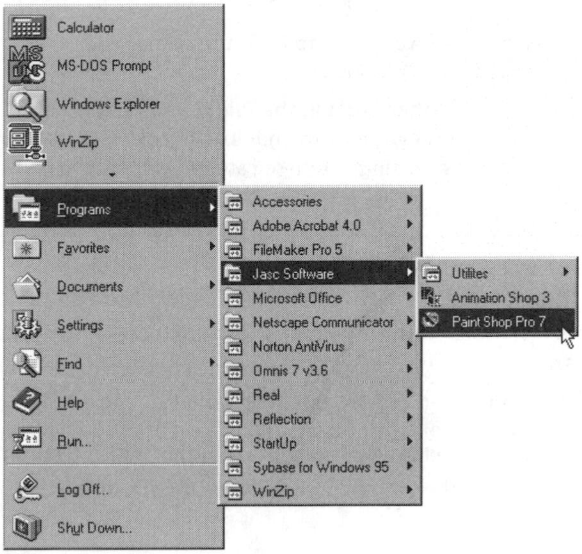

FIGURE 13.11
Starting Paint Shop Pro 7.

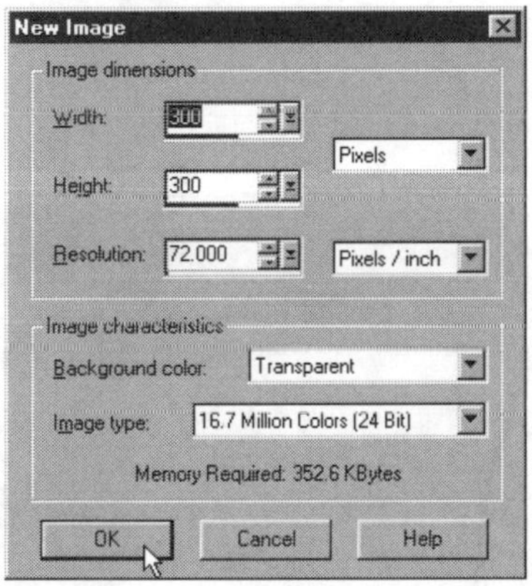

FIGURE 13.12
The New Image dialog box.

In the dialog box, the Width and Height fields define (in pixels) the width and height of the image you will create; you can edit these to your liking or ignore them and adjust the size of the image later. The Resolution box lets you raise or lower the resolution of the image; the default choice, 72 dpi, is a good one for creating images that look reasonably good online but don't inhabit very fat files.

13

> *Remember:* You want to keep the size of your image files low to make your page appear quickly to visitors online.
>
> The larger the values in the Width and Height fields, the higher the resolution, and the greater the number of colors, the larger the file. Always use the lowest settings in these categories that give you an image of acceptable quality.

The Image Type drop-down list offers five choices, from an image type that includes only 2 colors up to 16.7 million colors. Choose 16 colors for simple graphics with few colors, or 256 colors or 256 grays to create more complex, 8-bit images. (GIF files cannot contain more than 256 colors, but JPEG images can.)

Note that after you've made your selections in the Width, Height, and Image Type fields, the dialog box reports the approximate size of the file in bytes (on the Memory Required line).

After completing the New Image dialog box, click OK to begin painting. An empty window opens (see Figure 13.13), flanked by the toolboxes you use to paint and edit your new image.

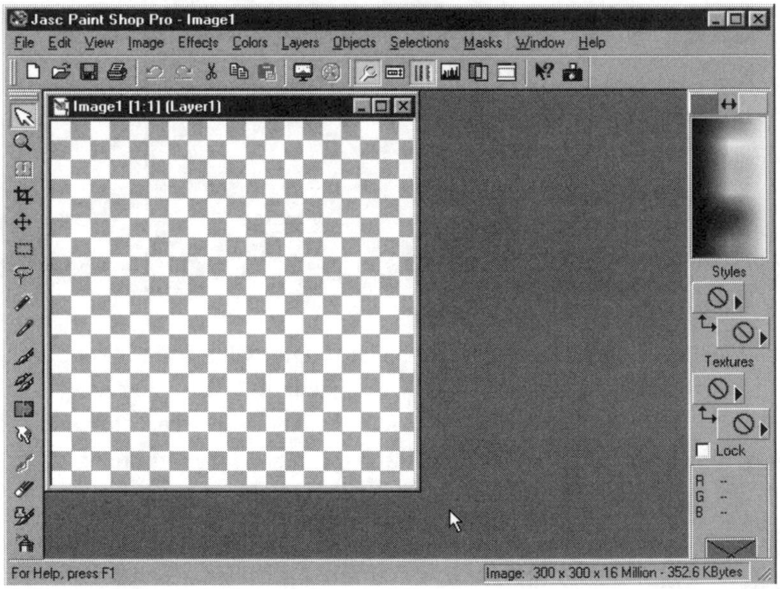

FIGURE 13.13
The New Image window and toolboxes.

Saving a Picture You've Created in GIF or JPEG Format

Soon after you begin creating your image, you need to save it and choose its file type. The following To Do shows how to save a picture in GIF or JPEG format in Paint Shop Pro.

To Do: Save an image and choose its file type

1. Click the Save button, or choose File, Save. The Save As dialog box appears.

> You're smart to store the image files for a page in the same folder in which you will store and edit the page itself (before publishing it on a server).
>
> At any point between Step 1 and Step 4, you can use the Save In list at the top of the Save As dialog box to navigate to the folder in which your Web page files are saved. After Step 4, the picture file is saved there.

FIGURE 13.14
Step 1: Choose File, Save.

2. Type a name for the image in the File Name box. Do not type a filename extension (such as `.gif`); that will be added automatically in Step 3.
3. Drop down the Save As Type list and choose CompuServe Graphics Interchange (GIF) or JPEG from the list. Observe that the appropriate filename extension is added automatically to the filename.

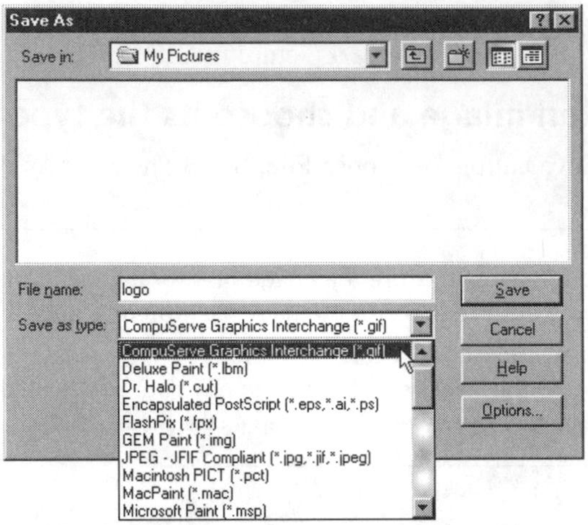

FIGURE 13.15
Step 3: Choose the file type.

4. Click the Save button in the Save As dialog box.

> There are two types of GIF files: GIF 87a and GIF 89a. Whenever a graphics program gives you the choice, use GIF89a, which supports interlacing and animation (GIF 87a does not).

Choosing GIF Interlacing

When saving a GIF file in Paint Shop Pro, you have the option to save it as an interlaced GIF file.

In the Paint Shop Pro Save As dialog box, after choosing the GIF format in the Save As Type list, click the Options button. In the dialog box that appears, click Version 89a and then click Interlaced (see Figure 13.16).

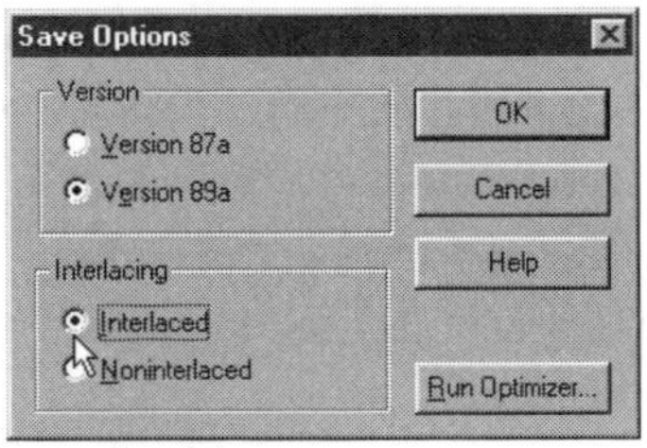

FIGURE 13.16
Choosing GIF interlacing in Paint Shop Pro.

> If you have already closed the Save As dialog box and need to reopen it to choose interlacing for a GIF image file, choose File, Save As.

Setting GIF Transparency

If you have saved a file in GIF Version 89a format (see the preceding section, "Choosing GIF Interlacing"), you can also add transparency.

To choose transparency options for the GIF file, choose Colors, Set Palette Transparency from the Paint Shop Pro menu bar. The dialog box shown in Figure 13.17 opens. Choose a transparency option:

No Transparency—Makes no color in the image transparent; all colors show.

Set the Transparency Value to the Current Background Color—Automatically determines the current background color and sets the transparency color to match so that the image background does not show. Use this option to omit backgrounds from images.

FIGURE 13.17
Choosing GIF transparency options in Paint Shop Pro.

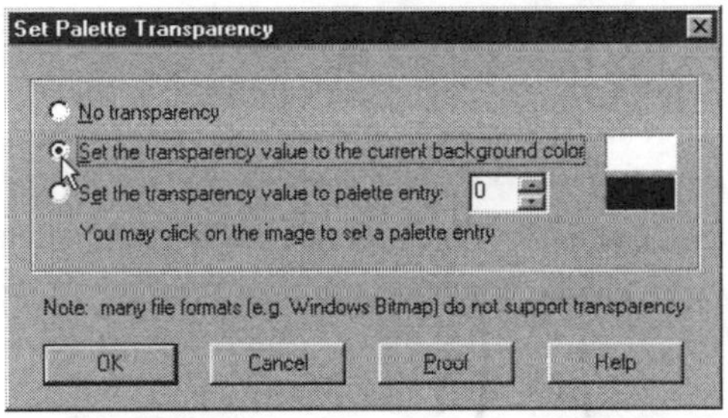

> If you make the background color transparent, never use that color in the foreground. Areas of the foreground using the same color as the background will be made transparent as well. (Of course, you can choose to make parts of the foreground transparent to achieve a special effect.)

Set the Transparency Value to Palette Entry—Enables you to select a specific color from those in the picture to use as the transparent color.

To test the transparency, click the Proof button in the Set Palette Transparency dialog box. After closing the dialog box, you can also test the transparency by choosing Colors, View Palette Transparency from the menu bar.

Summary

As you'll see in the next hour, getting your pictures into your pages is pretty simple. Nearly everything that can go wrong with pictures happens because something is wrong with the file—wrong type, wrong size, and so on. But that won't happen to you now that you know the rules.

Q&A

Q I see that some Web authoring programs can be used to change the size and other aspects of a picture. Should I do my "raw" image editing in a graphics editor like Paint Shop Pro and then fine-tune the picture in my Web authoring program?

A Web authoring programs vary in how well they edit pictures, and some work very well. In Hour 14, you'll learn how to use the Composer tools for changing size, shape, and other image properties. As a rule, you should make a picture exactly the size, shape, and color you want it to be in your graphics editor and then insert it in a page. Use the Web authoring tool only to adjust the picture's position on the page.

Sometimes, using the Web authoring program to edit other aspects of a picture can deliver unwanted results. For example, if you change the size of a GIF with a transparent background within a Web authoring program, often the transparency information is lost in the process. Such anomalies happen when the Web authoring program does not actually change the image file, but rather applies HTML coding around the picture that modifies the way a browser displays it.

HOUR 14

Adding Pictures (and Picture Backgrounds)

Pictures are like salt: Add the right amount in the right way, and your Web page becomes tastier—but add too much, and your visitors will wind up logging off the Internet to go get a soda.

In this hour, you'll learn not only how to add images (and image backgrounds) to your pages and to control the appearance of those images, but also how to use images wisely, for the best effects. At the end of the hour, you will be able to answer the following questions:

- How do I insert images into my Web pages?
- Can I control the alignment, the spacing, and even the size of the images?
- How do I create alternatives to images, for those whose browsers can't display pictures?
- How do I make an image into a link?
- How do I add a background image?
- Can I create fancy bullets for lists and snazzy horizontal lines?

Inserting a GIF or JPEG Image in Composer

Before beginning the steps to insert an image in a Web page, first prepare your image file or files as discussed in Hour 13, "Getting Pictures for Your Page." Be sure that the image file is stored in the same folder as the Web page file in which you will insert it. (If it isn't, move or copy it there before beginning the To Do.)

▼ To Do

To Do: Put an image in a page

1. Click in your page at the spot where you want to insert the image.
2. Click the Image button on the Composition toolbar.

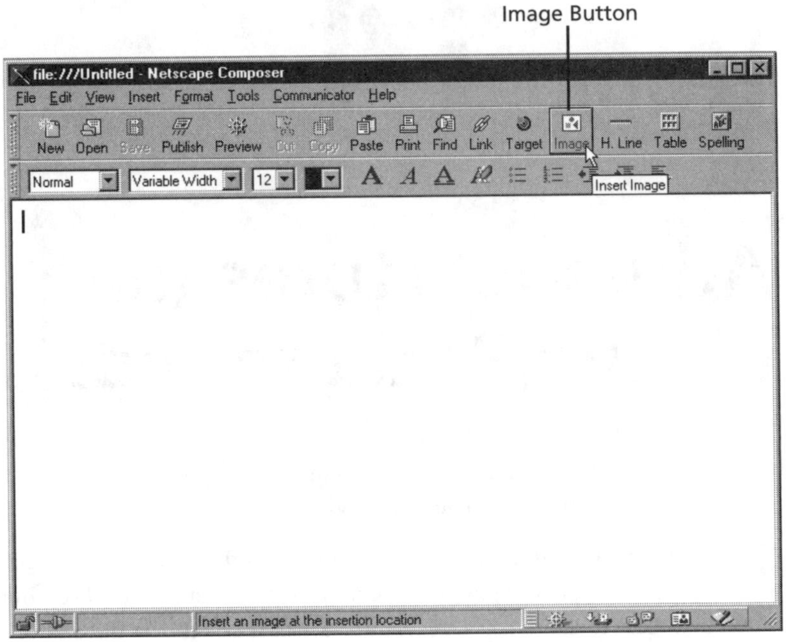

FIGURE 14.1
Step 2: Click Image.

3. Click the Choose File button.
4. Navigate to the folder containing the image file, click its name, and click Open.
5. The Image Properties box shows the filename in the Image Location window. If it's the image you want, click OK. (If not, click Choose File and find the right image.)

▼

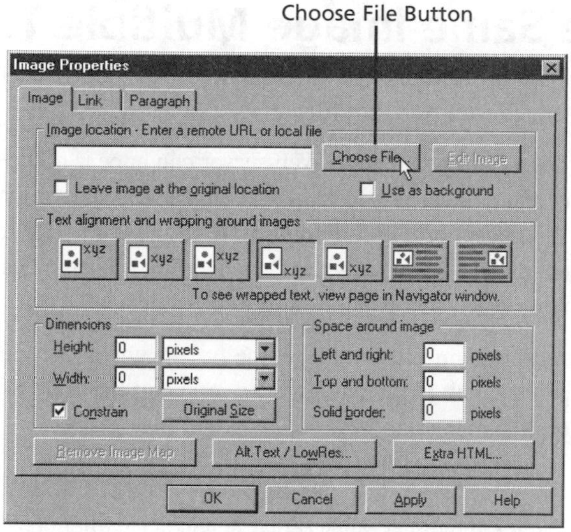

FIGURE 14.2
Step 3: Click Choose File.

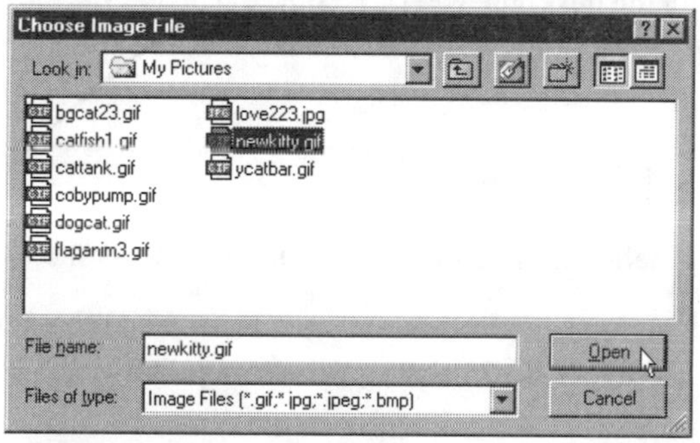

FIGURE 14.3
Step 4: Choose the file.

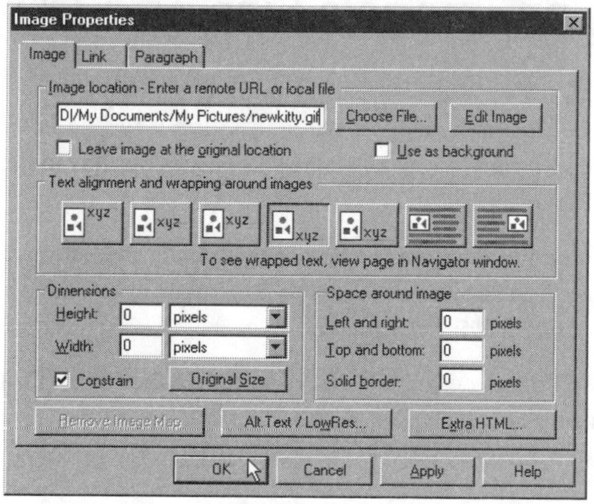

FIGURE 14.4
Step 5: Click OK.

Using the Same Image Multiple Times

If you want to use the same image multiple times in a page, you don't need multiple copies of the image with different filenames.

A single copy of an image file on a Web server can appear in the same page—or in several pages—as many times as you like. Just choose the same filename when inserting each copy of the image, or use copy-and-paste to insert multiple copies of the same image. This technique is especially useful when you use graphical bullets in a list (see "Inserting Fancy Bullets and Rules," later in this hour).

To use copy-and-paste, insert the image one time, right-click, and choose Copy from the menu that appears. Click in the page where you want the copy to go and then choose Edit, Paste from the menu bar.

> You can paste as many copies as you like without having to click Copy again. Until the next time you click Copy, the image stays in the Windows Clipboard, ready to be pasted anywhere you want it.

Deleting an Image

To delete an image, click it once to select it and then press the Delete key.

Note that deleting an image merely removes it from the Web page. The file itself is not deleted; it remains on your hard drive to be used another time.

Choosing an Image's Size and Other Properties

After you've inserted an image (or while inserting it for the first time), you can change its appearance in a variety of ways, all by choosing options in the Image Properties dialog box (see Figure 14.5).

The Image Properties dialog box opens while you are inserting an image, as shown earlier in this hour. You can open the dialog box later for an image you have already inserted by double-clicking the image.

The next several pages describe ways you can use the Image Properties dialog box to change a picture's appearance.

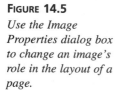

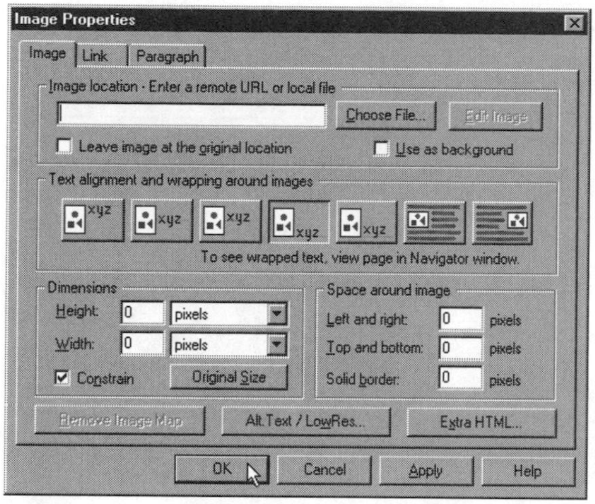

FIGURE 14.5
Use the Image Properties dialog box to change an image's role in the layout of a page.

Changing the Dimensions (Size and Shape) of an Image

From right within Composer, you can change the size of an image, and you can change its shape, stretching or squeezing (and distorting) it, as you learn to do shortly. But first…

As a rule, you get better results if you choose the size and shape of the image in the application used to create it or in a good image-editing program (such as Paint Shop Pro) rather than in Composer or most other Web authoring programs.

Why? Well, Composer can't really change the dimensions of an image. Instead, it applies tags to the HTML file that browsers use to resize the image when displaying it. A browser is not as sophisticated a graphics scaler as a real image-editing program, and the likelihood of unattractive "artifacts" in the scaled image (such as streaks through the image) or a loss of the transparency of a transparent GIF file is high.

With that caveat, the following To Do shows how to change the size and shape of an image in Composer, when doing so seems prudent to you.

To Do: Change the size or shape of an image

1. Double-click the image to open the Image Properties dialog box.
2. Observe the Height and Width boxes shown in the Dimensions area (the numbers show the number of screen pixels) and "guesstimate" how much to change those numbers. For example, if Width is 200 and you want to make the image half as large, you enter 100 for the width. (After you change the width, the height changes

automatically.) Click OK to close the dialog box and see how your picture looks at its new size.

If you don't change both the width and height of the image by exactly the same proportion, the image winds up stretched out of shape, in one dimension or the other. You may choose to do this on purpose, to achieve a particular effect (see Step 5). But if you want to change just the size of the image without changing its shape, make sure that the Constrain box is checked in the Image Properties dialog box.

When Constrain is checked, you need to change only one dimension. Change the width, and the height changes automatically to maintain the picture's original shape at its new size. Change the height, and the width changes automatically.

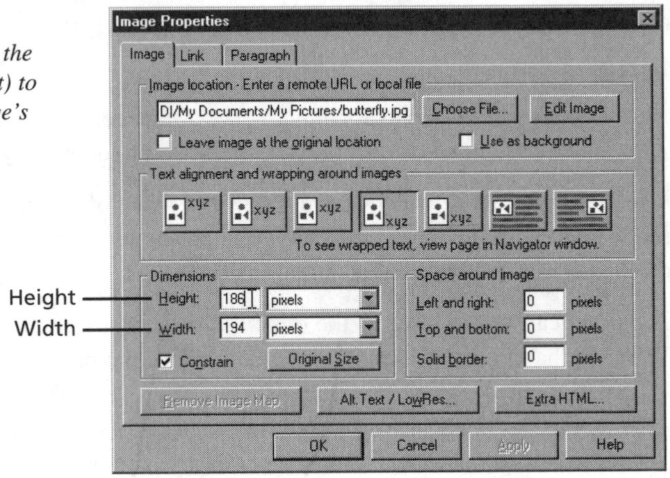

FIGURE 14.6
Step 2: Change the width (or height) to change an image's size.

3. To change the shape of the image, click to clear the Constrain box. Then change the width or height as desired and click OK to see the results.

FIGURE 14.7
Step 3: To change an image's shape, clear the Constrain box and change the width or height.

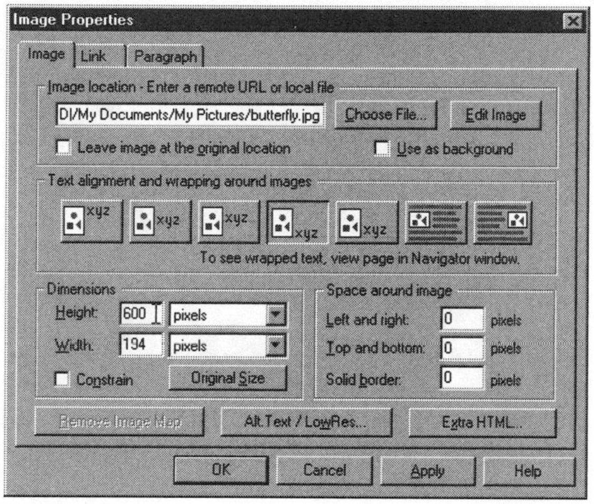

Controlling Alignment

A picture's *alignment* describes its position on the page and how it relates to any text adjacent to it.

By default, a picture aligns to the left side of the page (just like left-aligned text). The first line of any text immediately following the picture appears to the right of the picture, near its bottom. If the text runs for more than one line without an intervening paragraph break, all lines after the first line appear underneath the image. This default alignment is called *bottom* alignment (see Figure 14.8).

> To understand alignment options, you need to understand what the baseline of text is. The *baseline* is the line the letters sit on when you write them. Most letters appear entirely above that line, but a few—such as lowercase *j* and *y*—have descenders that drop down below the baseline.
>
> The default, bottom alignment, aligns the baseline with the bottom of the image so that any descenders drop lower than the bottom of the image.

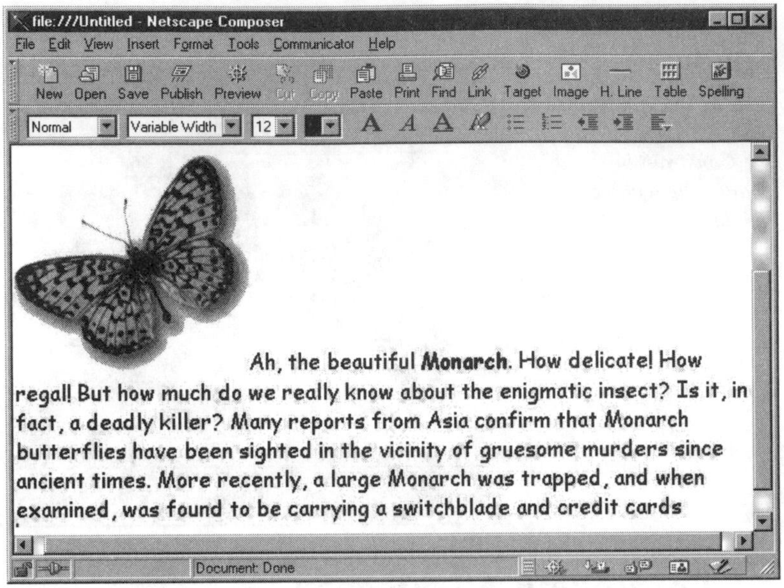
file:///Untitled - Netscape Composer
File Edit View Insert Format Tools Communicator Help
New Open Save Publish Preview Cut Copy Paste Print Find Link Target Image H. Line Table Spelling
Normal
Variable Width
12
Ah, the beautiful Monarch. How delicate! How regal! But how much do we really know about the enigmatic insect? Is it, in fact, a deadly killer? Many reports from Asia confirm that Monarch butterflies have been sighted in the vicinity of gruesome murders since ancient times. More recently, a large Monarch was trapped, and when examined, was found to be carrying a switchblade and credit cards
Document: Done

FIGURE 14.8
The default alignment for images, known as "bottom" alignment.

To change a picture's alignment, choose from the options in the Align Text to Image box in the Image Properties dialog box. The other choices (besides At the bottom) are:

- At the top—The first line of text appears to the right of the top of the image, with the top of the text aligned to the top of the image. Any lines after the first line appear underneath the image.
- In the center—The first line of text appears to the right of the image, with the baseline of the text aligned to the vertical center of the image. Any lines after the first line appear underneath the image.

The bottom two alignment options, Wrap to the Left and Wrap to the Right, are special "wrapping" options. Unlike all the other options, which can put only the first line of text alongside the image, right and left allow multiple lines of text to appear alongside a picture:

- left—Text wraps alongside the image, with the image to the left of the text (text on the right).
- right—Text wraps alongside the image, with the image to the right of the text (text on the left); see Figure 14.9.

FIGURE 14.9
Left alignment and right alignment (shown here) allow multiple lines of text to wrap alongside an image.

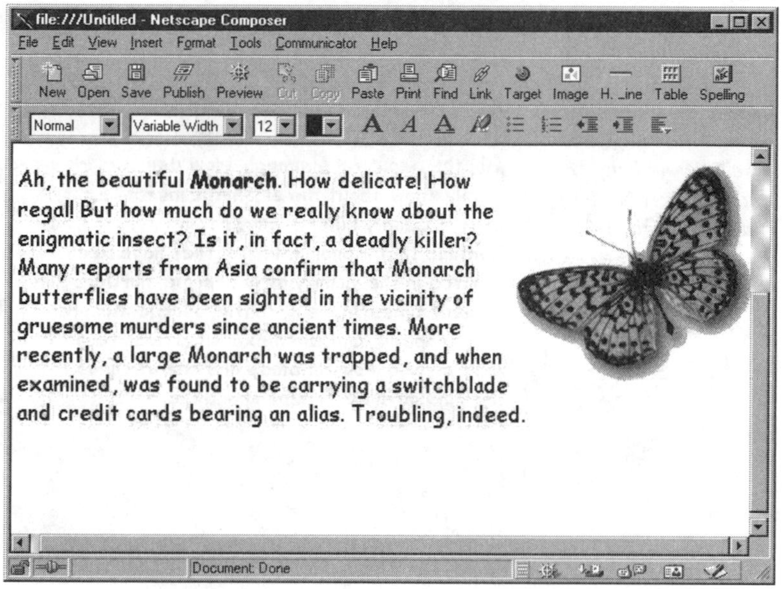
file:///Untitled - Netscape Composer
File Edit View Insert Format Tools Communicator Help
New Open Save Publish Preview Cut Copy Paste Print Find Link Target Image H. Line Table Spelling
Normal
Variable Width
12
Ah, the beautiful Monarch. How delicate! How regal! But how much do we really know about the enigmatic insect? Is it, in fact, a deadly killer? Many reports from Asia confirm that Monarch butterflies have been sighted in the vicinity of gruesome murders since ancient times. More recently, a large Monarch was trapped, and when examined, was found to be carrying a switchblade and credit cards bearing an alias. Troubling, indeed.
Document: Done

All the alignment options are represented reasonably accurately when you view a page in Composer, but sometimes the representation is not 100 percent accurate. Always evaluate your alignment formatting by viewing the page in a Web browser.

Controlling Spacing and Borders

To add a border around a picture, or to change the amount of space between the image and what's around it, use the spacing options in the Image Properties dialog box:

- To increase the space between the sides of the image and adjacent text, tables, or other objects, enter a number of pixels in the Left and Right boxes.
- To increase the space between the top and bottom of the image and adjacent text, tables, or other objects, enter a number of pixels in the Top and Bottom boxes.
- To add a black border all around the image (see Figure 14.10), enter in the Solid Border box a number of pixels for the thickness of the border.

Typing 4 in the Solid Border box makes a nice, bold border like the one shown in Figure 14.10. A lower number makes a finer border; a higher number, a thicker one. A border thicker than about 8 pixels is probably overkill.

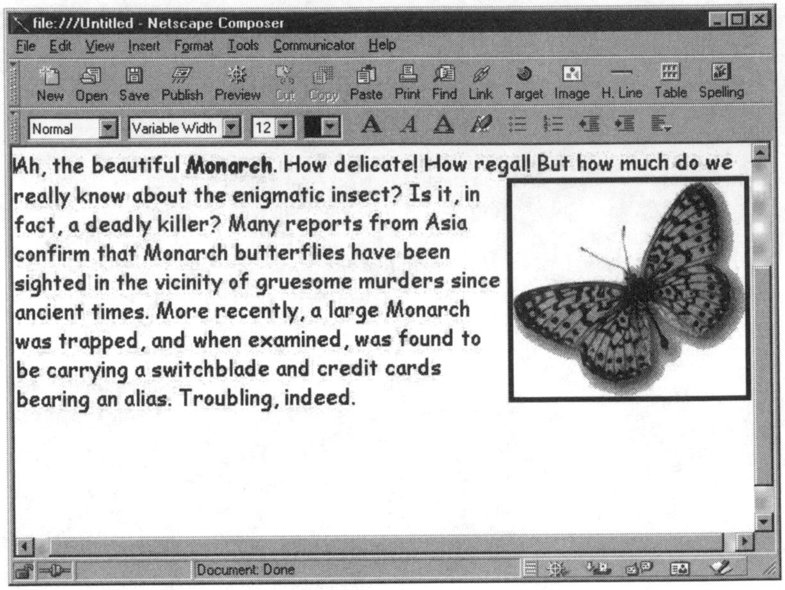
file:///Untitled - Netscape Composer
File Edit View Insert Format Tools Communicator Help
New Open Save Publish Preview Cut Copy Paste Print Find Link Target Image H. Line Table Spelling
Normal
Variable Width
12
Ah, the beautiful Monarch. How delicate! How regal! But how much do we really know about the enigmatic insect? Is it, in fact, a deadly killer? Many reports from Asia confirm that Monarch butterflies have been sighted in the vicinity of gruesome murders since ancient times. More recently, a large Monarch was trapped, and when examined, was found to be carrying a switchblade and credit cards bearing an alias. Troubling, indeed.
Document: Done

FIGURE 14.10
The same page shown in Figure 14.9 but with additional space around the image (30 pixels left and right) and a 4-pixel border indicated in the Image Properties dialog box.

Entering Alternative Text

You can help some visitors cope with your images by entering alternative text in the Image Properties dialog box (see Figure 14.11).

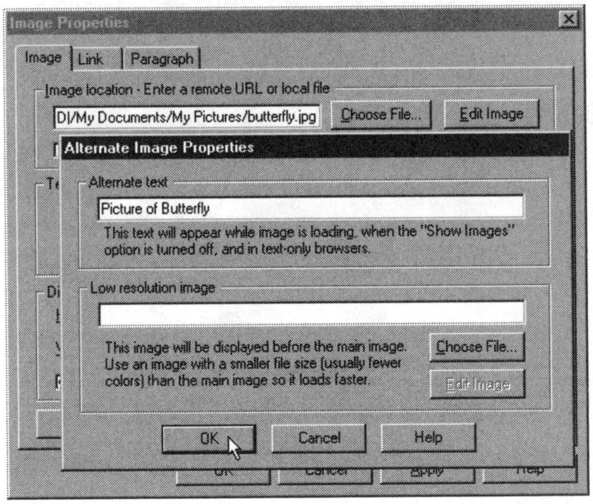
Image Properties
Image
Link
Paragraph
Image location - Enter a remote URL or local file
D|/My Documents/My Pictures/butterfly.jpg
Choose File...
Edit Image
Alternate Image Properties
Alternate text
Picture of Butterfly
This text will appear while image is loading, when the "Show Images" option is turned off, and in text-only browsers.
Low resolution image
This image will be displayed before the main image. Use an image with a smaller file size (usually fewer colors) than the main image so it loads faster.
Choose File...
Edit Image
OK
Cancel
Help

FIGURE 14.11
You can use alternative text to help some visitors with slow connections or non-graphical browsers.

Alternative text is any block of words you want to appear in place of the graphic in browsers that do not support graphics. Try to supply informative text to replace the idea that was originally communicated by the image. Also, many browsers that support text alternatives display an image placeholder, something like `<image>`, if you don't supply a text alternative representation. The text alternative is not only more informative in such browsers, but also better looking.

Entering Images in Table Cells

You put an image in a table cell (see Hour 8, "Organizing Text with Tables and Rules") exactly as you put one in a page. The only difference is that you must first click in the cell to position the edit cursor there. You can then click the Insert Image button and insert the picture exactly as you would anywhere else in a Web page.

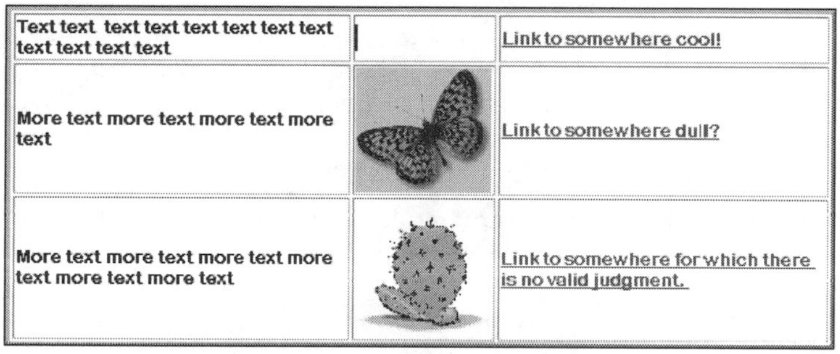

Text text text text text text text text text text text text
Link to somewhere cool!
More text more text more text more text
Link to somewhere dull?
More text more text more text more text more text more text
Link to somewhere for which there is no valid judgment.

FIGURE 14.12
To insert a picture in a table cell, click in the cell just before clicking Insert Image.

Inserting Fancy Bullets and Rules

No doubt you've seen some highfalutin' pages that feature cool, multicolored graphical bullets and horizontal lines. These objects are not actual bullets and lines of the kind you create with the list buttons and the H. Line button. Instead, they're just inline images that *look* like bullets and lines (see Figure 14.13).

> You'll find a great selection of GIF image files for fancy bullets and rules on the CD-ROM at the back of this book.

Line-type images, sometimes called *bars*, are simply inserted between paragraphs. The bullets are inserted before individual lines of text, using any paragraph style other than List. (If you use List, you get your cool bullets *plus* the list's bullets or numbers. Icky.)

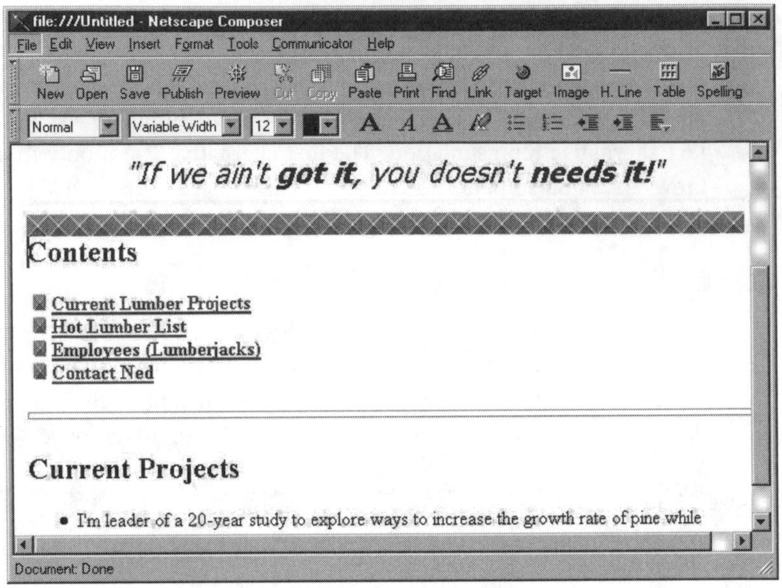

FIGURE 14.13
Fancy bullets and rules are just image files used in place of horizontal lines and list bullets.

To get the best results when inserting a bullet image next to a line of text, align the image using At the Center alignment.

Using an Image As a Link

As you learned in Hour 9, "Understanding Links," every link has two parts: the *link text* (the thing a visitor sees and clicks) and the *link location*, the URL (or local path and filename) to which the browser goes when the link is clicked.

Making an image into a link is just a matter of attaching the link location to an image. In fact, it's exactly like creating a text link; the only difference is that you select an image rather than a block of text before clicking the Link button.

To Do: Make an image into a link

1. Click to select the image you want to make into a link.
2. Click the Link button on the Composition toolbar.
3. Use the dialog box to create any of the types of links you learned to create in Hour 11, "More Ways to Link"—a link to a Web page, an email address, or an anchor, for example.

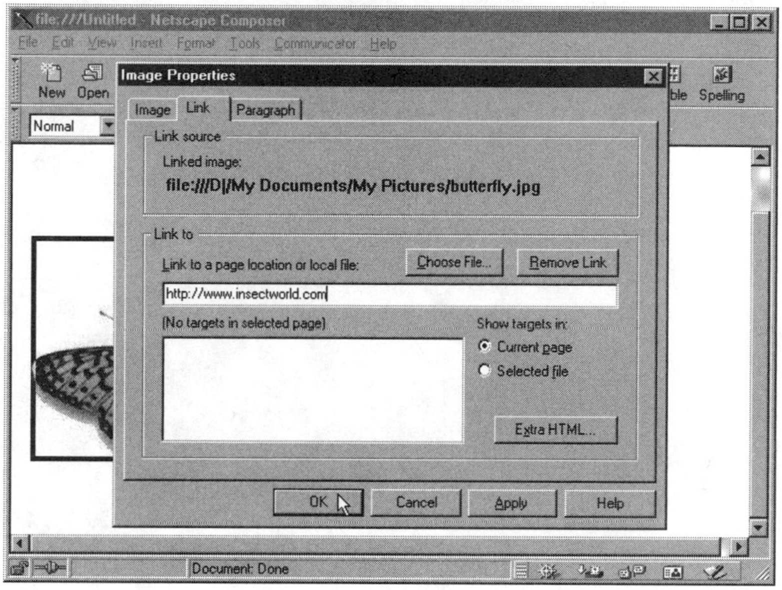

FIGURE 14.14
Step 3: Fill in the Link tab of the Image Properties dialog box for an image link exactly as you would for a text link.

Adding a Picture Background

As an alternative to a background color (which you learned to add in Hour 5, "Choosing a Title, Text, Colors, and Other Page Basics"), you can apply as a background a *tiled image*, an image file (GIF or JPEG) repeated across the entire background.

> An image background automatically supercedes a background color. If you create an image background, any selection you may have made for the background color is irrelevant.

When this image has been designed carefully to match up perfectly with its mates at all four corners, the tiling creates a seamless "texture" effect, as if one enormous image covered the background (see Figure 14.15). Fortunately, the effect is created from only one small image; accessing an image file large enough to cover a page would choke most Internet connections.

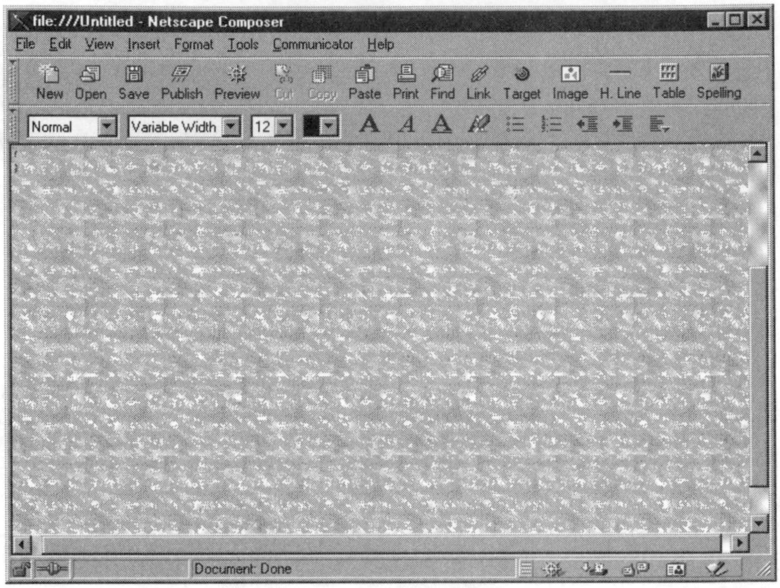

FIGURE 14.15
A tiled background texture.

You'll find a selection of image files for background textures on the CD-ROM at the back of this book.

You can choose, as an alternative to a background texture, to tile an image that doesn't match up perfectly with its copies at the edges. Using this technique, you can create some fun background effects, as shown in Figure 14.16.

Be careful with backgrounds. If you don't choose carefully, you can wind up making your text illegible, or at least hard on the eyes.

Use custom text colors (see Hour 5) to contrast the text with the background. Use light colors to stand out against dark backgrounds, and dark colors to stand out against light backgrounds.

Even with those precautions, a tiled-image background is usually too much when seen behind a page with lots of text on it. A way around this problem is to use a snazzy tile background behind your logo or brief text on a top page and then switch to a solid color or no background on text-heavy pages to which the top page links.

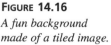

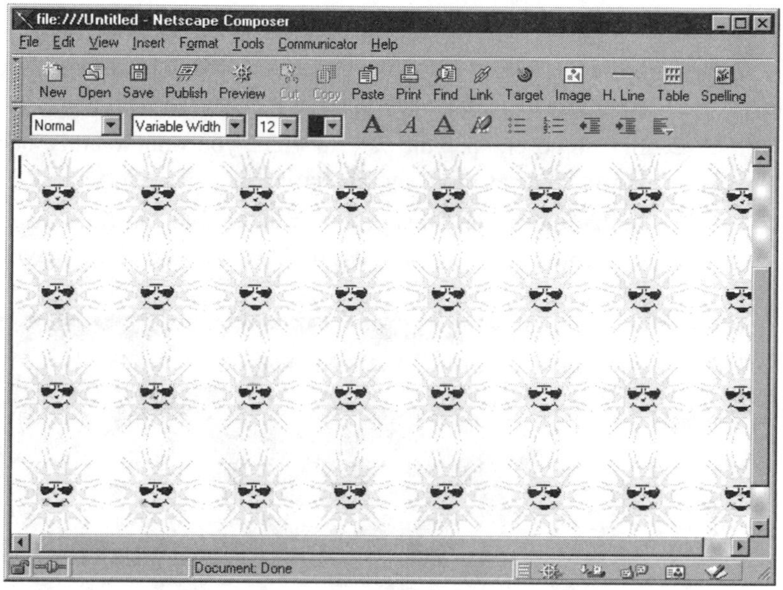

FIGURE 14.16
A fun background made of a tiled image.

Finally, you can use as a background a single, large image file that covers the entire page background (and thus requires no tiling). Be careful when using this technique to use an image with a low resolution and few colors to keep the image size small and the page's appearance fast.

Many "full page" background images do not actually cover the full background; rather, they often take the form over very tall, narrow bars. Because the bar is so tall, the browser does not tile it and left-aligns it on the page. The file itself is reasonably small, yet it lends a graphical flair to the whole page without obscuring text.

> Tiled background images automatically supercede a background color because they cover the whole background.
>
> But if you use a nontiled image and the image does not happen to fill the background, you might use a background color along with it. The background color affects only the portion of the background not covered by the image.

▼ To Do

To Do: Add a picture background

1. Store the GIF or JPEG image you want for a background in the same folder as the page in which you want to use it.
2. In Composer, open the page to which you want to add a background and click Format, Page Colors and Properties.
3. In the Background Image box on the Colors and Background tab, type the filename of the image you want to use (or click Choose File to navigate to it) and click OK.

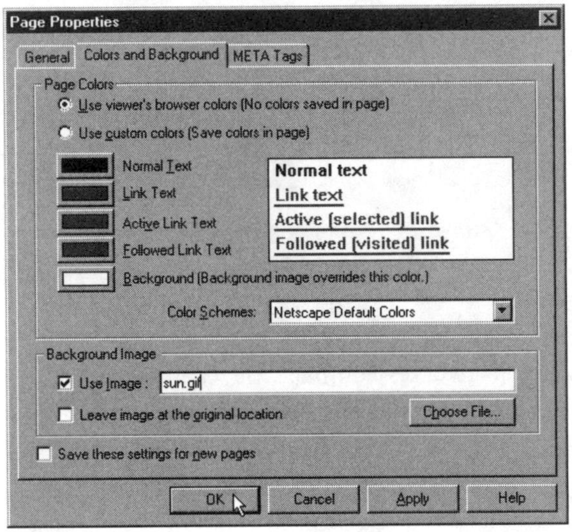

FIGURE 14.17
Step 3: Type the filename of the background image.

▲

Summary

In the cookie that is a Web page, images are the chocolate chips. And as we all know, the best cookie strikes just the right chip-to-cookie ratio—too many chips is as bad as none at all. (Replace with your favorite ratio-balancing analogy: pizza crust:cheese, peanut butter:jelly, RAM:processor speed, or longevity:fun, for example.)

The issue is not just whether you use graphics or how many you use, but *why* you use them. Do the images add something useful to your page—like photos of people the page is by or about or images of products and places described—or are they mere decoration? An image or two added for the sake of style is worthwhile, but only if the image succeeds in actually enhancing style. If the image seems like a generic one dropped there merely for the sake of having an image, dump it. Dress your page with careful text formatting, the natural beauty of solid organization, and strong writing.

Q&A

Q You sure are a downer about images. But on the coolest, award-winning pages out there, I see lots of graphics. Aren't you being a little puritanical here?

A Perhaps—and yes, some great, highly graphical sites are out there. But for every slickly produced, award-winning site, a hundred others overuse pointless graphics or obliterate text with poorly chosen background textures. The award winners use all their graphics smartly and to a purpose.

My point is not to discourage the use of images. I just want you to ask yourself the right questions before dumping any old image on your page. You can bet that the award winners do.

14

HOUR 15

Snazzing Up Your Page with Sound, Video, and Special Effects

At the simplest level, adding a little multimedia zip to your pages is extremely easy, requiring mostly Web authoring skills you already possess. But beyond a few simple tricks, Web multimedia gets pretty heavy and quickly escapes the scope of this book.

So, this hour offers two kinds of new wisdom: First, it shows how you can quickly add a little sizzle to your pages through some easy techniques. Then it introduces you to the big, fat, hairy world of external media, beginning (but by no means completing) your Web multimedia education without going so far as to blow any of your circuit breakers.

At the end of this hour, you'll be able to answer the following questions:

- How does external media work, and what can I do with it?
- How do I choose external media types to serve either the widest possible Web audience or a tightly targeted audience?
- How do I insert links to external media in my Web pages?
- How do I add the few available types of inline multimedia (such as inline video and background sounds)?

> A couple of important kinds of multimedia have been left out of this hour, both well within your capabilities and both coming up in later hours:
>
> You'll learn all about creating and using animated GIF images in Hour 16, "Creating Your Own Animations." In Hour 17, "Editing HTML," you'll learn how to use HTML Assistant Pro 2000, a program on the CD-ROM, to add video, sound, and scrolling marquees to your page by writing HTML code (that's not as scary as it sounds!).

About External Media

Unlike such *inline* multimedia files as background sounds or inline GIF images, *external* media files are not displayed or played automatically when a visitor accesses a Web page. Instead, external files are downloaded to the visitor's PC and displayed or played there only when the visitor executes a particular link.

Think of it this way: If it's integrated into the layout of the page (or plays automatically, if it's a sound), it's *inline*; if the visitor has to do something to show or play it, it's *external*.

New Term *External media* refers to media files—images, video clips, sound clips, and documents, for example—to which links in a Web page point.

Often, the browser does not play or display the file itself. Instead, a helper application or plug-in opens to do the job. Some browsers have native support for some types of files, but when the file is set up as external media, the effect is the same as if a helper application were used.

For example, Internet Explorer and Netscape Navigator both have native support for JPEG image files; these two programs can handle JPEGs as either inline or external media. But when a JPEG image is supplied as an external file, it has no home on the page—the browser doesn't know where to put it. So despite the browser's ability to display a JPEG image inline, the browser opens an empty window to show a JPEG image accessed as an external file (see Figure 15.1).

FIGURE 15.1
Viewing an external JPEG image through a browser with native JPEG support.

What if the visitor's browser has no native support and no helper application for a particular external media file? When the visitor clicks the link, the browser usually offers the option to download and save the file on a disk. That way, the visitor can install an appropriate application later to play the file offline. Because unplayable files are downloaded and saved, text-only browser users can still capture media files from the Web and then play them later in an application or a system that supports them.

Understanding Media Types

(Yes, I know, Dan Rather is a media type… but you won't learn about him here. Stay with me.)

Using techniques for embedding external media, you can build links to any type of file, from video and sound clips to the dynamic link library (DLL) files used by Microsoft Golf.

Although video and sound clips might be playable by the visitor, the DLL files from Golf are useless (except to Golf). The important question is not "What can I supply as external media?" but rather "What can the browsers and helper applications out there actually play or display?"

Unfortunately, external media file types have a tendency to be system-specific, or at least favored by certain systems. Some types of files play only in Windows, and others only in Macintosh, for example. More commonly, a type of file works across multiple systems but is favored by one system. For example, Video for Windows (`.avi`) video clips play natively in Windows but require a special player on a Macintosh.

When you're faced with a choice between formats that don't reach everyone, you have four options:

- Use the most widely supported format, even if it is not universally supported.
- Choose the file type most easily supported by your target audience. For example, professional graphic artists tend to use Macintoshes. If your page and its external media files are aimed at that community, choose file types that favor the Macintosh.
- Don't assume that visitors always have the latest software. For example, recent versions of Windows Media Player (which is often opened by Windows browsers to play files they don't play natively) play MP3 sound files and Mac (QuickTime) video clips. But older versions don't, and only a small slice of the Windows users online have upgraded to the latest version.
- Offer multiple versions of your media files, each in a different format (see the section "Tips for Proper Presentation," later in this hour).

Images

As explained in Hour 13, "Getting Pictures for Your Page," the main image file formats for inline graphics in Web pages are GIF and JPEG. Although GIF and JPEG images can be used inline, there's no reason that you can't offer them as external media instead; in fact, you have some good reasons to do so.

Suppose that you have lots of graphics you want to show—for example, pictures of products you sell or head shots of your employees or family. Inserting many such images inline dramatically increases the time required to transmit your full page to a visitor. In such a case, consider using a minimum number of inline images in a page that's compellingly organized and written. Then offer your images as external media, from a menu or from *thumbnails* (see the section "Tips for Proper Presentation," later in this hour).

Offering images as external media has other advantages as well. When you're using inline images but want to avoid building a page that takes a week to appear on the visitor's screen, you must compromise the appearance of the images by using fewer colors and making the images fairly small (covering a small area).

When images are external, you can publish the highest-quality images you want—even full-screen, photorealistic, 24-bit color JPEG images. (True—when the visitor clicks the link to view such images, the wait for such a picture to appear can be long. But by the time a visitor chooses to see external media, he or she has already been pulled into your document and is much more likely to wait patiently.) Professional artists who publish their portfolios on the Web nearly always offer their work as external JPEGs so that they can show the best.

Although GIF and JPEG are the only image formats supported inline, any other image format can be used externally. There is, however, one caveat: GIF and JPEG have been favored for a reason. They are broadly supported across the principal graphical systems—Windows, Macintosh, and X Windows. Other image file types tend to be supported by applications on one or two systems, but rarely on all three. So although you can offer these alternative image formats, you should convert these and publish them as GIF or JPEG files whenever possible.

- *Publisher's Paintbrush (PCX) and Windows Bitmap (BMP)* (the principal graphics formats used in Windows (3.1 and above)—Graphics created in the Windows Paint program or in Paint Shop Pro can be saved in either format. Any Windows-based graphical browser that uses helper applications can display external PCX and BMP files because Paint can be used as the helper. The Macintosh world has some application support for PCX files, but very little for BMP. As a rule, use PCX or BMP formats only when your intended audience includes only Windows users.
- *Tagged-Image File Format (TIF or TIFF)*—TIFF files are a longtime standard for scanned images, and most scanning software saves TIFF files (along with other formats). TIFF files are great for high-resolution images destined for printing but tend to be rather large as external media in comparison to other formats. TIFF files are used on all types of systems but are not widely supported by applications other than desktop publishing programs.
- *Macintosh Picture (PIC or PICT)*—A Macintosh picture file. The Macintosh has native support for PICT, so any Macintosh visitor to your page can display PICT files. But PICT support is rare beyond the Macintosh world.
- *PNG*—A cross-system format that can be displayed on many systems and browsers but is not yet recognized as a standard for inline Web graphics. Still, as a widely supported format, it's probably your third-best choice (after GIF and JPEG) for a widely viewable external image file format.
- *XBM*—An X Window bitmap image. X Window systems and most other graphical interfaces to Unix environments have native support for XBM, so almost any visitor using a Unix system with a graphical interface can display XBM files. However, XBM support is rare beyond the Unix world.

Video

Three principal video file formats appear on the Web. Each offers acceptable video quality (by the standards of computer-based viewing), and all three can include audio with the video. MPEG offers the best overall quality, but MPEG files are generally larger than comparable files for similar clips in the other formats.

The three video file formats are described below:

- *Video for Windows (AVI, or Audio-Video Interleave)*—AVI files, which include both picture and sound, are the standard for video clips in all versions of Windows. AVI is also the required format for inline video (see Hour 17). The Windows 98/Me/2000 Media Player program has native support for AVI, whereas Windows 3.1 users must install a Video for Windows player to play AVI files. Macintosh users can install players for AVI as well (or use a browser that supplies native AVI support, such as Internet Explorer), but outside the Windows world, MPEG and MOV files are supported far better.
- *Motion-Picture Experts Group (MPG, or MPEG)*—This format is an independent standard for high-quality audio and video. An MPEG player is required on any system type (recent versions of the Windows Media Player for Win 95/98/NT/Me/2000 can play MPEG files, but many users have not upgraded to that player). Still, because MPEG offers such high quality and because so many MPEG clips are on the Web, most surfers interested in using video have installed an MPEG player.
- *QuickTime (QT or MOV)*—QuickTime is the Macintosh video standard, the Apple counterpart to Video for Windows. All Macintoshes have native support for QuickTime, whereas users of other systems usually must install a player or plug-in (or use a browser that supplies native support). For example, Windows users can install a free QuickTime player from Apple, and the latest version of Windows Media Player can play QuickTime movies.

In addition to these standard file types, other types of video and audio file types that are common on the Web are *proprietary*—you can create them only if you purchase a particular vendor's program.

For example, you might have watched RealVideo clips or live broadcasts or listened to RealAudio in your travels online. You can create such files only with software purchased from the Real Networks company (`www.real.com`). You might also have visited "shocked" sites loaded with interactivity and multimedia and requiring a Shockwave plug-in in your browser. You can create such sites only with software from Macromedia (`www.macromedia.com`).

As you grow as an author, you might choose to begin working with such advanced formats. But their cost and complexity greatly exceed any real benefit to the beginning Web author. Stick with the nonproprietary audio and video formats for now. You can easily create these with the software included with most sound cards and video-capture cards for PCs.

Audio

Audio is perhaps the most confusing area of Web multimedia. Many formats are available now, and a few more emerge each year as developers try to improve the quality or download speed of audio information.

You can use Web search tools to search for archives of sound clips in much the same way you search for clip art.

More often, sound clips are found on pages to which the sound is related. For example, to find sound clips from your favorite TV show, you need to find a site about the TV show.

Although some browsers contain native support for some sound formats, the effect is the same as when a helper application is used. A pop-up window opens with controls for the sound, such as Play or Rewind. The following are the most common sound file types:

- *Basic audio (AU or SND)*—The most common sound format; several browsers and most audio player helpers provide native support for Basic audio. Although Basic audio offers only so-so sound, its combination of wide support and relatively small file size make it the recommended media type except when high audio quality is required.
- *Windows Sound Clip (WAV)*—The sound clip standard for Windows. The audio quality is about the same as Basic audio, but the format is not well supported outside Windows. WAV is best used for distributing sounds to Windows users and is the required format for background sounds (see Hour 17).

Using your PC's sound card and a microphone (or the sound card's audio inputs), you can record your own Windows wave files, for use as external sounds or as background sounds (see Hour 17).

Most sound cards include their own audio recording program; alternatively, you can use the built-in Windows sound recorder by clicking Start and then choosing (in Windows 98/Me/2000) Programs, Accessories, Entertainment, Sound Recorder. (In Windows 95, you open Sound Recorder by choosing Programs, Accessories, Multimedia, Sound Recorder.)

- *MP3*—Short for MPEG Level 3, a relatively new format that can carry CD-ROM–quality digital sound online. It's not as widely supported as the other sound formats yet, but might be within a year or two. MP3 support is included in the latest version of Windows Media Player, and dozens of shareware and freeware MP3 players are available online. You can also find shareware and freeware programs for recording your own MP3 files.

MP3 is the subject of ongoing controversy. Because of its CD-ROM–quality sound, the format has been widely used for distributing perfect copies of popular recordings—some authorized by the copyright holders, some not. The record industry is working feverishly to get some control of the flow of MP3 files online, and changes in the format are imminent.

To Do: Link to external media

1. Prepare the external media file and store it in the same folder as the Web page file.
2. Create the link source in either of two ways:
   - Compose text for the link source.
   - Insert an image for the link source.

FIGURE 15.2
Step 2: Create the link source.

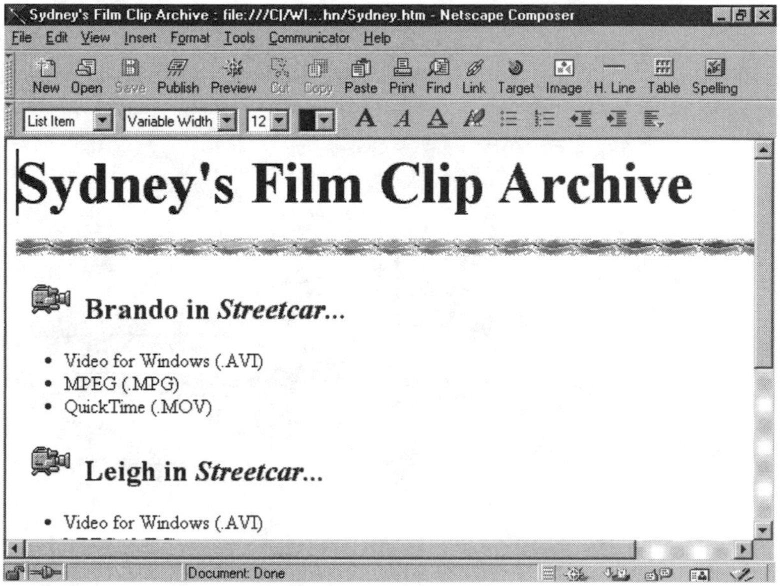

3. Select the link source (by highlighting the text or clicking the image).
4. Click the Link button on the toolbar.

FIGURE 15.3
Step 4: Click the Link button.

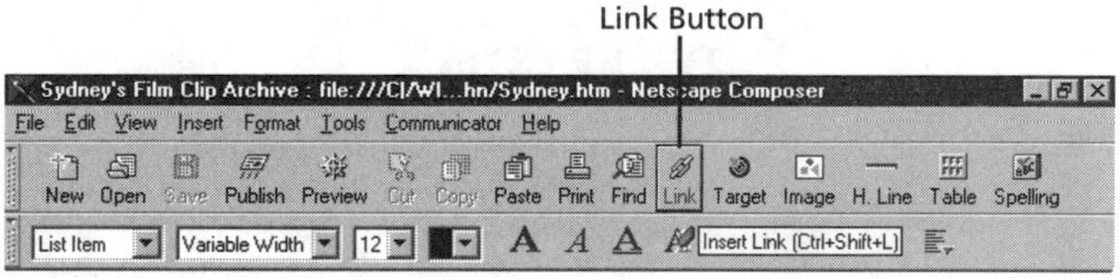

5. Click the Choose File button.
6. Open the Files of Type list and choose All Files.
7. Browse to the folder where the media file is located, select the file, and click the Open button.
8. Click OK on the Link tab of the Character Properties dialog box.

FIGURE 15.4
Step 6: Choose All Files from the Files of Type list.

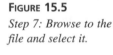

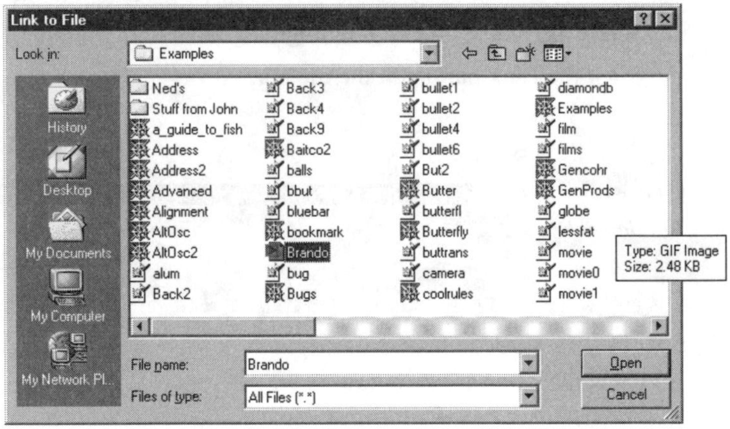

FIGURE 15.5
Step 7: Browse to the file and select it.

Tips for Proper Presentation

As you can see, making the link to external media is simpler than creating or acquiring the media file in the first place. But the secret to the effective use of external media isn't setting up the link and file. The secret is presenting the link to external media in an attractive, inviting, and useful way.

The next few sections offer tips for properly presenting your external media.

Show File Type and Size

Whenever you're offering external media, always show the file type and its size (see Figure 15.6) as part of the link (or very close to it) so that visitors can make two decisions before clicking a link in your document:

- Do I have the necessary software to play, display, or run a file of this type?
- Do I have the time or patience to download a file of this size?

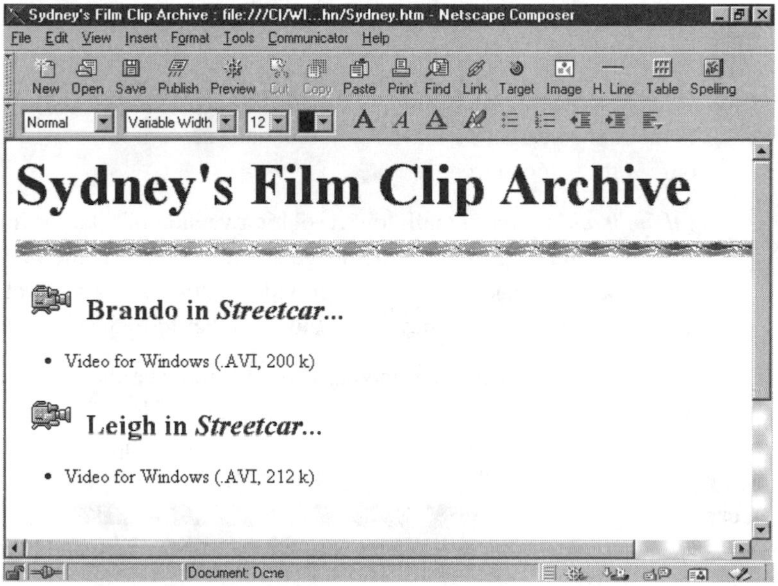

FIGURE 15.6
File type and size of an image linked to external media.

Keep in mind that many Web surfers are still novices, especially when it comes to dealing with external media types. Configuring helper applications baffles many browser users, so they just don't do it. You can make your document newbie-friendly if, in addition to showing the file size and type, you do the following:

- Describe what the file type means and what's required to use the file. Don't just say that the file is AVI; say that the file is a Video for Windows (AVI) file that requires Windows 95/98/NT/Me/2000 or a Video for Windows player in Windows 3.1 or Macintosh systems.
- Tell visitors where they can find the helper applications they need in order to play or display your file. If you know of a good source online, you can even provide a link to that source. That way, a visitor who wants to use your external media file but lacks the right software can jump to the helper application source, get the right

helper, and then return to your page. (The visitor can also download and save your external media file, go get the helper, and then play or display the file later, offline.)

Use Descriptive Images as Link Sources

In addition to labeling a link to external media with its file type, you should use an image that represents the file type as the link source. For example, a camera icon makes a great link source for any video clip. A sound-related icon, such as an ear or speaker, visually informs visitors that the link leads to a sound file.

Show Inline Thumbnails for Large External Images

As mentioned earlier in this hour, thumbnails are a great way to create meaningful link sources for external images.

A *thumbnail* is a very small, low-resolution version of a larger image. The thumbnail appears on the page as an inline image and also serves as the link source to the larger, full-resolution image. Thumbnails provide visitors with a general sense of what the full image looks like so that they can decide whether to bother downloading it.

As with any link to external media, you must indicate the file type and size along with the thumbnail. If a group of thumbnails all link to files of the same type and of about the same size, you can describe the files once for the group, as shown in Figure 15.7.

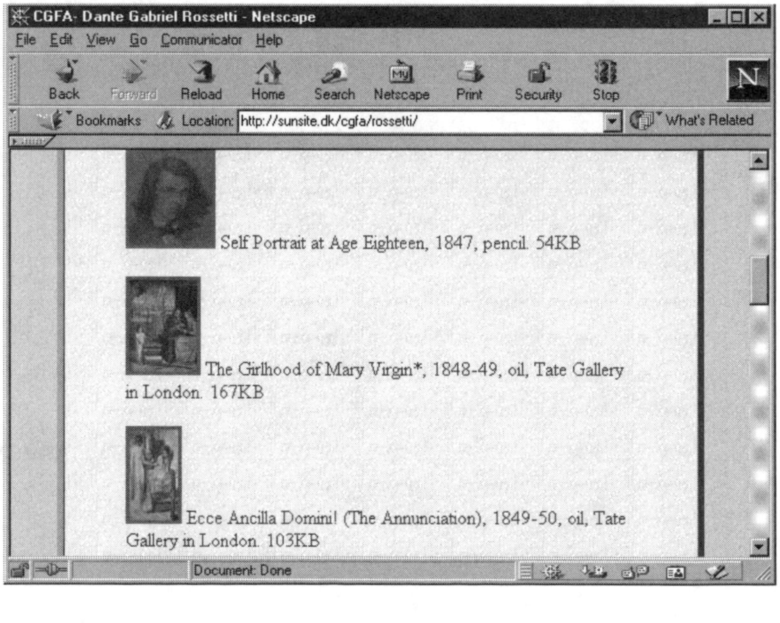

FIGURE 15.7
Thumbnails linked to larger JPEG images.

Summary

Embedding external media files in Composer is a snap: Make sure that the file is in the right place and build a link, and you're done. The only way you can blow it after that is if you forget to copy the media file to the server when you publish your page—and Composer can even make sure that you get that part right (see Hour 21, "Publishing Your Page").

The tricky part is creating or choosing the right type of file to reach either the broadest possible audience or the specific audience you most want to reach. PCs are more common in homes than Macintoshes, so if you're trying to reach homes, it helps to slant your file choices to whatever makes Windows happy. Many, many corporate users, especially those in engineering and technical departments, are on Unix systems with X Window interfaces. Web authors often overlook the Unix crowd when choosing media types. If your message is aimed at that crowd, try to aim your media files that way, too.

Q&A

Q If a video clip or other file I like is already available through a link on another Web page, can I simply link to it rather than supply my own file?

A Sure you can, and doing so is quite common. You do, however, have to follow a couple of rules:

First, as always, email the Webmaster of the site to which you will link and ask permission to link to the site and file.

Second, avoid linking directly to the file. Instead, link to the page on which the link appears. After all, the site providing the file is doing you a favor—the least you can do is give visitors a glimpse of the site's message before retrieving the link. Also, if the site is using the file in violation of a copyright (something that's difficult for you to find out), linking to the page rather than the file better insulates you from sharing the blame for the violation.

When you do create the link, you can use Composer's support for cut-and-paste to easily copy the link into your document (see Hour 10, "Making Links").

HOUR 16

Creating Your Own Animations

Ever visit a Web page where you see a spinning logo, steam rising from a picture of a coffee cup, or graphical rules that flash, strobe, and dance? You might not have known it, but you were experiencing *animated GIFs*, a special kind of inline GIF image file that moves when viewed through a Web browser.

You're about to learn how easy it is to create these puppies all by yourself. At the end of this hour, you will be able to answer the following questions:

- What's an animated GIF?
- How do I insert an animated GIF into a page?
- How do I create the various frames that serve as each step of the animation?
- How do I combine the frames into a single, animated file?
- How do I customize aspects of the way the animation plays, such as how quickly the animation flips through the frames?

About Animated GIFs

Animated GIFs are exactly what they sound like: GIF images that move. Unlike with other types of multimedia files discussed in this chapter, you can incorporate an animated GIF into the layout of a Web page and control the image's alignment, borders, and other formatting just like any other inline image [see Hour 14, "Adding Pictures (and Picture Backgrounds)"].

Unlike a regular GIF file, an animated GIF can *move*—well, a little. An animated GIF is not a suitable vehicle for a Disney film. Rather, animated GIFs provide very short, simple animations that add a little zip to a page without slowing its download to a crawl. A candle flickers. A cartoon bomb explodes. A horizontal line flashes and undulates. This kind of stuff is what animated GIFs do best.

The hands shown in Figure 16.1 are an animated GIF; they clap. (I can't prove it on paper, but it's true.) In this Web page, I paired this animated GIF with a *background sound* (see Hour 15, "Snazzing Up Your Page with Sound, Video, and Special Effects") of applause.

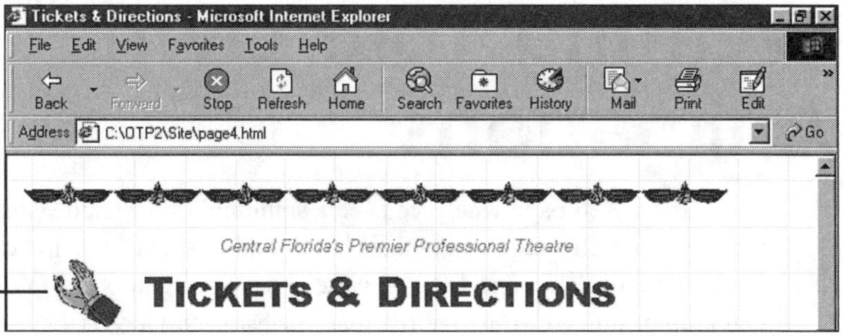

FIGURE 16.1
These hands clap (honest!).

> To find the addresses of some good clip art sites for animated GIFs, see Appendix B, "Online Resources for Web Authors."
>
> To learn how to copy an image—even an animated GIF—from a Web clip art library to your PC, see Chapter 13, "Getting Pictures for Your Page."

The best way for beginning authors to get animated GIFs is to pick them up as clip art. Dozens of clip sites on the Web feature animated GIFs (see Figure 16.2). You copy these from the Web (copyrights permitting!) by following the exact steps you use for doing so with any GIF file, animated or not (see Hour 13, "Getting Pictures for Your Page").

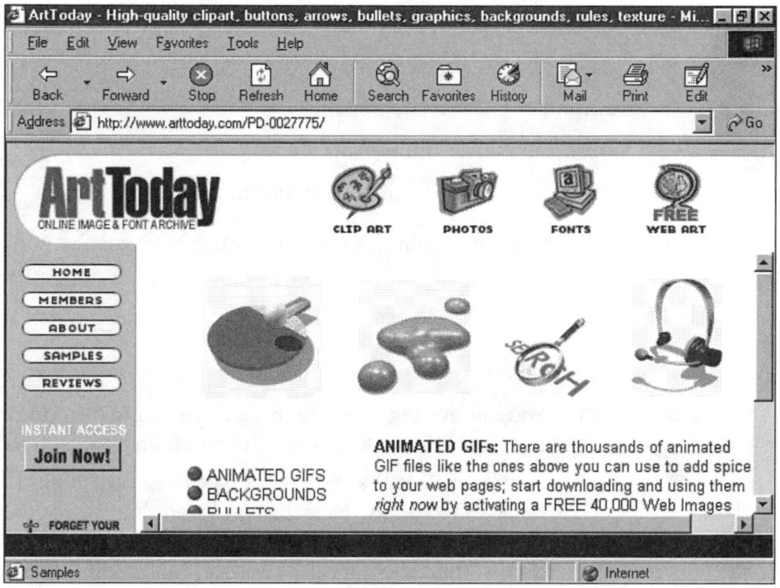

FIGURE 16.2
Animated GIFs are easy to find online, and you can copy them to your PC and use them in your pages using the same steps you use for non-animated pictures.

> You can use recent versions of Microsoft Word and Microsoft Publisher to create Web pages (see Hour 4, "Starting Pages in Other Programs"). Note that these programs include a clip art library on CD-ROM that contains a selection of motion clips, which are nifty little animations.
>
> The motion clips are not animated GIFs; they're another type of animated graphic. However, when you use Word (97, 98, or 2000) or Publisher (98 or 2000) to create a Web page, any motion clips you've inserted are automatically converted into animated GIFs.

Inserting Animated GIFs into Pages

After you have an animated GIF file you want to use, insert it in your Composer document just like any other inline image, by using the Image button.

> Composer does not include full WYSIWYG support for animated GIFs. When you insert an animated GIF in a page in Composer, the picture appears to be a static, non-animated one. When you preview the page in a browser, you see the animation play.

After inserting an animated GIF, you treat it in Composer like any other inline GIF image. Using exactly the same techniques used for ordinary GIFs, you can

- Position the GIF on the page
- Choose the way text aligns to it
- Add extra space or a border around the GIF

You make most of these changes using the Image Properties dialog box, which opens when you double-click the animated GIF image in your page. To learn more, review Hour 14.

> You can use the Windows drag-and-drop feature to drag an image (such as a clip art library) from a Web page into a page you're creating in Composer.
>
> I didn't explain that before, in part because I think that it's easier (and more reliable) to follow the steps I provided than to use drag-and-drop, especially when you consider all the finagling with window sizes you must do to make drag-and-drop practical.
>
> Another reason is that when you drag an animated GIF from one page to another, it loses its animation—it arrives in the page as an ordinary GIF. You can safely drag animated GIFs from one spot in a page to another, but not from page to page.

Creating Your Own Animated GIFs

If you want to create your own animated GIFs, you have two major steps to perform. Although an animated GIF is a single file, it is made up of multiple *frames*, just like a piece of movie film.

Each frame is slightly different from the others (see Figure 16.3); when the frames appear in rapid sequence, the illusion of a single image in motion is created. (Most animated GIFs are made up of a dozen frames or fewer.)

FIGURE 16.3
Like all animation, animated GIFs start out as a series of separate images, or frames.

The two steps in creating an animated GIF are

1. Creating the separate frames
2. Combining the frames into one animation file

Making the Frames

You create each frame as a separate GIF file. For example, using Paint Shop Pro, you could create a single, static GIF image of a closed blossom. After saving that image, you could edit it to show the blossom opening slightly and then choose File, Save As to save the edited version as a new file. You could continually edit and save new versions of the file to create a series of separate images that, viewed in sequence, show the flower bloom.

If you want a quick way to practice animation, create a series of images as described in the following To Do and then combine those images into an animation as described later in this hour. The simple animation you're creating makes your name appear to spin around.

To Do: Create a series of images for an animation

1. Open Paint Shop Pro from the Windows Start menu by choosing Programs, Jasc Software, Paint Shop Pro.
2. Start a new image (choose File, New).
3. In the New Image dialog box, enter or select:
   - 1 inch for both the width and height
   - 72 pixels per inch for the resolution
   - Background Color for the background color
   - 16 Colors for the image type

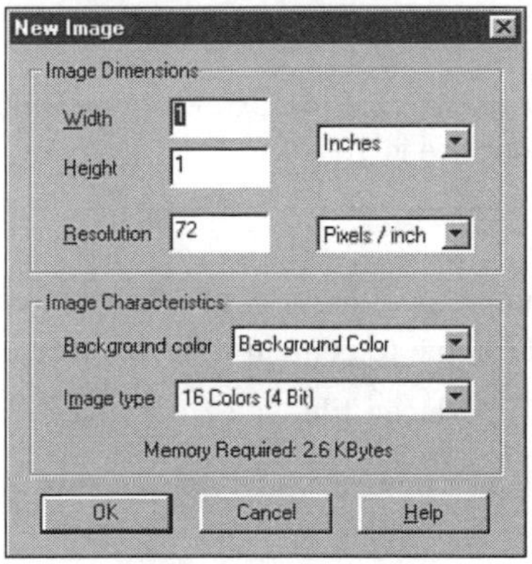

FIGURE 16.4
Step 3: Configure the first image file.

4. Click OK in the New Image dialog box and then choose View, Zoom In by 5 to make the image appear larger (so that it's easier to work with).
5. On the Tool Palette, click the Text tool.

FIGURE 16.5
Step 5: Click the Text tool.

6. Click anywhere in the image.
7. Choose any font and style you like, and choose a size of 16 or 18 (if your name is longer than four letters) or 20 if you have a short name. Then type your name and click OK.

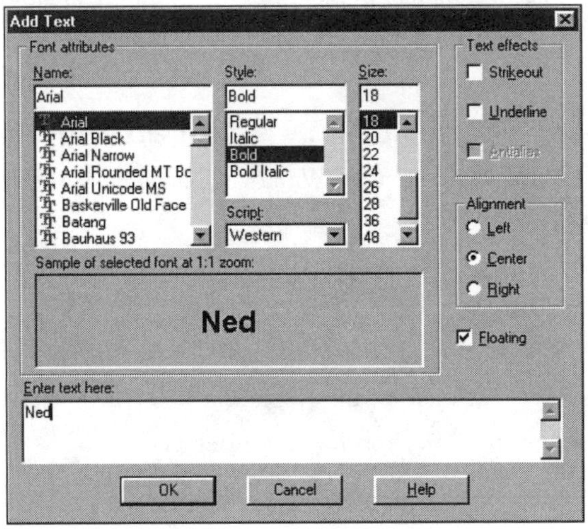

FIGURE 16.6
Step 7: Choose a font and size, and type your name.

If after Step 8 your name is too wide to fit in the window, start over and choose a smaller font size in Step 6.

8. Drag the outline of your name to where it is nicely centered in the window and click. Then right-click your name to cement it in its place.
9. Save the file as a GIF 89a interlaced file (see Hour 14). Name it **`name1.gif`**.

FIGURE 16.7
Step 9: Save the file as `name1.gif`.

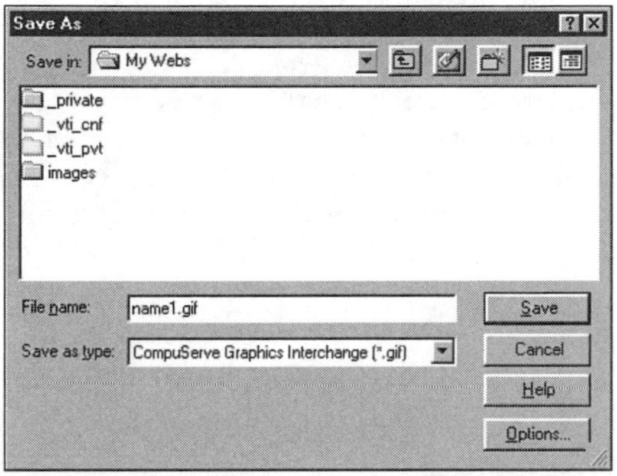

10. Choose Image, Rotate.
11. Click the Free option and type **`30`** (to rotate the image 30 degrees).

FIGURE 16.8
Step 11: Rotate 30 degrees.

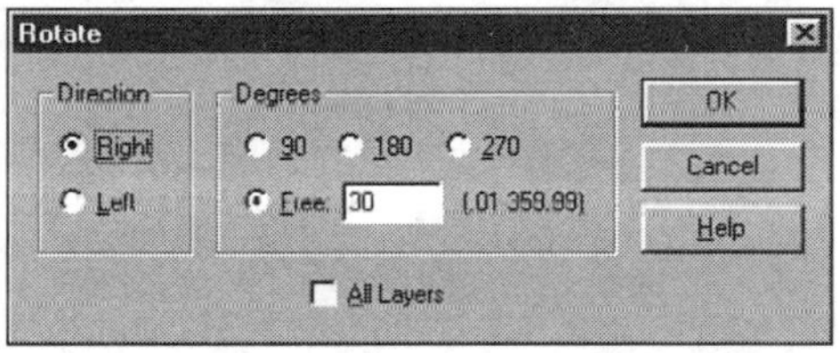

12. Choose File, Save As and save the file under a new name: **`name2.gif`**.
13. Repeat Steps 10–12 until you have rotated the name almost completely around. (Your last save should be **`name12.gif`**.)

Turning Multiple Frames into One Animation

After you've created the series of frames, you must combine them into a single animated GIF file. Doing so requires a special utility program.

One such program, Animation Shop, is included on the CD-ROM with this book. (The program is a part of Paint Shop Pro, so it is installed when you install Paint Shop Pro.) You can often acquire other, similar utilities from links on clip art sites that offer animated GIFs.

The following To Do shows how to use the Animation Shop Animation Wizard to combine a series of images into an animation.

> Animation Wizard offers quite a few options along the way for changing the way the animation is created. To help you learn quickly, and also because most of the time the preselected, default option is the one you want to choose anyway, I won't stop to explain every option. Besides, you can change any of these optional settings at any time after finishing the wizard.
>
> Leave most of these options alone until you gain some basic experience. When you want to know what each option does, consult the Animation Shop Help.

To Do: Combine GIF pictures into an animation

1. Open Animation Shop from the Windows Start menu by choosing Programs, Jasc Software, Animation Shop.
2. Choose File, Animation Wizard.
3. Click Next in this dialog box and also in the one after it.

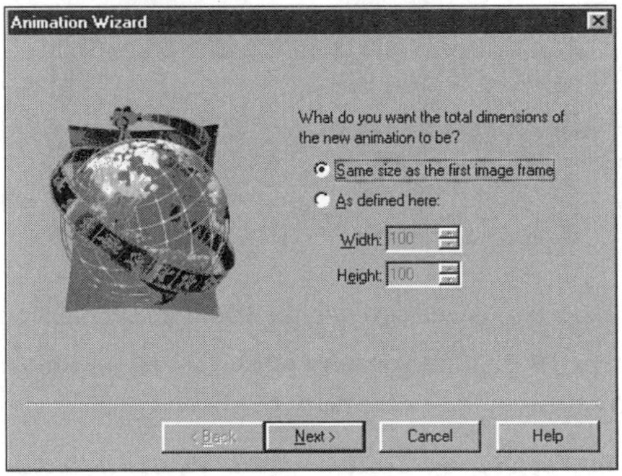

FIGURE 16.9
Step 3: Click Next in this dialog box and in the next one.

4. Choose Centered in the Frame and With the Canvas Color, and then click Next.
5. The wizard asks whether you want the animation to *loop* (play continuously, over and over, as long as the visitor views the page) or play a particular number of times and stop. Choose Yes, Repeat the Animation Indefinitely, and then click Next.

FIGURE 16.10
Step 4: Choose Centered in the Frame and With the Canvas Color, and then click Next.

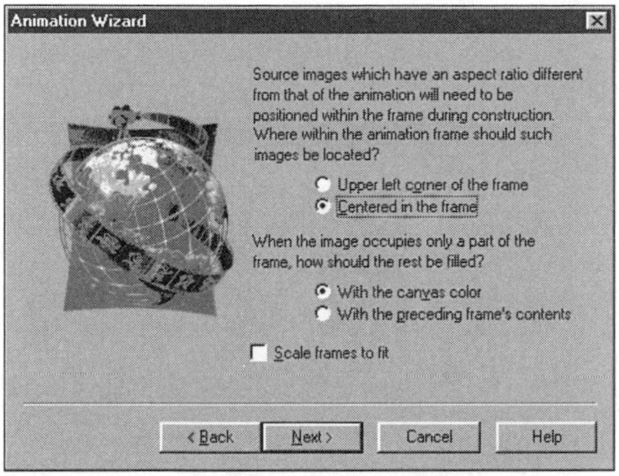
Animation Wizard
Source images which have an aspect ratio different from that of the animation will need to be positioned within the frame during construction. Where within the animation frame should such images be located?
Upper left corner of the frame
Centered in the frame
When the image occupies only a part of the frame, how should the rest be filled?
With the canvas color
With the preceding frame's contents
Scale frames to fit
< Back
Next >
Cancel
Help

The dialog box shown in Figure 16.11 also lets you choose the delay between frames. The higher the number you select, the more slowly the animation moves from frame to frame.

To achieve the smoothest animation, you want a high number of frames (10 or so) and a short delay (one one-hundredth of a second or so). When you have only a few frames, a short delay might make the animation whiz by too fast to see. The default setting of 10 one-hundredths of a second is a good choice for this example.

FIGURE 16.11
Step 5: Choose Yes and then click Next.

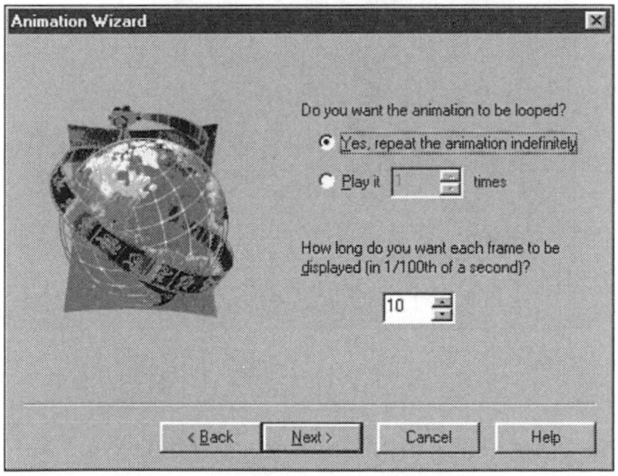
Animation Wizard
Do you want the animation to be looped?
Yes, repeat the animation indefinitely
Play it 1 times
How long do you want each frame to be displayed (in 1/100th of a second)?
10
< Back
Next >
Cancel
Help

6. The next screen prompts you to select the frame files. Click the Add Image button.
7. Browse to the folder where the “name” images you created are stored. Hold down the Ctrl key and select all the frame files. Then click the Open button.

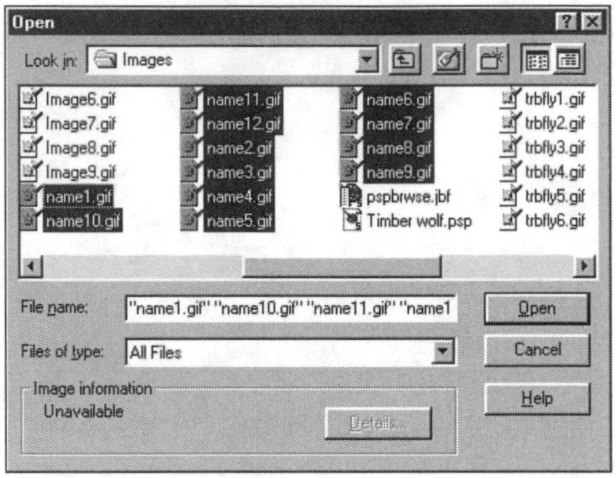

FIGURE 16.12
Step 7: Select the image files.

8. Rearrange the image filenames so that they’re in numerical order, from top to bottom. To move an image’s place in the order, click it to select it and then choose Move Up or Move Down. When you’re done, click Next.

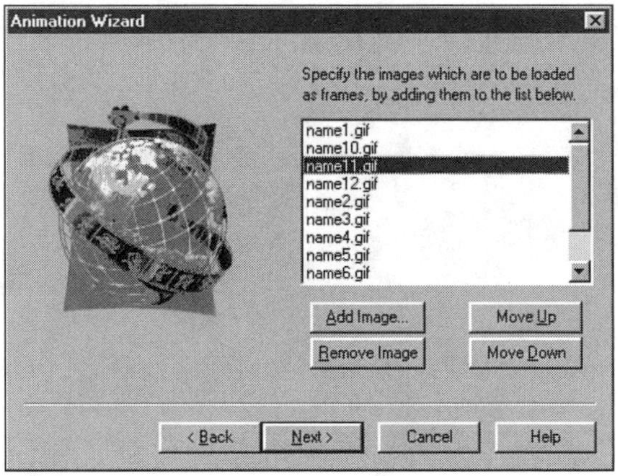

FIGURE 16.13
Step 8: Put the image files in order.

9. Click Finish. After a few moments, the frames of your animation appear.
10. Choose File, Save. Give the animation any name you like, but leave `.gif` as the filename extension. Click the Save button.

11. Now you get to choose Optimization. Optimization is important because it keeps the animation file from getting too large and slowing down your page. This small, simple animation won't be a size problem, so you can leave the slider at the top setting, Better Image Quality, and click Next.

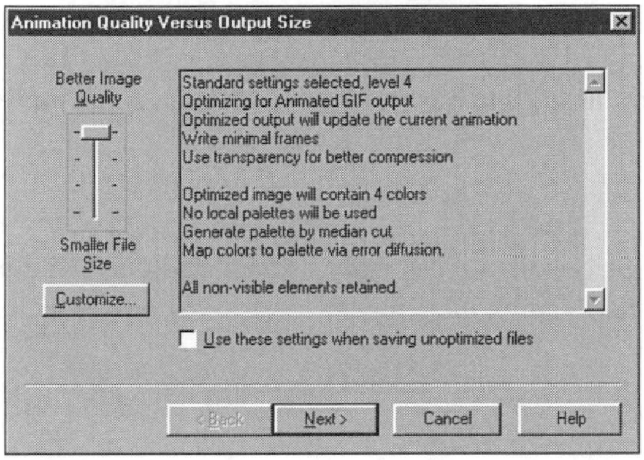

Figure 16.14
Step 11: Choose optimization settings.

When creating larger, more complex animations, you might prefer to move the slider down a notch or two, sacrificing image quality but creating a smaller file.

To change the optimization settings later, open the animation file in Animation Shop and choose File, Optimization Wizard.

12. Animation Shop creates the final file. Click Next.

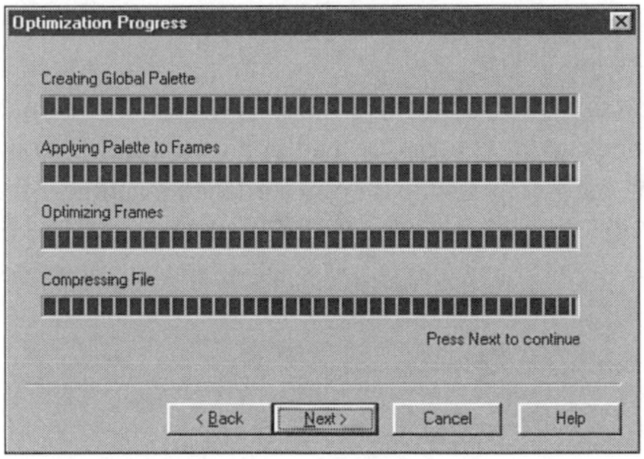

Figure 16.15
Step 12: Click Next.

13. Animation Shop reports the final size of the file and other statistics. Click Finish.
14. You can now do any of the following:
    - Choose View, Animation to watch your animation in Animation Shop.
    - Use the Animation Shop menus to change and fine-tune your animation.
    - Open Composer and insert in a Web page the animation file you just created. (You find it under the name you gave it in Step 10.) *Remember:* You have to view the page in a browser to see the animation move.

Summary

If you can make pictures, you can make an animated GIF. All it takes is creating a series of images and then binding them together. It's a fast, easy way to add a little action to a Web page.

Q&A

Q Do animated GIFs affect the download speed of a Web page?

A An animated GIF is an image file, and because it contains multiple frames, it is a larger file than a similar, non-animated GIF. As with any image, you must consider whether the effect of an animated GIF is worth the wait it can cause.

The major factors affecting the size (and thus the download time) of an animated GIF file are the number of frames it contains and the screen area it occupies. And, of course, if you build an animation from large, complex files with numerous colors, the animation file ends up large, too, despite optimization. Try to limit screen area and number frames while you're still creating an effective animation, and choose optimization settings carefully to get the best compromise between image quality and file size.

In addition to the extra download time, note that the animation can increase the memory demand and processor load in your visitor's browser. The impact is generally slight, but a visitor with an overburdened machine—for example, someone running Internet Explorer on a 486 PC with only 8MB of memory—might see a significant performance degradation when viewing animated GIFs.

Part V
Fine-Tuning Your Page

Hour

HOUR 17

Editing HTML

The easiest and most reliable way to create a Web page is to use a WYSIWYG editor—that's why I gave you Composer on the CD-ROM with this book, and that's why you've spent 16 hours with it.

No matter which editor Web authors use, they often reach a point where they want to do something that's perfectly possible in an HTML Web page but for which their WYSIWYG authoring program offers no buttons or menu items. If you reach that point, you might want to move beyond Composer into the realm of the HTML source file itself.

This hour introduces you to HTML source files and how new tags and attributes are applied. At the end of the hour, you'll be able to answer the following questions:

- How can I read and understand an HTML source file?
- How do I insert HTML codes from within Composer?
- What other tools can I use to edit HTML source code?
- How can I use HTML techniques to add three cool items to my Web pages: inline video, background sounds, and scrolling marquees?

Reading an HTML File

Recall from Hour 1, "Understanding Web Authoring," that an HTML source file consists of four basic elements:

- The text to be displayed on the page
- The filenames of inline images
- The URLs or filenames for links (and the text or image filenames for the link source)
- HTML tags and attributes, which tell browsers which lines are images, links, headings, or normal paragraphs, for example

The best way to learn about HTML is to study HTML files and compare them with the output in a browser. Figure 17.1 shows a basic Web page displayed in Netscape, and Figure 17.2 shows the HTML source file for the same page.

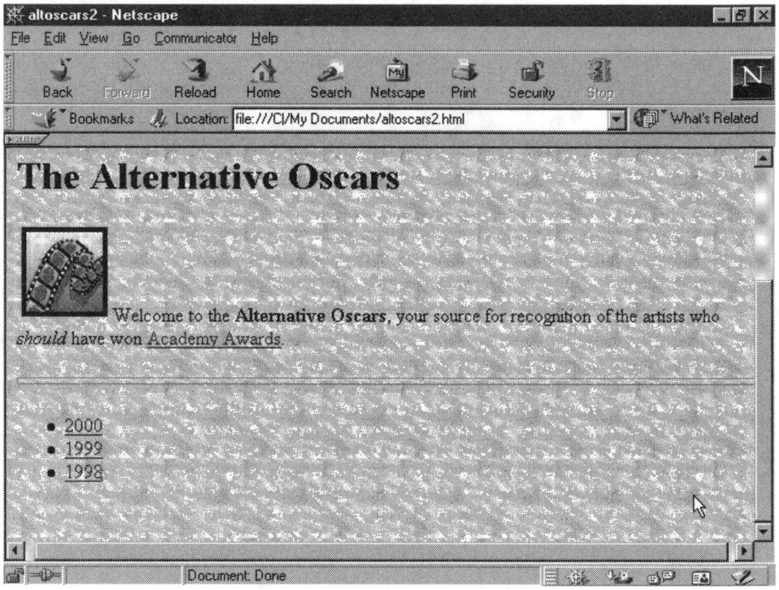

FIGURE 17.1
A basic Web page, as interpreted by a browser.

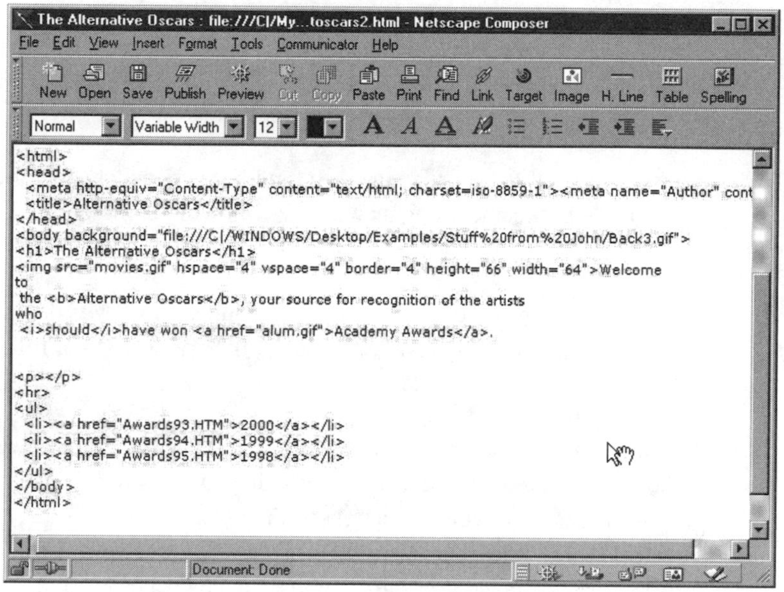
The Alternative Oscars : file:///C|/My...toscars2.html - Netscape Composer
File Edit View Insert Format Tools Communicator Help
New Open Save Publish Preview Cut Copy Paste Print Find Link Target Image H. Line Table Spelling
Normal Variable Width 12
<html>
<head>
<meta http-equiv="Content-Type" content="text/html; charset=iso-8859-1"><meta name="Author" cont
<title>Alternative Oscars</title>
</head>
<body background="file:///C|/WINDOWS/Desktop/Examples/Stuff%20from%20John/Back3.gif">
<h1>The Alternative Oscars</h1>
<img src="movies.gif" hspace="4" vspace="4" border="4" height="66" width="64">Welcome
to
the <b>Alternative Oscars</b>, your source for recognition of the artists
who
<i>should</i>have won <a href="alum.gif">Academy Awards</a>.
<p></p>
<hr>
<ul>
<li><a href="Awards93.HTM">2000</a></li>
<li><a href="Awards94.HTM">1999</a></li>
<li><a href="Awards95.HTM">1998</a></li>
</ul>
</body>
</html>
Document: Done

FIGURE 17.2
The HTML source code for the Web page shown in Figure 17.1.

> In Figure 17.2, notice that HTML tags are always enclosed within angle brackets (< >) and that each content element of the page—a paragraph or image filename—is surrounded by a pair of tags. Compare Figures 17.1 and 17.2 carefully, and you quickly see how HTML tags tell a browser what to do with the text and files that make up a Web page.
>
> Most Web pages contain more elaborate coding than what you see in the example illustrated by Figures 17.1 and 17.2. However, this example contains all the basics and shows how HTML tags are applied. When you understand this example, you'll know enough to apply virtually any other HTML tag.

While examining Figure 17.2, observe that you typically (but not always) need two HTML tags to identify a page element: one tag that has no slash (`/`) inside the first angle bracket and another that has a slash there. The no-slash version is used to mark the beginning of a page element, and the slash version (sometimes called the *close* tag) marks the end. For example, the tag `<HTML>` at the top of the file marks the beginning of the entire HTML document, and the close tag `</HTML>` marks the end.

> If you're wondering why you see some tags in uppercase letters and some in lowercase letters, see the "Q&A" section at the end of this hour.

Now take a look at how the tags, text, and filenames work together to build a page. Every HTML document begins with the following command:

```
<HTML>
```

This command tells the browser that it's reading an HTML document and should interpret it as such. Typically (but not always), the next tag is the following:

```
<HEAD>
```

This line informs the browser that what follows `<HEAD>` is header information. Information entered in the header is not displayed as part of the page but is important because it describes your document to the browser and to Web search engines and directories. The header portion of an HTML file created in Composer contains all the information you entered in the Composer Page Properties dialog box. This includes not only such standard elements as the document title, but also header elements created by Composer automatically. These are indicated with two types of tags:

```
<META NAME=...>
<HTTP-EQUIV>
```

The next two tags, `<TITLE>` and `</TITLE>`, surround the text of the Web page title. After the title and any other header lines, the tag `</HEAD>` informs the browser that the header is over. Next comes the body of the page, kicked off by the `<BODY>` tag. The body contains everything that's displayed on the page itself.

The first element of the body in Figure 17.2 is a heading. The heading tags are easy to remember: `<H1>` is a level 1 heading, `<H2>` is a level 2 heading, and so on. The first heading in the example is a level 1 heading:

```
<H1>The Alternative Oscars</H1>
```

Notice that the end of the heading is marked with `</H1>`.

The inline image (GIF file `movies.gif`) is indicated with the `<IMG SRC...>` tag, like the following:

```
<IMG SRC="movies.gif"...>
```

Note that the image filename must be enclosed in quotes. In Figure 17.2, optional *attributes* for spacing, image dimensions, and a border around the image appear between the beginning of the `<IMG SRC...>` tag and the close angle bracket (>) that ends it. Attributes are always optional and go inside the tag itself (between the angle brackets).

> The `<IMG SRC...>` tag requires no close tag.

Immediately following the end of the `<IMG SRC...>` tag comes a normal text paragraph (beginning with `Welcome`). Note that no tag is required in order to identify it; any text in an HTML document is assumed to be a normal paragraph unless tags indicate otherwise. However, keep in mind that while entering normal text, you cannot simply type a carriage return to start a new paragraph. To break a paragraph and begin a new one, you must enter the new-paragraph tag (`<P>`). Ending a paragraph with a close-paragraph tag (`</P>`) is proper, but doing so is not required.

Embedded within the normal paragraph are a few more tags:

- The set `<B>` and `</B>` surrounding `Alternative Oscars` applies bold character formatting.
- The set `<I>` and `</I>` surrounding `should` applies italic character formatting.
- The tag beginning with `<A HREF...` creates a link to another page, using the text `Academy Awards` as the link source. In the link, the `<A HREF=` portion indicates that, when activated by a reader, the link should open the file or URL named in quotes. The text between the close angle bracket following the filename and the close tag `</A>` is the text that is displayed in the page as the link source.

Following the normal paragraph is a new-paragraph tag that inserts a blank line before the horizontal line (`<HR>`) that follows. All by itself, the `<HR>` tag inserts a line; `width=100%` is an attribute, one of the optional properties you can apply to a horizontal line's properties extensions (see Hour 8, "Organizing Text with Tables and Rules").

The `<UL>` tag starts an unnumbered list. (Look for the `</UL>` tag that closes the list.) Each list item is surrounded by `<LI>` and `</LI>` and contains a link (`<A HREF`) to another page in the document.

At the bottom of the file, the `</BODY>` tag closes off the body and the `</HTML>` tag indicates the end of the HTML document.

That's it. To learn more about the HTML source code of pages you've created in Composer or any page you see on the Web, follow the steps in the next section.

Viewing the HTML Source Code of a Document

A great way to learn more about HTML is to study the source code for Web pages. You can study the source code for pages you view on the Web or look at the underlying source code for pages you create in Composer. You can even view the source code for a page you're editing, make a small change with the Composer menus or toolbar buttons, and then view the source code again to see how the HTML code has been changed. Give it a try!

To view the HTML source for a page you're looking at:

- In Internet Explorer, choose View, Source.
- In Netscape, choose View, Page Source.

Using Composer to Insert an HTML Tag

When you've built a document in Composer but need to add a tag here or there for which Composer offers no button or menu, the Composer Insert HTML Tag function allows you to do so conveniently, without having to fuss with the whole HTML source file.

To Do: Insert an HTML tag

1. Click in the page at the spot where you want the object or formatting applied by the tag to go.
2. Choose Insert, HTML Tag.
3. Type your entry and then click OK.

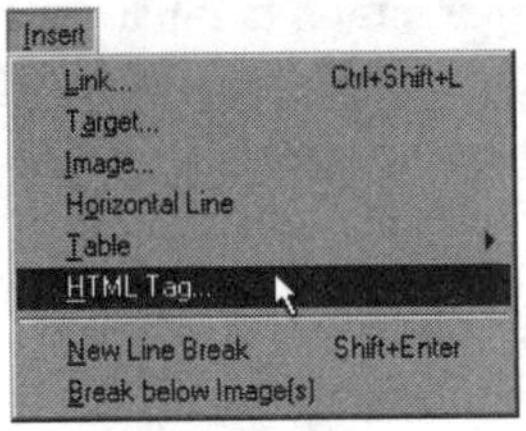

FIGURE 17.3
Step 2: Choose Insert, HTML Tag.

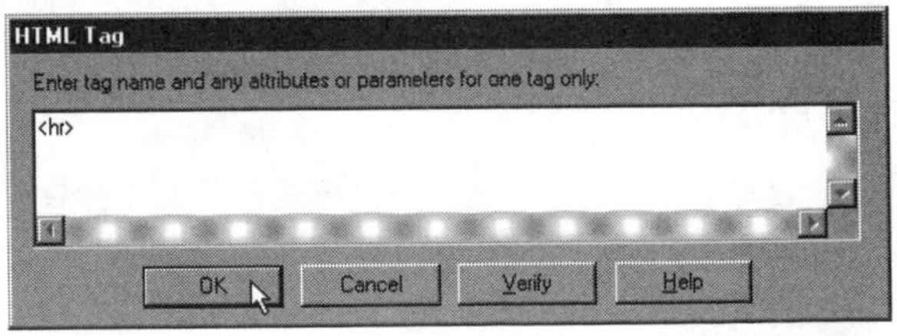

FIGURE 17.4
Step 3: Type the tag.

Adding Attributes with the Composer Advanced Edit Buttons

When performing many kinds of activities in dialog boxes in Composer—inserting or formatting an image, for example—you see an Extra HTML button somewhere in the dialog box, like the one shown in Figure 17.5. The button enables you to code attributes or other options manually into the HTML tag controlled by the dialog box.

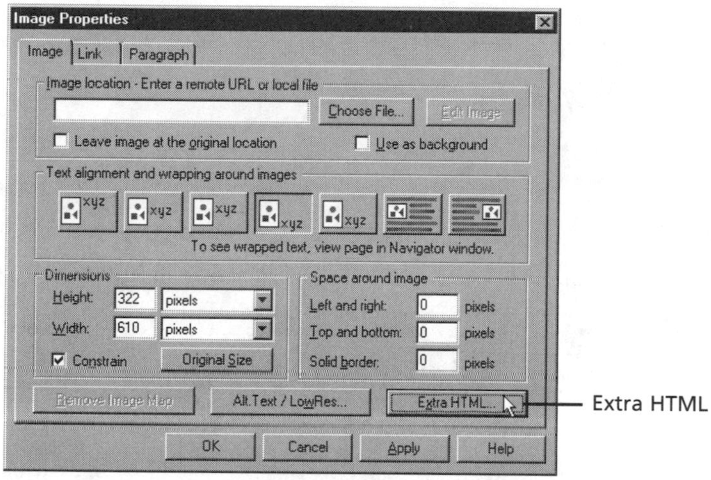

FIGURE 17.5
Where you see an Extra HTML button, you can click it to open a dialog box where you can add optional attributes.

However, the Extra HTML button has little immediate value when you're writing HTML. For the most part, all optional attributes you might want to use are already available in the dialog box. Also, the button enables you to insert any attributes or other code between the tag and its closing tag—for example, anywhere between `<TABLE>` and `</TABLE>` when you click the button in the Insert Table dialog box. However, this method does not give you control of the position of the added attributes among other attributes within the tags, and position is sometimes important.

I've told you about the Extra HTML button 'cause it's there and 'cause, for all I know, you might find it useful. But if you really want to apply attributes not featured on the Composer menus and toolbar buttons, I recommend steering clear of the Extra HTML button and editing the HTML source file, as described in the next section. Doing so, you develop greater skill and confidence working with HTML, and you avoid niggling little problems that the button can bring about.

Editing an HTML Source File Directly

The Composer Insert HTML Tag function is terrific for inserting a tag or two in a file, but for more serious HTML work, simply editing the HTML source file itself is easier.

Many Web authoring programs include an HTML source editor (but not Composer). But for basic changes, any text editor will do. Windows has a built-in text editor, Notepad (see Figure 17.6). To open Notepad, click the Windows Start button and choose Programs, Accessories, Notepad.

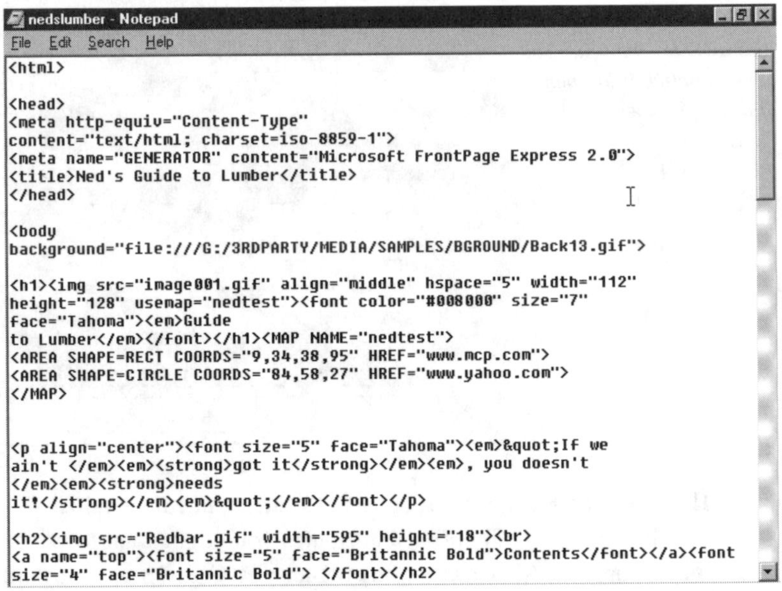


```
<html>

<head>
<meta http-equiv="Content-Type"
content="text/html; charset=iso-8859-1">
<meta name="GENERATOR" content="Microsoft FrontPage Express 2.0">
<title>Ned's Guide to Lumber</title>
</head>

<body
background="file:///G:/3RDPARTY/MEDIA/SAMPLES/BGROUND/Back13.gif">

<h1><img src="image001.gif" align="middle" hspace="5" width="112"
height="128" usemap="nedtest"><font color="#008000" size="7"
face="Tahoma"><em>Guide
to Lumber</em></font></h1><MAP NAME="nedtest">
<AREA SHAPE=RECT COORDS="9,34,38,95" HREF="www.mcp.com">
<AREA SHAPE=CIRCLE COORDS="84,58,27" HREF="www.yahoo.com">
</MAP>


<p align="center"><font size="5" face="Tahoma"><em>&quot;If we
ain't </em><em><strong>got it</strong></em><em>, you doesn't
</em><em><strong>needs
it!</strong></em><em>&quot;</em></font></p>

<h2><img src="Redbar.gif" width="595" height="18"><br>
<a name="top"><font size="5" face="Britannic Bold">Contents</font></a><font
size="4" face="Britannic Bold"> </font></h2>
```

FIGURE 17.6
You can use Windows notepad to edit HTML source code directly.

To open one of your Composer pages in Notepad to edit its HTML, open Notepad and then choose File, Open. In the Open dialog box, open the Files of Type list (see Figure 17.7) and choose All files (doing so makes HTML files, and all other file types, appear in the lists of files the Open dialog shows). Then browse to your file and click the Open button.

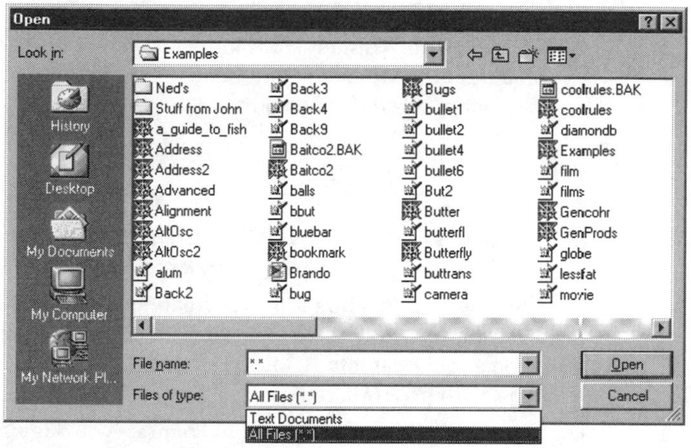

FIGURE 17.7
Choose All Files from the File of type list to choose an HTML file to edit.

About HTML Assistant Pro

Some WYSIWYG editors do all the HTML work for you (behind the scenes), and some flat HTML editors and text editors let you edit the source code, but give you little or no help with it. Somewhere between those two extremes lie professional HTML editing tools like HTML Assistant Pro, which is included on the CD-ROM at the back of this book (see Figure 17.8).

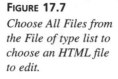

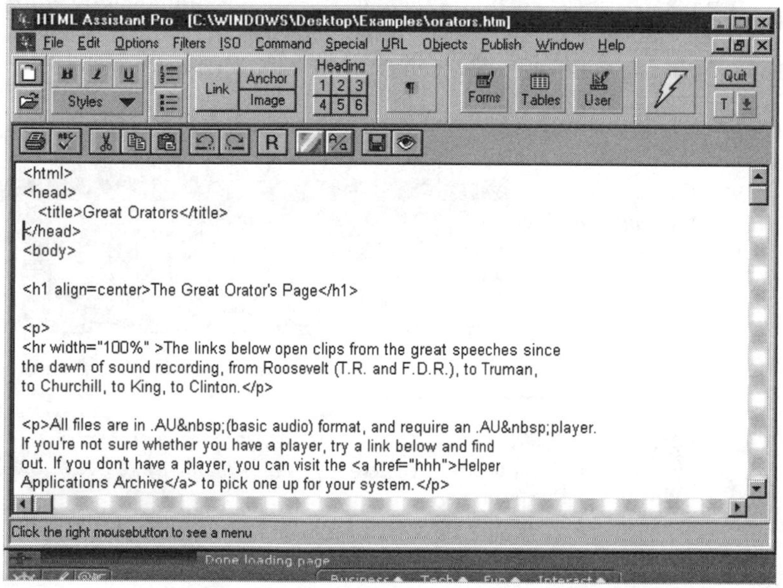

FIGURE 17.8
HTML code being edited in HTML Assistant.

> To open HTML Assistant Pro, choose Programs, HTML Assistant Pro 2000, Pro 2000 from the Windows Start menu. (If the Welcome screen appears, click the Continue with Mission button.)

> For readers of this book, HTML Assistant Pro provides another important benefit—one that requires no HTML coding.
>
> Composer includes no facility for creating Web pages with *frames*—pages divided into two or three separate panels that each show a different file. Using a tool built into HTML Assistant Pro, you can easily produce a frames page, with no HTML coding.
>
> In Hour 18, "Dividing a Page into Frames," you'll learn how to create frames in HTML Assistant Pro.

Although an HTML editor produces and edits simple text files, it also offers menus and toolbar buttons to make entering tags more convenient and accurate.

For example, in HTML Assistant Pro, you apply the tags for bold character formatting by simply highlighting text and then clicking the B button on the toolbar (see Figure 17.9). Rather than see the text turn bold (as you do in a WYSIWYG editor), you see the bold tags (<B>, </B>) appear around the text. These editors don't show you the effects of your coding (you need to view the file in a browser to check its appearance), but they do make working with raw HTML easier, and they help ensure that you enter the codes correctly.

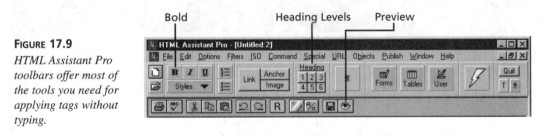

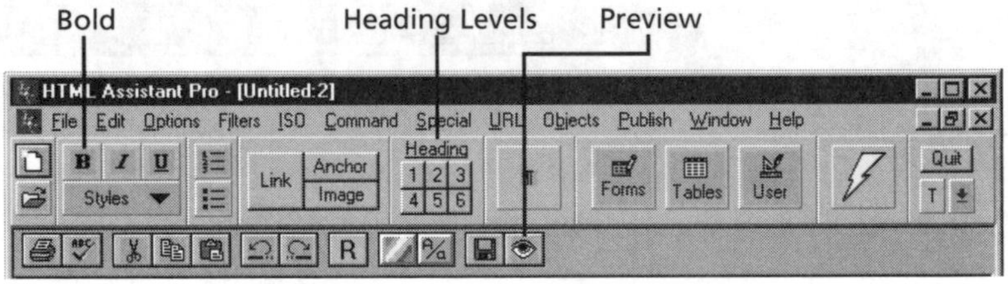

FIGURE 17.9
HTML Assistant Pro toolbars offer most of the tools you need for applying tags without typing.

> When working in HTML Assistant Pro, you can click the Preview button on the toolbar (the creepy eye; refer to Figure 17.9) to view the page in the default browser on your PC.

Typically, you compose in HTML Assistant Pro by typing only the text you want to display (or entering filenames for images or URLs for links), highlighting the text with your mouse, and then clicking a toolbar button to apply a set of tags to the selected text. The tags are displayed instantly in the document. For example, you could type a line of text and then click a number (1–6) under Heading on the top toolbar to assign heading tags to the text.

Note too that you needn't manually code such structure tags as `<HTML>`, `<HEAD>`, or `<BODY>`; HTML Assistant Pro adds these automatically when you create the file.

> In Hour 24, "Developing Your Authoring Skills," you'll learn about other Web authoring environments, such as Microsoft FrontPage, which you can add to your arsenal as your skills advance.
>
> If you need to do lots of HTML coding to do stuff Composer doesn't do, consider moving up to one of these professional-level Web authoring tools so that you can perform the same tasks more conveniently and in true WYSIWYG fashion.

Editing Composer Pages in HTML Assistant Pro

Before you can begin using HTML Assistant Pro to edit pages you've created in Composer, you need to know how to open a Composer page in HTML Assistant Pro.

Begin by opening HTML Assistant Pro. Choose File, Open to display the Open dialog box (see Figure 17.10); then browse to and open your Composer file.

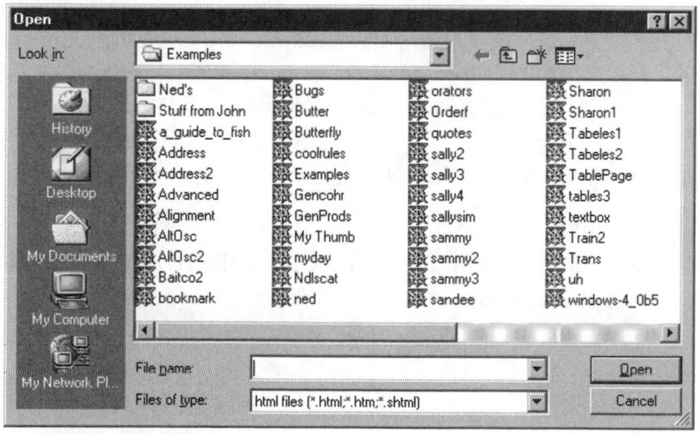

FIGURE 17.10
Choose File, Open to browse for and open a Composer page in HTML Assistant Pro.

When finished editing the HTML of your page, save the file by choosing File, Save. Then re-open the page in Composer (to continue editing) or Navigator (to view the results).

> Many of the HTML features you can add in HTML Assistant Pro cannot be previewed in Composer. You can view the proper effects of your HTML work in Navigator, but in Composer, some tags added by HTML Assistant Pro will show up not as they would appear online, but instead indicated by little yellow tag icons. These tags simply mean that you've used tags a browser would understand, but Composer doesn't.

Using HTML Assistant Pro to Add Sound and Video to Your Web Pages

As you learned in Hour 15, Composer's ability to add media files to your pages is pretty much limited to pictures. But by using HTML Assistant Pro in concert with Composer, you can easily insert inline video files, background sounds, and scrolling marquees to your pages. The following To Do's show how.

> Before you can add a video clip or background sound, you need to have a video (.AVI) file (for video) or a Windows Wave (WAV) sound file (for sound). If you are unfamiliar with these file types, see Hours 13 and 15.

To Do: Add a background sound

> Composer can't play background sounds. View the page in Internet Explorer to hear the sound. (Make sure your speakers are switched on!)

1. Store your Wave file in the same folder where the Web page is stored.
2. Open the Web page file in HTML Assistant Pro.
3. Click at the end of a line anywhere in the BODY section of the file and press Enter to start a new line.

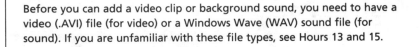

4. Choose Special, Sound Attributes.
5. In the Loop section of the Sound Attributes dialog box, select the number of times you want the sound to play, or choose Infinite to make the sound play repeatedly for as long as the visitor displays the page.

FIGURE 17.11
Step 5: Choose Loop options to control how many times the sound plays.

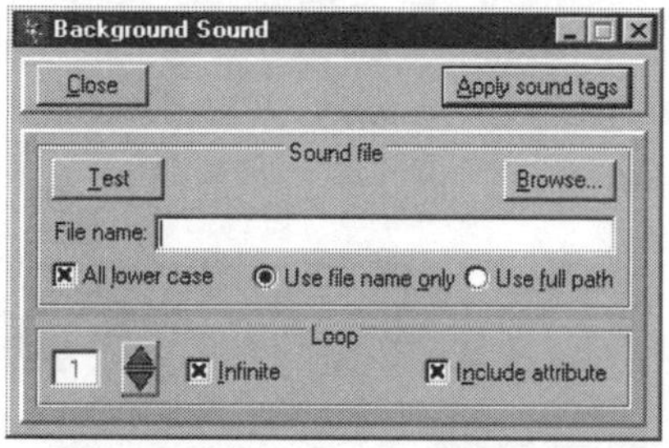

6. Click the Apply sound tags button.

17

Creating a Times Square-Style Animated Marquee

NEW TERM A *marquee* is a short slice of animated text that scrolls through a Web page. The effect is like the scrolling marquee on the *New York Times* building in Manhattan, the one people in movies are always watching for bulletins during a crisis. Marquees are a fast way to add a little action to a page, and are usually used for text you really want the visitor to notice.

> At this writing, scrolling marquees are enabled by a Microsoft extension, and are supported in Internet Explorer but not in Netscape Navigator or in other browsers. Navigator users will see your marquee text as regular, static text on the page.

To Do: Insert a marquee

1. Open the Web page file in HTML Assistant Pro.
2. Study the BODY section of the HTML code to locate the place in the page layout where you want the marquee to appear.

3. Click at the end of a line and press Enter to start a new line.
4. Choose Special, Apply Marquee Attributes.
5. Choose options for how you want your marquee to behave. For example, choose Scroll to make the text scroll across the page, Slide to make it slide back and forth, or Alternate to alternate between sliding and scrolling. In the Loop box, choose the number of times you want the marquee to do its thing before stopping, or choose Infinite to make the marquee scroll (or slide) repeatedly for as long as the visitor displays the page.

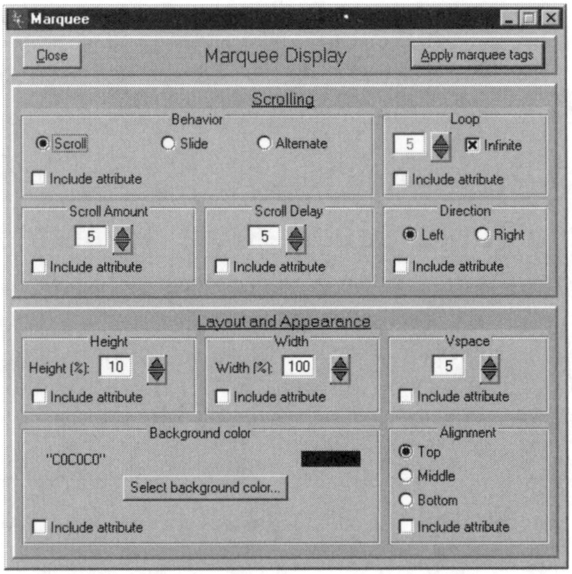

FIGURE 17.12
Step 5: Choose options for how you want your marquee to behave.

6. Click Apply Marquee Tags. You'll see a fresh set of tags with the cursor positioned between them.
7. Right where the cursor is, type the text for the marquee.

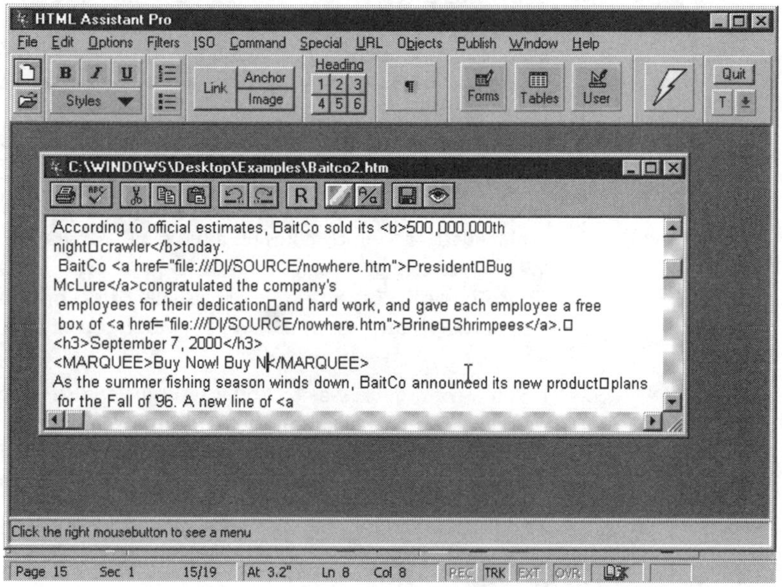
HTML Assistant Pro
File Edit Options Filters ISO Command Special URL Objects Publish Window Help
Link
Anchor
Image
Heading
Styles
Forms
Tables
User
Quit
C:\WINDOWS\Desktop\Examples\Baitco2.htm
According to official estimates, BaitCo sold its <b>500,000,000th
night□crawler</b>today.
BaitCo <a href="file:///D|/SOURCE/nowhere.htm">President□Bug
McLure</a>congratulated the company's
employees for their dedication□and hard work, and gave each employee a free
box of <a href="file:///D|/SOURCE/nowhere.htm">Brine□Shrimpees</a>.□
<h3>September 7, 2000</h3>
<MARQUEE>Buy Now! Buy N</MARQUEE>
As the summer fishing season winds down, BaitCo announced its new product□plans
for the Fall of '96. A new line of <a
Click the right mousebutton to see a menu
Page 15 Sec 1 15/19 At 3.2" Ln 8 Col 8 REC TRK EXT OVR

FIGURE 17.13
Step 7: Type the text for the marquee between the tags.

Inserting an Inline Video Clip

OK, I'll tell you how to add an inline video clip (a video clip that appears within the page layout, like an image), because HTML Assistant Pro provides such a handy way to do it. But that doesn't mean I recommend it….

Here are the problems, in no particular order: 1) The clips work only when the page is viewed through Internet Explorer, not in Navigator or in any other browser; 2) An inline clip may dramatically slow down the performance of your page, annoying visitors (unless they have a really fast Internet connection, such as cable Internet or DSL), and 3) A nice inline picture or animation (see Hour 16) really makes more sense. Save video for external presentation (see "About External Media," later in this hour).

That said, I know you…. There's just no holding you back, is there? The following To Do shows how to add an inline video clip.

Before you insert a video clip, you must have one on-hand, in AVI format (using the filename extension `.avi`). You can find such clips online in clip art libraries (see Appendix B, "Online Resources for Web Authors"), or you can create your own AVI files if you have a video capture card in your PC. You can plug a camcorder or VCR into a port on the capture card, play a tape in the VCR or camcorder, and use the card's software to save the incoming video in an AVI file.

Keep in mind that video files are very large. A mere minute can take up several megabytes, which takes up a big chunk of your allotted space on the Web server and also forces long waits for those with slower Internet connections. The video capture software usually offers options for keeping the file size down, at the cost of making the video clip smaller (in onscreen area) and fuzzier.

If you want a quick way to find an AVI file to use for practice (without downloading one from the Web), use the Windows Find facility and search for `*.avi`. Odds are the search will turn up a few AVI files you didn't even know you had, deposited on your PC by various programs or Web sites.

To Do

To Do: Insert inline video

1. Store the AVI file in the same folder as the Web page (or copy it there).
2. Open the Web page file in HTML Assistant Pro.
3. Study the BODY section of the HTML code to locate the place in the page layout where you want the video clip to appear.
4. Click at the end of a line and press Enter to start a new line.
5. Choose Special, Video Clip.
6. In the Video Clip URL section of the dialog box, choose Use file name only.

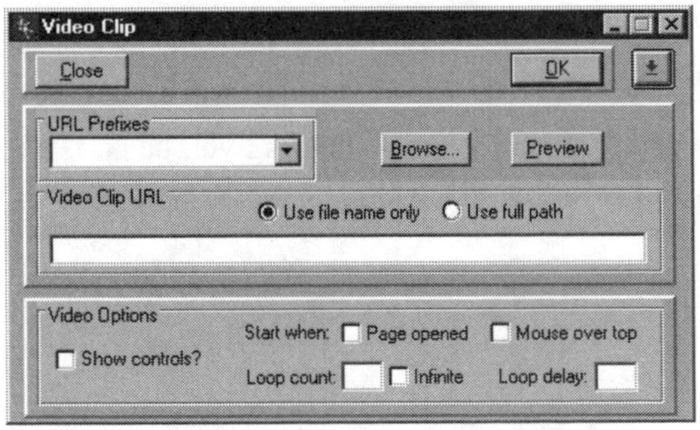

FIGURE 17.14
Steps 6: Choose Use file name only.

7. Click the Browse button, navigate to the video clip, and click the Open button.
8. Click OK on the Video Clip dialog box.

Summary

Coding HTML is no great challenge. In fact, the beauty of HTML is that coding simple stuff—such as text paragraphs, links, and inline images—is actually simple, and coding more complex elements builds naturally on the skills required for the easy stuff.

As a Composer author, you won't spend much time coding the simple stuff because Composer offers buttons and menus for all of it. Instead, you can lay out most of your document in Composer and then use Insert HTML Tag or an HTML editor to code the rest.

Q&A

Q I noticed in some of the HTML source code examples you showed that the lines of code in the header were indented. What does indenting do?

A Nothing. The indenting of blocks of HTML code has no effect on the display of the page; the indenting is there for the same reason some editors color-code the HTML when showing it to you. Authors (and most editors) indent portions of code to make the structure of the file easier to understand when a person reads it. Browsers don't care; they pay no attention to indents in HTML source code, so do whatever works best for you.

Q I've also noticed that tags are sometimes typed in uppercase letters (`<TITLE>`) and other times lowercase (`<title>`). Does it matter which I use?

A Browsers today don't care whether you use uppercase tags, lowercase tags, or both—they pay no attention to the case of the letters used in tags, and the tags have the same effect either way. You might have noticed that Composer uses lowercase tags (refer to Figure 17.8) and that HTML Assistant uses uppercase tags (refer to Figure 17.9). Same dif.

For years, the accepted convention among Web authors was to use uppercase tags. Because most of the text content of a page was likely to be lowercase (with uppercase letters only at the beginnings of sentences and on proper nouns), the experts of the time thought that using uppercase tags helped the author easily distinguish tags from content. That's the same reason, in this hour, that I mostly used uppercase tags—so that they stand out from my description around them.

Given that you'll probably spend most of your HTML coding time editing HTML files originally produced by programs, staying flexible and cultivating the ability to work either way pays off. In fact, you might want to always do the opposite of what the program does; for example, when editing the all-lowercase HTML code that Composer creates, write your edits in uppercase—that makes it easier to see what you've changed if you need to resolve a problem later.

Eventually, all coding is likely to be required to be lowercase. That's because HTML will one day be supplanted by a new standard, XHTML (see Hour 24), in which tags must be lowercase. But that's still a while away.

Q I've looked at the source for some pages on the Web, and I've seen lines of text preceded by a `<!-` tag. The text doesn't seem to be part of the header, but it is displayed nowhere in the browser view of the page. *Que pasa, mi amigo*?

A Any text preceded by `<!-` is a *comment*, a note inserted in the file to explain something to anyone who might read the HTML source code. Comments are inserted by programmers in all types of program code, including HTML, to help others (or even the programmer) understand the code when reading it. Comments have no effect on the display or actions of the document, and the text within comments is hidden when the browser displays the document. (In Composer, you can add comments to the HTML by choosing Insert, Comment.)

HOUR 18

Dividing a Page into Frames

If you've hit frame-based pages in your browsing, you know that they're cool. They make your display look like the control panel of a jet fighter—so many different, independent chunks of information stimulating your brain at one time. (If you're not sure what I mean, peek ahead to Figure 18.1.)

It's like the picture-in-picture feature on a new television, for people with eyes so info-hungry that just one program—or one page—at a time provides inadequate sensory input. Of course, frames also greatly expand the author's ability to offer a variety of page-navigation scenarios to visitors.

At the end of this hour, you'll be able to answer the following questions:

- What's a frames page really made of, behind the scenes?
- How can I easily create a frames page by using HTML Assistant Pro and Composer together (with no HTML coding!)?
- How can I create and edit frames in HTML?
- How do I help visitors who don't have frames-capable browsers?

What Does It Take to Make a Frames Page?

In a frame-based page, the content of each frame is contained in a separate HTML page (see Figure 18.1). If the page features three frames, it has at least three separate HTML files, one to appear in each frame.

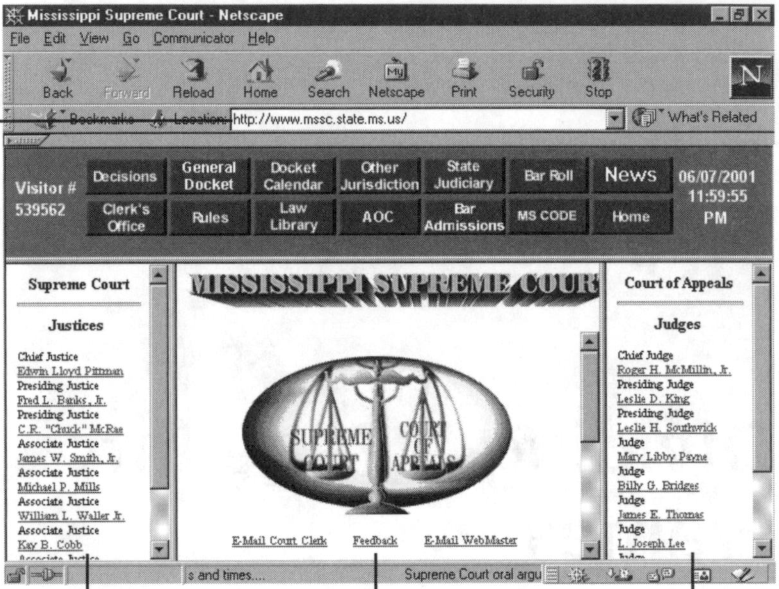

FIGURE 18.1
A frame-based page.

In addition to those "content" HTML files, another HTML file ties all the others together—the frame definition page.

NEW TERM The *frame definition page* is a special HTML file that creates and controls a frame-based Web page. The file contains the filename of the HTML file that's to be displayed in each frame, plus tags dictating the number and size of the frames.

Creating a frame-based page requires three basic steps:

1. Create the various individual HTML pages to be displayed within the frames.
2. Create the frame definition page to define the number, size, and other aspects of the frames.
3. Tie one HTML file to each frame.

> When publishing and publicizing your frame-based page, you direct visitors to the frame definition page, not to any of the content files displayed within the frames.

The Frame Definition Page

The frame definition page supplies no content to the page; it merely specifies how the page will be split up and which HTML page will be displayed in each frame.

In Figure 18.1, the URL shown in the address box is that of the frame definition page; that's the URL a visitor accesses to open the page. The frame definition page then takes care of displaying the pages within the frames.

> In the frame definition page, you can insert a message to be displayed only to visitors who can't see links. (See the section "Accommodating the Frame-Intolerant," later in this hour.)

The Frame Content

A separate HTML file, which you compose like any other Web page, supplies the content of each frame. You create and format these pages like any other Web page file; however, when composing files to be displayed in frames, you must try to account for the size and shape of the frame in which you plan to display it.)

Browsers help adjust content for frames: They automatically shorten horizontal lines and wrap text to fit within a frame. Alignment properties are also preserved in a frame; for example, if your text is centered in the page when you compose it, the browser centers the text within the frame when displaying it. However, browsers cannot adjust the positions or spacing of images (or images used as rules or bullets); images often make framing difficult.

> Note that each page in a frame can have its own, unique background image or color, defined in the content file.

Frames are not created in Composer, but you can create your content files in Composer and tie them together under a frame definition page you create with HTML or another tool (as you do in the next To Do) and then check your work by previewing the page in Netscape or another browser.

Browsers automatically add scrollbars to a frame when the contents exceed the frame size. But a frames page showing a collection of fragmentary files and scrollbars is unappealing, and visitors tire quickly of excessive scrolling—especially horizontal scrolling to read wide text. Whenever practical, make the content fit the frame—or vice versa.

Using HTML Assistant Pro to Create a Frames Page

Because Composer contains no built-in tools for making frames, you need to code the frames directly in HTML or bring in another tool to help. The easier method is to bring in another tool, and—lucky you—you have one: HTML Assistant Pro, included on the CD-ROM at the back of this book.

> The following To Do assumes that you have already installed HTML Assistant Pro from the CD-ROM at the back of this book. If you have not, see Appendix A, "Setting Up the Programs on the CD-ROM."

To Do

To Do: Build a frames page with Composer and HTML Assistant Pro

1. In Composer, compose the content pages to be displayed in the frames. Try to organize and format them, if possible, in a way that minimizes the need for visitors to scroll them in their frames. (Keep in mind that you can always fine-tune them later, after seeing how they look in their frames.)
2. Open HTML Assistant Pro by choosing Programs, HTML Assistant Pro 2000, Pro 2000 from the Windows Start menu. (If the Welcome screen appears, click the Continue with Mission button.)
3. Choose Special, QuickFrames from the menu bar.
4. Click the picture that matches the style of frames page you want to create.
5. In the picture of the frame, click in any frame.

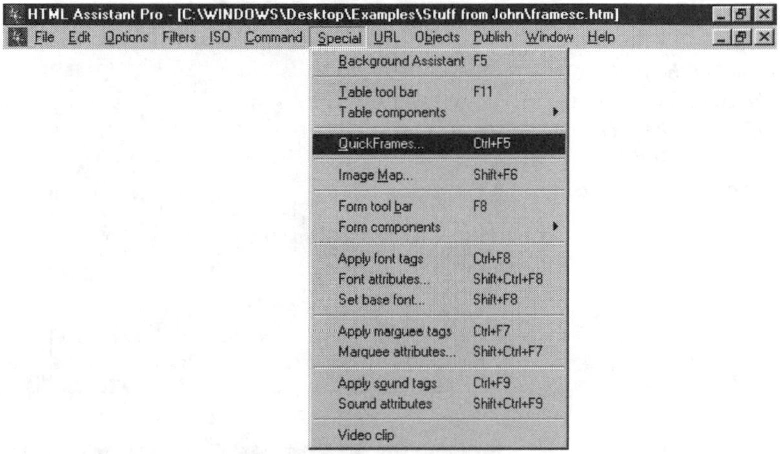

FIGURE 18.2
Step 3: Choose Special, QuickFrames in HTML Assistant Pro.

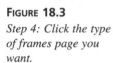

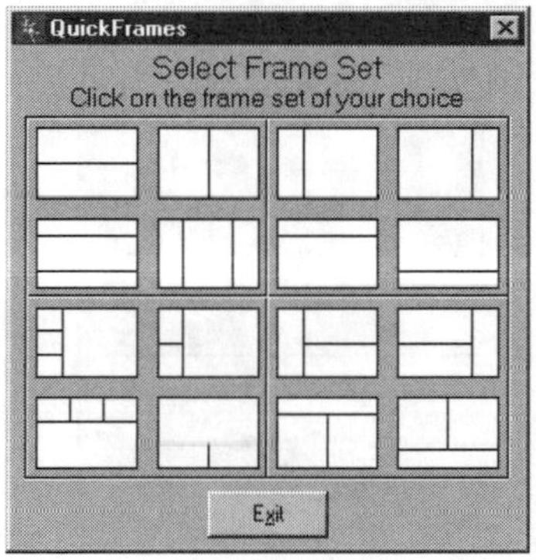

FIGURE 18.3
Step 4: Click the type of frames page you want.

6. Under URL Prefix, click None; under File Name, click File Name Only.
7. Under Source URL, type the filename of the HTML file you want displayed in the frame you clicked in Step 5. (Or click Browse to browse for it.)
8. Repeat Steps 5–7 for all other frames in the picture.
9. When you have supplied a filename for all frames, click the Create Frame Set button.

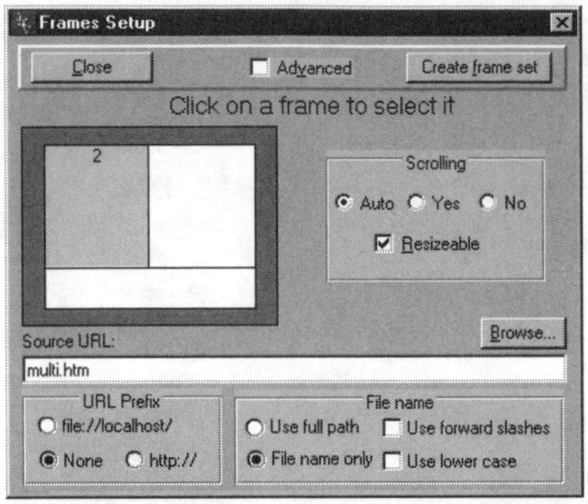

FIGURE 18.4
Steps 5–7: Click a frame in the picture, choose a few options, and enter the filename of the HTML file to appear in that frame.

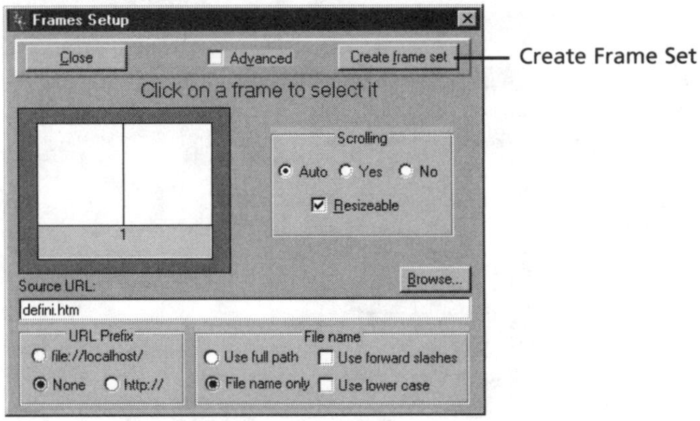

FIGURE 18.5
Step 9: Click Create Frame Set.

10. Choose File, Save, and save the new frame definition page. Be sure to save it in the same folder as its content files (the ones created in Step 1).

> If you want to change the number or organization of the frames after creating the frame definition page in HTML Assistant Pro, you must edit the HTML directly; no easy dialog box appears for revising the frames.
>
> An easier technique, however, is to simply create a new frame definition page (choosing new options along the way) and incorporate the same content files as in the preceding version. Doing so takes only a minute or two and is quicker than fussing with the code.

11. Still in HTML Assistant, click the Preview button to see the page displayed in your default browser.

FIGURE 18.6
Step 11: Click the Preview button to view the frames page in your browser.

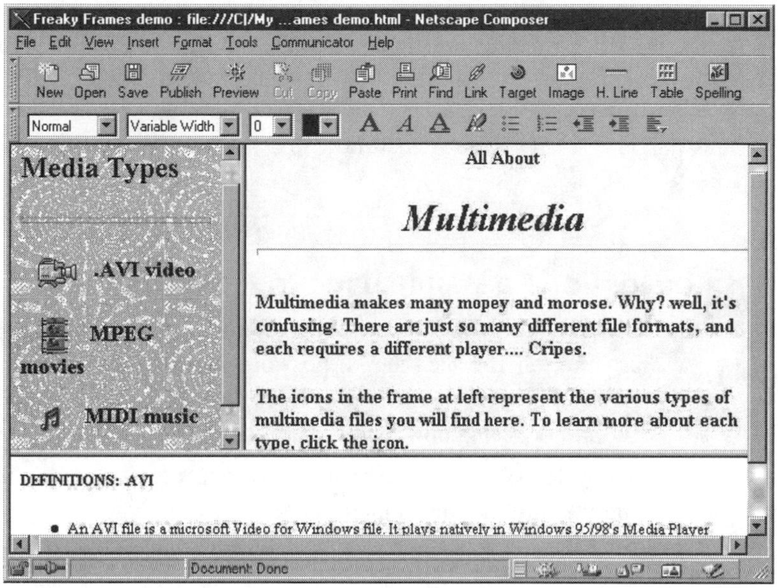

12. Leave your browser open, and open Composer.
13. Make any changes you want to the content files to improve their appearance in their frames. After changing a file, save it in Composer and open the frame definition page in Composer or in your browser to check your work.

When you publish a frames page to the Web (see Hour 21, "Publishing Your Page"), you must be certain to publish the frame definition page and each of the separate content pages.

Even though you can't view the frames in Composer, you can open the frame definition page in Composer and use the Composer publishing tools to publish the frame definition page. You can finish up by publishing each of the content pages separately.

You can also publish your frames page simply by uploading all its files via FTP or using the publishing tools in HTML Assistant Pro.

After publishing, when publicizing your page (see Hour 23, "Publicizing Your Site"), be sure to direct visitors to the address of the frame definition page, not to any of the content pages.

Creating Frames in HTML

Most folks' frames needs are more than satisfied by HTML Assistant Pro, as shown in the preceding To Do. But if you want greater control over your frames, you want to edit the HTML source directly, in either HTML Assistant Pro or n another tool.

> If you don't know how to edit HTML, see Hour 17, "Editing HTML."

To Do: Code a simple page in HTML

1. In Composer, compose the content pages to be displayed in the frames. Try to organize and format them, if possible, in a way that minimizes the need for visitors to scroll them in their frames. (Keep in mind that you can always fine-tune them later, after seeing how they look in their frames.)
2. In any HTML editor, create a new HTML file, including the required structure tags and the title for your frames page:

```
<HTML>
<HEAD>
<TITLE>Frames Demo</TITLE>
</HEAD>
   <BODY>
   </BODY>
</HTML>
```

3. Replace the <BODY> tags with <FRAMESET> tags, as shown in the following code. (Note that in a frame definition page, the <FRAMESET> block replaces the <BODY> block, and you cannot include a <BODY> block anywhere in the file.)

```
<HTML>
<HEAD>
<TITLE>Frames Demo</TITLE>
</HEAD>
   <FRAMESET>
   </FRAMESET>
</HTML>
```

The <FRAMESET> tags enclose the entire definition of the frames. All further coding is inserted between these tags.

4. The frames page is split into two columns without any rows. Therefore, in the <FRAMESET> tag, you add the COLS attribute. Suppose that you want the first column to be narrow (30 percent of the window) and the second column to take up the remainder of the window.

```
</FRAMESET>
```

> In the <FRAMESET> tag in the example, COLS="*,70%" or COLS="30%,70%" would have the same effect as the entry shown.

5. Having defined the frames, you define their content by adding the <FRAME SRC> tag and the filenames of the content files (in quotes). In the columns on the page, the files are displayed in the same order (from left to right) in which they appear in the <FRAMESET> block (from top to bottom). In the following example, the page file MULTI.HTM is displayed in the first (left) column:

```
<FRAMESET COLS="30%,*">
    <FRAME SRC="MULTI.HTM">
    <FRAME SRC="DESCRIP.HTM">
</FRAMESET>
```


6. Review the completed code of the frame definition page:

```
<HTML>
<HEAD>
   <TITLE>Frames Demo</TITLE>
</HEAD>
   <FRAMESET COLS="30%,*">
       <FRAME SRC="MULTI.HTM">
       <FRAME SRC="DESCRIP.HTM">
   </FRAMESET>
</HTML>
```

7. Choose File, Save, and save the new frame definition page. Be sure to save it in the same folder as its content files (the ones created in Step 1).

8. Test your new page by opening the frame definition page in your browser.

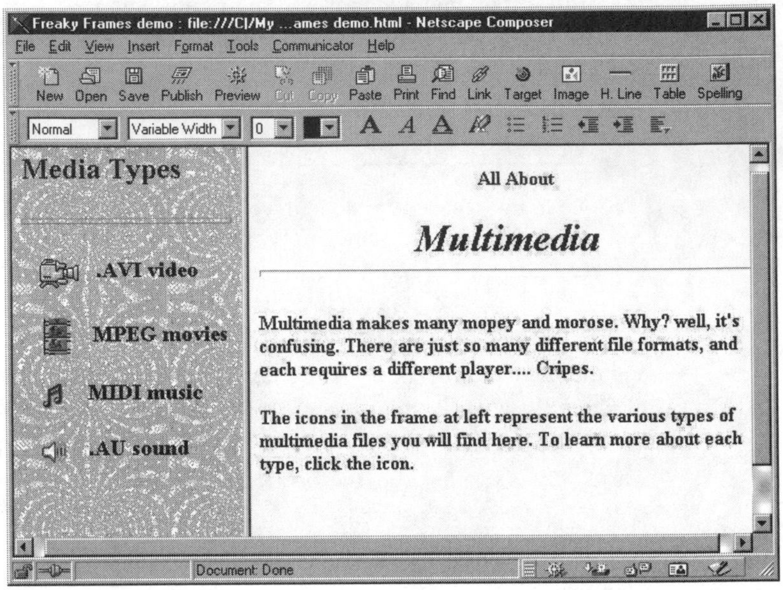
Freaky Frames demo : file:///C|/My ...ames demo.html - Netscape Composer
File Edit View Insert Format Tools Communicator Help
New Open Save Publish Preview Cut Copy Paste Print Find Link Target Image H. Line Table Spelling
Normal
Variable Width
Media Types
.AVI video
MPEG movies
MIDI music
.AU sound
All About
Multimedia
Multimedia makes many mopey and morose. Why? well, it's confusing. There are just so many different file formats, and each requires a different player.... Cripes.
The icons in the frame at left represent the various types of multimedia files you will find here. To learn more about each type, click the icon.
Document: Done

FIGURE 18.7
Step 11: Test the page in a browser.

Specifying the Frame in Which a Linked Page Opens

If you code your frame definition pages as shown up to this point in the hour, a link that appears in any of the pages opens its corresponding file in the same frame that holds the link. In other words, if I click a link that's shown in the upper-left frame, the page opened by that link also appears in the upper-left frame, replacing the file that was there.

If you want a link in one frame to open a new page in *another* frame, you must do two things:

- In the `<FRAME SRC>` lines of the frameset, give each frame a name.
- In the links within the content files, indicate the name of the frame in which the linked file should open.

Naming the Frames

Using the page created in the preceding To Do as a starting point, name the frames. Add the `NAME=` attribute to the `<FRAME SRC>` tag after the filename (and a blank space), as shown in the following code:

```
<FRAMESET ROWS="75%,*")
<FRAMESET COLS"30%,*")
<FRAME SRC="MULTI.HTM" NAME="Icons">
<FRAME SRC="DESCRIP.HTM" NAME="Text">
</FRAMESET>
<FRAME SRC="DEFINI.HTM" NAME="Definitions">
</FRAMESET>
```

It doesn't matter what you call the frames, as long as you give each one a unique name. The frame names are not displayed on the page, just in the source code.

> To name frames while creating them in the Frames Setup dialog box in HTML Assistant Pro, click the Advanced check box. Doing so expands the dialog box to reveal a box in which you can type a name for each frame.

Making Links Point to Frame Names

After naming the frames, you must edit the links within the content files to add the *target*: the name of the frame in which the linked files should open.

To code your targets in HTML, you must add the `TARGET=` attribute and the frame name (in quotes) to the link, following the filename, as in the following example:

```
<A HREF="avidef.htm" TARGET="Definitions"></a>
```

When the link shown is executed, the file `AVIDEF.HTM` opens in the frame named `Definitions` (the bottom frame), replacing `DEFINI.HTM`.

Suppose that you want every link in the `MULTI.HTM` file to open its file in the `Text` frame. When all links are to open in the same frame, you can save time by using the `<BASE TARGET>` tag in the content file's header. All links in a file containing a `<BASE TARGET>` tag open their files in the frame named by `<BASE TARGET>`; you do not need to add any `TARGET` attributes to the link tags, as in the following example:

```
<HTML>
<HEAD>
<TITLE>
<BASE TARGET="Text">
</HEAD>
<BODY>
page definition goes here
</BODY>
</HTML>
```

All links in the sample content file open their files in the `Text` frame.

Accommodating the Frame-Intolerant

For all that frames can deliver, they can also make you pay.

Frames generally slow down initial access to a page (because the browser must download multiple files) and, when poorly designed, force visitors to do lots of scrolling simply to read the contents of a single page. Frames are supported in all versions of Internet Explorer and Netscape Navigator released since about 1997 and in some—but not all—other browsers.

Besides all that, many folks online (especially relative newcomers to the Web) simply don't like navigating frames pages; they find them confusing.

For all these reasons, many authors who create frames pages also create a non-frames version, with identical content, and give visitors a choice of which version to view. The easiest way to do this task is to create a non-frames page that contains links to each of exactly the same, separate content pages also opened by the frame definition page.

Another useful touch is to add a "noframes" message to the frame definition page. When a visitor using a non-frames-capable browser opens the frame definition page, the message appears in place of the frames. The message can include a link to the non-frames version; for example:

```
Sorry, your browser does not support frames. To view the non-frames version of
the Web site, click here.
```

Two easy ways to create the `noframes` message are

- Open the frame definition page in HTML Assistant Pro and look for the `<NOFRAMES>` tag near the bottom of the file. Replace the sample text there (`This is where to put text that browsers without frames support will display`) with your message and URL.
- Open the frame definition page in Composer. Because Composer does not support frames, it shows the sample `noframes` message created by HTML Assistant Pro—it acts, in effect, like a non-frames-capable browser. You can edit the message right there in Composer, add your URL pointing to the non-frames version, and then save the file.

Summary

Frames are an exercise in careful choices and organization. Most important among the choices is deciding whether to even use frames. When you're committed to using frames, always try to supply a useful `<NOFRAME>` message and an alternative version for the frameless.

Q&A

Q Sometimes, my browser adds scrollbars to my frames when they're not really necessary. What can I do about that?

A By default, browsers add scrollbars whenever a file's contents seem to exceed the frame. You might be able to eliminate the problem by adjusting the formatting of the content file or the size of the frame in which it is displayed so that the content sits comfortably in the frame.

Keep in mind, however, that just because everything fits in your display, this does not mean it will always do so in every visitor's browser. Variations in font size, display resolution, and other display factors can cause material that fits in a frame on your computer to exceed the frame on someone else's. Leaving scrollbars enabled helps ensure that all frames-capable visitors can navigate your page.

If you're confident that scrollbars are unnecessary, but they still show up, you can prevent them in two ways: In HTML Assistant Pro, when defining the content page to use for each frame (look back at Figure 18.4), click the No option in the Scrolling box. Or, you can edit the HTML directly and add the `SCROLLING="NO"` attribute to the `<FRAME SRC>` line for the frame, as shown in the following line:

```
<FRAME SRC="sample.htm" SCROLLING="NO">
```

By the way, you can force browsers to display scrollbars on a frame, even when the browser considers them unnecessary, by either choosing the Yes option in HTML Assistant Pro or adding `SCROLLING="YES"` to the `<FRAME SRC>` line.

Q I've seen pages online that appear to have frames (parts of the page seem to operate independently of others), but no borders or scrollbars appear between frames. How do I do these?

A Doing it in HTML Assistant Pro is easiest. When defining the frames, click the Advanced check box at the top of the Frames Setup dialog box. The dialog box expands to reveal more options below. For each frame, click the frame in the picture and then clear the check box labeled Border in the expanded area.

That step removes borders, but scrollbars still appear if the selection under Scrolling is Auto or Yes. To prevent the scrollbars from appearing, choose No.

HOUR 19

Designing Fill-in-the-Blanks Forms

You know forms. They're those fill-in-the-blanks parts of Web pages you use to enter search terms, register with a Web site, make e-purchases, and much more. In fact, Web forms are really the only way a Web visitor can send information to a Web site *through* the Web (email doesn't count).

A signature containing your email address (see Hour 10, "Making Links") is sufficient for providing visitors with a way to send you comments and questions. But if your site is visited hundreds or thousands of times a day or you want to collect orders or mailing list signups online, you need a more efficient method—a way to collect all the information sent by visitors, store it in a database, and then work with it in a meaningful way. That's what forms make possible.

At the end of this hour, you will be able to answer the following questions:

- What's involved in creating a form, and why do most beginners need to enlist the aid of a server administrator to get the whole job done?
- How do I create the easy part of a form, the part you actually see in the Web page?
- What do I have to do to get the tricky part of a form (the data processing) done?

> The material in this hour requires a basic understanding of HTML and basic familiarity with HTML Assistant Pro, a demo version of which is included on the CD-ROM with this book. If you lack this knowledge, you skipped Hour 17, "Editing HTML." Tsk, tsk. Go take a quick tour of Hour 17, and then come back. I'll wait.

Understanding Forms

A *form* is a Web page (or a part of a Web page) that collects information from your visitors by prompting them to select options from lists, check boxes, and other such *form fields* (see Figure 19.1). When done supplying information, the visitor clicks a Submit button to send the data to the server to be processed. (An optional *Reset* button also is often provided; this button clears all the forms entries a visitor has made so that he or she can start over, if necessary.)

FIGURE 19.1
Forms use fields to collect information from visitors.

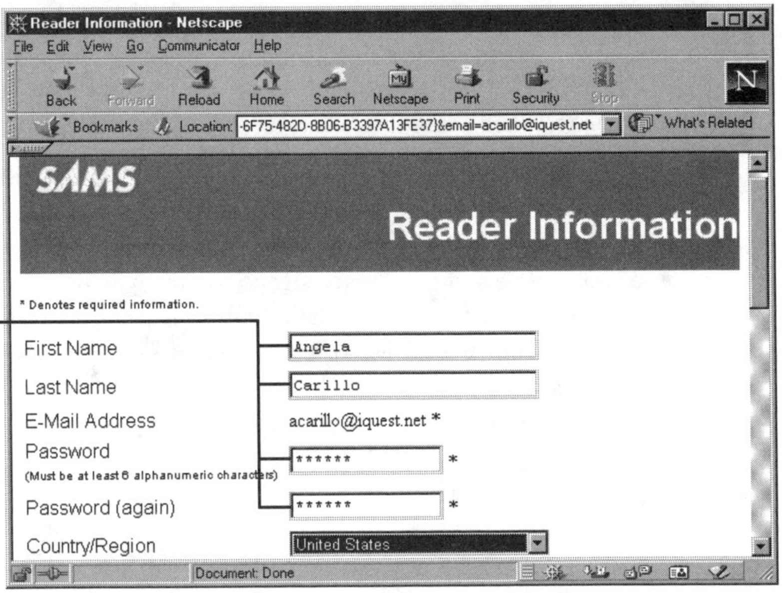

Creating the part of a form you *see* is easy—in fact, HTML Assistant Pro 2000 (included on the CD-ROM and introduced in Hour 17) can even create one for you, in several different ways. But the part you see is only half the form; the other half consists of various behind-the-scenes programming for collecting and processing the data visitors enter and storing it in a form that's useful to you.

That processing can happen in several different ways; for example, if you use Microsoft FrontPage as your authoring tool and if the Web server on which you publish the page containing the form is equipped with the Microsoft software *FrontPage Extensions*, you can configure nearly all aspects of processing from within FrontPage, and you will need no other programming to process your form.

But if you do not use FrontPage and the extensions, a short program called a *script* must be custom-written to process your form, and that script must be properly set up on the Web server. The script can be programmed in any of several different programming languages (CGI scripts, created in the Perl programming language, are the most common). Such programming generally exceeds the capabilities and ambitions of beginning Web authors—although, if you're so inclined, plenty of good books can teach you.

For beginners, I think that the best approach is this: You worry about what appears onscreen, and you let someone else worry about the scripting.

If you will publish on your Internet provider's Web server, you can simply define the form's onscreen appearance (as you learn to do in this hour) and then talk with your Internet provider about how you want the data handled. In all likelihood, the Internet provider will have a script already written that can be modified to suit your particular needs.

Creating the Visible Form

Alas, Composer includes no tools for making forms. But HTML Assistant Pro 2000 (included on the CD-ROM and introduced in Hour 17) provides easy-to-use tools for creating the form.

Although the data processing aspects of forms can be tricky, creating the form itself in HTML Assistant Pro is a snap. The next several pages show several different ways you can quickly produce any type of form you desire.

Building a Fast, Easy Form with a Template

HTML Assistant Pro includes a form template you can use to create a new form in a snap. Based on your selections in a simple dialog box, HTML Assistant Pro builds a basic form for you. You can start your page in HTML Assistant Pro, create the form, and then finish the page in Composer, or you can switch from Composer to HTML Assistant Pro to add the form and then jump back to Composer when your form has been added.

> Composer cannot give you a WYSIWYG view of your form. To preview your form, you must view the page in a browser. In Composer, the form fields are indicated with yellow tag icons, like all HTML tags that Composer does not recognize.

To Do: Add a simple form with HTML Assistant Pro

1. Open HTML Assistant Pro by clicking the Windows Start button and choosing Programs, HTML Assistant Pro 2000, Pro 2000.
2. Choose File, Open to open a page.
3. Browse to and select a page you've been working on in Composer.

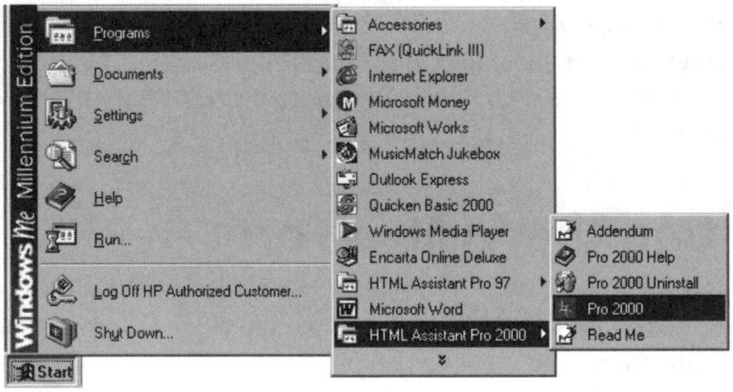

FIGURE 19.2
Step 1: Open HTML Assistant Pro 2000.

FIGURE 19.3
Step 3: Choose a file to add a form to.

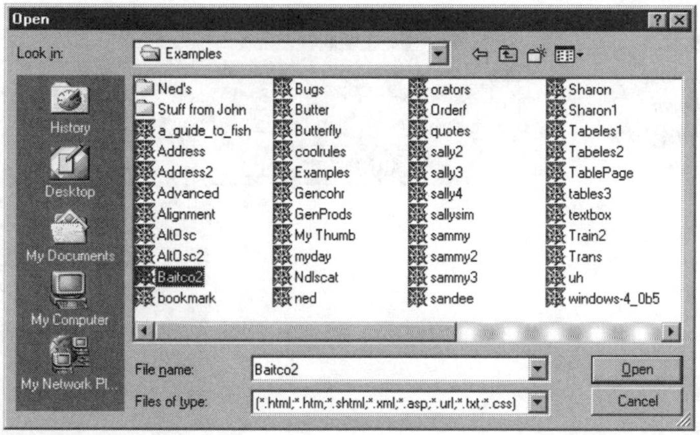

4. Look carefully at the Body section of the HTML, and locate the spot in the page where you'll want to insert the form.

FIGURE 19.4
Step 4: Find the area within the page where you want to add a form.

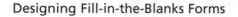

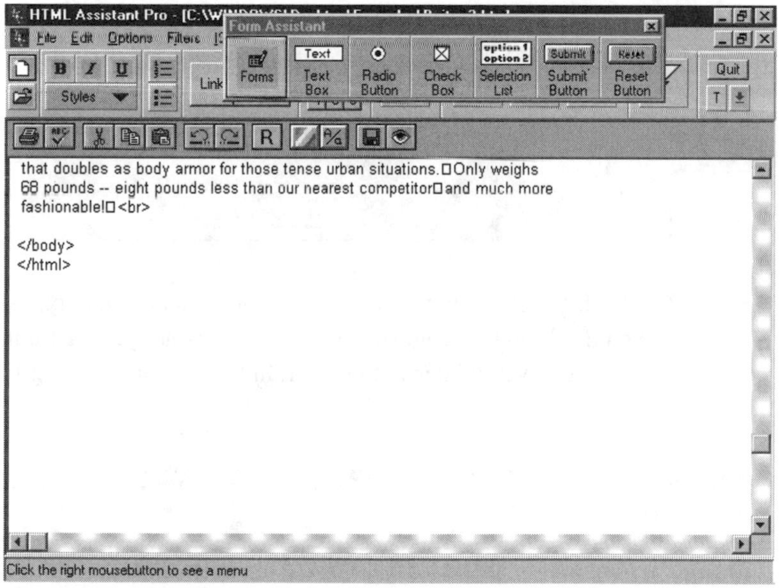

5. Click at that spot and choose Special, Form Components, Form from the menu bar.

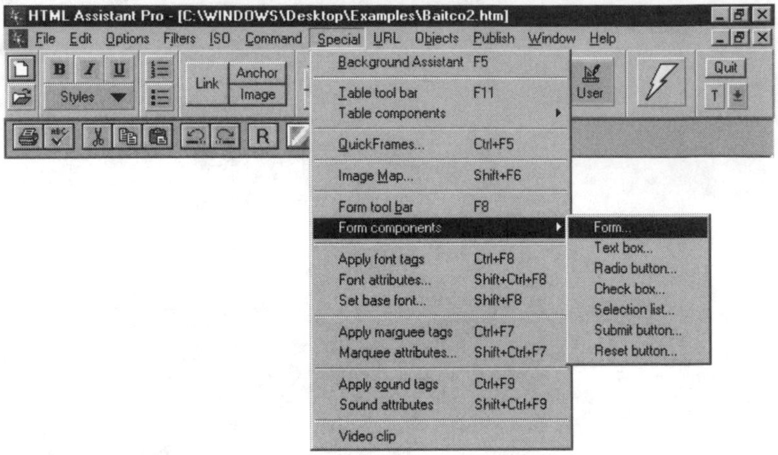

FIGURE 19.5
Step 5: Choose Special, Form Components, Form.

6. Click the Create a Form Template button.

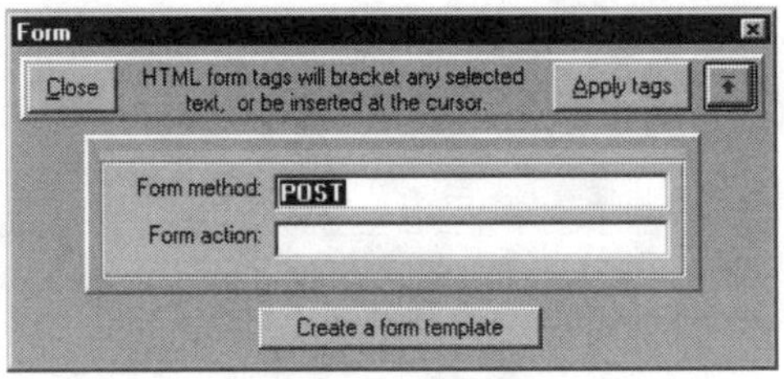

FIGURE 19.6
Step 6: Click Create a Form Template.

7. Check the check boxes next to any form "data input" types you want to include. (If you don't quite recognize what these items are yet, just don't worry about it. They're covered later in this hour, in the section "Adding Form Fields.") When finished, click OK.

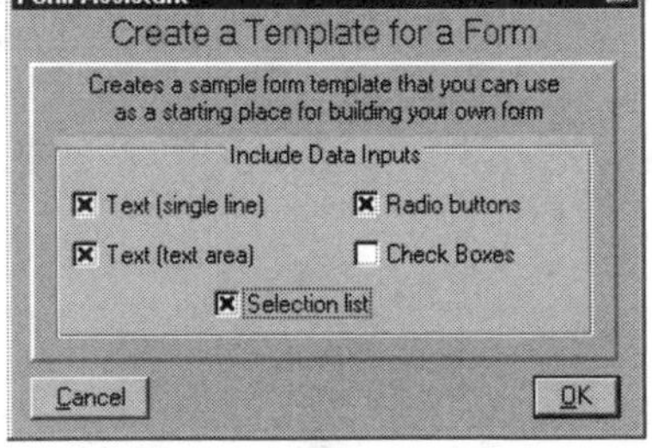

FIGURE 19.7
Step 7: Check the check boxes for the form fields to include.

8. To view the results, click the Preview button (the button with an eye icon on the far right side).

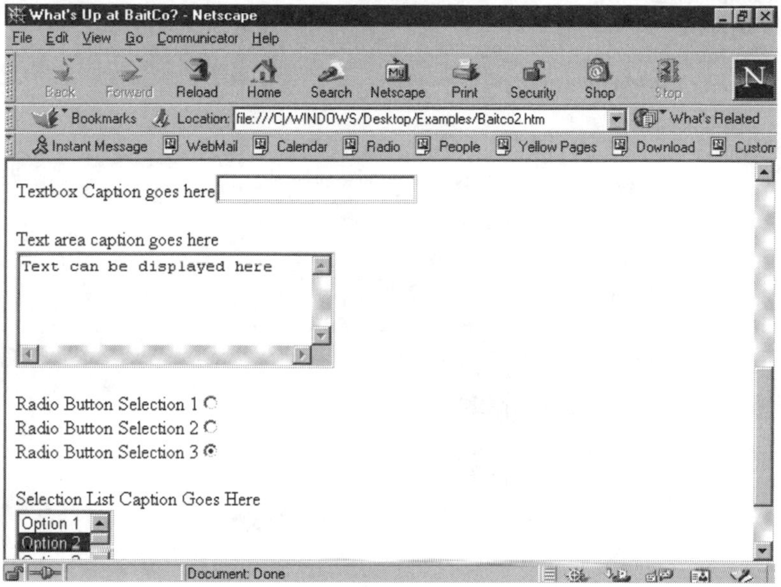

FIGURE 19.8
Step 8: Preview in Netscape to see your form.

To Do: Edit your form labels in Composer

The form added by HTML Assistant Pro has boilerplate text all over it, stuff like "Option 1" and "Text Goes Here." Obviously, you want to change these labels, or *captions*, to text that means something to you and your visitors.

You can do this right in HTML Assistant, if you're comfortable rooting around in HTML. But because you'll do most of your other authoring in Composer, you might as well switch over and do the work there:

1. Open Composer, and open in Composer the file you added a form to.
2. Composer displays its tag icons where the form fields are; the other text, before and after each tag, is the boilerplate text you can replace.

> The labels that begin with the word *Option* are the individual options on a drop-down list.

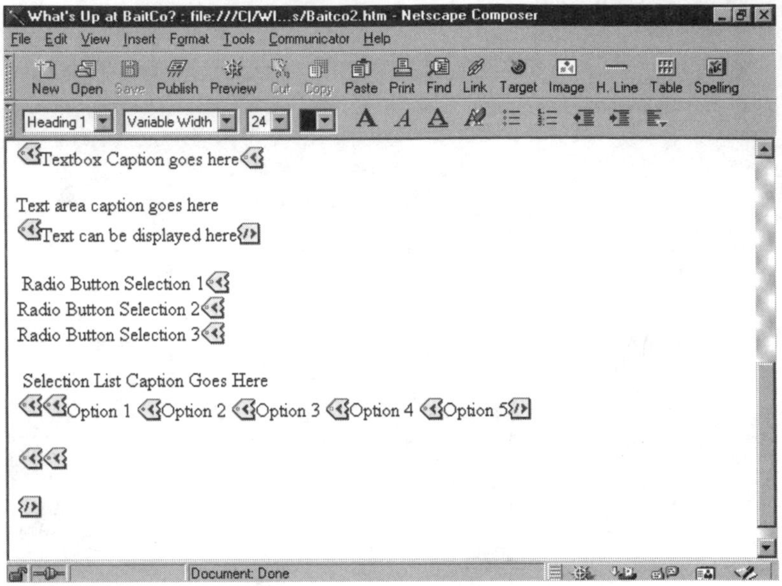

FIGURE 19.9
Composer displays your form's labels, plus tag icons representing the form fields.

3. Highlight any block of text.
4. Type its replacement.

> In the boilerplate form field labels on your HTML Assistant–built form, watch for the word *can*, as in "Text can be displayed here." That word tips you off that the label in that case is not required. You can replace the text containing *can*, but you might also erase it altogether.

Adding Form Fields

Besides providing a template for making forms, HTML Assistant offers the Form Assistant toolbar (see Figure 19.10), from which you can quickly create forms containing precisely the fields you require.

FIGURE 19.10
Use the Form Assistant toolbar to add individual fields to a form.

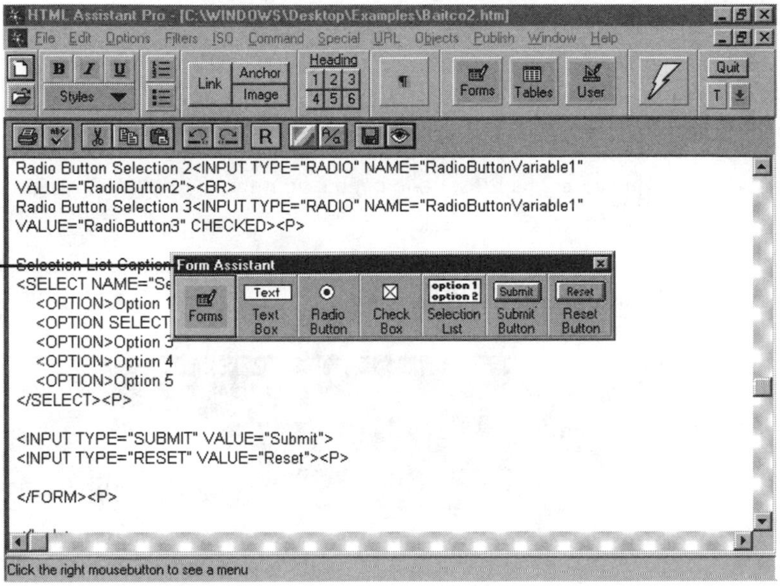

To display the Form Assistant toolbar, choose Special, Form tool bar from the HTML Assistant Pro menu bar.

To add fields, you click buttons on the Form Assistant toolbar:

Text Box

Radio Button

Check Box

Selection List

Submit Button

Reset Button

To Do: Insert form fields

1. Open the page file in HTML Assistant Pro.
2. Choose Special, Form tool bar to display the Form Assistant toolbar.
3. Examine the HTML code carefully, to locate the section where your form is located. The form code begins with the tag `<FORM...>` and ends with the tag `</FORM>`.
4. Examining the form field tags already in place, locate and click in the spot where you want to add a new field.

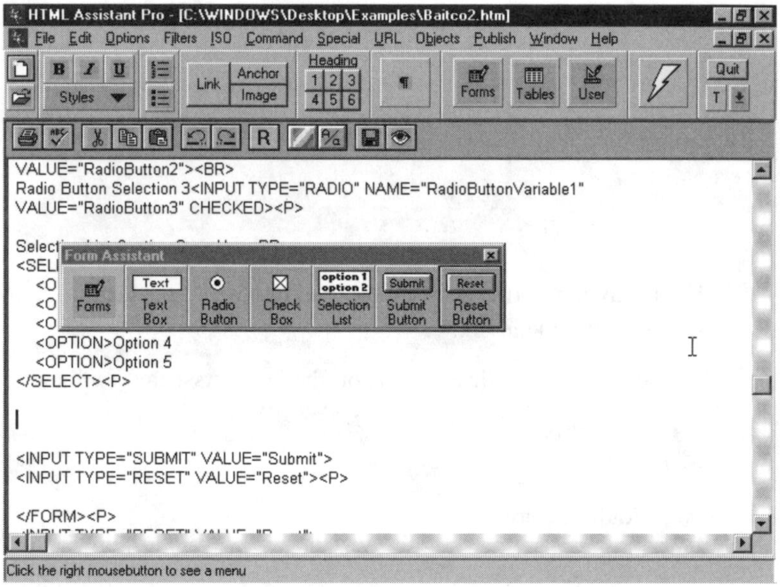

FIGURE 19.11
Step 4: Choose the spot in the code where you will add a new form field.

5. Press Enter to start a new line on which to add the field.
6. On the Form Assistant toolbar, click the button for the form field you want to add.

Customizing Fields

When adding form fields, you can customize their appearance or action. For example, when adding a text box, you can choose to make it a multiline text box rather than the default single-line text box, to give your visitors room to type longer input.

To choose options for a form field while creating it, don't click the button for the field on the Form Assistant toolbar. Instead, right-click the button. An options dialog box (different for each form field) appears (see Figure 19.12). Choose your options and then click the Apply Tags button in the dialog box.

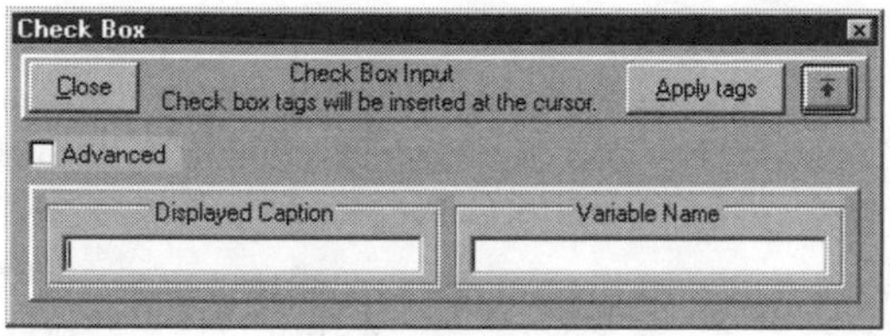

FIGURE 19.12
Right-click a button on the Form Assistant toolbar to see options for customizing that field.

Again, the exact options you see vary, depending on the type of field you double-clicked. Most options are self-explanatory. You can expand these dialog boxes by clicking the Advanced check box you see in each dialog box (see Figure 19.13).

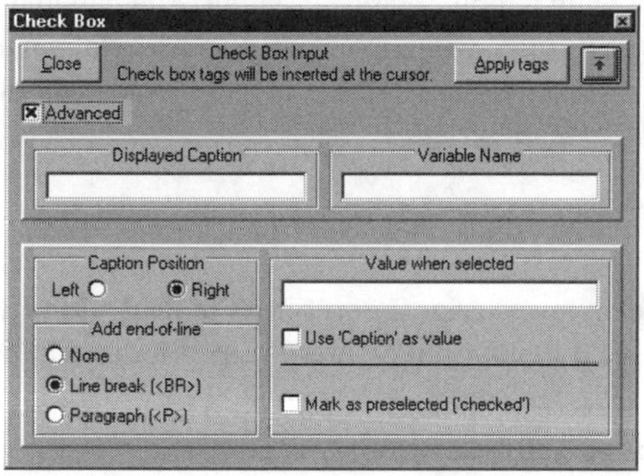

FIGURE 19.13
Click the Advanced check box to see advanced options for a form field.

> One option you see in most dialog boxes for customizing form fields is Variable Name. This name, which does not appear in your page, is used by the CGI programmer to determine what happens to the data the visitor will type there.
>
> For example, the variable name for a text box intended to collect the visitor's first name could be FIRSTNAME. Choosing these variables enables you to communicate more effectively with your CGI programmer, giving you the ability to tell him or her exactly what you want done with each piece of input collected.

However, you'll see two important options, especially when you've clicked the Advanced check box that might not be so self-explanatory:

- *Value*—In one-line and scrolling text boxes, this is an optional, default form entry you offer your visitors to save them time. For example, if you predict that most visitors will probably make a particular entry in a text box, you can make that entry appear to be pre-entered on the form. The visitor can always change that entry, but if the initial value is what he would have chosen or typed anyway, he can skip that field. Some Web authors also use the Initial Value field to display within the form an instruction for using the form ("Type your address here").

- *Mark As Preselected*—In lists, check boxes, and radio buttons, you can specify that a particular field or list item is automatically selected so that visitors who would have made the same selection can skip the field.

Summary

As you can see, building a form is easy—even fun. And building the data-handling can be fun, too—but you must be willing to commit yourself to moving a notch higher in your technical expertise. See Hour 24, "Developing Your Authoring Skills," for some suggestions on how to learn scripting.

Q&A

Q So if I write my own script, I don't need to deal with my server administrator when building a form, right? 'Cause I saw him once, and…he scares me.

A No, you still need to work closely with the administrator of the Web server to set your form up properly.

Different servers have different rules in force about what kinds of processing users are permitted to do and where on the server the programs must be stored, for example. These policies are essential to safeguarding the server from computer theft and vandalism.

In fact, security is one reason some server administrators don't install the FrontPage Extensions, even though the extensions make it easier for users of Microsoft FrontPage to program their own forms processing. Some administrators believe the extensions make it too easy for just anyone to run a program on the server.

Don't be afraid of your server administrator. The next time you see him, just call him Spock, and you'll be fast friends.

HOUR 20

Putting Multiple Links in One Picture

You've seen 'em—those cool-looking pictures and button bars in Web pages that contain multiple links. Click one button or one part of the picture and you go one place; click another part, you go somewhere else. It's a pro touch.

But it's not out of your league, now that you have 19 hours of Web authoring training already under your belt. In this hour, you learn how to apply some of the HTML skills from Hour 17, "Editing HTML," and scripting skills from Hour 19, "Designing Fill-in-the-Blanks Forms," to make these multilink pictures happen. At the end of this hour, you'll be able to answer the following questions:

- How do *imagemaps*—those inline images with multiple links—work, anyhow?
- What's the difference between a *server-side* imagemap and a *client-side* imagemap?
- How can I add imagemaps to my Web pages, using Composer in tandem with MapEdit, another program on the CD-ROM?

About Imagemaps

You know that an image file can serve as a link source; clicking the image activates the link. By creating an imagemap, you can make different areas within one image activate different links. Figure 20.1 shows an imagemap.

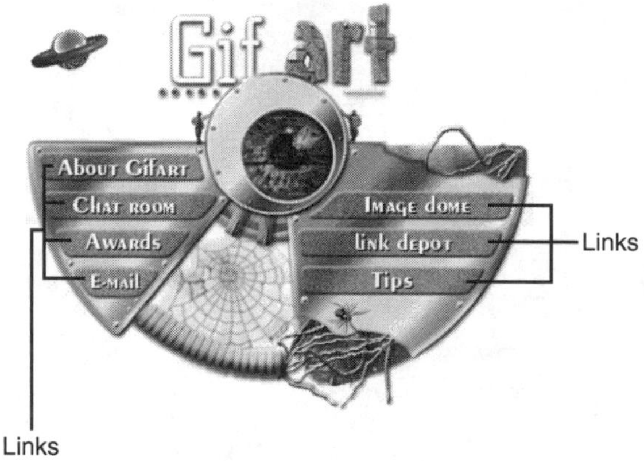

FIGURE 20.1
Clicking on different parts of this imagemap activates different links.

NEW TERM An *imagemap* is an inline image containing multiple links, each of which is activated when the visitor clicks a different area of the image.

Imagemaps are used for fancy jobs, such as maps—click a country or state and a link opens a document about it. But imagemaps have more mundane uses as well; for example, most button bars you see online are imagemaps. The whole bar is one big GIF file, but the imagemap assigns a separate URL to each button.

> The links in an imagemap can point anywhere that any other link can point: to another Web page, to an email address, to a bookmark (*target*), or to a file for download or display, for example.

Server-Side Versus Client-Side

An imagemap can be written as a server-based, imagemapping script, or it can be coded into the HTML file itself to be run by the browser, or *client*. When the imagemap code is inserted directly into the HTML file, it's a *client-side* imagemap. When a script on the server is required, the code is a *server-side* imagemap.

> To learn more about scripts, see Hour 19, "Designing Fill-in-the-Blank Forms."

Which should you create? Here's the full poop: Client-side imagemaps are much easier to create than server-side imagemaps. Client-side imagemaps work only when the page is viewed through an imagemap-compatible browser, but, fortunately, the overwhelming majority of folks online today use browsers that can handle client-side imagemaps. Client-side imagemaps are supported by

- Every version of Internet Explorer since its debut
- Netscape Navigator versions 2 and later

These browsers (which together represent about 90 percent of the browsers used on the Web) support not only client-side imagemaps, but also server-side imagemaps.

A very small proportion of folks online—those using graphical browsers other than the ones I listed—cannot use client-side imagemaps, but *can* use server-side imagemaps. Of course, those using text-only browsers cannot use any kind of picture links, including any sort of imagemap, whether client or server.

As you know from Hour 19, writing scripts requires more technical expertise than most beginning Web authors care to develop. On top of that, publishing your scripts on a server requires close collaboration with the administrator of the Web server where your pages will be published to ensure that you write your script in a language the server supports and follow other rules that vary from server to server. Server-side imagemaps require much more work than client-side imagemaps and expand the reach of your page by only a tiny proportion.

Given that, I recommend doing what most Web authors do these days:

- Stick to client-side imagemaps.
- Make sure that a block of text links on the page repeats all links that are in any imagemap (or other picture link) on the same page (see Figure 20.2).

Your client-side imagemaps will work great for nearly all visitors. And the text links will serve not only visitors whose browsers don't support client-side imagemaps, but also those with text-only browsers and those who have turned off the display of images in their browsers to speed up surfing.

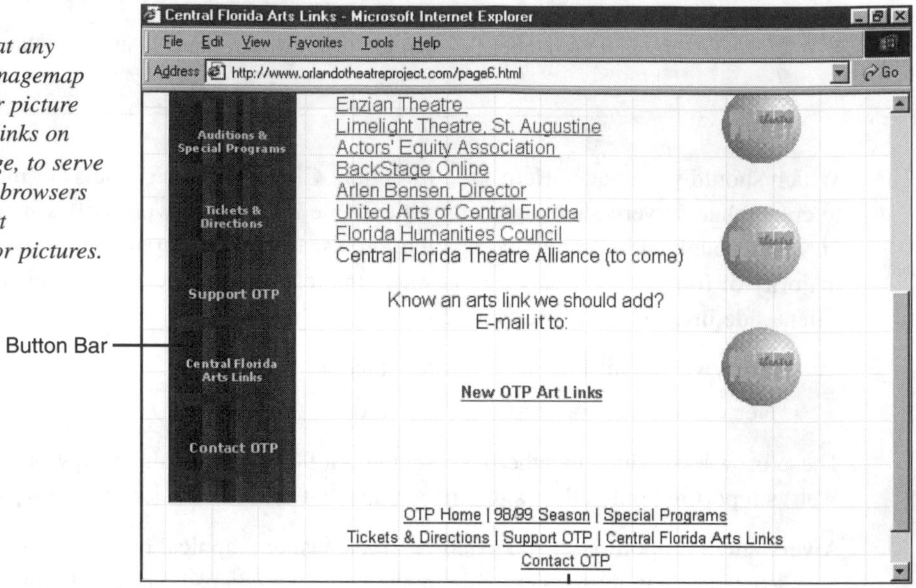

FIGURE 20.2
Always repeat any links in an imagemap (or any other picture link) in text links on the same page, to serve those whose browsers don't support imagemaps or pictures.

> If you decide to ignore my advice and develop server-side imagemaps, note that the imagemap creator included on the CD-ROM with this book, MapEdit, can be used to create either server-side or client-side imagemaps.

Choosing (or Creating) Images Suited for Imagemapping

You can use any GIF or JPEG image for an imagemap, whether it's one you created or a copyright-free piece of clip art. The best image for an imagemap is one that's clearly and obviously divided into distinct regions.

After seeing the image, a visitor *must* instinctively expect different regions to lead to different places. If the image's regions are not clearly defined, a visitor might assume that the image is a picture link leading only one place and click it without carefully choosing a region. Or the visitor might not even realize that the picture contains any links and fail to exploit the useful tool you have so thoughtfully provided.

For example, consider the image shown in Figure 20.3. This image is a poor choice for an imagemap because it does not appear to have distinct segments or regions. The image shown in Figure 20.4 is a better choice because it is divided naturally into identifiable shapes that visitors will naturally assume contain different links.

FIGURE 20.3
This image would make a poor imagemap. How could you tell which parts to click?

FIGURE 20.4
This image, clearly divided into distinct regions, is a better choice.

Creating an Imagemap

The CD-ROM at the back of this book contains MapEdit, a program for adding imagemaps to existing HTML files.

To use MapEdit to create a client-side imagemap, you first create your page (in Composer or another tool) and insert in the page the image you will use for the imagemap. You then open the page in MapEdit to turn the image into an imagemap, as described in the following To Do.

In general, you should finish all other aspects of the page (in Composer or in another Web authoring program) before using MapEdit to make one or more images in the page into imagemaps.

Why? Well, if you change the size or shape or any other aspects of an image in the page after you create the imagemap, the imagemap might not work properly anymore. In practice, you can probably do some manipulation of the page safely after adding the imagemap, but it's hard to predict which kinds of changes will create problems later and which won't. You should leave MapEdit for the final step.

20

> If, after creating an imagemap, you decide that you must make major changes to the page (or if you've already made such changes and discover that your imagemap no longer works properly), the best solution is to reopen the page and image in MapEdit (as described in Steps 2 through 5 of the To Do) and adjust the regions as needed.

To Do: Create a client-side imagemap in MapEdit

1. Using Composer or another tool, create the page and insert in it the image that will become the imagemap.
2. Open MapEdit from the Windows Start menu by choosing Programs, MapEdit, MapEdit.
3. Choose File, Open HTML Document.
4. Navigate to and select the file of the Web page you created in Step 1 and then click Open.
5. The list shows all the image files in the page. Click the one that will serve as the imagemap and then click OK.

Select Inline Image
Select the image to be mapped. You can create a map corresponding to any inline image mentioned in the HTML document.
tomato.gif
tomatoes.gif
OK
Cancel

FIGURE 20.5
Step 5: From the images shown in the page you opened in Step 4, choose the one for the imagemap.

6. Consider the general shape of the first region to which you want to attach a link: Is it more or less circular or rectangular, or is it a more irregular polygon? Decide what the closest shape is and then click that shape in the toolbar.
7. Click and drag to draw a shape that generally covers the region:
   - For a circle, click in the center of the region and drag outward. When the shape generally covers the region, click once.
   - For a rectangle, click in the upper-right corner of the region and drag diagonally toward the lower-right corner. When the shape generally covers the region, click once.

- For a polygon, click one corner of the region and drag to another corner to draw a line. Click the corner you've arrived at to stop that line and then drag to the next corner. Continue until you have drawn a shape completely around the region and then right-click.

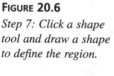

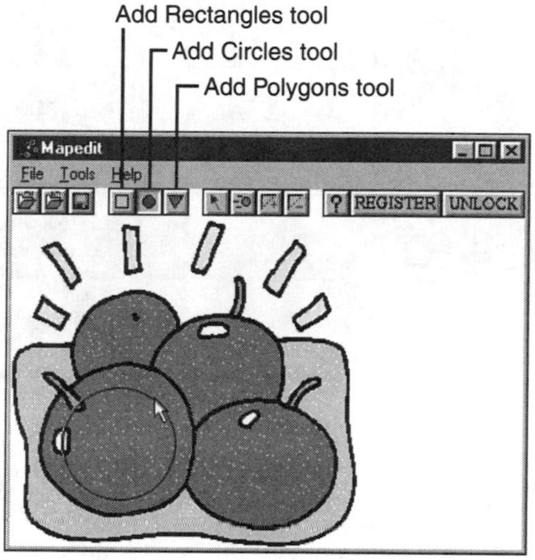

FIGURE 20.6
Step 7: Click a shape tool and draw a shape to define the region.

> If you don't like the point where you started a shape, press Esc to clear the shape and start over.

> In Steps 6 and 7, don't fuss too much over trying to perfectly match a shape to a region.
>
> As long as the shape you draw roughly covers the region and does not overlap with other shapes you draw for other regions, it's no big deal if some gaps occur between the shapes covering regions or if the shape covers a little bit of space outside the region.
>
> Understanding this, you find that in most cases you can use the Circle or Rectangle tools to draw your rough shapes, resorting to the more laborious Polygon tool for only special circumstances.

8. Fill in the URL to which a visitor should be taken when clicking this region and click OK.

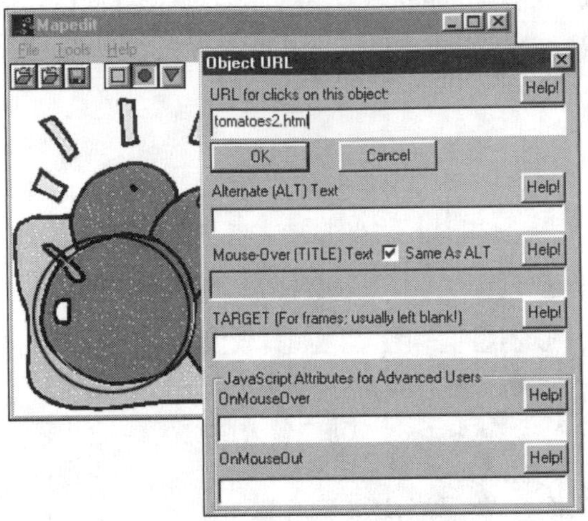

FIGURE 20.7
Step 8: Fill in the URL to which this region points.

The TARGET field in the dialog box shown in Figure 20.7 is not for entering the name of a bookmark (see Hour 11, "More Ways to Link") as you might expect, but rather for choosing the *target frame*.

If the HTML file you opened in Step 2 will be part of a frames-based Web page, you can enter in the TARGET field the name of the frame in which you want the file or page opened by this link to appear. See Hour 18, "Dividing a Page into Frames."

9. Repeat Steps 6, 7, and 8 for each region in the image. (You can use different kinds of shapes and different kinds of URLs for different regions.)

FIGURE 20.8
Step 9: Complete the regions.

10. Choose File, Save HTML Document to save the Web page file with its new imagemap added to it.
11. Preview the file in a Web browser to test the links.

> In Step 8 of the To Do, you can enter any type of URL: one pointing to a Web site or Web page (for example, `http://www.samspublishing.com`), the filename of another Web page in your Web site, stored in the same folder (`page2.html`), a link to an email address (`mailto:me@server.com`), or the name of a file for downloading (`resume.doc`).
>
> To make the link point to a particular bookmark (*target*), add a hash mark and the bookmark name (`#Chapter3`) to the URL as described in Hour 11.

Summary

Imagemaps are pretty cool and not too hard to make. Just be sure that you choose an image in which the regions to which you attach links are easy for visitors to recognize.

Q&A

Q Can I edit my imagemaps later, after creating them?

A Sure. Repeat Steps 2–5 of the To Do, and then use the MapEdit tools to make any changes you like.

Q Not that I necessarily want to, but assume that I do want to use MapEdit to create a server-side imagemap. How would I do it?

A. Begin by creating a client-side imagemap, just as described in the To Do "Create a client-side imagemap in MapEdit" in this hour. Still in MapEdit, choose File, Export Old Server Map. The imagemap script is saved in its own file.

After saving the file, show it to the administrator of your Web server to find out whether any changes must be made to make it work properly on the server, and to learn the rules for publishing scripts on the server, such as in which directory your script must be stored.

PART VI

Getting it Online

Hour

Hour 21

Publishing Your Page

You didn't become a Web author just to share your accomplishments with your canary. Of course, you want to get your work on a Web server so that it can be visited, loved, and lauded by those burgeoning Web masses.

Composer is a big help with publishing. By setting up a few defaults and properly organizing your files, you wind up with the ability to publish your pages (and then update them later) with a few quick clicks.

At the end of this hour, you'll be able to answer the following questions:

- Where do I publish?
- What should I do before publishing to make sure that everything's ready?
- How do I use Composer to make publishing my page easy?
- After my page is online, how do I check it out?

About Web Servers

As you've known for about 20 hours, you need space on the hard disk of a Web server to publish your page on the Web.

By now, you probably already know where you intend to publish your page. Nearly all Internet accounts—whether with a regular Internet service provider or with an online service, like AOL—now include a few megabytes of Web server space in the deal (see Figure 21.1). Most folks publish their first Web pages in the space supplied by their Internet providers.

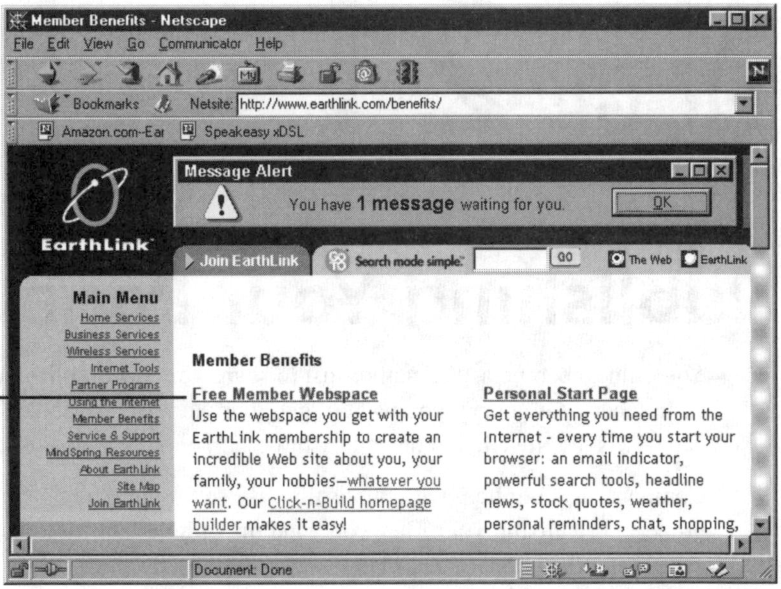

FIGURE 21.1
Most folks just starting out with Web publishing should use any Web server space that comes free with their Internet or online service account.

Note that Web space suppliers usually make a distinction between personal home pages and commercial pages (those used to promote a business). On the assumption that a commercial page generally gets more traffic than a personal one, suppliers might charge a higher rate for space used by a commercial page.

If your Internet provider gives you free space, the provider might require that the space be used for only a personal page and might charge an additional monthly fee if you use the space for commercial purposes. (Exceptions may be made for not-for-profits; talk to your provider.)

In case your Internet provider offers no server space to you, here are some other ways to pick up Web server space:

> Before choosing a provider for Web space, visit that company's Web page a few times at different hours. If the server sends pages slowly at certain hours or seems to be unavailable from time to time, look for a better-equipped provider.

At work or school—Your employer or school might have a Web server on which you are permitted to store your page. Certainly, if your page is strictly work related (or school related), you're most likely to gain permission to publish it on the server for free.

However, note that free access to corporate and university servers is diminishing rapidly as demand grows and as organizations look for ways to earn money from their Internet connections. Also, many university systems, as well as some corporate systems, are overtaxed and might have outdated server hardware or inadequate connection speeds. Using a slow or unreliable system provides poor service to your visitors; forking over a few dollars a month for space on a fast commercial server might be a better choice in the long run than using free space on a poor server.

From a Web hosting service—A growing number of companies online offer Web space "hosting services." Many such services are just Internet providers making a few bucks on the side by leasing server space, often for just a few dollars a month.

You can also find "free" server space offered by a variety of companies sometimes called *online communities*. In exchange for your free space, you agree to include required advertising on your pages (see Figure 21.2). For more about these communities, see Hour 3, "Getting a Head-Start with Templates."

> Finding Web hosting services by surfing is easy. You can enter the search term *Web hosting* in any search engine or visit the HostSearch site (`www.hostsearch.com`), a search tool specifically for finding server space (see Figure 21.3).
>
> Some hosting services are set up to offer free or low-cost space for pages with particular worthy topics: the arts or nonprofit organizations, for example.

FIGURE 21.2
You can get "free" Web hosting services—just remember that they reserve the right to post advertisements on your Web pages, for your visitors to see.

FIGURE 21.3
The HostSearch page helps you find Web server space that matches your needs.

The build-your-own method—If your Web page requires extra-tight security (for online sales) or makes extensive use of CGI scripts (especially for forms), an in-house Web server might be your answer. Building your own Web server is a more practical solution than ever (even for relatively small companies), thanks to lower-priced server computers (especially Pentium-based PCs); cheaper, simpler server software (primarily from Microsoft, although free, open-source alternatives are also available); and the wide availability of high-speed data lines (such as ISDN or T1).

> Setting up a Web server is not cheap. The hardware and software for a decent server is coming down rapidly, to a reasonable cost for a small business (less than $5,000). But the 24-hour, high-speed dedicated Internet connection that a Web server demands might cost more than four times that much—every month. Although effectively administering a Web server is getting easier all the time, the job essentially demands one or more full-time experts.
>
> The combined cost of server, connection, and staff now falls within the means of most companies with more than 100 employees, or smaller companies whose line of business makes Web service a high priority. For other small companies and for individuals, however, leasing space on someone else's server is a far more sensible option.
>
> Increasingly, commercial hosting services not only provide space, but can also supply (for a higher fee) e-commerce services. The hosting company can take care of processing orders and credit card transactions for you, so you can set up an online store without having to worry about all the e-details.

How Much Space Do I Need?

Good question. Odds are that you need very little, starting out.

As I've reminded you over the past 20 hours, the more a page contains, the bigger its file. Pictures (and picture backgrounds) dramatically increase the amount of space a page requires (and the time it takes to appear to a visitor). Sound, video, and large file downloads also might dramatically increase the amount of space you need.

If you have followed the tips I've offered for keeping the performance of your page sprightly, you'll find that each page occupies very little space. A basic page—a screenful or two of text graced with two or three small picture files and maybe a picture background—typically requires less than 100KB of server space (often much less). You can store at least a dozen such basic Web pages in 1MB of server space. (There are 1024 kilobytes in a megabyte).

Most Internet providers and online services supply at least 3MB of free space to each customer; many supply as much as 10MB. That's enough to store 100 basic pages and have a few megs left over for a short video clip or two.

The following To Do shows how to determine the minimum amount of disk space required by your page files.

> The following To Do assumes that you have stored all the files for the page—the HTML file or files and picture files, for example—in the same folder on your hard disk.

To Do: Find out how much space your files need

1. In Windows, open the folder in which your Web page files are stored.
2. Press and hold the Ctrl key and click one by one all the files that are a part of the page. (The folder shouldn't have any files that aren't part of the page, but if it does, don't click those.)
3. When all the files are highlighted, you see the amount of space they occupy reported at the bottom of the folder window. The Web page in this example (which includes two screenfuls of text, two pictures, and a picture background) requires only 5.16KB of space!

FIGURE 21.4
Step 3: Read the size of the combined files.

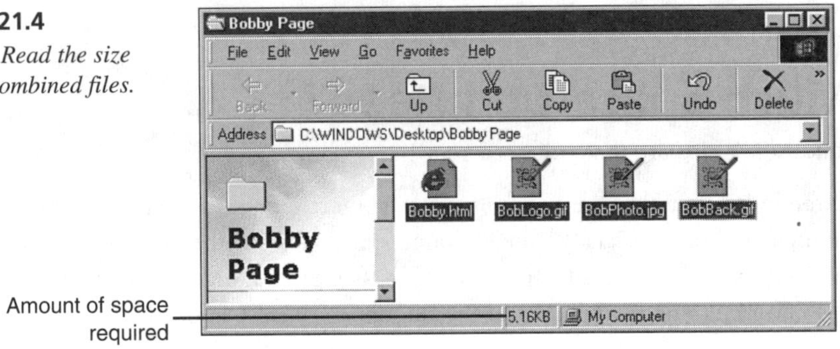

Preparing to Publish

Before publishing, you want to have acquired your server space and given your page a final once-over. (Even if you miss a mistake, you can easily fix it later and publish the correction, as described in Hour 23, "Testing and Maintaining Your Page Online.")

The last thing you need to do before publishing is to get some important information from whomever is supplying your Web server space. Specifically, you need to know:

- *The name of the communications protocol required for uploading your files*—Many servers allow you to use the Web protocol (HTTP) for uploading files, whereas some require that files be uploaded via FTP. (Composer supports both methods.)
- *The complete address and path where your files will be stored*—You need to know the complete URL of the directory in which your files will be stored, including the server name, the path to your directory, and the name of your directory. Ideally, you have your own separate directory for all your files. Having your own directory prevents conflicts that might arise if any other file on the system (a page, image, or other file) uses the same filename as one of your files.

> It's standard practice to name the top page of a multipage Web site `index.htm` (or `index.html`).
>
> Unless you have your own directory on the server, though, do not name any page `index.htm` (or `index.html`). Although this name is often used for the top page in a multipage Web page, if the directory already contains a file named `index.htm`, the server rejects yours—or overwrites the other!

- *The rules or restrictions for filenames on the server*—Different server platforms have different rules for filenames. For example, DOS-based servers and some UNIX servers do not permit filenames longer than eight characters or file extensions of more than three characters. Ideally, you find out about these types of restrictions before you create and name your files. But, if you composed your page without first finding out about the server, you should check for naming restrictions and change any filenames as needed.

> If you find that you must alter any filenames, be sure to check and adjust any links between pages before and after publishing.

- *Your unique username and password for gaining upload access to the server*—Your server supplier should give you a username and password for uploading your files.

> If you get server space from your Internet provider, the username and password you use to publish will probably be the same ones you always use to connect to the Internet.

Publishing from Composer

Most server providers prefer that you *upload*—copy your Web files from your PC to the Web server—using an Internet tool named FTP.

If you're familiar with FTP, you can always do it that way. But the publishing facilities built in to Composer can be much easier to use. More important, when you make changes to your pages online (as you learn to do in Hour 23), Composer can publish those changes in about two clicks.

Even if you do know FTP, I recommend giving the Composer publishing tools a shot anyway. (If you don't already know FTP, you have no need to learn now—at least for publishing purposes.)

To Do: Publish a page

1. Connect to the Internet.
2. In Composer, open the HTML file you want to publish.
3. Click the Publish button on the Composer toolbar to open the Publish dialog box.
4. The page's title and HTML filename already appear in the box. Fill in the rest of the Publish dialog box with the address to which you will publish and the username and password your server provider gave you.
5. In the area at the bottom of the Publish dialog box, make sure that all the files required for your Website have been included. If you've followed the advice given throughout this book—store all HTML files, pictures, and whatever in the same folder—this job is easy; simply select the All Files in Page's Folder option to send all files to the server.

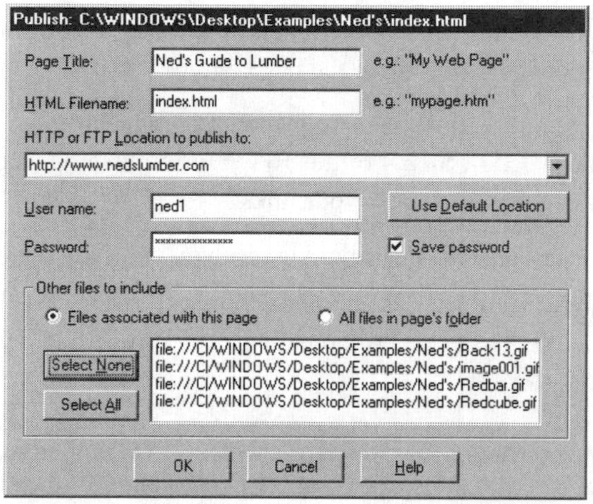

FIGURE 21.5
Step 4: Complete the dialog box by filling in the address to publish to, your server username, and your password.

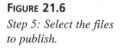

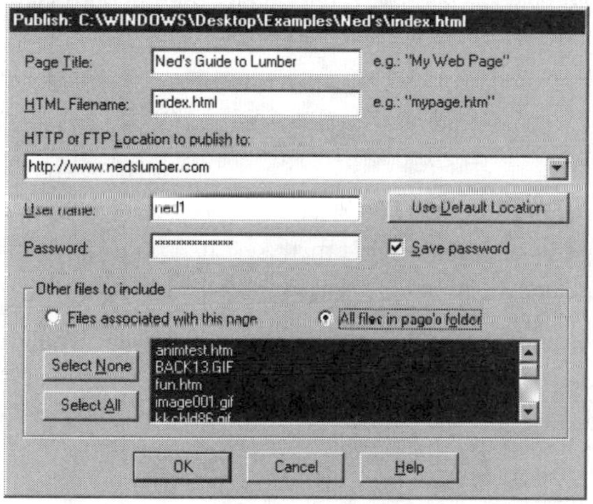

FIGURE 21.6
Step 5: Select the files to publish.

> If you do not want to send all the files in the folder to the server, leave the All Files in Folder option unselected. Press and hold the Ctrl key and select one by one all the files in the folder you want to upload.

6. Click OK. In a few moments, a message appears and reports that the files have been uploaded. They are now on the Web, available to all.

Viewing Your Page Through the Internet

After you publish, you must test your page through the Web, viewing it exactly as your visitors will. Besides, it's fun to see the page online.

To view your page online, just open your browser, connect to the Internet, and go to the same address you typed in Step 4 of the To Do for publishing. Explore your page, evaluating its appearance and testing all your links.

- If you find any mistakes or anything else you want to change, see Hour 23.
- If you want to learn how to announce your page to the world (so that visitors can discover it), see Hour 22, "Announcing Your Web Presence."

> If you named your top page `index.html` (as suggested in Part II of this book), that page opens automatically whenever a visitor surfs to the server directory without specifying a filename. For example, if the user enters the URL `www.server.com/sally/` in his browser, the `index.html` file in the `sally` directory opens automatically.

Summary

Publishing is a simple activity (and relatively foolproof) as long as you've taken care in the preparation of your page. Simple mistakes, like putting files for the same page in different directories, are the kinds of things that most often cause publishing problems.

If you are careful with your filenames and locations, obey your server's rules, and follow the publishing steps, you'll find publishing one of the more satisfying aspects of authoring—the reward for a job well done.

Q&A

Q I want my own dot-com, as in `www.steve.com`. How do I get one o' those guys?

A You need your own Internet domain, which is a little more ambitious than first-time Web authors are ready for. But by now, you're probably ready (if you have the cash) and certainly motivated. You learn how to get a domain in Hour 24, "Developing Your Authoring Skills."

Q What if the HTML standard changes? Will my page suddenly not work in browsers that conform to a new standard or support new extensions?

A Updates to HTML are backward compatible; in other words, when HTML changes, new tags and attributes are added, as are new ways to do old things. But older approaches and tags still work indefinitely.

In Hour 23, you'll learn about testing your page's HTML online. In Hour 24, you'll learn that HTML is not only still evolving, but it's also morphing into something new: *XHTML.*

Q How do I update my page when it changes?

A That, too, is coming in Hour 23. First, you need to learn how to announce your newly published page to the world; see Hour 22.

HOUR 22

Announcing Your Web Presence

After your page is on the server, it doesn't do you much good if nobody knows that it's there. You need to get the word out so that anyone who might have an interest in your page knows that it's there and can find it easily.

In this hour, you learn how to announce your page to the world. At the end of the hour, you'll be able to answer the following questions:

- Where are the major Web search pages on which my page should be listed?
- How do I get listed on the search pages?
- In what other ways can I publicize my page?
- How do I broadcast an email announcement to my friends, family, or clients?

Listing Your Page in Web Search Pages

Two kinds of people are on the Web whom you might want to know about your Web page—the people you know and the people you don't know.

You will inform directly the people you know, as you learn to do later in this hour. The most efficient way to inform the people you don't know is to get your page listed on the major Internet search services, including

- *Yahoo!* `www.yahoo.com`
- *Excite* (see Figure 22.1) `www.excite.com`
- *Lycos* `www.lycos.com`
- *Alta Vista* `www.altavista.com`
- *WebCrawler* `www.webcrawler.com`

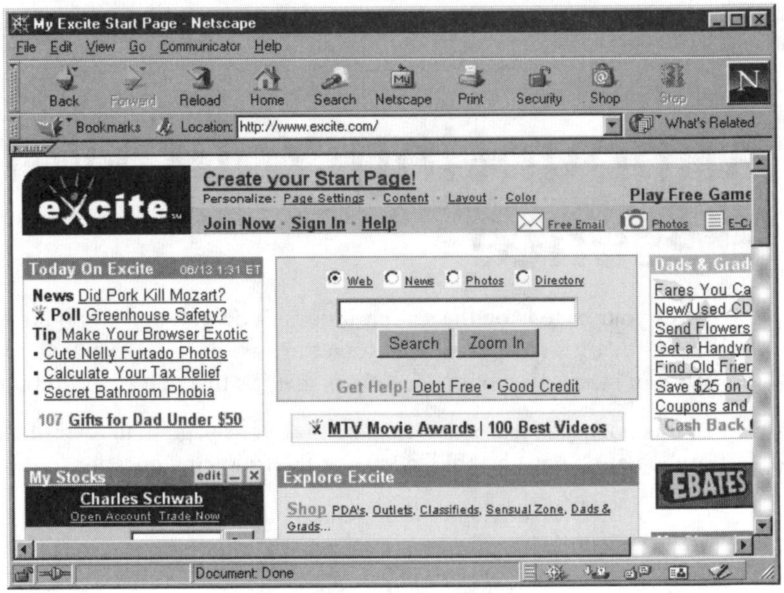

FIGURE 22.1
Excite, one of the Web search pages to which you'll want to add your page.

> If your page covers a particular subject, you should use the search pages to find other pages about the same subject and explore them.
>
> Many such pages offer a list of links to related pages; when you find this type of page, you can email its Webmaster to ask that a link to your page be added to the list. (An email link to the Webmaster usually appears on the same page as the links.) You can also add to your Web site your own list of links to related pages, thus returning the favor.

When your page is properly listed by these services, folks will find your page whenever they search for something related to your page's subject, title, or *keywords* (see Hour 5, "Choosing a Title, Text Colors, and Other Page Basics").

Some search pages find your page all by themselves. Services such as Excite and Alta Vista use programs, sometimes called *spiders* or *crawlers*, to methodically search the Web and add new pages to their search pages.

By adding your pages to these and other search pages manually, you get them listed more quickly and you improve the chances that they'll be categorized properly—which improves the chances that your page will be found by people who actually want to see it.

Each search page has different rules for adding new pages. You always begin by navigating to the search page's top page. From there, by hunting around, you can usually find instructions, a button, or some other indication of how to add a site.

> When adding the URL of a business site to search pages, do searches to find out how your competitors are listed. Then, be sure that your page is associated with the same categories or keywords.
>
> That way, whenever anyone does a search that finds your competitors, that person finds you, too.

To Do: Add your site to Yahoo!

1. Go to Yahoo! at `www.yahoo.com`.
2. Explore the Yahoo! categories and choose the precise category in which your page belongs.
3. Scroll to the bottom of the page and click Suggest a Site.
4. Read the Suggest a Site page for tips on properly listing your page with Yahoo!

> If the category you chose in Step 2 is too broad, Yahoo! displays a message to that effect and asks you to choose another, more specific category before proceeding.

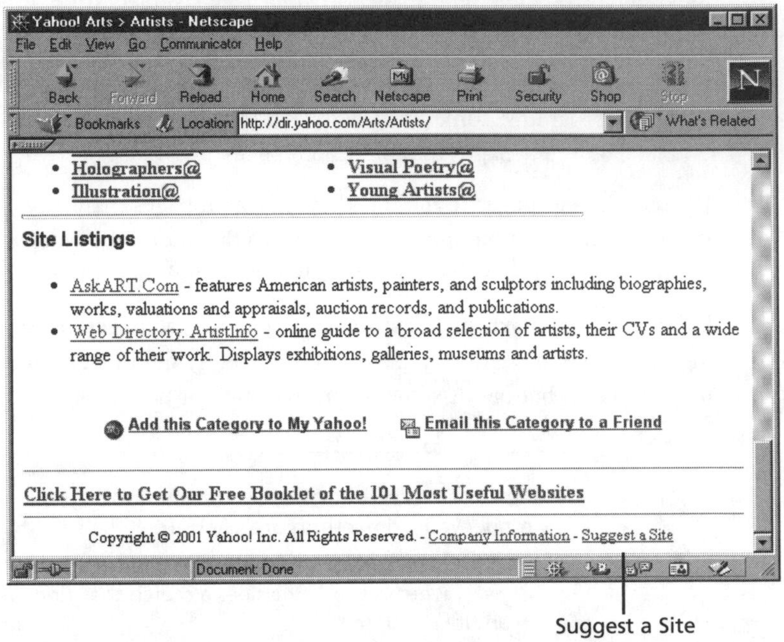
Yahoo! Arts > Artists - Netscape
File Edit View Go Communicator Help
Back Forward Reload Home Search Netscape Print Security Shop Stop
Bookmarks Location: http://dir.yahoo.com/Arts/Artists/
What's Related
Holographers@
Illustration@
Visual Poetry@
Young Artists@
Site Listings
AskART.Com - features American artists, painters, and sculptors including biographies, works, valuations and appraisals, auction records, and publications.
Web Directory: ArtistInfo - online guide to a broad selection of artists, their CVs and a wide range of their work. Displays exhibitions, galleries, museums and artists.
Add this Category to My Yahoo!
Email this Category to a Friend
Click Here to Get Our Free Booklet of the 101 Most Useful Websites
Copyright © 2001 Yahoo! Inc. All Rights Reserved. - Company Information - Suggest a Site
Document: Done
Suggest a Site

FIGURE 22.2
Step 3: Click Suggest a Site at the bottom of the Yahoo! category that fits your page.

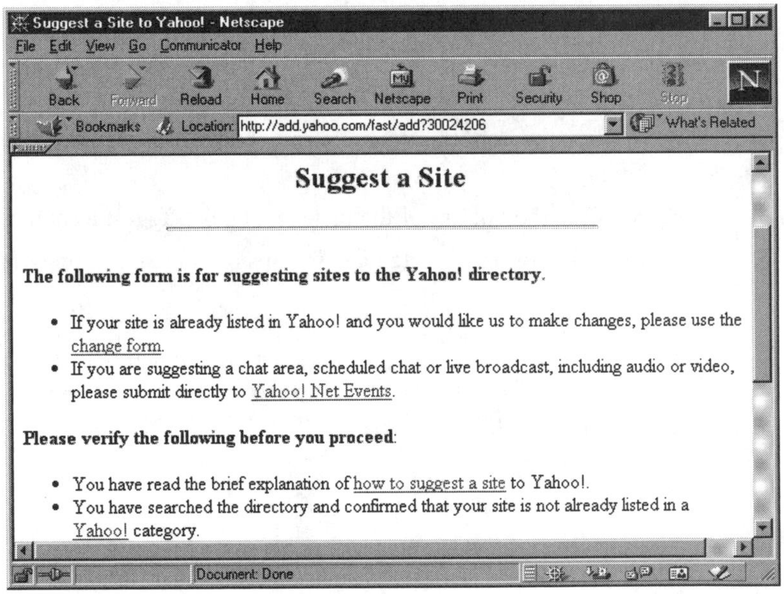
Suggest a Site to Yahoo! - Netscape
File Edit View Go Communicator Help
Back Forward Reload Home Search Netscape Print Security Shop Stop
Bookmarks Location: http://add.yahoo.com/fast/add?30024206
What's Related
Suggest a Site
The following form is for suggesting sites to the Yahoo! directory.
If your site is already listed in Yahoo! and you would like us to make changes, please use the change form.
If you are suggesting a chat area, scheduled chat or live broadcast, including audio or video, please submit directly to Yahoo! Net Events.
Please verify the following before you proceed:
You have read the brief explanation of how to suggest a site to Yahoo!.
You have searched the directory and confirmed that your site is not already listed in a Yahoo! category.
Document: Done

FIGURE 22.3
Step 4: Study the Suggest a Site instructions.

5. Scroll to the bottom of the Suggest a Site page and click Proceed to Step 1.

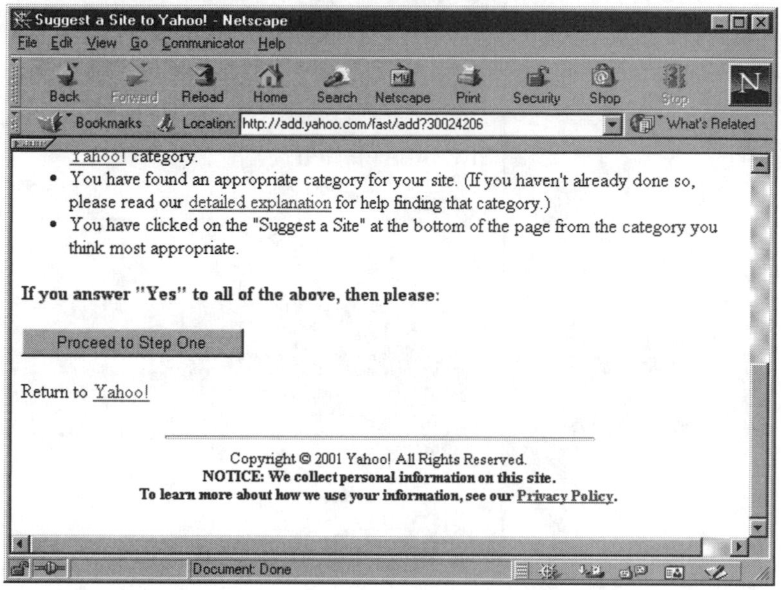
Suggest a Site to Yahoo! - Netscape
File Edit View Go Communicator Help
Back Forward Reload Home Search Netscape Print Security Shop Stop
Bookmarks Location: http://add.yahoo.com/fast/add?30024206
What's Related
Yahoo! category.
You have found an appropriate category for your site. (If you haven't already done so, please read our detailed explanation for help finding that category.)
You have clicked on the "Suggest a Site" at the bottom of the page from the category you think most appropriate.
If you answer "Yes" to all of the above, then please:
Proceed to Step One
Return to Yahoo!
Copyright © 2001 Yahoo! All Rights Reserved.
NOTICE: We collect personal information on this site.
To learn more about how we use your information, see our Privacy Policy.
Document: Done

FIGURE 22.4
Step 5: Click Proceed to Step 1.

6. Yahoo presents a choice of submission: a free, standard submission and a business express submission that expedites your submission for a one-time fee. For now, for practice, click the button for Standard submission.
7. Scroll down to the Site Information form and type the title and URL of your page or site, plus a brief description.

> The description you type in Step 7 appears in the search results whenever someone's Yahoo! search finds your page. Word your description carefully, to help searchers determine whether your page contains what they want. Be sure also to include in the description keywords related to the page's topic.

8. At the bottom of the Suggest a Site page, click Proceed to Step 2.
9. Continue through Steps 2, 3, and 4, filling in all information requested and clicking the button at the bottom of the page to proceed to each new step.

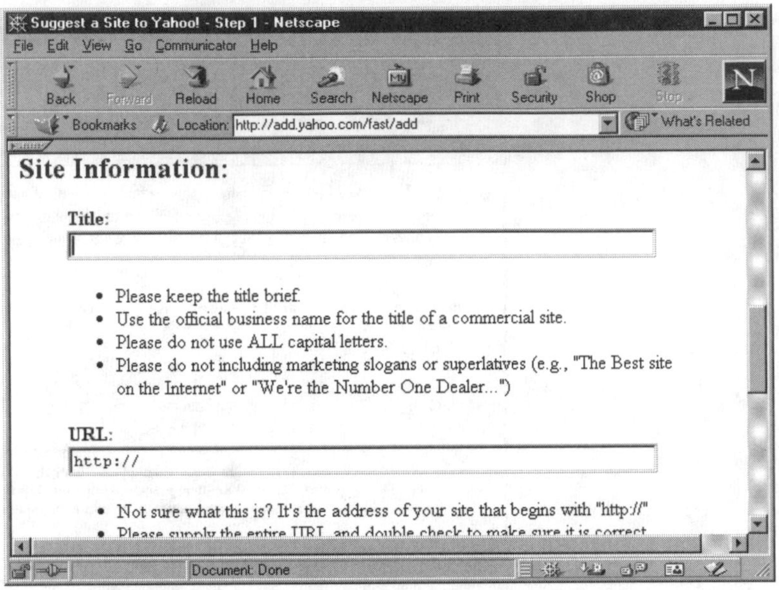
Suggest a Site to Yahoo! - Step 1 - Netscape
File Edit View Go Communicator Help
Back Forward Reload Home Search Netscape Print Security Shop Stop
Bookmarks Location: http://add.yahoo.com/fast/add What's Related
Site Information:
Title:
Please keep the title brief.
Use the official business name for the title of a commercial site.
Please do not use ALL capital letters.
Please do not including marketing slogans or superlatives (e.g., "The Best site on the Internet" or "We're the Number One Dealer...")
URL:
http://
Not sure what this is? It's the address of your site that begins with "http://"
Document: Done

FIGURE 22.5
Step 7: Fill in your page's title and URL.

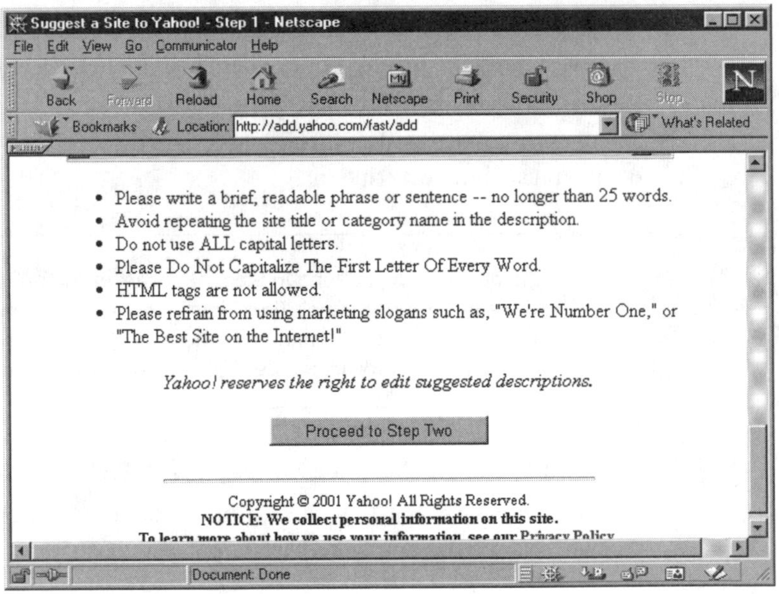
Suggest a Site to Yahoo! - Step 1 - Netscape
File Edit View Go Communicator Help
Back Forward Reload Home Search Netscape Print Security Shop Stop
Bookmarks Location: http://add.yahoo.com/fast/add What's Related
Please write a brief, readable phrase or sentence -- no longer than 25 words.
Avoid repeating the site title or category name in the description.
Do not use ALL capital letters.
Please Do Not Capitalize The First Letter Of Every Word.
HTML tags are not allowed.
Please refrain from using marketing slogans such as, "We're Number One," or "The Best Site on the Internet!"
Yahoo! reserves the right to edit suggested descriptions.
Proceed to Step Two
Copyright © 2001 Yahoo! All Rights Reserved.
NOTICE: We collect personal information on this site.
Document: Done

FIGURE 22.6
Step 8: Proceed to Step 2.

22

When you add a site to many search pages, including Yahoo! and Excite, the URL does not show up in the search page immediately. You might have to wait two weeks or longer before your addition becomes official.

▼ To Do

To Do: Add your site to Excite!

Like all spider-based search tools, Excite crawls around the Web cataloging its contents, and it eventually catalogs your site. But by suggesting your site, you get it listed more quickly.

1. In your Web browser, go to Excite at www.excite.com.

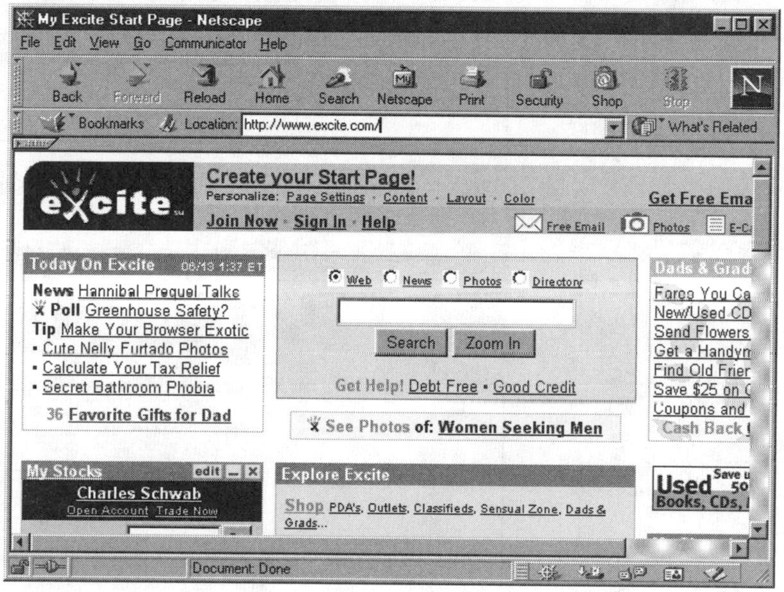

FIGURE 22.7
Step 1: Go to Excite.

2. Scroll to the bottom of the page and choose Submit a Site.
3. Excite offers three submission options: two options (for a fee) that put your page not only in the Excite listings, but also in many other search engines, and a free option for listing just in Excite. To use the free option, scroll to the bottom of the page and click on `submit`.

▼

FIGURE 22.8
Step 2: Choose Submit a Site.

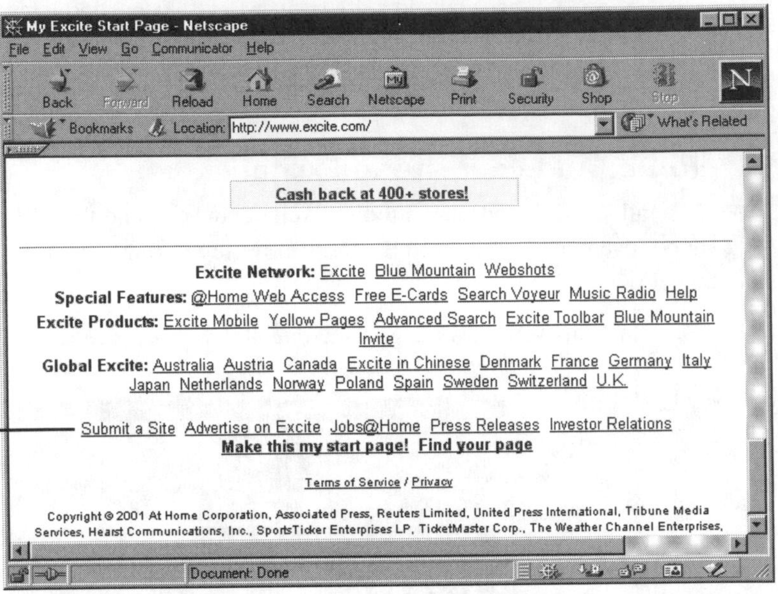

FIGURE 22.9
Step 3: Click on `submit`.

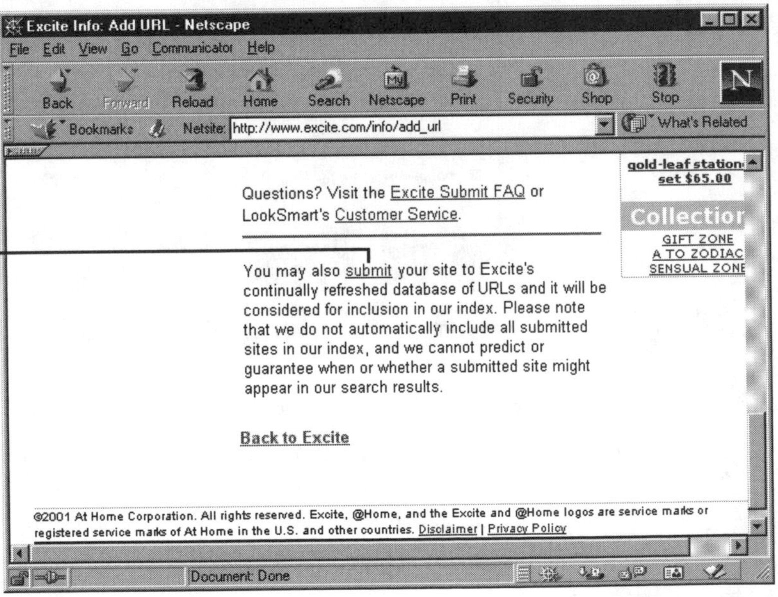

4. Scroll to the bottom of the page and fill in the form with the URL of your page (or top page of your site), your email address (so that Excite can contact you if necessary), the language the page uses, your general location in the world, and the general category. Then click Send.

FIGURE 22.10
Step 4: Fill in the form and click Send.

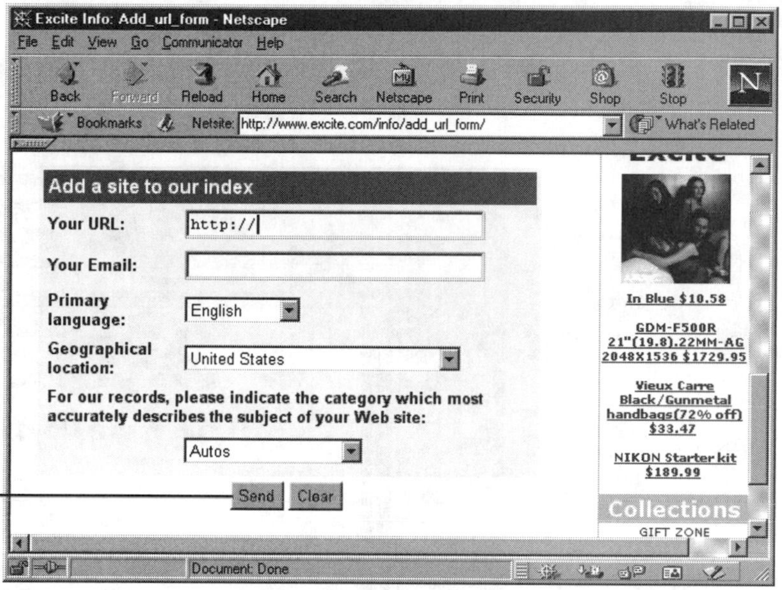

To make sure that your page is located and properly cataloged by Web spiders, be sure to carefully and thoughtfully phrase the page's title, description, and keywords in the Page Properties dialog box. Refer to Hour 5 for help.

Getting in Multiple Search Pages at Once

Over the past couple years, some commercial services have emerged that offer (most for a fee) to list your site with many of the most popular search pages and spiders, all in one quick step.

This type of service charges from as little as $10 to more than $100. Note that these services submit not only to the major search engines, but also to hundreds of topic-specific search pages.

> You can find more Web promotion sites by entering the term `site submission` or `web promotion` in any general-purpose search page.

Check out these sites:

- *Site-See* (see Figure 22.11) `www.site-see.com`
- *Submit It!* `www.submit-it.com/`

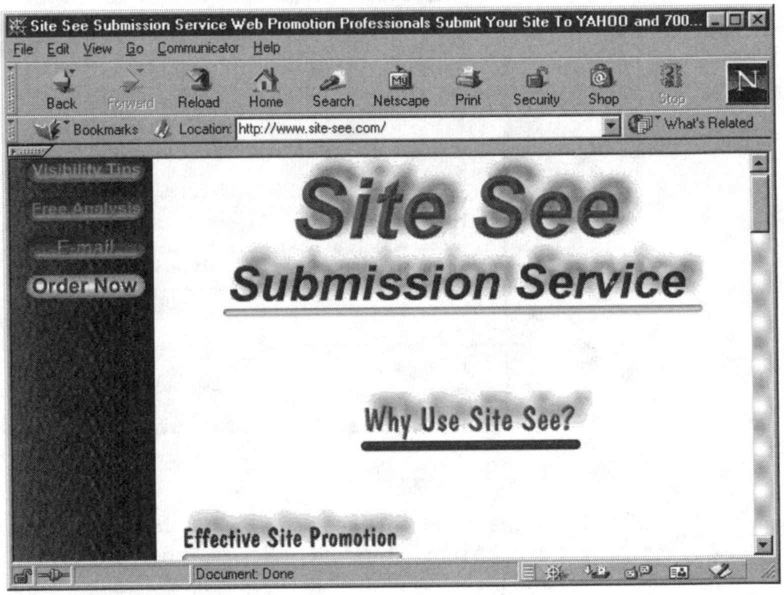

FIGURE 22.11
Site-See, one of the many site-submission services available online.

Publicizing Your Page off the Web

Don't forget that not all the ways to publicize your Web pages are on the Web (or even online). Be sure to list your Web site address:

- In your email signature
- On your business cards
- On personal or company stationery
- In company advertising and marketing collateral

Remember: In theory (and in reality, too!), everyone among your acquaintances who visits your Web page has Internet access and probably has, therefore, an email address, too.

A great way to make a targeted announcement to people you know is to broadcast an email message announcing your page's URL.

To broadcast an email message, compose the message and include in the To: portion of the message header the email address of everyone you want to receive the message (see Figure 22.12). In most email programs, you separate the addresses with semicolons (;), as shown.

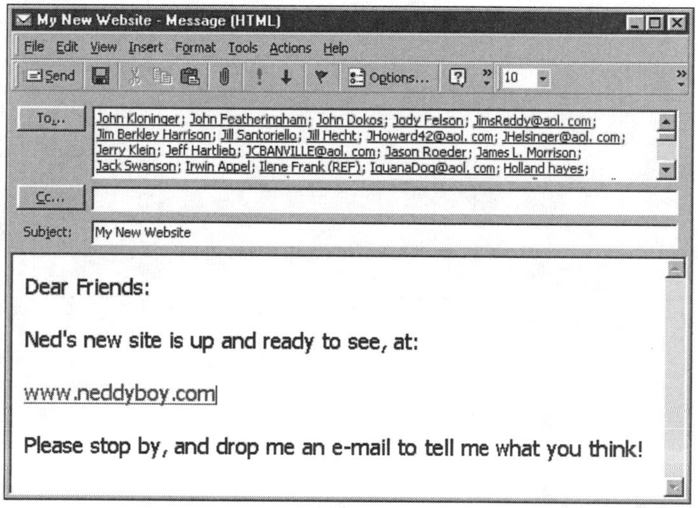

FIGURE 22.12
Broadcasting an email message to announce your page.

Summary

If a page falls on the Web and no one is around to hear it, does it make a sound? I dunno. I shouldn't ask dumb questions I can't answer. The point is that after you create and publish a Web page, your job isn't done. It pays to advertise.

Q&A

Q Do I have to check or update my listings on the search pages?

A After adding your page to the search pages (and after the addition has been made formal on search pages that make you wait a few days), you should always find your listing and test it to make sure that it works as advertised.

After that, you can pretty much forget about it, unless you change your Web page's address or filename. Whenever you make this type of change, you must change your listings in the search pages to match.

HOUR 23

Testing and Maintaining Your Page Online

You haven't simply published a Web page. You've established a Web presence—hopefully one that will expand and evolve with time (most do). After your page is online, you should know how to update it—so that you can improve and enlarge it over time—and how to test it so that you can keep it performing reliably for your visitors.

At the end of this hour, you'll be able to answer the following questions:

- How do I ensure that my Web page looks good, no matter what browser the visitor is using?
- How do I check out how my page looks when viewed by visitors using varying display resolutions?
- How do I keep my links working smoothly?
- How do I evaluate my page's ease of use for visitors?
- How do I update my page whenever I need to (or when I just plain feel like it)?

Testing Your Pages

Okay, as you've worked on your page, you've evaluated its appearance by previewing it in Netscape, and by now you've checked out the page online through Netscape. So that means it's perfect, right?

Not necessarily. You might not be aware of all sorts of little glitches until you go looking for them. The next few sections show you how to thoroughly test your page after it's online so that you can make sure that your visitors have precisely the experience you want them to have.

Testing Browser Variability

You know that your page looks and functions fine when viewed through Netscape. But what about the rest of the Web population—those using earlier versions of Netscape or those using various versions of Internet Explorer or any of a dozen other browsers? How will your page look to them? Figures 23.1 through 23.4 illustrate how exactly the same page can appear dramatically different in different browsers.

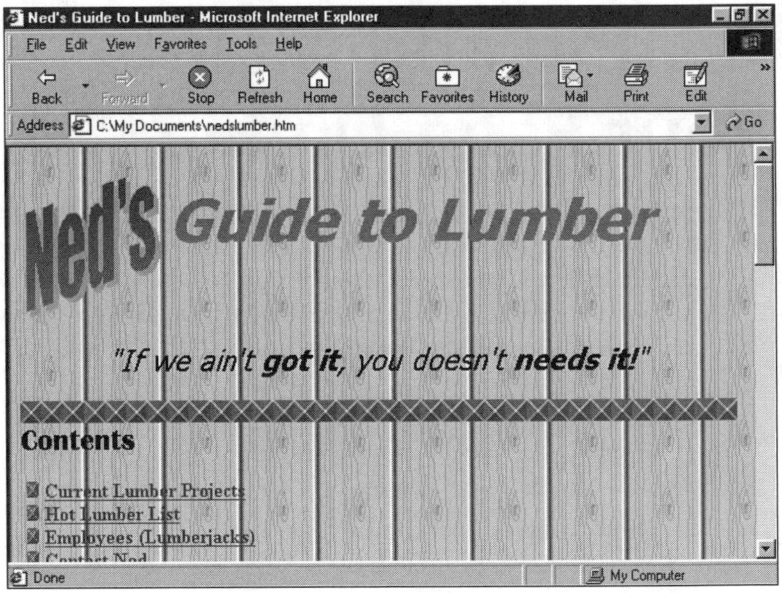

FIGURE 23.1
Ned's Lumber, as seen through Internet Explorer 5.

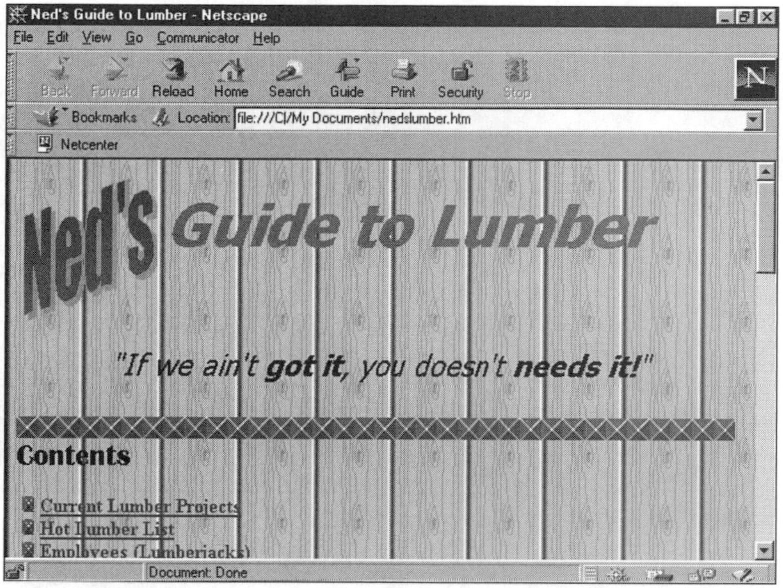

FIGURE 23.2
Ned's Lumber, as seen through Netscape Navigator 4.

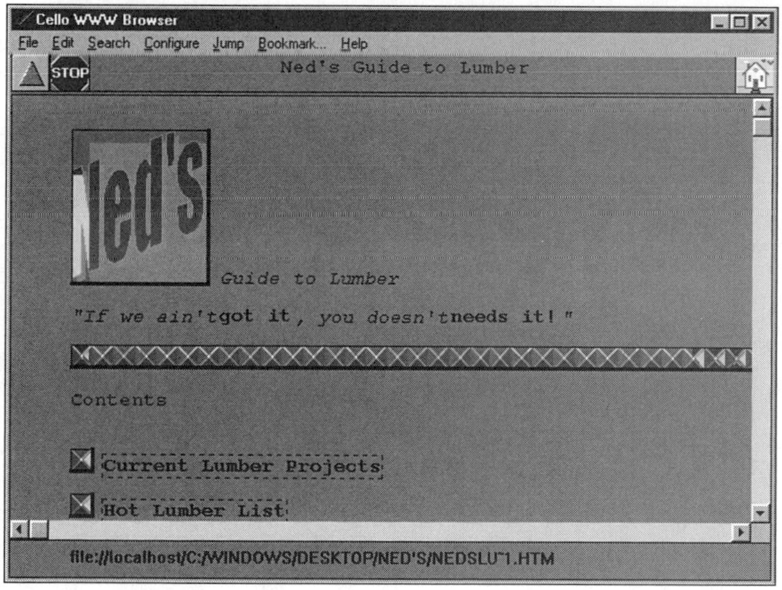

FIGURE 23.3
Ned's Lumber, as seen through Cello.

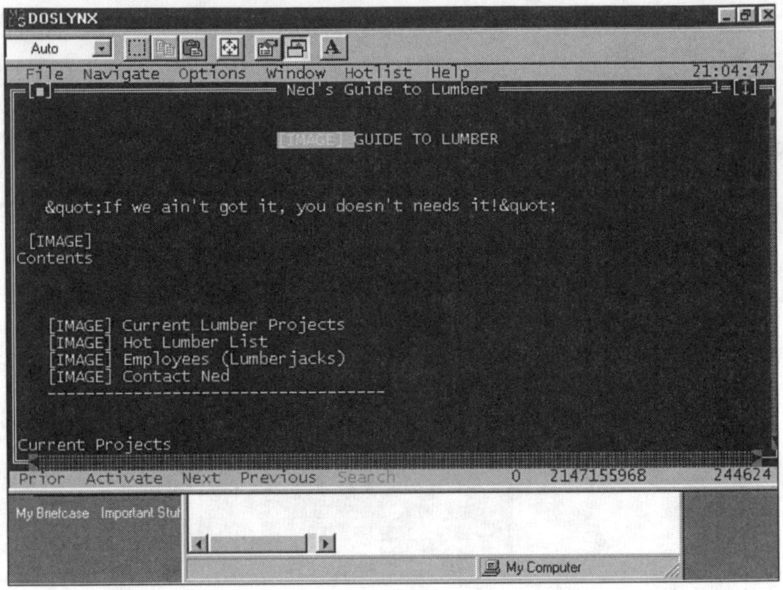

FIGURE 23.4
Ned's Lumber, as seen through DOSLynx.

To make sure that your page's appearance is acceptable to all, you should view your page online through a variety of different browsers, just to see if any serious problems arise when using browsers other than Netscape 4. If you discover any problems in a particular browser environment, you must decide whether to adjust your page to eliminate the problem (which may involve compromising some of your formatting or other fancy features) or to sacrifice the performance of your page for one segment of the audience to preserve its performance for another.

> Don't worry about whether the page looks identical through all sorts of browsers. It won't, and it doesn't have to. The question is "Does the page look okay in every browser?" Is all the text legible? Do the links work? If a picture or other element does not appear, does something else on the page fulfill the same function?
>
> For example, if a bunch of links in an imagemap do not appear (or don't work) when displayed through a particular browser, are duplicate text links available? If your company logo doesn't show up, is the company name presented in a heading? If the background doesn't show up, is all the text legible without it?

You should keep some other browsers around to see how the other half sees you. You can download many different browsers from the Web for free. A good place to start is the Tucows Internet software directory (`www.tucows.com`), from which you can download many different browsers (see Figure 23.5).

> You can also find in Appendix B, "Online Resources for Web Authors," the download addresses for various shareware and freeware browsers.

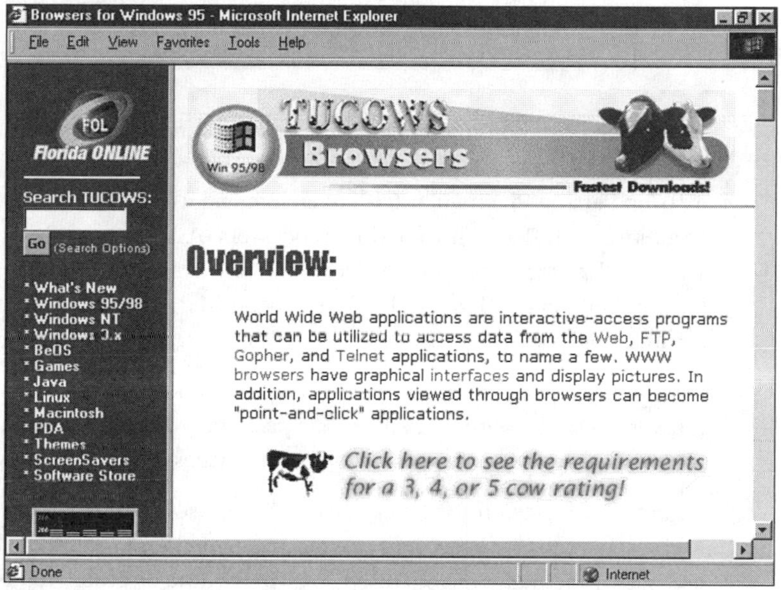

FIGURE 23.5
The Tucows directory at `www.tucows.com` *is a good place to pick up various browsers for testing.*

Which browsers should you test in? Well, the overwhelming majority of the folks online browse the Web through Internet Explorer or Netscape Navigator, so you need to test in the latest version of each of those "Big Two" browsers, at least.

Keep in mind that not everybody keeps up with the latest browser versions, so a page that looks fine in the current version of Internet Explorer or Netscape might show some trouble when viewed through a browser from just a year or two ago.

If you rummage through the CD-ROMs you have lying around (especially any that were bundled with computer books), you might find some that have older versions of Internet Explorer or Navigator you can use for testing your pages.

> You often see outdated computer books for sale, sometimes for as little as $2, in big bins at bookstores. (It breaks my heart.)
>
> Often, those books include CD-ROMs that have obsolete versions of various Web browsers. For a few bucks, you can pick up some old browser versions for testing and also pick up a lovely artifact of computer history. For example, if you find the first edition of this book in the blowout bin, you get a 1998 version of Netscape Communicator (including the Netscape Web authoring tool, Composer, which you'll learn more about in Hour 24, "Developing Your Authoring Skills").
>
> Check the book's copyright date before buying; a browser from any year before 1997 is probably too old to bother with.

Also, each of these browsers is available in different versions for different types of computers. For PCs alone, you can get Internet Explorer in three different "current" versions: a 16-bit version, the regular 64-bit version, and a 128-bit version for top-of-the-line PCs, like those with Pentium III and IV processors. Add to these the various Internet Explorer versions for other system types (such as Macintosh), and you must realize that you really have more than one Internet Explorer to consider. (Several different Netscape versions are available too.)

If your page looks okay in the most recent versions of Netscape and Internet Explorer (all versions released within about the past two years), you can rest assured that your page probably looks okay to most—but not necessarily all—folks on the Web.

After you've tested for the Netscape and Microsoft worlds, about 10 to 20 percent of Web users remain whose view of your page you don't know. Of those, many probably use one of the many flavors of NCSA Mosaic, the original Web browser, now largely defunct.

Beyond Mosaic, you may want to test in

- Older, graphical browsers that don't support recent Netscape or Microsoft extensions, such as Cello (refer to Figure 23.3)
- Text-only browsers, such as DOSLynx (refer to Figure 23.4)

Although these types of browsers are on their way out, you need to test in them and adjust your page as needed if you really want it to behave properly for absolutely all potential visitors. However, you must accept that doing so inevitably forces you to restrict your page to the most minimal formatting.

If you're really concerned about reaching everyone, supply your page in two versions: a fancy, extension-rich version and a very plain HTML 2–based version—and offer either from a universally visible top page. This is also a great way to accommodate differing connection speeds and patience levels. The version provided for older browsers usually also includes little or no multimedia, so those with slow Internet connections can enjoy your pages without waiting an eternity for them to appear (see Figure 23.6).

FIGURE 23.6
To take advantage of advanced formatting while still supporting older browsers, you can create two versions of your pages—one simple, the other fancy—and give your visitors a choice between the two, from the top page.

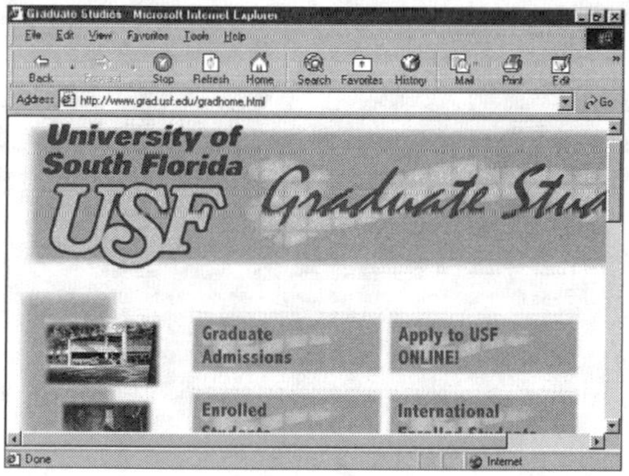

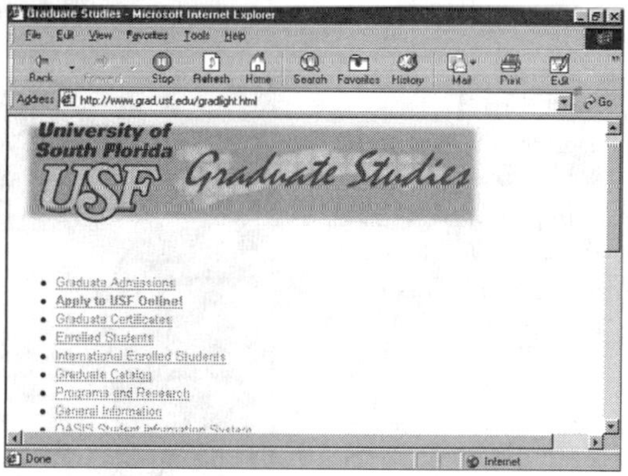

Testing at Different Resolutions

Within the past year or so, it has become standard practice to design Web pages to look their best when displayed on a computer screen running at 800×600 resolution, the most common setting now used by most folks on PCs and Macintoshes.

The compromise is effective: Users of computers running at the minimum Windows resolution of 640×480 need only do a little scrolling to see all of an 800×600 Web page, and the page appears acceptably large to those using higher resolutions.

Figures 23.7 through 23.9 show how the same Web page (one designed for 800×600) appears to visitors at three different resolutions.

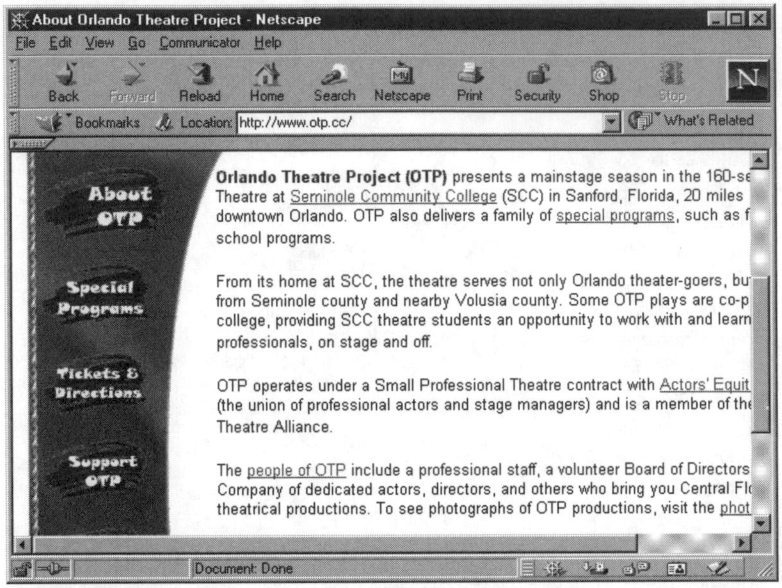
About Orlando Theatre Project - Netscape
File Edit View Go Communicator Help
Back Forward Reload Home Search Netscape Print Security Shop Stop
Bookmarks Location: http://www.otp.cc/
What's Related
Document: Done

FIGURE 23.7
A page designed for 800×600 resolution on a display running at 640×480. The visitor must scroll to see the whole page.

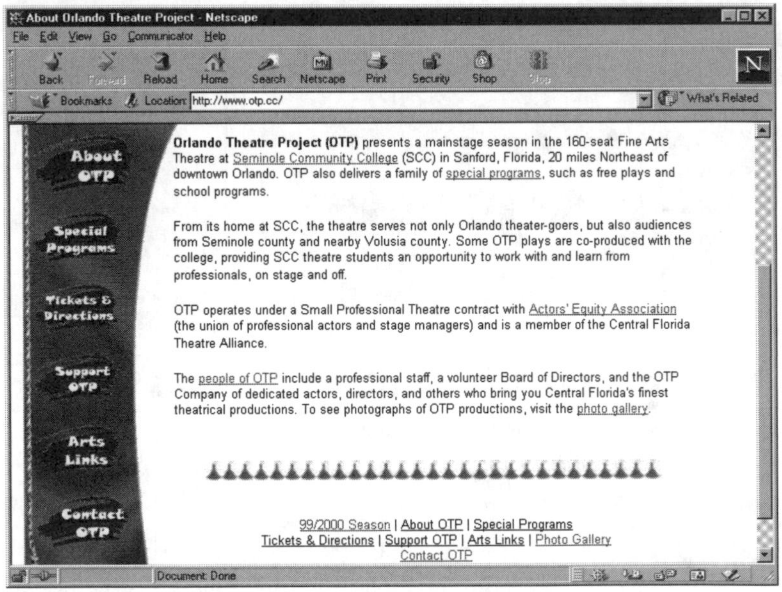
About Orlando Theatre Project - Netscape
File Edit View Go Communicator Help
Back Forward Reload Home Search Netscape Print Security Shop Stop
Bookmarks Location: http://www.otp.cc/
What's Related
Orlando Theatre Project (OTP) presents a mainstage season in the 160-seat Fine Arts Theatre at Seminole Community College (SCC) in Sanford, Florida, 20 miles Northeast of downtown Orlando. OTP also delivers a family of special programs, such as free plays and school programs.
From its home at SCC, the theatre serves not only Orlando theater-goers, but also audiences from Seminole county and nearby Volusia county. Some OTP plays are co-produced with the college, providing SCC theatre students an opportunity to work with and learn from professionals, on stage and off.
OTP operates under a Small Professional Theatre contract with Actors' Equity Association (the union of professional actors and stage managers) and is a member of the Central Florida Theatre Alliance.
The people of OTP include a professional staff, a volunteer Board of Directors, and the OTP Company of dedicated actors, directors, and others who bring you Central Florida's finest theatrical productions. To see photographs of OTP productions, visit the photo gallery.
99/2000 Season | About OTP | Special Programs
Tickets & Directions | Support OTP | Arts Links | Photo Gallery
Contact OTP
Document: Done

FIGURE 23.8
A page designed for 800×600 resolution on a display running at 800×600. The page image neatly fills the window.

FIGURE 23.9
A page designed for 800×600 resolution on a display running at 1024×768.

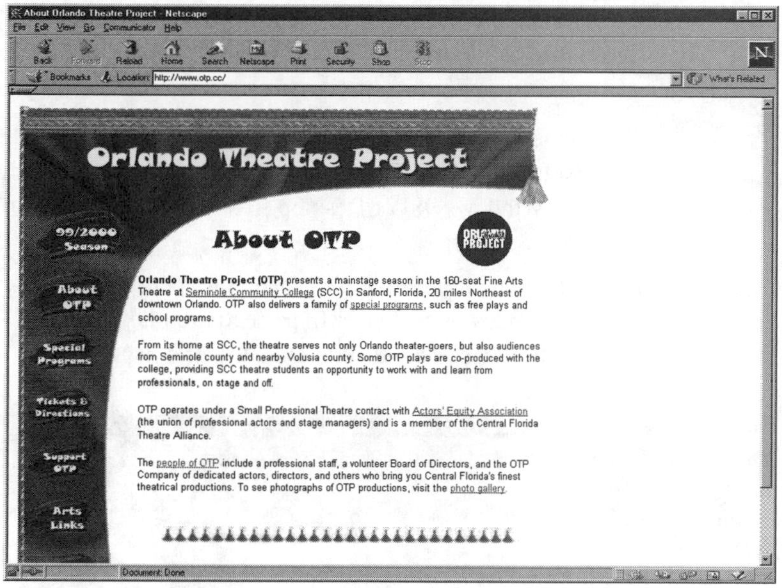
About Orlando Theatre Project - Netscape
File Edit View Go Communicator Help
Back Forward Reload Home Search Netscape Print Security Shop Stop
Bookmarks Location: http://www.otp.cc/
What's Related
Orlando Theatre Project
99/2000 Season
About OTP
Special Programs
Tickets & Directions
Support OTP
Arts Links
About OTP
Orlando Theatre Project (OTP) presents a mainstage season in the 160-seat Fine Arts Theatre at Seminole Community College (SCC) in Sanford, Florida, 20 miles Northeast of downtown Orlando. OTP also delivers a family of special programs, such as free plays and school programs.
From its home at SCC, the theatre serves not only Orlando theater-goers, but also audiences from Seminole county and nearby Volusia county. Some OTP plays are co-produced with the college, providing SCC theatre students an opportunity to work with and learn from professionals, on stage and off.
OTP operates under a Small Professional Theatre contract with Actors' Equity Association (the union of professional actors and stage managers) and is a member of the Central Florida Theatre Alliance.
The people of OTP include a professional staff, a volunteer Board of Directors, and the OTP Company of dedicated actors, directors, and others who bring you Central Florida's finest theatrical productions. To see photographs of OTP productions, visit the photo gallery.
Document: Done

You may recall that I recommend running your PC at 800×600 when using Netscape Composer. If you do and you design pages to look good on your own screen, you're designing for 800×600 without even having to think about it!

Display resolution is a factor only when pages contain pictures, tables, forms, or frames. The layout of a page containing only text is automatically fit to the size of the window in which it is displayed.

Tables and horizontal lines automatically refit themselves to varying resolutions when you have specified their width as a percentage of the window, not as a number of pixels (see Hour 8, "Organizing Text with Tables and Rules"). However, when a table contains pictures, the results of that refit may not be appealing. Always test such pages at varying resolutions.

When evaluating your page, you're smart to check out how it looks at varying resolutions. To do that, you must change your display resolution in Windows and then view the page:

- To change your display resolution, open Windows Control Panel and double-click the Display icon. Choose the Settings tab and drag the slider control labeled Screen Area (in Windows 98) or Desktop Area (in Windows 95) to the resolution you want (see Figure 23.10).
- After changing the resolution, when you open your browser you might find that the browser window is no longer fit perfectly to maximized full-screen size. To make the browser fill the screen, double-click the title bar at the top of the browser window.

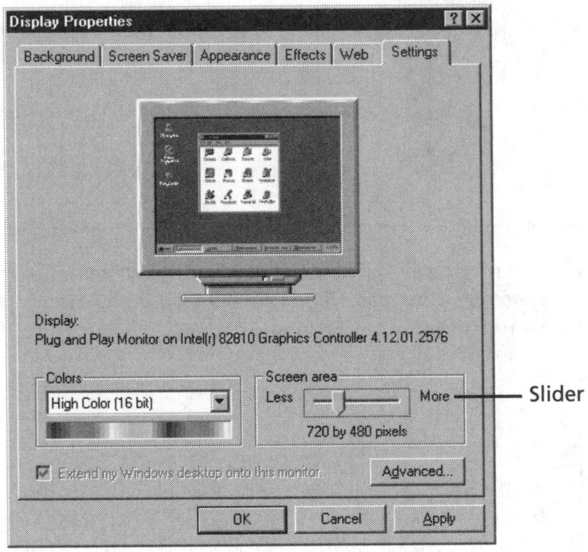

FIGURE 23.10
Drag the slider control under Screen Area to change the display resolution in Windows.

> If you think that changing resolutions this way is a pain, you can download a free program named BrowserSizer from ApplyThis Software, at `www.vasile.com/racecar/stampware/browsersizer/`.
>
> BrowserSizer provides a simple menu from which you can easily change the size of the browser window (either Internet Explorer or Netscape Navigator) to a size that mimics the way the browser would appear at a particular resolution. This program gives you a fast and simple way to check your page's appearance in varying resolutions.

Testing Link Validity

Finally, you *must* test all the links in your page.

After you've verified the links among your own files—between your pages and to images and external media—you needn't recheck them unless you change a file. Retesting all such links whenever you make *any* changes to your Web site is a good practice. Even seemingly small changes to a single page can sometimes inadvertently scramble links.

When your page contains *external* links—links to other people's Web pages or to any file other than those you control on the server—you need to check these links often because the files they point to might have moved or their names might have changed. I recommend checking all external links at least once a month.

Evaluating Your Page's Ergonomics

The preceding sections in this hour have explained only how to check your page's technical integrity. What about its fuzzy qualities—its look, its feel, its *mise-en-scéne*? And what about its interaction with visitors? Can they find what they came for? Do they see the parts of your message you want them to see? Do they naturally follow paths through your page to certain items, or are they frustrated by lots of blind alleys and backtracking?

The best way to answer these questions is to gather some friends (ideally friends who don't already know too much about your page or its subject) and cooperative strangers and watch them browse your page (no coaching!). Watch what they choose to click and what they skip. Note whenever they move down a path and fail to find what they expected or hoped to find. And, of course, listen to their comments.

Finally, remember always to use a signature with your email address. That way, people can send you comments and constructive criticisms.

> Here's one final way to check out your pages: Any time, any place that you have an opportunity to visit your pages away from home, do it. In particular, look for opportunities to test your pages through other types of computers (such as Macintoshes) and varying connection speeds. You may find such opportunities
>
> - When visiting friends who use the Internet
> - At a local library that has a public Internet terminal
> - At work

Updating Your Page

Okay, you've found some stuff you want to fix or updates to make. What's the procedure?

Begin by editing the original files on your PC in Composer. (You cannot edit the copies of the files that are on the Web server; you must work with what's on your PC.)

After making all your changes and testing the results offline in one or more browsers on your PC, start the publishing steps exactly as you did in Hour 21, "Publishing Your Page." Click the Publish button on the Composer toolbar to open the Publish dialog box (see Figure 23.11).

Here's the cool part: Composer remembers the server name and all the other stuff you entered when you originally published the page. As long as you change nothing in the Publish dialog box (see Figure 23.11) and simply click its OK button, that's all you have to do. The changed files are uploaded to the server, replacing the old pages and using the same settings you entered when you first published this page. (Depending on how your server and Internet account are set up, you might be prompted to sign on to the Internet or to supply your authentication information, but that's the most you have to do.)

> Of course, you must retest your page after uploading changes. But you knew that, right?

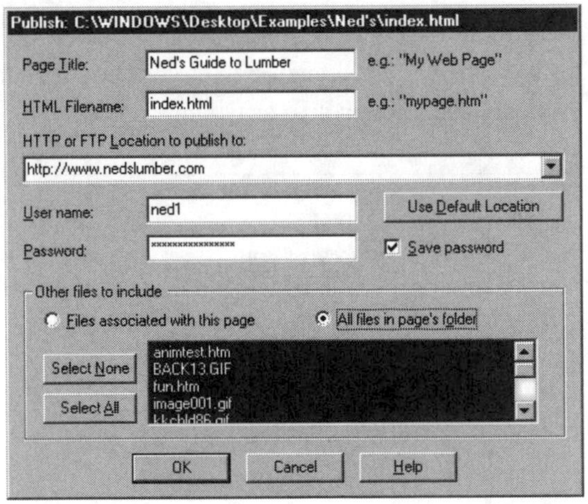

FIGURE 23.11
Click OK in the Publish dialog box (without changing anything) to publish changes to a Web page.

Summary

Evaluating and updating your Web pages is no big deal, and it's a critical step in making sure that your page does the job for which you created it.

Perhaps more important, testing and updating your page are important practices in improving as a Web author. Each time you republish your pages, they get better and better and you gain experience and confidence. So get in the habit of seeing your pages not as "finished" works that you upload and forget, but rather as works in progress, regularly benefiting from your enhancements and fine-tuning.

Q&A

Q My page works great in both Internet Explorer and Netscape Navigator, but shows some problems in other browsers. The problem is that I don't want to give up the cool stuff in my pages just to make them compatible with everybody's browser. What do I do?

A Many Web authors in that situation put a disclaimer on the top page, saying "This page is best viewed with Internet Explorer" or words to that effect. Often, the disclaimer is accompanied by a link to Microsoft or Netscape for downloading a compatible browser. The disclaimer says, in effect, "If you wanna enjoy everything my page offers, go get an up-to-date browser."

A few years ago, I would have called that practice a cop-out, a callous disregard for those not willing to dance to Microsoft's or Netscape's tune. But like it or not, so much of the Web today works properly only through one of these browsers that anybody using another browser is likely to be encountering problems with more than half the pages he or she visits. That person has already decided to accept that many pages won't look quite right to him, which takes you off the hook (a little).

Q I installed some other browsers for testing, and now when I go online one of those browsers opens rather than Netscape. And when I do use Netscape, it doesn't work right. How do I get Netscape back?

A Most browsers want to be your only browser, so when you install them, they have a bad habit of making themselves the default browser on your PC, the one that opens automatically for most Internet activities.

The easiest way to make Netscape the default browser again is to reinstall it from the CD-ROM, which should also fix any little troubles that may have cropped up since you installed the other browsers.

That won't get rid of the other browsers, which will remain ready for your Web page testing. But it will make Netscape the default Web browser again so that the other browsers don't appear unless you deliberately open them.

HOUR 24

Developing Your Authoring Skills

This is it—*la chapitre finale*. And guess what? I tell you nothing here that immediately adds to your authoring skill set. (I know—it's a cheap trick. It's like when they forced you to show up for the last day of high school and then let you goof off all day anyway.)

What you do get in this hour is a graduation speech, or, rather, a send-off with a purpose. If you've hit most or all of this tutorial, you've built a solid foundation as an author. But there's always more to learn, always that one new trick that can make a good Web page into a great one. You now possess all the prerequisites needed to understand more advanced authoring information that you might find in other books or on the Web. So in this last hurrah, you find tips for developing your new skills.

At the end of this hour, you'll be able to answer the following questions:

- How can I get my own dot-com, my own *domain*, as the address of the pages I publish?
- When I outgrow Composer, what's next?

- What practices can help me grow as a Web author, no matter what tools I use?
- What can I read now to take me to the next level?

Getting Your Own Domain (Your Own Dot-Com)

If you simply take some space on someone else's server, your page is accessible through the Web, but it doesn't have the sort of catchy Web address that gives you a Web identity, such as `www.buick.com`. Instead, your page's address is expressed as a directory on the server; for example, `www.serviceco.com/neddyboy/fredo/`.

If you want to have your own Internet name, you must register your own Internet *domain* and then have that domain set up on the server on which you will publish your pages.

> When you check to see whether the domain you want to use is available (as you will in the next To Do), you might receive a message that the name is available for purchase or lease, for a particular sum.
>
> Because a domain costs only $70, a number of companies have snapped up every domain name they can think of that anyone might want to use. But they have no intention of using the names; they intend to sell them, often for much more than $70.

Because the technical details of setting up your domain on the server must be taken care of by whomever controls your server, I recommend having your Internet provider (or whoever else controls the server you use) take care of both registering and setting up your domain for you. Most providers will register a domain for a small fee, or even for free.

Whether you set up your domain yourself or have someone else do it, you still must pay some fees to Network Solutions (or one of the other domain registration services; see Tip on next page), the organization that manages domains for the Internet. At the time of this writing, Network Solutions charges $70 to establish the domain, which includes two years of keeping the domain. After that, you must pay $35 per year to maintain it. Typically, if your provider sets up your domain, it can also collect the fees and forward them to Network Solutions for you.

> FYI, Network Solutions is no longer the only source for registering a domain name, although it remains the largest. There are others you may use, including `register.com`, `siteleader.com`, and `worldwidedomains.com`. The process for registering on all such sites is similar, but prices may vary, so check 'em out.

Although you might need help setting up the domain, you can choose the name all by yourself. The trick is that the domain must be absolutely unique—it can't be the same as any other domain already in use. You can use the Network Solutions Web site to find out whether the domain you want is available, as described in the following To Do.

> The final part of the domain name can be `.com` or `.cc` (both for commercial sites, the most common), `.org` (organization, like a foundation or other not-for-profit), `.edu` (educational institution), or `.net` (network). If you're not sure what to use, you're probably a `.com`.
>
> Being a `.com`, as opposed to an `.org` or other domain type, has an advantage. The `.com` suffix is so common that many Web users—particularly newcomers—have a habit of assuming that all addresses end in `.com`. Tell people that your page is at `www.nedco.org`, and a surprising number of them will try to reach you at `www.nedco.com` and never understand why you're not there.

To Do

To Do: Choose a domain name

1. Think about what you want your Internet domain to be; for example, `www.cathy-corp.com`. Have a few options ready, in case one or more are already taken.
2. Visit the Network Solutions Web site at `www.networksolutions.com`.
3. In the Search for a Domain Name box at the top of the page, type the domain you chose in Step 1 and click the Go! button to the right of the box.

> When typing your proposed domain in Step 3, don't precede it with the `http://` or the `www` part. These elements are part of a typical Web site address, but not really part of the domain. For example, if you want your Web site address to be `http://www.wild.com`, just type `wild` in Step 3 and use the list box provided to choose the `.com` suffix.

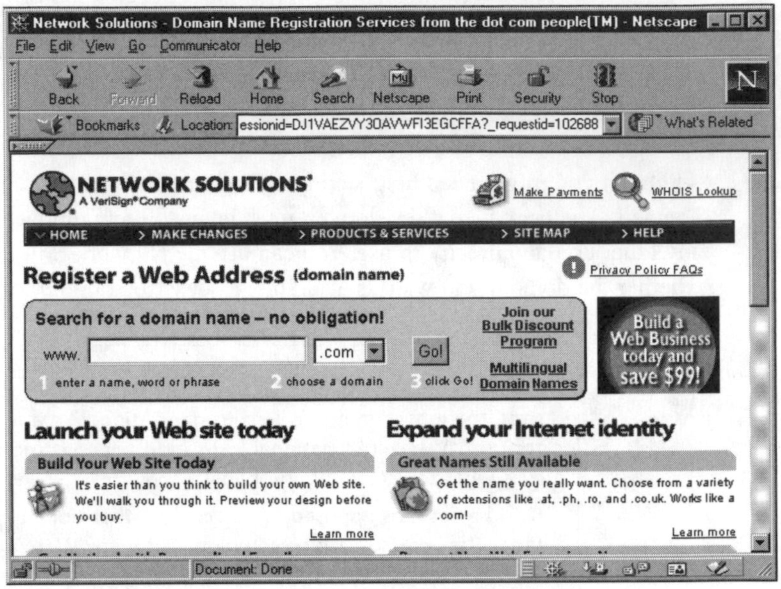

FIGURE 24.1
Step 2: Visit Network Solutions at `www.networksolutions.com`.

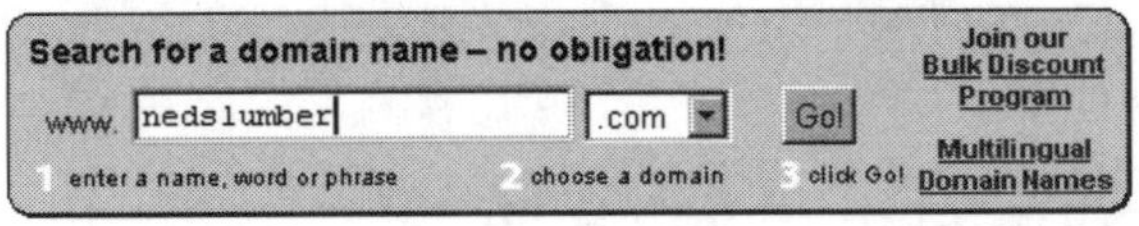

FIGURE 24.2
Step 3: Type your chosen domain in the Search box.

4. A report appears, telling you that your chosen name is or is not available. It also shows alternative domain names you might want to consider registering, either instead of or in addition to your favorite.

> Why register one or more of the alternative names? Well, businesses protective of their name recognition who don't want to take any chances that potential customers will wind up at the site of a shrewd competitor with a too-close domain name often buy up not only the most likely domain name, but also all other similar names. Those businesses then use a Redirect option to automatically funnel all visitors from the alternative domain names to the company's main site.

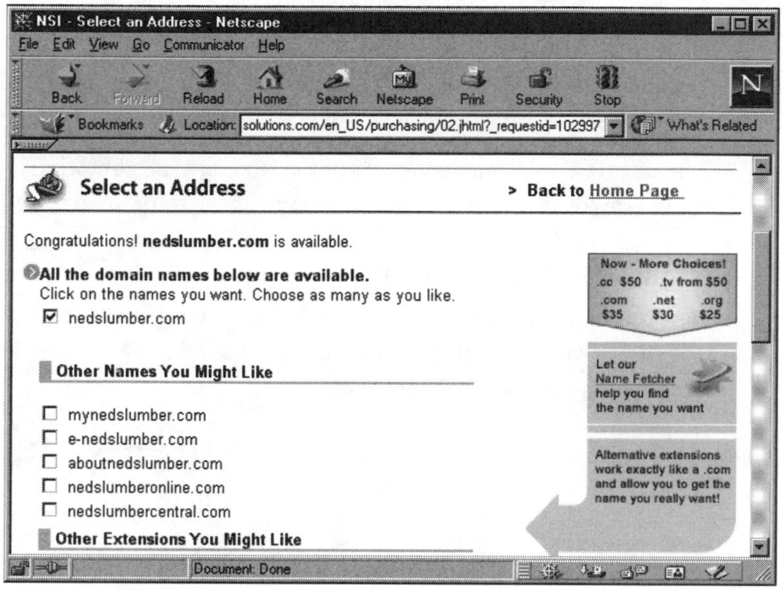

FIGURE 24.3
Step 4: The site tells you whether the domain is available or taken.

- If the name *is* available, proceed to Step 5.
- If the name *is not* available, you can scroll the page to reveal the box labeled Search for More Web Addresses and try a different name there or choose from among any available alternatives displayed on the report.

5. Contact your server provider as soon as possible and fill out the paperwork to register the domain. (If you're feeling brave, you can scroll to the bottom of the page and click the Continue button to buy the domain yourself. Your server provider can still set up your domain on his server.)

> After you set up your domain, you have all new settings to use when you publish pages: a new server address and new username and password, for example. The person who sets up your domain on the server gives you this information; don't forget to use it when you start publishing to your new domain.

Advancing to New Authoring Tools and Techniques

Sculptors start with Play-Doh and work their way up to marble. Like a sculptor, if you continue authoring, your needs will one day advance beyond Composer's capabilities.

The next few pages describe two of the leading Web authoring environments and related tools. Any of them would make a fitting next step for an experienced Composer author.

Microsoft FrontPage

If you've cut your authoring teeth in Composer, a logical step up is to FrontPage, the Microsoft Web authoring environment for Microsoft Windows. Figure 24.4 shows FrontPage (Version 2002) in action.

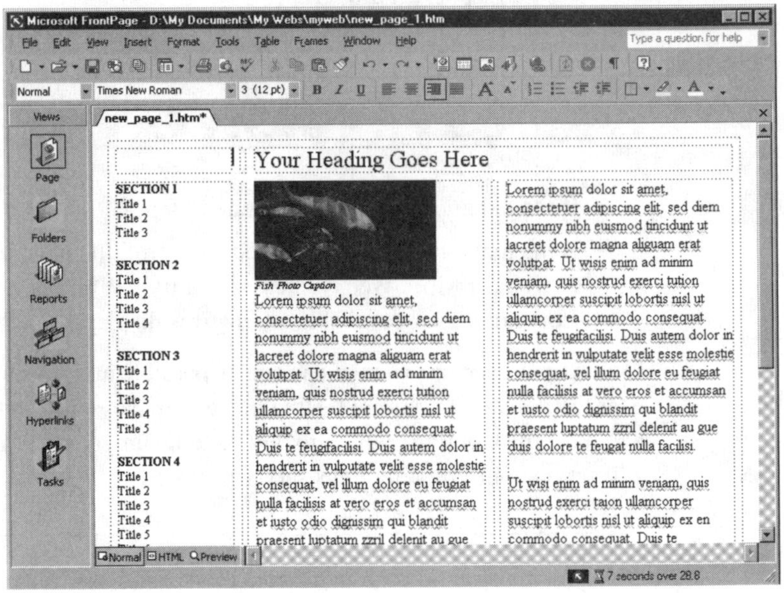

FIGURE 24.4
FrontPage, the Microsoft commercial Web authoring software.

You can get FrontPage 2002 in the Developer's edition of Microsoft Office XP (bundled with Word 2002, Excel 2002, and so on) or by itself.

Why FrontPage? Well, performing many of the basic tasks you already know about is similar in both Composer and FrontPage. You don't have to relearn how to do many things you already know how to do. That frees you up to move ahead to the things FrontPage does that Composer doesn't do.

For example, you insert a picture in FrontPage almost exactly as you do in Composer. But after you insert that picture, a Picture toolbar appears automatically whenever a picture is selected. The toolbar offers buttons for all sorts of advanced stuff, like adjusting the contrast and brightness of the picture or positioning the picture *absolutely*—locking it into an exact spot on the page, as you would in a desktop publishing program.

FrontPage also adds a site-management facility that's especially valuable when you begin to manage Web sites with many interlinked pages. The facility can show you a diagram of a whole Web site and of the interrelationships among the pages (see Figure 24.5). From this view, you can add and delete pages to and from the site and move pages around. FrontPage automatically updates the links and navigation bars on other pages in the site so that everything still works together properly.

FIGURE 24.5
FrontPage features a site-management facility.

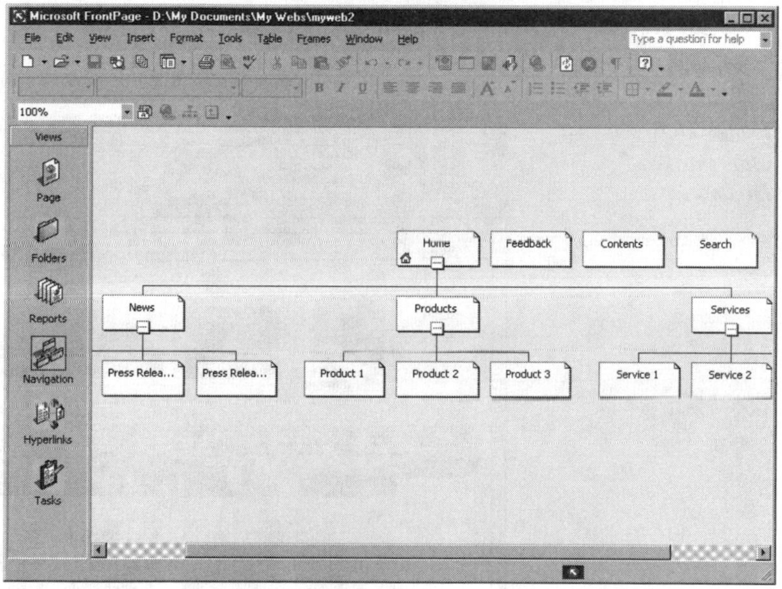

You can learn more about FrontPage at `www.microsoft.com/frontpage/`.

You can order a trial version of FrontPage on CD at `http://www.microsoft.com/frontpage/evaluation/trial.htm`.

> If you have ambitions to become a professional Web author in a company, you have another good reason to learn how to use FrontPage.
>
> Most companies want the Web authors they hire to be able to use a range of Web authoring tools and to possess other skills (such as Java or CGI programming). But FrontPage is now the most widely used Web authoring application, so knowing how to use it is essential for any job-hunting author.

Macromedia Dreamweaver

Dreamweaver (see Figure 24.6) "…is the solution for professional Web site design and production," according to its maker, Macromedia. What that really means is that it's an all-around Web authoring tool that includes advanced graphics creation, editing facilities, site management, and more.

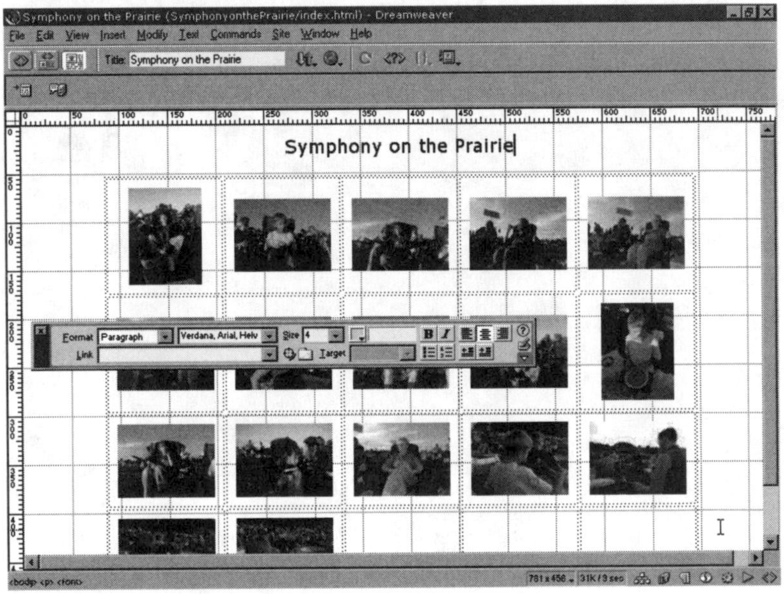

FIGURE 24.6
Macromedia Dreamweaver.

Dreamweaver is similar to FrontPage in most respects, but a little more powerful, a little more difficult to learn and use, and more expensive. Although FrontPage suits both beginners and pros, Dreamweaver is really for ambitious Web authoring professionals who want every bell and whistle at their command.

You can learn more about Dreamweaver at `www.macromedia.com/software/dreamweaver/`.

You can download a free trial at `www.macromedia.com/software/dreamweaver/trial/`.

The Future of Web Authoring: XHTML

Every time the HTML standard changes, new formatting tricks and other capabilities are available to apply in Web pages and everybody runs out to get new tools (or learn new tags) to apply those features. To some extent, your "moving up" as a Web author depends a great deal on how and when HTML "moves up."

The current HTML standard is HTML 4.01, and an HTML 5 won't be created. Instead, HTML is merging with another document-formatting standard, XML (eXtensible Markup Language), to create a new standard for the Web pages of the future: XHTML (eXtensible Hyper Text Markup Language). In fact, you can already see some XHTML-based Web pages online.

For general Web authoring, XHTML will be very similar to HTML. But the new language will be applied much more broadly than the old and will be used to enable browser-like features in such devices as digital TVs, portable phones, and even auto PCs (computers you use in your car). Estimates are that by 2002, 75 percent of the viewing of Internet documents will take place on these types of alternative platforms. To accommodate this change, XHTML is being designed to be highly *portable* (able to work on lots of different kinds of devices) while also being *extensible* (easily upgradable with new capabilities).

As a Web author, you will see a few years pass before you have to think much about XHTML, and by that time WYSIWYG tools will crank out XHTML the same way that tools like Composer crank out HTML today. (Very simple tools already are available for converting existing HTML files to XHTML format.) If you plan to do Web authoring in the long term, keep your eye on XHTML. It is the future.

How to Grow as a Web Author

What can you do next? How will you advance to the next level? More important, how can you keep a keen edge on the skills you've already mastered? Here are a few important habits you can adopt to prosper and grow.

Observe

When on the Web, don't just browse. Think about the pages you visit. Study them carefully, not at a technical level but rather at an aesthetic one. If a page impresses you, ask yourself why. Is it the images, the layout, the writing, the colors, or some combination of these factors? Bookmark sites that impress you and visit them often. Make a mental catalog of what grabs (or loses) your interest as a browser. Odds are that many other people respond the same way.

Dissect

When a page really impresses you, save it on your PC (in Internet Explorer, choose File, Save As) and then study it offline. Consider such questions as:

- What types of image files were used, and what properties are applied to them?
- What is the flow of text elements and properties on the page?
- What special techniques show up in the HTML code if you view the source file?
- In a multipage Web site, how much information is on a page?
- How many pages are there, and in what ways are they interlinked?

For Further Reading

Here are some Sams titles that make excellent advanced reading following this tutorial:

Sams Teach Yourself HTML and XHTML in 24 Hours, by Dick Oliver

Sams Teach Yourself Microsoft FrontPage 2002 in 24 Hours, by Rogers Cadenhead

Sams Teach Yourself Macromedia Dreamweaver 4 in 24 Hours, by Betsy Bruce

Sams Teach Yourself Web Publishing with HTML and XHTML in 21 Days, by Laura Lemay)

The Bridges of Madison County, by Robert James Waller—just to get your mind off Web authoring

Summary

You've picked up a great start, and now you know as much about Web authoring as you might ever need. But there's always more to learn, always room to grow.

In the meantime, thanks for the 24 hours. Please come back to this book for a refresher any time. We're always open.

PART VII
Appendixes

Appendix

APPENDIX A

Using the Programs on the Bonus CD-ROM

This appendix describes how to get started with the valuable programs and files on the bonus CD-ROM inside the back cover of this book. The appendix is split into two sections:

- "Setting Up the Programs" explains how to copy the programs and files from the CD-ROM to your computer's hard drive so that you can use them at any time without the CD-ROM.
- "What's on the CD-ROM?" describes each program, tells how to start the program after it has been installed, and tells where in this book you can learn more about using the program.

> The programs on the bonus CD-ROM require a computer running Windows 95, Windows 98, Windows Me, Windows NT, Windows 2000, or Windows XP.

Setting Up the Programs

To install any of the programs and files on the bonus CD-ROM, begin in Windows and close any programs that are running (except Windows). Then follow these steps:

1. Insert into your CD-ROM drive the *Sams Teach Yourself to Create Web Pages in 24 Hours* CD-ROM.
2. Wait a few moments. If a screen with this book's title appears, go on to Step 3. (If not, open My Computer from your Windows desktop and double-click the icon for your CD-ROM drive.)
3. On the screen that shows the book's title, click the CD Menu link in the upper-right corner.

   On the CD-ROM menu, you find links and icons for all the programs and other useful files on the CD-ROM. A group of icons for installing several programs appears in the lower-left corner of the CD-ROM menu; links for installing all other programs and files appear in a list along the right side of the menu.

> To learn more about any program before installing it, consult the "What's on the CD?" section, later in this appendix.

4. To install anything you see on the CD-ROM menu, click its icon or link. The Installation Wizard for the program you selected opens and leads you step-by-step through the installation of the program you selected. Simply follow the instructions that appear.
5. When you have finished installing a program, the CD-ROM menu reappears so that you can install another program, if you want.
6. When you've finished installing programs, click the Exit link at the bottom of the CD-ROM menu. Then click Yes on the credits screen when prompted with "Exit the CD?"

> Some programs might prompt you to restart your computer to complete the installation. If you must restart, but still want to install more programs, repeat Steps 1–3 to redisplay the CD-ROM menu.

What's on the CD-ROM?

The following sections describe all the programs and files on the CD-ROM at the back of this book.

Netscape Communicator

Netscape Communicator is the Netscape all-purpose Internet suite. Communicator includes not only a Web browser, email program, and newsreader, but also Composer, the principle Web authoring tool used in the examples and exercises in this book. You can use Composer to create Web pages and use Netscape to evaluate those pages (and, of course, to surf the Web!)

JPEG Graphics

A great selection of graphics is included on the CD-ROM. You can use these graphics in Web pages you create or use them to practice the techniques you learn in this book:

- To locate the graphics files when adding them to a Web page, insert the CD-ROM (and close the CD-ROM installation program, if it opens) and look in the following folders:

  D:\WebGfx contains three folders: Banners (Web banners), Buttons (various styles of navigation buttons you can attach links to), and Textures (background pictures).

  D:\Fun contains a collection of fun images.

  D:\Photos contains three folders of photographic images: Animals, Everyday, and People.

  D:\Backgrounds contains more great images for picture backgrounds.

  D:\Business contains business-related photographs.

- To learn more about using these files in Web pages you create, see Hours 13–16 and Hour 20.

HTML Assistant Pro 2000

Supplied here in a trial version of HTML Assistant Pro 2000 is a full-featured editor for composing and editing HTML, the underlying code used in Web pages. This program is not used as the principle Web authoring tool in this book because Composer is a better choice for beginners. But as a companion to Composer, HTML Assistant Pro is valuable for creating Web pages divided up into frames and also for general HTML editing tasks:

- To start HTML Assistant Pro from the Windows Start menu, choose Programs, HTML Assistant Pro 2000, Pro 2000.
- To learn more about using HTML Assistant Pro to edit HTML files, see Hour 17, "Editing HTML."
- To learn more about using HTML Assistant Pro to create Web pages divided into multiple frames, see Hour 18, "Dividing a Page into Frames."

MapEdit

Supplied here in a trial version, MapEdit is a tool for creating the type of images you see in Web pages, wherein clicking different parts of the image activates different links. MapEdit is a handy companion to FrontPage Express for adding button bars and other sophisticated features to Web pages you create:

- To start MapEdit from the Windows Start menu, choose Programs, MapEdit, MapEdit.
- To learn more about using MapEdit to put multiple links in one picture, see Hour 20, "Putting Multiple Links in One Picture."

Paint Shop Pro (with Animation Shop)

Supplied here in a trial version, Paint Shop Pro is a sophisticated image drawing, painting, editing, and conversion tool. You can use it to create new images for inclusion in your Web document or to convert, edit, or prepare images you've acquired from other sources. Paint Shop Pro includes a companion product, Animation Shop, which you can use to create animated graphics for your Web pages.

- To start Paint Shop Pro from the Windows Start menu, choose Programs, Paint Shop Pro, Paint Shop Pro. To start Animation Shop from the Windows Start menu, choose Programs, Paint Shop Pro, Animation Shop.
- To learn more about using Paint Shop Pro to create graphics, see Hours 13, "Getting Pictures for Your Page," and Hour 16, "Creating Your Own Animations." To learn how to create animations with Animation Shop, see Hour 16.

NetZip

Supplied here in a trial version, NetZip is a Windows compression and decompression utility that allows you to conveniently decompress ZIP files and other compressed formats commonly downloaded from the Internet.

This capability is important for decompressing Web authoring programs and graphics collections you may download from the Internet, and also for compressing large files you offer to others online. When you install NetZip in a Windows environment, it automatically updates the File Types registry so that when you open any ZIP file, NetZip opens automatically to decompress the file and extract any separate files within the ZIP archive.

- To start NetZip, double-click any ZIP file.

Adobe Acrobat Reader

This program enables a Web browser (Internet Explorer or Netscape Navigator) to display documents stored in Adobe Acrobat (PDF) format, a format commonly used for documents distributed through the Web.

APPENDIX B

Online Resources for Web Authors

Browsers and Other Net-Surfing Programs

- Cello

  `www.law.cornell.edu/cello/cellofaq.html`

- Client Software Directory

  `www.w3.org/hypertext/WWW/Clients.html`

- Microsoft Internet Explorer

  `www.microsoft.com/windows/ie/`

- NeoPlanet

  `www.neoplanet.com`

- Netscape Communicator (Composer)

  `www.netscape.com/download`

- Opera
  www.opera.com
- Stroud's CWSApps List—Browsers
  cws.internet.com/browsers.html

General Web Authoring

- Builder.com
  builder.cnet.com
- Developer.com
  www.developer.com
- Free Tools for Web Site Construction
  freeware.intrastar.net/htmladd.htm
- Jonny's HTML Headquarters
  www.webhelp.org/main.html
- Netscape Developer's Edge
  developer.netscape.com
- PageResource.com
  www.pageresource.com
- Web Developer's Virtual Library
  Wdvl.com
- Web Toolbox
  www.rtis.com/nat/user/toolbox

Clip Art, Animation, and Templates

- ABC Giant Web Graphics and Fonts
  www.abcgiant.com/
- Absolute Designs
  www.absolutedesigns.com
- Animation City
  www.animationcity.net
- Animation Factory
  www.animfactory.com

- Barry's Clip Art Server
  `www.barrysclipart.com`
- Clipart.com
  `www.clipart.com`
- Clip Art Universe
  `www.nzwwa.com/mirror/clipart/`
- Dragon's Free Web Graphics
  `www.silet.com`
- GIFart.com
  `www.gifart.com`
- Web Diner
  `www.webdiner.com`

Java

- FreeWare Java
  `www.freewarejava.com`
- Java Applet Directory
  `www.gamelan.com`
- Java Boutique
  `javaboutique.internet.com`
- Java Repository
  `java.wiwi.uni-frankfurt.de`
- Sun Microsystems Java Home Page
  `java.sun.com`
- Yahoo Java Directory
  `www.yahoo.com/Computers_and_Internet/Programming_Languages/Java/`

General-Purpose Software Download Sites

- Download.com
  `download.cnet.com`
- Freeware Files
  `www.freewarefiles.com`

- Shareware.com
  `shareware.cnet.com`
- Shareware Junkies
  `www.sharewarejunkies.com`
- Tucows
  `www.tucows.com`

Plug-Ins, Helpers, and Other Browser Accessories

- Adobe Acrobat Reader
  `www.adobe.com/products/acrobat/`
- Macromedia Shockwave and Flash
  `www.macromedia.com/software/`
- Microsoft Free Downloads
  `www.microsoft.com/downloads/default.asp`
- Plug-In Plaza
  `browserwatch.internet.com/plug-in.html`
- Plug-In Gallery and Demo Links
  `www2.gol.com/users/oyamada`
- RealAudio/RealVideo
  `www.real.com`

GLOSSARY

alignment The way text or another object is placed within a page layout. Left-aligned text lines up to the left margin, right-aligned text lines up to the right margin, and centered text is centered between the left and right margins.

anchor An invisible marker in a Web page that provides a spot to which a *link* can point so that a link can take a *visitor* straight to a specific spot within a page.

animated GIF A special kind of computer image file that plays as a brief animated clip when viewed through a *browser*. See also *GIF*.

applet A small program or application, particularly one written in *Java.*

background A color or image that covers the entire area behind the text and pictures of a Web page.

browser A program that enables you to view Web pages, such as *Internet Explorer* or *Netscape.*

bulleted list A list of items in which each item is preceded by a marker, a "bullet" or some other symbol character. See also *numbered list.*

cell The individual boxes that make up a *table*. One cell appears at each intersection of one row and one column.

CGI (Common Gateway Interface) One method for creating scripts that make some advanced Web page features work, such as *forms*. See also *Java* and *JavaScript.*

character formatting Formatting that changes the style of text characters, such as applying *fonts* or bold or italic.

check box A small, square box used to select objects in a program or a Web page *form*. Clicking an empty check box inserts a check mark there, indicating that the object or option next to the check box is selected.

client A software tool for using a particular type of Internet resource. A client interacts with a server on which the resource is located. Browsers are clients.

clip art Graphics, photos, and sometimes other media, such as sound and video clips, published in collections for convenient use in creating Web pages and other publications.

close tag An HTML *tag* required at the end of a block of code beginning with certain tags. Close tags begin with `</`.

Communicator See *Netscape*.

Composer A Web authoring program, included on the CD-ROM with this book, that's part of the Netscape Internet program suite. See also *Netscape.*

dialog box A box that pops up in Windows programs to provide the options necessary for completing a particular task. Different tasks display different dialog boxes.

domain The address of a computer on the Internet. A user's Internet address is made up of a username and a domain name. Every Web server has its own, unique domain and can play host to other domains.

download The act of copying information from a server computer to your computer. See also *upload.*

Dynamic HTML (DHTML) A set of enhancements to the standard *HTML* Web language that enable a Web page to include a variety of advanced features and formatting. (DHTML features function only when the page is viewed through a DHTML-compatible browser, such as Netscape Navigator versions 4.5 and above and Microsoft Internet Explorer versions 4 and above.)

email Short for *electronic mail*. A system that enables a person to compose a message on a computer and transmit that message through a computer network, such as the *Internet*, to another computer user.

email address The Internet address used in an email program to send email to a particular Internet user. The address is typically made up of a username, an `@` sign, and a domain name (`user@domain`).

Explorer See *Internet Explorer.*

extensions Nonstandard enhancements to HTML that can add features to Web pages. The features can be viewed only through browsers that support the extensions. See also *FrontPage extensions*.

FAQ file Short for Frequently Asked Questions file. A computer file, often made available on the Internet, containing the answers to frequently asked questions about a particular topic or Web site.

flame A hostile message, often sent through email or posted in newsgroups, from an Internet user in reaction to a breach of netiquette.

font A particular style of text.

font size The relative size in which text appears onscreen.

form A part of a Web page in which users can type entries or make selections that are then collected and processed. Forms require either the *FrontPage Extensions* or a *script* on the server to be processed.

frame definition document An HTML document whose purpose is to define the *frames* in a frame-based document as well as to identify the content files to go in each frame.

frames Multiple panes in a browser window, each of which displays a different Web page file. Web authors design frames pages to enable visitors to use the frames together as a single, multidimensional Web page.

freeware Software available to anyone, free of charge (unlike shareware, which requires payment).

FrontPage A Web-page authoring program from Microsoft, sold by itself and sometimes included in the *Microsoft Office* suite.

FrontPage extensions A set of programs that, when installed on a Web server, enables *forms* and some components in Web pages created in *FrontPage* to perform their tasks without the aid of a *script*.

FTP Short for File Transfer Protocol. The basic method for copying a file from one computer to another through the Internet, often used for publishing Web page files by *uploading* them to a server.

GIF A form of computer image file, using the file extension `.GIF`, commonly used for *inline images* in Web pages. See also *animated GIF.*

heading A short line of text, often set large and in bold, that marks the start of a particular section of a document, such as a Web page.

horizontal line In a Web page, a straight line that divides sections of the page horizontally. Sometimes also known as a horizontal rule.

HTML (Hyper Text Markup Language) The document formatting language used to create Web pages. The files produced by Web authoring programs like *Composer* are HTML files.

HTTP (HyperText Transfer Protocol) The standard protocol used for communications between servers and clients on the World Wide Web.

hyperlink See *link.*

imagemap A picture in a Web page that contains multiple *links*; clicking different parts of the picture activates different links.

inline image An image that appears within the layout of a Web page.

Internet Explorer A browser for the World Wide Web, created by Microsoft.

internetwork A set of networks and individual computers connected so that they can communicate and share information. The Internet is a very large internetwork.

intranet An internal corporate network, usually a local area network, which is based on Internet technologies such as TCP/IP and Web *browsers.*

Java A general-purpose programming language sometimes used to add advanced capabilities to Web pages.

JavaScript A programming language for creating *scripts* that add functions to Web pages.

JPEG A form of image file, using the file extension `.JPG`, commonly used for inline images (and sometimes for picture backgrounds) in Web pages.

link Short for *hyperlink*, an object in a Web page that takes the visitor to another page or an *anchor* in a page, downloads a file, or starts some other action.

link source The part of a link that a visitor actually sees in a Web page and clicks to activate the link. (The other part of a link is the *URL.*) A link source can be some text, an *inline image*, or a part of an *imagemap.*

list box In a *dialog box*, *toolbar*, or Web page *form*, a small box with a downward-pointing arrow at its right end. Clicking the arrow opens a list of options the user can click to select one to appear in the box.

mailto: link A link in a Web page that, when clicked by a visitor, opens the visitor's email program and creates a new message preaddressed to a particular person.

marquee A line of text that repeatedly scrolls across part of a Web page, used as an attention-getting device.

Netscape Short for Netscape Communications, a software company (now owned by the America Online service) that developed and markets a popular Word Wide Web program suite called *Netscape Communicator*, which is included on the CD-ROM with this book along with its *Composer* Web authoring program.

network A set of computers interconnected so that they can communicate and share information. Connected networks together form an *internetwork*.

newsgroup An Internet resource through which people post and read messages related to a specific topic.

numbered list A list of items in which each item is preceded by a number and the numbers go up as the list goes down. See also *bulleted list*.

paragraph Any block of text uninterrupted by a paragraph mark (¶).

paragraph break The space between two paragraphs, in which a hidden paragraph mark appears.

paragraph formatting Text formatting, such as *paragraph styles* or *alignment*, that can be applied to only a whole paragraph or paragraphs, never to only selected characters within a paragraph, such as *character formatting*.

paragraph style The principal form of text formatting on a Web page. Paragraph styles include six levels of *Headings*, a style for Normal text, and several different styles for creating lists.

password A secret code, known only to the user, that allows the user to access a computer that is protected by a security system.

script An external program opened by a link in a Web page to perform some special function.

search page A Web page on which a visitor can search the Web or other Internet resource for particular information.

server A networked computer that serves a particular type of information to users or performs a particular function. On the Internet, servers called Web servers store Web page files and deliver them through the Internet to *browsers* on demand.

shareware Software programs that users are permitted to acquire and evaluate for free. Shareware is different from *freeware* in that, if a person likes the shareware program and plans to use it on a regular basis, he or she is expected to send a fee to the programmer.

signature A block of text on a Web page, usually near the bottom, that identifies the page's author or the *Webmaster*. Signatures often include a *mailto: link* to the author's email address.

style See *paragraph style.*

symbol A character that's not on the keyboard, such as a copyright symbol.

spider A program that searches methodically through a portion of the Internet to build a database that can be searched by a *search page*.

table A box or grid used to arrange text or pictures in neat rows and columns.

tag A code in the *HTML* language.

TCP/IP (Transmission Control Protocol/Internet Protocol) The fundamental Internetworking protocol that makes the Internet work.

template A preformatted Web page (containing sample text and pictures) that a Web author copies and edits to conveniently create a new page.

title The name that identifies a particular Web page. A Web page's title appears in the title bar at the top of the browser window.

toolbar In a program, a row of icons, buttons, and *list boxes*, usually near the top of the program's window, you can click to perform common tasks.

undo A feature of some programs that enables you to reverse an action you performed by clicking a button on a *toolbar* or choosing a menu item. Undo is useful for undoing mistakes.

Unix A computer operating system widely used by Web servers.

upload The act of copying information *to* a server computer from your computer. See also *download.*

URL Short for Uniform (or Universal) Resource Locator. A method of standardizing the addresses of different types of Internet resources so that they can all be accessed easily from within a Web browser.

username An identification name for a user, used in tandem with a *password* to gain access to a computer or network that's protected by a security system.

visitor A casual way a Web author may refer to the people who will access his or her creations through the *Internet* or an *intranet.*

Webmaster The person responsible for the management and maintenance of a particular Web page or Web site, sometimes (but not always) also the Web page's author.

Web site A group of individual Web pages linked together into a single, multipage document. Web site also is sometimes used to describe a whole Web *server* or all pages on a particular *domain*.

wizard Automated routines, used throughout Windows, for conveniently performing a step-by-step procedure.

Yahoo! A popular *search page.*

INDEX

A

H

I

Q

R

S

U

V

W

X

Y